The Art of
Instrument
Flying

TAB
PRACTICAL
FLYING SERIES

The Art of
Instrument
Flying

J.R. Williams

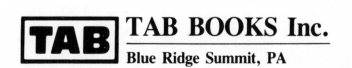
TAB BOOKS Inc.

Blue Ridge Summit, PA

FIRST EDITION

FIRST PRINTING

Library of Congress Cataloging in Publication Data

Williams, J. R., 1934-
    The art of instrument flying / by J.R. Williams.
      p. cm.
    Revised. ed. of: IFR by the book II. REV. and updated. C1983.
    Includes index.
    ISBN 0-8306-2018-4   ISBN 0-8306-2418-X (pbk.)
  1. Instrument flying. I. Williams, J. R., 1934- IFR by the
book II. II. Title.
TL711.B6W545 1988   88-11916
629.132'52—dc19   CIP

Questions regarding the content of this book
should be addressed to:

    Reader Inquiry Branch
    TAB BOOKS Inc.
    Blue Ridge Summit, PA 17294-0214

Contents

Acknowledgments

No one just sits down at a typewriter and pounds out this type of book. It comes from years of experience and the help of numerous people. Therefore, I would like to acknowledge as much of this help as the passage of years will allow me to remember. The list is by no means complete, and to those I have omitted, I apologize.

In chronological order, none of this would have been possible without the help and support of my late mother and father, both of whom taught me that anything worth having is worth working for. They must have wondered many times if their number one son would ever settle down and amount to anything.

Then there was K. Russell Smith of the Smith Flying Service in Forty-Fort, Pennsylvania, who owned the J-3s, PA-11s, and the Cessna 150 and 172 that became my early classrooms. They were assigned to me by the late Ms. Gene Reynolds, who took care of her chicks like a mother hen, although they were ruled over by my primary and advanced flight instructor, the late John L. (Jack) Green with his ever present cigar.

When I advanced into the instrument phase, I was tutored by Andy Perugino and Myrttyn Mack, both severe taskmasters who taught me to feel at home in a totally alien environment.

I will never forget my FAA friends at the Allentown, Pennsylvania, General Aviation District Office (GADO). Both John Doster, who is the present head of the facility, and the late Clarence Claybaugh not only flew check flights with me, but spent many additional hours answering questions both on the ground and in the air. Their patient reinforcement and improvement of techniques I had learned from my instructors, plus their hammering on what seemed to be minor points, certainly helped take off a lot of rough edges.

As an airline copilot (especially in an operation where you make a dozen landings a day and there are only about 50 captains) you learn something from everyone you fly with. Some of these things you accept as good practices, and others you discard as not quite so good. But, if there is any semblance of professionalism in my flying, it was put there by watching and absorbing the styles of five fine gentlemen, now all retired: Captains Paul Hundsdorf, Bruce S. Mac-Bride, Emile J. Pepin, C.E. White, and Arthur Daegling. Art happened to be so close to me on the seniority list that I only flew with him once or twice, but we spent hours together discussing various flying philosophies, and I learned a great deal. He is a long-time student of aeronautical history and a pilot par excellence.

Throughout the book I mention the help I have received from Jeppesen Sanderson, Inc., but here I would like to specifically acknowledge the late Jack H. Davis, Vice President, Services, and his successor, James E. Terpstra, Director, Flight Information Development, both of whom have personally given me every assistance I ever asked for.

This project would never have gotten off the ground had it not been for my former editor (and now my very good friend) at *Private Pilot*, Dennis Shattuck, who thought enough of my writing abilities to suggest a series of articles for his magazine and was magnanimous enough to subsequently release the rights to me so I could put everything together into a book form.

It was Howie Keefe, the world-famous unlimited racing pilot and past-owner of the modified P-51 *Miss America*, who suggested the chapter on the NOS charts. He not only gave me the charts to use but showed me through his facilities at the Air Chart Co. in Venice, California, and spent a full day explaining how charts are developed. He also explained how he developed the concept for his simplified, time-saving method of chart revisions.

And I also want to acknowledge M. Gene Dow, at that time the owner/publisher of the General Aviation Press, who published the first volume, and Norval Kennedy, who edited it.

Proofreading technical books, especially when the proofreader has no knowledge of the subject matter, has to be pure drudgery. I owe a lot to my wife, Jaslyn, for whom such a task was truly a labor of love.

Finally, I would like to thank Jeff Worsinger, Aviation Acquisitions Editor of TAB BOOKS Inc., who has been so helpful in breathing life into this present edition.

Introduction

The first edition of this book was printed in March of 1980. It met with widespread approval and ended up winning the Best Technical Book award for the Western Region of the Aviation/Space Writers Association in 1981. There were suggestions that we incorporate explanations of the National Ocean Service (NOS) approach charts along with those of the Jeppesen charts, and these were added to the second edition in order to make it as useful as possible to the greatest number of people. This third edition was improved further by the addition of a glossary containing terms of special interest to the instrument pilot.

This book is the culmination of many years of work, study, and experience—most of which has been quite enjoyable.

The intent of this project is not to prime you to pass your instrument pilot written exam. It contains no questions or answers. Nor is it intended to prepare you for a career as an instrument repair technician. There are enough other books on the market that will do those things for you.

Instead, it is intended to talk you though the actual "hands on" flying of an aircraft, from the basics through the actual approaches, using only your radios and instruments. In addition, I hope that you will be able to glean some of the nuances of the professional airman. To accomplish these goals I hope that as you read these pages you will be able to picture yourself at the controls of your own aircraft and that you can actually imagine that I am by your side talking you through the various maneuvers.

All of the chart formats and instrument procedures are based on U.S. Federal Aviation Regulations (FARs) and procedures, which can be quite different from the International Civil Aviation Organization (ICAO) terminologies and procedures used in other countries. If enough readers indicate an interest in ICAO procedures, perhaps they will be incorporated in a future edition.

Before I am called a "male chauvinist," let me state that there are many fine female pilots. Many of them are flying in the airline industry and perform as well or better than their male counterparts. I use the term "he" throughout the book in the generic sense. It has been done to make for easier writing, editing, and reading, and no offense is intended.

For the instrument approaches, I have relied on material from Jeppesen Sanderson Inc., because I feel that this material is the most frequently used in the aviation industry. I like their format as well as their method of revisions, although as I mentioned earlier, I will be explaining the various symbols shown on both the Jeppesen and NOS charts so that you will have no trouble making the transition from one "brand" to the other.

Remember, however, that aviation is a rapidly changing industry, and regulations and chart formats keep changing in order to keep pace. What is in these pages was current when I wrote these words, but some of the regulatory or format information might be outdated by the time you read this, so it will be your responsibility to keep up with these changes as they come about.

Because there are more similarities in aircraft than differences, I have attempted to write this book in general enough terms so you will be able to easily adapt your flying skills to any aircraft you will be operating.

1

Instrument Interpretation

INSTRUMENT FLIGHT IS AN EXCITING, PRECISE CHALLENGE, BUT MOST IMPORtantly, it is a psychological challenge. When you, as an instrument pilot, can psychologically accept two facts, you will have most of your problems licked.

Fact One is that your aircraft doesn't know the difference between day and night, or VFR and IFR conditions—it flies the same in all cases. From your first flight lesson you should have learned that when you move the yoke or stick to the left, the left wing will roll away from you. If you push the left rudder pedal, the nose will yaw to the left. At slow speeds, such as when landing or taking off, this yaw will control your heading, while at higher speeds it will counteract the adverse yaw created by the drag of the aileron on the outside wing. If you pull back on the stick or yoke, you pull the nose toward you. Opposite control forces will move the aircraft in the opposite directions. Using power, your other control, only one thing is certain. If you reduce power sufficiently, your aircraft will descend, regardless of how you move the other controls.

I have intentionally avoided using the terms ''up'' and ''down,'' as related to the horizon. When flying, you can be in any attitude when you initiate a control input, and if you have enough speed and/or power, the aircraft will react as indicated above.

This becomes an important point to remember. Your aircraft will almost always react the same way to these control inputs, whether IFR or VFR, single or multiengine, recip or jet, J-3 Cub or C-5A. These are the physical facts of flight.

Fact Two is simply that you must learn to believe your instruments. A few simple maneuvers are usually enough to prove to the most cynical pilot that seat-of-the-pants flying doesn't work too well when outside visual cues are obscured. It is not enough, though, to just look at one instrument and base your conclusions as to what the aircraft is doing on that one glance. To fly your aircraft accurately, you must be able to look at each of your instruments in a systematic fashion and interpret them properly. To interpret properly, you look for trends. I'll go into this in depth later.

Once you put your mind at ease, you will be able to proceed much more efficiently with the proper scan and interpretation of the instruments and to quickly initiate the proper corrective responses.

Because of the wide range of flight and navigational instruments available today this discussion will have to be made in generalities. My points will be basic in nature. There might be some slight variations depending upon the equipment in the aircraft you'll be flying. But in the majority of cases, the principle explored here will work for everyone.

These discussions will not tell you how to read each instrument. That in itself would take a book. There are at least three different types of altimeters, two types of vertical speed indicators, plus many variations of attitude indicators and other instruments.

TRIM, PRESSURE, AND CONTROL DISPLACEMENT

When learning to fly, every student has a difficult time with two techniques: separating control pressure from control displacement, and the proper use of trim tabs.

Trim is the easiest of the two to explain. My explanation of trim is this: the proper use of trim, in each trim-equipped control axis, is to remove the existing pressure from the associated cockpit flight control in such a manner that the aircraft will continue in the desired flight path or attitude with little or no assistance from the pilot.

It is also easy to explain how to trim to accomplish this. Manipulate the cockpit controls to elicit the desired flight path or attitude from the aircraft. Then operate the trim control for each trim-equipped axis, one at a time, until the pressure being exerted on the control is eliminated. To double check, remove your hand or foot from the control. If the aircraft continues as desired, the trim is proper. Note that you do not fly the aircraft with the trim. You merely use it to remove the pressure from the controls. To try to fly the aircraft with the trim will usually result in the trim and the aircraft ending up 180 degrees out of phase. The proper use of trim is very important to good instrument flight.

Differentiation of control pressure and control displacement is difficult to explain and to teach, and I have found that many people never really learn it.

Properly learned and executed, this differentiation is what separates the aircraft drivers from the aircraft pilots. Many times, control pressure will not result in any noticeable control displacement; it is merely a light touch in the direction you want the control to move.

You cannot feel these pressures if you're gripping the yoke tightly. If you do that, you deaden some of the nerve endings that are necessary for this sense of feel. RELAX. That's one of the most important words for any pilot. Turn loose of the yoke, flex your hand a few times to restore the blood circulation, then place your hand—lightly—back on the wheel. Don't clamp it tightly. Allow some space between your hand and the yoke all the way around. That way, if the aircraft is out of trim, you will feel the pressure at once.

Although many times the aircraft driver will deliver a very precise flight, the aircraft pilot will give the smoothest flight, with precision as well. RELAX— that's the word. Remember, everyone reading this has carried passengers, or will someday. When you do, although your primary consideration has to be safety, your secondary consideration should be passenger comfort. Your passenger should not know when your aircraft leaves the blocks and should have minimal sense of taxiing to the runway, braking, takeoff, cruise, descent, landing, and taxiing into the ramp and stopping on the blocks. This goes for J-3 Cubs as well as 747s. It's the mark of a good pilot.

This is not to say that you don't displace the controls, for you certainly do. The slower you fly, the more displacement is necessary to achieve the same pressure, and when recovering from unusual attitudes, you use a lot of displacement and throw pressure out the window.

Although some of your instruments have lags related to them, a good instrument pilot should imagine that he has a string connected between the controls and the instrument he wants to move and that proper control pressure will move the instrument in concert with the pressure, even eliminating the inherent lag.

VISUAL AND INSTRUMENT CORRELATION

A current—and ongoing—question among instructor pilots is how much instrument integration instruction a student pilot should receive, and how soon he should begin receiving it.

My personal feeling on this is that the student pilot should be taught to use his instruments and to correlate them with his external visual references from Lesson One. At no time, however, should the necessity of adequate heads-up flying be minimized. I have always felt that no student should be soloed until he can take off, fly the pattern, and land with a simulated blockage of his pitot-static system. As much stress should be placed on the full use of his senses (sound of wind and engine, and visual height separation) as in the days of open-cockpit biplane trainers.

From the beginning, though, the student should be shown the similarities between the instrument and the visual cues, such cues as the attitude indicator showing wings level, the outside horizon being level, etc.

He should also be shown how to interpret this information. For example, if your aircraft is flying wings-level with the nose on the horizon, and your attitude indicator shows the same, does this mean that you are actually flying straight and level? The answer is, "Of course not." If you encounter an updraft or downdraft (wind shear), or if your power is too high or too low, your aircraft can climb or descend accordingly and still be in a level flight attitude. Visually, the ground will appear to come nearer or sink away. On instruments you will notice the vertical speed indicator deflect up or down, with a corresponding change in the altimeter. If the instrument changes are due to changes in power setting, you will also notice improper airspeeds and a change in engine sound, and the power instruments will show a change in RPM and/or manifold pressure.

Here's another example. Does a nose-high attitude indicate a climb? Not unless you have added sufficient power. In slow flight the aircraft has to assume a nose-high attitude to maintain altitude.

All of these relationships should be pointed out to the student from the beginning. What we should be teaching the students, in other words, is that one visual cue, or the indication of one instrument, is not enough. You must derive information from as many sources as possible in order to accurately interpret the flight path and attitude of the aircraft.

INSTRUMENT SCAN AND INTERPRETATION

If you were able to see the precise flight path of an aircraft, you would see that it is maintained by a series of corrections to the controls to make the aircraft follow the desired track. The smaller and more frequent these corrections are, the closer the aircraft will conform to the desired path.

In order to make small corrections, you must receive a large input of information in a short period of time, interpret it correctly, and then make the desired control response in a timely fashion.

How do you do this? You learn to scan the instruments and to interpret what you see. As you practice this procedure, you learn to give bare notice to those instruments that indicate what they should, while devoting most of your attention to those instruments that have deviated—they will stand out like a soldier out of step.

The two major errors most commonly made in instrument scanning are omitting necessary instruments from the scan and spending too much time looking at one instrument. An instrument is omitted from the scan because the pilot is spending too much time worrying about another one, so these errors are usually interrelated.

At one time or other, we are all guilty of having unwanted heading changes of 15-20° or unwanted altitude deviations of ±100-150 feet. How much time would such inadvertent changes take? Unless your aircraft encounters exceptional trim changes, wind shears, updrafts, downdrafts, or power changes, your normal rate of climb (or descent) in unpressurized aircraft is rarely more than 500 FPM. At this rate, it would take 10-12 seconds for your altimeter to change by 100-150 feet. This means that for 10-12 seconds you have omitted the vertical speed indicator, altimeter, and attitude indicator from your scan. Ten to twelve seconds of daydreaming is a long time—but we all do it. How can we avoid it? By practice and hard work, of course. Keep your eyes constantly moving over your instruments. SCAN.

Proper Instrument Scanning

You must have a systematic approach to your scan. In most situations the attitude indicator will be your prime instrument, just as in most situations the outside horizon will be your prime visual aid. Some people will argue with this idea, but I feel it's easier to learn to fly on instruments by keeping one of the instruments as a primary one that you can always fall back on.

Your scan will almost always begin with the attitude indicator and proceed to the supporting instruments for the aspect of flight that you're focusing on. You will scan the other instruments as well, but your major concern will be those that support the flight characteristics that you are most interested in at the time.

For example, in level flight your scan would begin with the attitude indicator, and then, while attempting to hold a constant attitude, you would glance at the altimeter, the vertical speed indicator, the airspeed indicator, the power setting, and back to the attitude indicator. Hopefully, by the time you get back to the attitude indicator, it will still be indicating the same as the first time you glanced at it. You will then repeat the scan of the instruments mentioned above.

Provided that your attitude and power have remained constant, one of three trends will have been established: descent, level flight, or climb. One cue that you will look for is the airspeed. Is it higher, lower, or normal for your power setting? Notice that I have not yet made mention of the position of the attitude indicator; it is enough that you hold the attitude indicator constant. At this point a lower airspeed at a given power setting would indicate a climb (or flight through a strong downdraft). This will be confirmed by the second scan of the vertical speed indicator and the altimeter. The second and third scans determine the trend. If the trend indicates a climb or descent when you want level flight, you will have to correct it. This correction should be accomplished in two *smooth* steps (notice the word I stress). The first step is to stop the unwanted trend. The second step is to begin a trend back to the desired flight situation.

In the example above, you began to climb slightly. If your power setting is proper for level flight, you will stop your climb by a slight change of the pitch attitude shown on your attitude indicator. You do this by relaxing enough back pressure (or by adding enough forward pressure) on the yoke to cause the imaginary string leading to the vertical speed indicator and altimeter to move the needles to a level flight indication.

Although an experienced pilot would actually be doing all of these things simultaneously, as a student, you will have to try to control one instrument at a time while learning. Because the attitude indicator has the least lag, it is the easiest instrument to control.

After you have made your slight change, you again try to hold the attitude indicator constant at the desired attitude and scan the other instruments again. Your change will have accomplished one of three things: (1) if you did not change the pitch attitude sufficiently, you will continue climbing, but at a reduced rate; (2) if you made an overcorrection, you will descend, and your airspeed will increase; or (3) if you have changed the pitch the proper amount, your altimeter and vertical speed indicator should indicate level flight, and your airspeed will begin to increase. After you have stopped the unwanted trend, you can apply another small correction to reverse the previous trend and get your aircraft back to its desired flight path or attitude.

As you learn to control the vertical speed better through smooth corrections, and to coordinate that with corrections to the attitude indicator, you will find that more of your corrections will be of the latter type.

The smaller and smoother you can make your corrections, the less chance you will have of developing vertigo (spatial disorientation), the smoother ride you will afford your passengers, and the more accurately you will fly your aircraft.

INSTRUMENT ERRORS

Earlier I said that I had intentionally made no mention of the initial attitude indication. This is because you must think of the attitude indicator as a *relative* instrument rather than as an absolute indicator of the aircraft performance. Your aircraft (and its attitude indicator) can be nose-low or nose-high, and depending on loading (center of gravity) and speed, still be in level flight.

The attitude indication on instruments will also change due to precession of the gyro as well as from acceleration and deceleration errors. For example, if you have been climbing for a long while, the attitude indicator gets used to indicating a nose-high attitude and will continue to indicate slightly more nose-high than normal for a few minutes after you have leveled off and established cruise airspeed. Therefore, all attitude corrections are made to the previous indication, not to the actual attitude.

Gyro precession and acceleration errors are inherent gyro instrument errors you learn to live with, and with proper scanning procedures they become relatively unimportant. Non-gyro instruments are also subject to errors. You have all undoubtedly heard of altimeter and vertical speed instrument lag. By horsing the controls abruptly you can get a momentary instrument reaction opposite to the aircraft's reaction, but if you make slow, smooth corrections as mentioned earlier, this lag becomes barely noticeable.

There are many books that go into depth on instruments, their construction, and the reasons for their errors. My purpose here is only to tell you how to live with them.

AIRSPEED CONTROL

For the remainder of this chapter, I will concentrate on changing airspeed while maintaining level flight. The purpose of this is to teach the relationships among power setting, pitch attitude, airspeed, and trim.

One nice thing that you will learn about trim is that it is closely related to airspeed, and that once trimmed for a given speed and center of gravity (CG), the aircraft will tend to remain at the same airspeed regardless of your power setting. When you reduce power, the airspeed will want to decrease, but if you are trimmed for the higher speed, the nose will lower instead, and you will begin to lose altitude. If your plane is fairly stable, it will porpoise a few times, and eventually the speed and the rate of descent should stabilize.

From this point on in these discussions you will be attempting to maintain exact altitudes, airspeeds, headings, and rates of climb or descent. Here the allowable margin of error will be ±0. I realize that the FAA Practical Test Standards are more lenient, but you will not achieve a high level of competence by training for minimum performance. You should be striving for perfection from the start. You'll never achieve it—but you should try.

Let's begin with this thought. In level flight, any given power setting should result in a specific airspeed and corresponding pitch attitude (instrument error disregarded). Ideally then, at cruise power and airspeed, your attitude indicator should show precisely level flight.

Because the four forces working on an aircraft (lift, thrust, drag, and gravity) must always be in balance, anytime one of the them varies, the other three will change to bring all four back into equilibrium.

If you increase power and maintain pitch, the thrust will overcome drag and your speed will increase until the drag and thrust balance each other out. At the same time, the increased speed (with no deliberate change of attitude) will increase lift. This, in turn, will cause your aircraft to climb until the lift is balanced out by gravity again. To counteract this climbing effect, as your speed increases, you must slowly lower your pitch attitude to maintain level flight. To do this you will apply forward pressure on the yoke—enough pressure to keep the vertical speed indicator at zero, and the altimeter at the required altitude. The more the speed increases, the more forward pressure you will have to exert on the yoke. The opposite occurs if you reduce power while trying to maintain altitude.

John Doster, director of the FAA GADO at Allentown-Bethlehem-Easton Airport in Pennsylvania, has always felt that the level turn is the best training maneuver to teach aircraft control.

He would begin by asking each of his thousands of students and flight certificate candidates what causes an aircraft to turn. There was—and is—only one correct answer: lift.

As the ailerons deflect to roll into a turn, the lowered aileron on the up-wing causes increased drag, which turns the nose of the plane slightly in the direction opposite the turn. Rudder pressure has to be added to counteract this yawing tendency.

As the aircraft banks, part of the lift that up to now has balanced out gravity (to maintain level flight) is vectored to the inside of the bank, *lifting* the aircraft into the turn.

Inertia is a factor for a little while. The aircraft maintains level flight until the vertical component of lift decreases enough to allow gravity to take over, causing the aircraft to descend. As this occurs, back pressure has to be applied to the yoke to increase the angle-of-attack of the wing, thereby inducing enough added lift to maintain the desired altitude. Unfortunately, this added lift also increases drag, and the plane begins to slow down unless enough thrust is applied to overcome the increased drag and keep all four forces in balance.

The opposite situation occurs when rolling out of the turn. First, the rudder has to be applied again to counteract yaw. As the aircraft rolls to a wings-level attitude, inertia again works on it momentarily. Then the plane wants to begin climbing, due to the increased vertical component of lift.

This climbing tendency can be overcome by forward pressure on the yoke (decreasing the angle-of-attack) but when you do this, the power you added previously begins to overcome drag, and your airspeed increases, unless you reduce power again.

John Doster feels that the best training maneuvers for any pilot are turns of various degrees of bank and duration, with zero permissible altitude and airspeed fluctuation.

As I mentioned above, when your airspeed changes, so will the control pressures, and here's where it's very important to retrim the aircraft. Remember— your aim is to have the aircraft trimmed in such a manner that it will maintain the desired path and attitude if you momentarily take your hands off the controls.

By learning how to maintain level flight while varying the pitch and power settings, you also learn how to slow down to approach speed before actually beginning your descent. This will be of importance when you get into the approach phase of instrument flight.

During all phases of instrument flight, try to keep changes as simple as possible. When beginning an approach, try not to go from cruise speed/attitude/power to approach speed/attitude/power all at once. You can control your aircraft easier if you first slow to approach speed/attitude while still maintaining level flight and then begin a descent by easing off a little power, lowering some flaps, or extending the landing gear.

For practice, try flying level, with and without the hood, varying the airspeed from five knots above stall speed to five knots above cruise speed. Trim the aircraft as the speed changes so that once your speed has stabilized, the aircraft will fly practically hands-off. When you do this without the hood, compare your aircraft's nose and wingtip positions (i.e., their relationship with the horizon) to what is presented on the attitude indicator. Naturally, you should have an instructor or safety pilot with you to scan outside at all times.

Develop your instrument scan by covering one pitch instrument at a time and flying with the remaining ones to learn their interrelationship. With the attitude indicator covered, try to develop a touch and smoothness on the yoke that will minimize the instrument lag inherent in the vertical speed indicator and the altimeter.

2

Vertigo Awareness

THERE ARE ONLY TWO TYPES OF INSTRUMENT PILOTS. THOSE WHO HAVE SUF-
fered from vertigo—and those who will.

Your eyes are a most important factor in maintaining equilibrium in flight.
You will have a tendency to lose your orientation if your supporting senses conflict with what you see.

One source of this conflict during instrument conditions is the reflection of
anticollision lights on clouds or on the aircraft's wings and canopy. These flickers
make you feel as if you are turning. You can even be bothered by the airplane's
shadow, projected onto clouds in an otherwise dark night sky. The easiest way
to correct this problem is to turn off the rotating beacon and/or strobe lights until
you get over the feeling.

Climbing or descending through an area of broken clouds, either IFR or VFR,
can give you the impression that your airspeed and altitude are changing rapidly.
This is especially prevalent when flying over water on a bright hazy day, or through
areas of heavy haze, when you lose the horizon. Your best bet in such situations
is to go on instruments immediately.

Many times when banking soon after takeoff on a dark night, or when leaving
a bright area and proceeding over dark water, desert, mountains, or forests, you
will get the impression that the stars are actually lights on the ground. Other times,
ground lights that you know are lower than your altitude will appear to be higher.
Both of these impressions will cause you to develop symptoms of vertigo that
can be overcome only by going on the gauges at once. I have long felt that, for

this very reason, an instrument ticket should be a prerequisite for night flying. There is a long list of night accidents in which the probable cause was the pilot's inability to maintain orientation due to a loss of visual landmarks.

In addition to sight, we possess the postural senses of touch, pressure, and tension, and the motion-sensing organs of the inner ear. The postural senses cannot detect an unchanging velocity; there must be acceleration or deceleration. Without the sense of sight to help us, the 2-G centrifugal force of a steep turn feels identical to a 2-G pull-up from a dive, and a wing load of ±1-2 G's often feels the same whether caused by in-flight turbulence or by rough control pressures related to leveling off, climbing, or beginning descents.

Most of the complications we have with spatial disorientation, though, begin in the inner ear.

THE INNER EAR

Basically, the inner ear consists of a reservoir, called the common sac, to which are fitted three hollow rings called the semicircular canals. These semicircular canals are oriented in each of three planes, and the entire unit is filled with fluid. Very fine hairs, called sensory hairs, project into the fluid within the semicircular canals.

Picture yourself holding a glass of water. If you twist the glass, the water will tend to stay where it is at first. If you were to tape a few hairs to the inside of the glass (similar to the sensory hairs inside the semicircular canals) and then twist it, the water would stand still at first, and the hairs would drag backwards in the water.

The same thing happens in the inner ear. If you begin turning, the semicircular canals begin turning with you, but because of the laws of inertia, the fluid in the canal (in the plane of rotation associated with your motion) resists moving at first, and the sensory hairs are deflected as they drag in the fluid. The hairs send a signal to the brain, telling the brain that you are moving.

If you continue turning (or accelerating or decelerating) at the same rate, the fluid will begin moving and after a while it will move at the same rate as the canal. At this time, the sensory hairs will return to their static position and your brain will sense that your turn, etc., has stopped, even though your aircraft and your body are still turning.

Then, when you begin to roll out of the turn, the opposite will happen. The semicircular canal will move in the opposite direction, and the hairs will deflect to tell the brain that you are moving in the opposite direction. In the case of rolling in and out of a turn, this will work out fine as long as you roll smoothly. But, if you roll out abruptly, after you stop the roll the fluid will continue moving, carrying the hairs in the opposite direction again. Even though you are flying straight and level, your brain thinks that you are in another turn.

As long as you can see the outside horizon, or the attitude indicator and the directional gyro, you will not be too confused. Under visual conditions, the out-

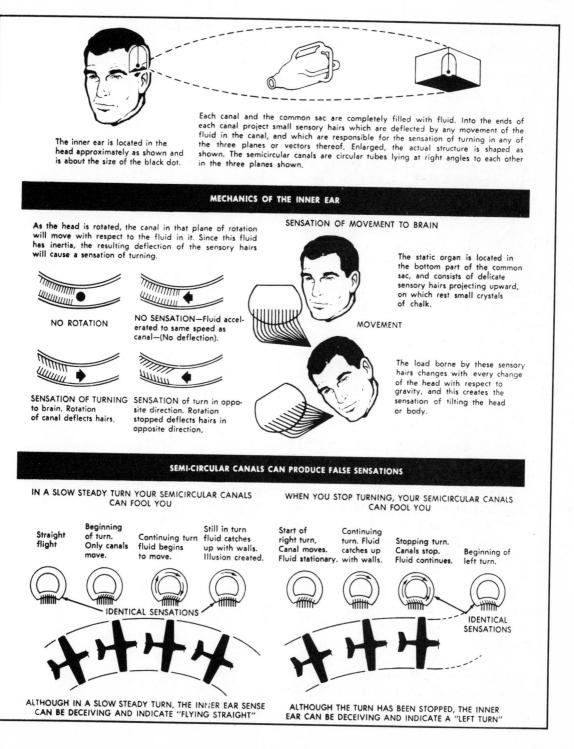

The inner ear is located in the head approximately as shown and is about the size of the black dot.

Each canal and the common sac are completely filled with fluid. Into the ends of each canal project small sensory hairs which are deflected by any movement of the fluid in the canal, and which are responsible for the sensation of turning in any of the three planes or vectors thereof. Enlarged, the actual structure is shaped as shown. The semicircular canals are circular tubes lying at right angles to each other in the three planes shown.

MECHANICS OF THE INNER EAR

As the head is rotated, the canal in that plane of rotation will move with respect to the fluid in it. Since this fluid has inertia, the resulting deflection of the sensory hairs will cause a sensation of turning.

NO ROTATION

NO SENSATION—Fluid accelerated to same speed as canal—(No deflection).

SENSATION OF TURNING to brain. Rotation of canal deflects hairs.

SENSATION of turn in opposite direction. Rotation stopped deflects hairs in opposite direction.

SENSATION OF MOVEMENT TO BRAIN

The static organ is located in the bottom part of the common sac, and consists of delicate sensory hairs projecting upward, on which rest small crystals of chalk.

MOVEMENT

The load borne by these sensory hairs changes with every change of the head with respect to gravity, and this creates the sensation of tilting the head or body.

SEMI-CIRCULAR CANALS CAN PRODUCE FALSE SENSATIONS

IN A SLOW STEADY TURN YOUR SEMICIRCULAR CANALS CAN FOOL YOU

WHEN YOU STOP TURNING, YOUR SEMICIRCULAR CANALS CAN FOOL YOU

Straight flight

Beginning of turn. Only canals move.

Continuing turn fluid begins to move.

Still in turn fluid catches up with walls. Illusion created.

Start of right turn. Canal moves. Fluid stationary.

Continuing turn. Fluid catches up with walls.

Stopping turn. Canals stop. Fluid continues.

Beginning of left turn.

IDENTICAL SENSATIONS

IDENTICAL SENSATIONS

ALTHOUGH IN A SLOW STEADY TURN, THE INNER EAR SENSE CAN BE DECEIVING AND INDICATE "FLYING STRAIGHT"

ALTHOUGH THE TURN HAS BEEN STOPPED, THE INNER EAR CAN BE DECEIVING AND INDICATE A "LEFT TURN"

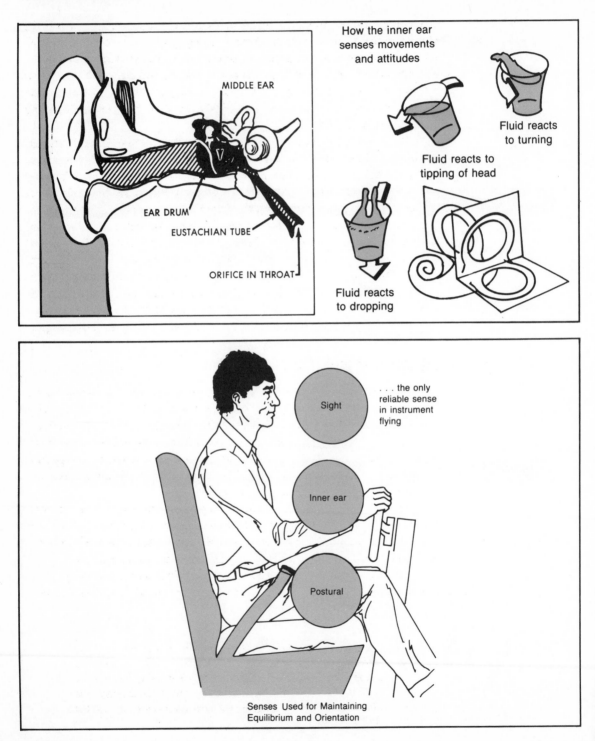

MIDDLE EAR

EAR DRUM

EUSTACHIAN TUBE

ORIFICE IN THROAT

How the inner ear
senses movements
and attitudes

Fluid reacts
to turning

Fluid reacts to
tipping of head

Fluid reacts
to dropping

Sight

. . . the only
reliable sense
in instrument
flying

Inner ear

Postural

Senses Used for Maintaining
Equilibrium and Orientation

side horizon alone will suffice to tell you when you are turning; you will see objects on the horizon or on the ground as they pass across your view. When you're on instruments, you need two gauges to give you the same information. The attitude indicator or the turn-and-bank indicator will tell you if you are in a bank, and the directional gyro will confirm that you are actually turning; the numbers rotating past the lubber line will take the place of the objects going by on the outside horizon.

If you close your eyes while making a smooth entry into the turn, roll out suddenly, and then open your eyes and look only at the instruments, the instruments will tell you just the opposite of what your inner ear has been saying, and you will be primed for vertigo. This can happen if you allow yourself to bank too steeply during an instrument turn, then notice your error and overcontrol, snapping quickly back to the desired angle of bank. In such a situation, if you doubt the instruments, you will find that you become dizzy and unable to control your muscle functions. By the time you realize that the attitude indicator is telling you the true attitude, it might be too late. One part of your brain is trying to tell your muscles to roll out of the turn, but another part of your brain has become so confused that it refuses to allow the muscles to respond. In this situation, you are experiencing extreme vertigo, and you are set up for a catastrophe.

BELIEVING THE INSTRUMENTS

The only way to overcome vertigo is to understand it, catch it at its outset, and believe the instruments. You must train yourself to disregard all of the false senses and try to rely solely on the instruments. This takes patience and practice. You must also remember that instruments can fail from time to time, so you must be able to reinforce what some of the instruments are telling you by interpreting other instruments in the same group. The more experience you have, the less your chance will be of succumbing to vertigo.

There are some specific maneuvers designed to induce vertigo, and though each is designed to produce a specific sensation, any sensation at all will help you learn that you can't trust your senses. Be certain that these maneuvers are only undertaken with an instructor or qualified safety pilot on board.

These maneuvers will: (1) show you the absolute need to rely on your instruments, and (2) give you an understanding of how head movements, in various aircraft attitudes, cause disorientation.

- While flying straight and level, close your eyes and have the instructor skid right or left while holding the wings level. You will feel as though your body is actually tilting in the direction opposite the skid. As soon as you feel that you are tilting, tell the instructor what direction you're tilting in, and open your eyes to see what the aircraft is doing.

- While flying straight and level with the aircraft slowed down to approach airspeed, close your eyes. Have the instructor increase the speed to climb speed while maintaining a straight-and-level attitude. You'll feel as though you're climbing. This is important to remember when executing a missed approach from low airspeeds, especially if you have to divert your head from the instruments to reset a radio or to check a chart for a procedural point.

- From a straight-and-level attitude, close your eyes and have the instructor execute a slow roll into a well-coordinated 45-degree banked turn. Hold this 1.5-G turn for 90°. Because of the gravity forces in the turn, you will feel as though the aircraft is climbing. Keep your eyes closed and have the instructor roll out of the turn slowly and with coordinated pressures. Because of the decrease in gravity forces, by the time you have rolled halfway out, you will feel as though you are descending.

The reason for these sensations is that, with a lack of visual reference, if the rate of angular acceleration is less than 2° per sec.-sec., the body is unable to detect a change of direction in any of the three planes of motion. Therefore, the change of gravity forces, usually associated with climbing or diving, is all that will be felt.

You can experience a false sense of reversal in motion by using the following maneuver:

- With your eyes closed while straight and level, have your instructor smoothly and positively roll into a 45-degree bank while using opposite rudder pressure to keep the nose on a point. If the roll rate is suddenly stopped, you will feel as though you are actually rotating in the opposite direction, and a recovery based solely on your senses could be fatal. This demonstration, when properly executed, will drive home the need for smooth, well-coordinated control usage, and a firm need for a belief only in your instruments.

The next two demonstrations can also be shown by strapping the student in a rotating chair. Whether done in a rotating chair or in flight, the results will be extreme disorientation, causing a quick and forceable—almost violent—movement of the head and body, upward and backward, and to the side opposite the rotation. Naturally, if this reaction were applied to the controls of an aircraft in flight, you could get into a lot of trouble.

- From straight-and-level flight, either close your eyes or look down at the floor. The instructor should roll positively into a coordinated bank of 45° (or begin spinning the chair). As the aircraft is rolling into the bank, bend your head and body down and look to either side, and then immediately straighten up and sit normally. The instructor should stop the bank (or stop the chair rotation) just as you reach the normally seated position.

- Watch as the plane is rolled into a steep, descending spiral. After 15 seconds or so, bend your head and body down and look to either side as you did in the first maneuver, and again immediately resume the normal seated position.

The disorientation may be severe. You may even become nauseated. This could easily happen in a real-life situation if the plane begins turning as you are looking for a chart or book in your flight case. The reaction is usually more severe when you are forced to look down and to the rear. This is one of the reasons I advocate placing all charts and paperwork in some handy location such as on top of the glareshield where you can reach them without turning your head and body.

Normal vertigo can only be overcome by familiarity with your instruments, belief in them, and continuous practice. The more you fly on instruments, the less susceptible you will be to false sensations.

3

Physiological Factors

TO COMBINE WHAT YOU'VE LEARNED SO FAR, WE'LL INCORPORATE ALL OF THE flight instruments into your scan to enable you to maintain altitude, speed, and heading, and to establish climbs and descents.

Before getting into that, however, let's discuss a few more physiological factors that will affect your flight performance in general and your instrument capabilities in particular.

The effects of pressure changes on pilots are well known, and we have all been advised not to fly with a cold or when we have ear or sinus blockage. We must also take care after scuba diving as we can set ourselves up for the bends if we fly at too high a cabin altitude too soon after diving.

DRUGS

A second problem when flying with a slight cold deals with the effect of medication on your system. Drugs, even the over-the-counter variety, which would have little or no effect on you on the ground, can end up having disastrous results when you fly. This is especially true when you're on instruments.

Some types of drugs and their effects on you are:

ANTIHISTAMINES may cause dizziness, drowsiness, headaches, and/or nausea, and they usually also affect vision.

BARBITURATES, as they wear off, bring about sleepiness that often goes unrecognized. They also affect motor and thinking functions.

DIET PILLS are responsible for nervousness and impaired judgment.

MUSCLE RELAXANTS, by their nature, cause weakness as well as sleepiness and vertigo.

STIMULANTS, like diet pills, cause nervousness and impaired judgment as well as blurred vision.

TRANQUILIZERS also cause blurred vision and sleepiness.

Some of these pills can be bought without a prescription, and many times your family doctor will prescribe medication containing these or other ingredients detrimental to the safe operation of aircraft. Ask your doctor about the effects his medication may have on your ability to fly. If you have any doubt, or if you're thinking of taking an over-the-counter pill in some part of the country where you don't have a doctor, contact the local FAA medical examiner for advice. If, for some reason, you're unable to get medical advice, stay away from the driver's seat of an aircraft for at least 24 hours after taking any pills.

ALCOHOL, CIGARETTES, AND HYPOXIA

Another serious physiological problem stems from the consumption of alcoholic beverages. It takes only 25 percent as much alcohol to impair flying skills as it does to impair driving skills. One or two drinks will decrease your flying ability below safe standards, and in instrument conditions this danger is multiplied. Alcohol, which is readily absorbed into the bloodstream, interferes with the normal use of oxygen by the tissues. As you climb, it causes you to suffer effects similar to hypoxia (oxygen starvation) which brings us to our next subject.

There are two kinds of hypoxia: that caused by foreign or toxic substances in the blood, and that caused by reduced atmospheric pressure.

Oxygen is carried through the bloodstream by a substance called hemoglobin. A certain amount of pressure in the lungs is required to combine the hemoglobin with the oxygen. The higher you go, the lower the pressure, and the less oxygen is absorbed. Not only that, the higher you go, the less oxygen is available in any given volume of air that you inhale.

For all practical purposes, you can consider 10,000 feet MSL as the upper limit for safe, long-range flight for a normal, healthy body without supplemental oxygen. The FAA allows you to fly at 12,500 feet MSL without any supplemental oxygen at all. Now, if you have any physiological problems at all you may not be able to even handle 10,000 feet safely, and I have already mentioned that alcohol will interfere with your body's normal use of oxygen and this will affect your susceptibility to hypoxia.

Another very serious detrimental habit is smoking. Three cigarettes at sea level can raise your physiological altitude to 8000 feet MSL before you even set foot in an aircraft. This, then, can noticeably affect your body's tolerance of altitudes.

What is it about smoking that affects your body? Carbon monoxide—that colorless, odorless, tasteless, killer chemical. It is absorbed by the hemoglobin in the bloodstream 200 times easier than oxygen. Every bit of carbon monoxide that is absorbed by the hemoglobin takes the place of that much needed oxygen, and once in the bloodstream, it cannot be cleared out by just a little suck on the oxygen mask. It is harder to *remove* carbon monoxide from the bloodstream than it is to absorb it.

Carbon monoxide can be absorbed into the bloodstream from sources other than cigarettes. One prevalent source is exhaust gas from a cracked exhaust pipe. Another is the smoke from your passengers' cigarettes. In fact, recent findings tend to support the contention that the nonsmoker suffers more from this "passive" smoke in a confined area than does the smoker.

The greatest danger of hypoxia, from whatever source, is the way it numbs the brain so that the person suffering from it can black out, recover, and have no recollection of the experience, except for a possible headache. In fact, unless you have some definite proof to show him, he will argue about the fact that he was unconscious. United Airlines made an interesting training film showing some of their personnel in a decompression chamber, and it is a sobering and frightening experience to watch the film. You develop a healthy respect for the dangers of hypoxia.

Hypoxia brings about the following symptoms, although not necessarily in the following order:

Dizziness (not always apparent as it is more often just a little lightheadedness)

Tingling (again not always noticed because the person sometimes feels as though that part of the body is "falling asleep")

Blurry vision (often confused with fatigue or tired eyes)

Feeling of warmth ("who turned on the heater?")

Euphoria (a feeling of well-being—here's where the brain remains for some reason, feeling nothing else)

Mental confusion

Inability to concentrate

Loss of judgment

Slow reflexes

Clumsiness, and finally

Loss of consciousness (and eventually death, unless oxygen is administered)

Even then, some irreparable damage may have been suffered by the brain. Naturally, through all of the adverse symptoms mentioned above, the subject is very susceptible to vertigo.

A final physiological problem, in which many symptoms are the same as hypoxia, is hyperventilation. This occurs when you get excited and begin breathing quickly and heavily. In so doing, your body gets rid of too much carbon dioxide (a waste product of muscular exertion). A body requires a certain balance between the oxygen and carbon dioxide in the blood. Too much oxygen in relation to the carbon dioxide will cause dizziness and faintness. Take a few fast deep breaths and see for yourself.

People tend to hyperventilate when they get into tight situations involving stress and fear. The best protection against this problem is to learn to relax, calmly appraise the situation, don't allow yourself to panic, don't fall for "sucker holes," don't try flying when conditions are minimal, practice your instrument skills, know your aircraft, know your own capabilities, and force yourself to breath slowly and steadily.

4

Attitude
Instrument Flying

SO MUCH FOR PSYCHOLOGICAL AND PHYSIOLOGICAL FACTORS. NOW BACK TO instrument flying.

HEADING CONTROL

Let's take a look now at controlling your heading. To start off with, we'll work with just the heading instruments and concentrate on making turns at the standard rates without worrying too much about altitudes. We'll tie everything together later.

The heading instruments consist of the attitude indicator, needle/ball (sometimes called the turn/slip or slip/skid) or turn coordinator, and the heading indicators. The heading indicators will consist of at least the magnetic compass and the directional gyro. Sometimes you'll find slaved gyros, flux gate compasses, and/or automatic sensing azimuths for your Automatic Direction Finders.

The primary turn instrument will still be the attitude indicator because the aircraft can't turn unless it is banking. (This isn't exactly true, as rudder pressure may cause the plane to skid and this will cause the heading to change somewhat, but for the most part, it is the sideways lift vector of the banked wing that lifts you through the turn.)

Remember that you set your attitude by relative pitch indications on the attitude indicator. When you turn, you also use the attitude indicator as the prime instrument, only now you set a relative bank indication on it.

The amount of bank you will use will depend on the number of degrees you have to turn, the amount of airspace you have to work in, the time you have to spend in the turn, and the speed of the aircraft. The greater the speed, the steeper you will have to bank to get the same rate of turn. A good rule of thumb to use for most aircraft is one degree of bank for each degree you want to turn, up to the angle of bank necessary for a standard-rate turn.

You should practice rolling into and out of your banks at the same roll rate. This will be helpful in rolling out on the proper headings so that you can expedite your turns and at the same time prevent overshooting desired headings. For example, if your roll rate is such that you turn through 10° before your bank is established, you should use the same roll rate when rolling out of the turn and begin the rollout 10° prior to your intended heading. The key to this is a constant roll rate.

OVERCOMING COMPASS ERRORS

Directional gyros, slaved gyros, and flux gate compasses are, for the most part, direct-reading indicators. The only error you have to be concerned with is the precessional error of the directional gyro. To eliminate that, merely reset the directional gyro to the magnetic indication every 10 minutes or so. To do this accurately, your aircraft must be flying straight and level, and at a constant airspeed. Otherwise, the magnetic compass may be inaccurate.

Magnetic compasses are prone to two errors: northerly turning error and acceleration error. Both of these errors result from magnetic dip, which is greatest near the poles and least near the equator. This dip is caused by the needle trying to align itself parallel to the magnetic force field of the earth.

When you decide to turn, you roll the aircraft into a bank, and as you do so, the magnetic compass card tilts also. When it does, the north-seeking end of the compass tends to dip to the low side of the bank. This error is greatest when you are heading north or south, and least when heading east or west.

The effect on the compass, when heading north, is to cause an initial apparent turn opposite to the direction of the actual turn. When heading south this error will show the airplane to be turning in the proper direction, but it will cause the magnetic compass to indicate a faster turn than you are making. When heading north or south, the magnitude of this error will approximate the degree of latitude. As mentioned above, it will be minimal when you are heading east or west. Through practice and interpolation, you should be able to roll out right on course when you apply your roll-rate lead, plus the amount of error, for the desired heading.

The acceleration error is most noticeable when accelerating or decelerating on an east or west heading. It also occurs when climbing and descending on these headings. (There should be no appreciable acceleration error on a north or south heading.) When accelerating or descending, the compass card will turn to the north, and when decelerating or climbing it will turn to the south. You can remember the errors easier by thinking of the word "ANDS"—*A*ccelerate, *N*orth; *D*ecelerate, *S*outh.

To keep all of these errors constant you must make smooth, coordinated turns. If the errors are constant, you will be able to compensate for them. In addition, the bank should be limited to less than 18° to prevent the magnetic compass card from binding. You should practice flying to specific headings using only the magnetic compass. After a while, you will find that you can roll out consistently on course with an accuracy of ±2½°.

STANDARD-RATE TURNS

After you perfect this technique, you should develop the ability to execute standard-rate turns. A standard-rate turn for normal general aviation aircraft, is one of 3° per second. This means that it will require two minutes to execute a 360-degree circle. For slower aircraft this turn rate will require a bank angle of 10-25°. High-performance aircraft require steeper banks. High speeds can even require a four-minute (or half-standard-rate) turn to keep the bank angle from becoming excessive. The maximum bank angle you'll want to make on instruments is 30°, and most flight command systems will limit the aircraft to 27°.

One instrument that will help maintain a constant standard-rate turn is the turn coordinator or its equivalent. Today, most general aviation aircraft use a two-minute turn indicator. As all instruments have certain errors, it becomes necessary to determine the exact needle position on your turn coordinator to result in a standard-rate turn. To do this, roll smoothly into a turn and place the low wing of the airplane figure on the turn index. Check the bank angle on the attitude indicator. Fly through 360°, timing your turn as you pass through a few of the cardinal headings. Continue through another 360°, readjusting the angle of bank as necessary to complete a 360-degree turn in two minutes at your normal cruising airspeed. The resultant needle position and attitude indicator position should show a three-degree-per-second turn every time. Time the turn coordinator in both directions.

Above I mentioned timing the turn through a few cardinal headings. Perhaps I should explain that. If you are turning at a rate of 3° per second, you should turn through 30° in 10 seconds, 45° in 15 seconds, and 60° in 20 seconds, so as you are turning, you won't have to fly the entire 360° to see if your angle of bank is resulting in the desired rate of turn. But, once you have adjusted and readjusted your bank angle to get the desired results, it is still necessary to go through a complete 360-degree turn to ascertain that it is correct.

Once you have accomplished this experiment, you should be able to establish a standard-rate turn by using either the turn coordinator or the attitude indicator. Naturally, when both instruments are working, you will constantly use one as a cross-check against the other, but if one fails, you should still be able to complete the turn. Not only that, but by rolling into and out of turns smoothly and slowly, always at the same roll rate, you should be able to roll out on any heading—or be able to make a turn of any number of degrees—without reference to the compasses, just by timing the turns. Believe me, this ability has saved many pilots when their magnetic compasses have sprung leaks. To execute a timed turn properly, begin timing just as you begin rolling into the turn, and begin rolling out again at the end of the timing period.

The ball on the turn coordinator will help you keep the turn coordinated. It should always be centered. If the ball is on the high side of the turn, it indicates a skid. If it is on the low side, it indicates a slip. In either case, "step on the ball" to center it. First, take all pressure off the rudder pedals, which will usually eliminate 70 percent of the skid. Then apply just enough rudder pressure to center the ball, pressing the rudder pedal on the same side to which the ball is deflected.

As explained in Chapter 1, apply smooth pressure to the aileron and rudder to roll slowly into a coordinated turn. As the aircraft reaches the desired angle of bank as indicated both by the turn coordinator and the attitude indicator, the speed will decay somewhat due to some of the lift being used to turn the plane. As it occurs, the nose will begin to drop, as evidenced by the attitude indicator. About this time, the vertical speed indicator will indicate a descent, and if you wait much longer the altimeter will begin unwinding. Apply back pressure to the yoke to hold the proper nose attitude on the attitude indicator and then trim off the back pressure, cross-checking the compasses, turn coordinator, and attitude indicator for the proper rate of turn. It will be necessary to add a small amount of power to maintain the desired speed due to the increased drag produced by the increased angle-of-attack.

As you approach the desired heading, apply smooth, coordinated pressure to the opposite aileron and rudder to roll out of the turn on the proper heading. As you near a wings-level attitude, the upward lift vector will increase and the nose will tend to rise. Stop this by applying forward pressure on the yoke, and then by trimming off the pressure. It will also be necessary to ease off the extra power applied when entering the turn.

The most common errors committed while rolling into and out of turns are:

- Rolling in and out of turns at varying roll rates.

- Omitting the attitude indicator from the scan, allowing the nose to lower after entering the turns, or to rise after rolling out.

- Anticipating an altitude loss entering turns, or a gain when rolling out, and reacting too soon, causing the opposite results.

Practice should consist of perfecting turns using the magnetic compass, perfecting timed turns, and rolling in and out of turns smoothly and at a consistent roll rate.

STRAIGHT-AND-LEVEL FLIGHT

Combining the pitch instruments with the heading instruments, try to fly straight and level.

The first thing to do is to get the attitude indicator (AI) to show a wings-level, nose-level attitude with the power set for cruise. You must program both a heading and an altitude in your mind. As you scan the instruments, if you find the airspeed is higher or lower than normal for the power you have set, check the altimeter and vertical speed indicator (VSI) for any deviation. If none is noted, check your power control to determine if it has slipped in or out.

If you do have a change of altitude, make a slight pitch change, referencing the AI, to try to stop the unwanted trend. It will be important to remember the new pitch position of the AI. After making the slight pitch change, you should scan the directional gyro (DG) and needle/ball (or turn coordinator, as the case may be). If the needle is upright (or the airplane figure is wings-level), the ball is centered, and the AI indicates wings-level, you should have no change in the heading.

If your heading has changed, and is still changing, the turn needle will be deflected and the ball will probably be off center. To stop the turn, apply aileron pressure opposite the direction of the turn needle deflection, and use pressure on the rudder pedals to keep the ball centered.

If you apply slow, smooth pressures, you may imagine that the turn needle (or airplane figure) is directly connected to the yoke or stick, and you can almost "will" it to the center by the light pressure you are exerting on the yoke. When the needle centers, glance at the AI to note the wing position. That will be your new wings-level reference for straight flight, at least momentarily, until any precession has worked out of the gyro.

Now, return your scan to the pitch instruments. The altitude deviation should have stopped due to your corrective pitch change, and now you can make another pitch change to bring the aircraft back to your desired altitude. This pitch change should result in a vertical speed equal to twice the altitude change required, up to a maximum of 500 FPM. In other words, if your altitude is off by 100 feet, you should climb or descend by 200 FPM until you return to your desired altitude. This will take 30 seconds, during which time you will go back to the heading indicators and begin a slight correction back to the desired heading.

Straight-and-level flight is probably the hardest to master, perhaps because most pilots become complacent and feel that it's too easy. Once you're able to fly fairly straight and level at cruise power and speed, start varying your speed as you did before, only this time keep your heading by scanning the heading instruments.

From straight-and-level flight at cruise power, reduce to approach speed, maintaining both heading and altitude. Slowly and smoothly reduce the power to slightly less than required for approach speed. As the airspeed begins to decrease, you will notice a tendency for the pitch attitude to lower, accompanied by the VSI showing a descent. You should apply back pressure smoothly, raising the pitch attitude on the AI at a rate necessary to maintain a zero indication on the VSI and altimeter. This back pressure should be trimmed off as necessary.

At the same time, the ball will tend to move to the left and the nose will tend to yaw to the right. This can be corrected by either easing the pressure off the right rudder pedal, or by applying sufficient pressure to the left rudder pedal, as the case may be, to keep the ball centered. Properly executed, this maneuver should result in no change of heading.

When the airspeed reads three to five knots above the approach speed, the power should be advanced smoothly to the approach speed power that you learned earlier. The pitch attitude and power setting will be a close approximation and may have to be adjusted slightly to keep you at the proper airspeed and altitude.

Now, increase your speed back to cruise, while at the same time maintaining heading and altitude. To do this, increase the power smoothly to the climb power setting and reverse the previous procedures. Keep the ball centered by using a little right rudder pressure as the power is increased. When the airspeed reaches cruise, smoothly reduce to cruise power.

CLIMBS AND DESCENTS

Once you are able to do these maneuvers fairly well, try a climb, straight ahead. To initiate a climb, apply slight back pressure to the yoke to set a climb attitude indication on the AI. As the airspeed decreases, the increasing back pressure on the yoke should be trimmed off. When the airspeed reads five knots above climb airspeed, slowly and smoothly advance the power lever to the climb power setting. This procedure will result in a smooth transition from level flight to a climb attitude.

Throughout this maneuver, the right rudder pressure will have to be slowly increased to keep the ball centered and to hold the desired heading. If the aircraft has a rudder trim tab, this pressure should be trimmed off. Pitch attitude should be readjusted as necessary to establish and maintain a 500-FPM minute rate of climb on the VSI.

During the last 100 feet of climb, the pitch attitude should be gradually changed to level off at the desired altitude. As the airspeed increases, the pitch control pressure should be removed through the use of trim. When the airspeed reaches cruise speed, the power should be smoothly reduced to cruise power, and the rudder pressure should be removed to keep the ball centered.

So far so good. Now for descents. There are at least three different airspeeds commonly used during descents. You should learn to use them all.

The first, and easiest, is merely to lower the pitch attitude, and retrim as needed, to establish a 500-FPM rate of descent on the VSI, allowing the airspeed to increase and reducing power only if the airspeed approaches the red line, or V_{ne}. This is a good descent procedure to use in calm air. But instrument flight is seldom conducted in calm air, so a slower descent, your second choice, is made by merely reducing the power sufficiently to establish a 500-FPM descent at cruise airspeed. In this case, very little pitch trim will be necessary. As you near your desired altitude, slight nose-up pressure (trimmed off) and re-establishment of cruise power should hold the airspeed constant.

The last type of descent is made at approach speed. From level flight and approach speed/power, you can lower the gear and/or flaps and retrim to establish the required descent rate, reduce power as you did in the preceding method, or use a combination of these methods. The important thing is to reduce to approach speed and level flight first. The fewer attitude, speed, and configuration changes you have to make at one time, the easier it becomes to do it right.

If you have to use drag devices (gear and/or flaps) to establish your descent, when you near the desired altitude, maintain it by retracting the drag devices or by increasing power. Establishing your new altitude by retraction of drag devices requires a longer lead time than by power changes, and usually tends to confuse—and, in some cases, alarm—your passengers.

All of these procedures should be practiced first in straight flight, and then combined with turns to specific headings, until they can be accomplished smoothly, with little or no noticeable change of gravity forces and with minimum instrument deviation. The turns should be practiced using (1) the directional gyro (2) the magnetic compass, and (3) time, separately and in combination. Altitude changes should be practiced using (1) the altimeter and (2) time.

In short, you must practice, practice, practice, until the procedures become second nature and your instrument scan becomes automatic.

Some of the most common errors are:

- Omission of one or more instruments from the scan.

- Gazing too long at one instrument, called "instrument fixation." This is sometimes caused by staring at the instrument while waiting for a change to take place.

- Anticipating the need for corrective pressures and applying them before they are needed. This is especially prevalent when rolling into or out of turns.

- Misinterpreting the instruments, resulting in such errors as unnecessary power changes. For example, you see the airspeed is too high, so you reduce power, not noticing that the increased airspeed is due to a loss of altitude and that simply leveling off by applying back pressure will slow the airspeed.

- Personal tension transferred to the controls, resulting in inability to sense unwanted pressures. From time to time, flex your hands and feet to restore circulation.

- Erratic and excessive control displacement, resulting in excessive instrument deflections, instrument lag, and gravity forces, leading to vertigo.

- Improper trim techniques.

5

Airspeed/Altitude Control

SOME YEARS BACK, MAYBE BACK IN THE BEGINNING OF TIME AS FAR AS AIRplanes are concerned, someone thinking about flight in general, or instrument flight in particular, came up with the idea that the elevator controlled the airspeed, while the power controlled the altitude. This started a controversy that has lasted ever since, sort of like, "Which came first, the chicken or the egg?"

This concept has been widely taught throughout the industry, and it has created a lot of confusion. One young instructor, so the story goes, was hired by an airline for the express purpose of teaching this new idea to the airline's pilots. He was busy transitioning a grizzled, 20,000-hour DC-3 captain into a DC-6 while at the same time teaching the captain this new instrument technique.

The way I heard the story, after the first landing and while taxiing back for another takeoff, the disgruntled captain turned to the instructor and said, "O.K. Sonny, let me make sure of this. This yoke's supposed to control my airspeed, while the throttles will control the altitude, is that right?"

"That's it, Captain," the instructor beamed. "Now you're getting the point."

Being cleared for takeoff, the captain maneuvered onto the active runway and began pumping the yoke back and forth, with the throttles at idle.

"What are you doing, Captain?" the young instructor asked.

"Well, Sonny," the grey-beard muttered with a sly smile, "I'm pumping up some airspeed, and when I get to V_r, I want you to grab them four throttles and jam in a little altitude."

Well, we've all laughed at the joke, but most of us accepted the theory and became proficient at it. Then along came the flight directors, the devices that not only told us that we were above or below the glide slope, but also how much of a pitch correction to make to intercept it again. All of a sudden altitude was controlled by the elevator again, and the throttles, quite naturally, handled the airspeed. Sure, the logical answer is that they're interrelated and that you can seldom change one without also changing the other.

Finally, and at long last, the FAA has come out with a very logical breakdown that should do a lot to eliminate the confusion and controversy. Basically, the "new" correct premise is this: when power is variable and available, then the power controls the speed and the elevators control the altitude or rate of altitude change. This means that in level flight, rate climbs or descents, and instrument approaches, the power will control the speed.

When the power is fixed, or not available, the elevator will control either speed or rate of altitude change, such as full throttle takeoffs, or during descents when the engine(s) have failed or are at zero thrust (idle descents).

Hopefully, this will end most of the controversy. Try it out, you'll like it—and it's logical.

FLYING THE PARTIAL PANEL

What will you do if the AI and DG both quit? You will be left with the basic panel, which is called by many people the "partial panel," or the needle-ball-and-airspeed group. For many years these were *all* the instruments that were available to pilots. Today, a partial panel is used as part of the instrument flight test.

I can remember (sounds like an old man, doesn't it?) when I learned to fly. I took my primary training in a Piper PA-11, which was basically a J-3 Cub with a 90-hp engine. One day, my instructor told me that we would learn to fly on instruments. He briefed me very quickly on the then-current (1962) method of partial-panel flying, called the one-two-three method. In this method, the pilot would:

1. Use only the rudder to center the needle.
2. Use only the ailerons to center the ball.
3. Use only the elevators to maintain the proper airspeed.

The altitude would be controlled by the power, but for some reason it was never considered as Step #4. Maybe it was thought to be so obvious that it didn't need to be made part of the method.

In any event, this method resulted in the most uncomfortable, uncoordinated, mechanical, vertigo-inducing type of flight you can imagine, and the first time I tried it I was all over the sky.

One day it came to me (perhaps after reading it in a book, although I don't remember) that the turn needle looked like the stick in the PA-11 and that I would try to make the needle move in relation to the movement of the stick. That part worked fine, and so did the advice to "step on the ball" to center it.

From then on, I had no more trouble controlling an aircraft on instruments. Things just seemed to fall naturally into place, and I found the procedure resulted in well-coordinated, smooth flight, even in the PA-11.

When I progressed to aircraft that used yokes instead of sticks, I pretended that when I moved the wheel I was really moving a stick and the procedure still worked well. Now that so many aircraft are equipped with turn coordinators, it's easy to visualize in a direct manner again. If you picture the sides of the wheel as being connected to the wings of the turn coordinator (or to the AI for that matter), it becomes a simple matter of "pushing" downward on the left side of the yoke to force the left side of the turn coordinator (or the AI) down.

What all of this really boils down to is that it makes no difference where your visual cues, concerning the attitude of the aircraft, come from. Whether it's VFR, IFR on a full panel, or IFR on a partial panel, you should always fly the aircraft the same way, and for the best results and smoothest flight, this way should be a smooth and coordinated manipulation of all of the controls, with a minimum of aircraft attitude change.

In the previous chapters I talked about the instruments that support the AI. Now, assume that, due to severe turbulence or other factors, your AI has tumbled, or has otherwise become disabled, that the DG has packed up, and that you are all alone in a big sky filled with soft, white fluffy clouds that you can't see through. You are on partial panel. Here's where the gentle pressures and proper scanning techniques that you have been practicing become really important.

Think back to the earlier lessons where you became so good at applying smooth control pressure that you were able to make the VSI act as a direct extension of the yoke. Now, under partial panel, use the same techniques to control altitude, climb, and descent. In level flight, you will control airspeed by power, and altitude by pressure exerted on the elevator. All of your turns will be timed turns, based on the needle and ball, backed up with the magnetic compass.

UNUSUAL ATTITUDES

There may be times when, due to inattention or turbulence, you may end up in an unusual attitude. These attitudes will normally be one of two types: the power-on spiral (FIG. 5-1) or the climbing approach to a stall (FIG. 5-2). In either case, the cause, or the result, may leave you with an unreliable AI, so recovery should be based on the partial panel.

The indications of a power-on spiral would be: extreme deflection of the turn needle (the ball may end up being almost anywhere, but it will usually be near the center); high, and usually increasing, airspeed; altimeter unwinding at a rapid

AIRSPEED INCREASING   DIVING RIGHT TURN   LOSING ALTITUDE

Fig. 5-1. *Unusual attitude: power-on spiral.*

rate; and VSI indicating a high rate of descent, perhaps even pegged-out.

The recovery must be smooth and coordinated, but it will usually be somewhat mechanical. The first step should be to reduce the power. This will flatten the blades of a constant-speed propeller, producing some drag, and it will either pull the fixed-pitch propeller out of the red line area or prevent it from going in.

Secondly, roll out to wings-level. To do this, apply aileron opposite to the deflection of the turn needle (in other words, push the needle back to an upright position, or the wings of a turn coordinator to a level position), and smoothly apply rudder pressure as necessary to center the ball and to keep it centered.

As the wings roll level, the upward lift coefficient of the wings will increase, tending to make the nose pitch up, thereby reducing the dive angle. In fact, the increased airspeed may cause the nose to pitch high enough to cause a rapid climb and resultant stall. If the aircraft had been trimmed for level flight before the spiral, and the trim had not been changed, you will not have to use any back pressure at all to level off. In fact, until the airspeed drops down to cruise you will very possibly need slight forward pressure to prevent a pitch-up. In any event, be very careful that you do not allow the G-forces to get too great during the pullout, whether the aircraft is recovering itself or you have had to apply some back pressure.

As you pull level, check the airspeed indicator. When it first reverses its trend (that is, when it stops increasing and just begins to decrease), the aircraft is, for all practical purposes, in a level flight attitude *for that airspeed*. At this point, the altimeter will have stopped unwinding. Hold that attitude (hold the yoke in that specific position regardless of pressure) for a few moments, and then begin controlling the altitude with the elevator, cross-checking the VSI and airspeed. This part of the recovery will be mostly mechanical. When the airspeed slows down to within 10 MPH of cruise speed, increase the power smoothly to the cruise power setting.

After the aircraft is back under control and trimmed out properly, begin a smooth climb back to the desired altitude. To do this, apply smooth back pressure to the yoke to bring the VSI to the desired rate of climb. When the airspeed slows down to about 5 MPH above climb speed, add power smoothly to the climb power setting, and fly the airspeed indicator or VSI, depending on which instrument is the most desirable based on the aircraft capabilities at that altitude.

In the initial recovery for this unusual attitude, follow three steps:

1. Power reduction,

2. Roll (bank) recovery, and finally,

3. Pitch recovery.

If you try to pull out of the dive without first rolling the wings level, you will tighten the spiral. This will increase the speed, the rate of descent, and the wing loading, and will greatly increase the chances of folding the wings.

Sometimes, once the wings are level, you may have a tendency to try to level out faster by applying excessive back pressure, which may result in another unusual attitude, an approach to a stall. This can be recognized by a rapidly decreasing airspeed, a high rate of climb, an increasing altitude (which may be leveling off if you're close to, or in, a stall), and possibly a turn indication on the needle/ball.

To initiate the recovery you should shove the throttle(s) in rapidly, but smoothly, to the full power setting, while at the same time pushing forward slightly on the yoke (or by relaxing back pressure as the case may be). Finally, center the needle/ball with smooth, coordinated control pressures.

How much pitch control displacement is necessary? As in the spiral, only enough to stop the airspeed indication from decreasing, or make it begin increasing if it has already stopped decreasing. In other words, just enough to make a perceptible change in the airspeed. When this change occurs, you'll be roughly in a level flight attitude.

Fig. 5-2. *Unusual attitude: approach to a stall.*

If you've waited too long to notice the approach to a stall, and the stall break itself has occurred, you must lower the nose a little more to hasten the recovery and to prevent a secondary stall. When near stall speed, it's very important to keep the ball centered to avoid entering a spin.

Again, and this must be reemphasized, just as in a spiral, when the airspeed has shown a definite change of trend you are near level flight *for that specific airspeed*, and you should fly the altimeter and VSI until the airspeed approaches cruise, at which time you should readjust your throttle(s) to cruise power and retrim. Once under control, you should return smoothly to the desired altitude.

Although I have mentioned pitch and power changes as two separate steps in the recovery from an approach to a stall, these two steps are normally combined into one smooth, but largely mechanical, action. The same holds true for the recovery from a power-on spiral. You really make the recovery the same as if you're in visual conditions.

In both recoveries demonstrated, the altitude gained or lost should be recovered (or at least the recovery attempt should be initiated) before you worry too much about the heading. In most cases, the altitude will be the most critical problem. If you try to do too many things at one time, especially on a partial panel, you can very easily end up doing more harm than good, and may create confusion, vertigo, and more unusual attitudes.

Remember, *during unusual attitudes treat the AI and DG as if they have tumbled, because chances are they have.* You must base your recovery on your primary instruments, adding the AI and DG to your scan only when you are absolutely certain that they have regained their reliability.

INSTRUMENT TAKEOFFS

This leads us to the final topic for this chapter, the instrument takeoff (ITO).

The ITO is basically a training maneuver. If the weather is really zero/zero, not even the birds will take off, let alone intelligent pilots. After all, where could you go if you had to make an emergency landing shortly after takeoff?

I can only think of a few instances when you would be justified in making an actual ITO, for example, if your airport is socked in by a strictly local condition, such as a ground fog, where the tops are only a few hundred feet high, and there's another field nearby that's open. Even then you'd be taking a chance, but at least it would be well calculated.

In making an ITO, taxi onto the runway, line up with the centerline, and let the plane roll a few feet to make sure that the nosewheel, or the tailwheel, as the case may be, is rolling straight. Set the DG to the painted runway heading, even though the magnetic compass may be reading differently. You can, and will, always reset the DG later, but on takeoff it's easier to steer to a specific mark on the face of the DG.

Next, set the attitude indicator to the proper aircraft attitude, which is approximately nose level with a tricycle gear, but nose high (near normal climb attitude) in a taildragger.

Be sure that the gyros are uncaged and up to speed. Remember that it takes up to five minutes for gyros to spin up to a reliable speed.

Finally, advance the throttle(s) smoothly to maximum allowable power (takeoff power), while keeping all pressure off the brakes. Do not attempt to steer with the brakes. As in visual takeoffs, you will be correcting the heading with rudder pressure. There will be a psychological tendency to overcontrol your heading at first, because you will feel that you are about to tear out all of the runway lights. By paying more attention to the action of the DG on your next visual takeoff you will see what the normal reactions are like and be more able to relate them to the ITO.

As your airspeed approaches climb speed, establish a climb attitude on the AI. This will be about the same attitude whether you are in a tailwheel or nosewheel aircraft. In a taildragger, you will have to lift the tailwheel off the ground first, but just bring it off slightly, nowhere near the amount you do on a normal visual takeoff. For this reason you should practice this technique a few times under visual conditions to see what it feels like and looks like before trying it under the hood.

Remember, as the aircraft lifts off, the AI will precess and show a slightly higher nose attitude. Scanning the AI and VSI should be quick because you're holding the heading with the DG and the needle/ball. Improper interpretation of the AI at liftoff can result in touching back down. The first 150 feet of altitude will be fairly critical. Above that, you will be well out of ground effect, and the instrument precession and lag should have pretty much recovered.

ITOs are a lot of fun, and while they may not be the most practical maneuver, they do a lot of good toward teaching good instrument scanning techniques. They also help build confidence.

6

Practice, Practice, Practice

NOW THAT WE'VE WORKED THROUGH MOST OF THE BASICS, ONE BY ONE, LET'S combine them in some practice problems to make use of all the basic flying skills you'll need to keep the aircraft in the air. In addition, let's begin adding the clock to your scan. The clock is quite necessary in an actual IFR flight, and it is one of the culprits that greatly interferes with the scan of many pilots—they tend to stare at it waiting for it to move while flying a timed portion of a flight.

The problems you will be working with in this chapter are designed to make aircraft control and instrument scan second nature, while the use of the clock will add some external pressure to prepare you for the more advanced portion of instrument flight.

At the end of this chapter you will be working with a problem that utilizes a VOR. This is designed to get your mind working rapidly on factors away from the actual instrument panel.

The first problem is fairly simple, incorporating airspeed control, level turns, descents, and climbs. You should fly each of these patterns visually the first time to get an idea of what's happening. Then fly them with a full panel until you are really good at them, and finally, finish up using only a partial panel.

A BASIC MANEUVER

Begin flying the problem illustrated in FIG. 6-1 from a cruise power, cruise airspeed, straight-and-level configuration. If there is any appreciable wind, you

Fig. 6-1

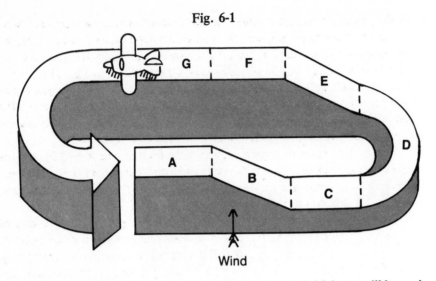

Wind

should begin the problem by flying crosswind so that the initial turn will be made downwind. The reason you do this is to remain in the same relative practice area.

Take a look now at FIG. 6-1 and follow along:

Segment A: Slow to approach airspeed, and fly straight and level for one minute.

Segment B: Begin a descent for one minute at approach airspeed and a 500-FPM rate of descent.

Segment C: Level off, and fly one minute at approach airspeed. Here you should be 500 feet lower than when you began the maneuver at A.

Segment D: Make a level, standard-rate turn. Remember that a standard-rate turn is 3° per second. Make this turn for one minute, which should result in a turn of 180°.

Segment E: Climb for one minute at climb airspeed and a 500-FPM rate of climb.

Segment F: Here you should be at your initial altitude. At this point, accelerate to cruise airspeed and cruise power.

Segment G: Make a standard-rate level turn for one minute, rolling out on your initial heading.

When you fly this pattern the second time, you should make the turns in the opposite direction, and alternate the directions of the turns from then on, not only for the practice of different turns, but also to remain in the same practice area.

During the descent segment (B) you should use as many different aircraft configurations as you can. In other words, make one simulated approach in the clean configuration, using only power to adjust the rate of descent. Then, if you have retractable gear, make a descent by lowering the gear, adjusting power as necessary to maintain a 500-FPM descent. Finally, use various flap settings, with and without the gear, paying attention to the specific pitch attitude and the approximate power setting needed for each type of descent.

If you have retractable gear, try flying the level turn segment (D) with the gear down and the flaps in both the clean and the proper maneuvering positions. No matter what configuration you are using in segment D, you have to remember to clean up the aircraft when you begin the climb in segment E.

Learn the aircraft thoroughly. It's necessary to practice this pattern of maneuvers until controlling the aircraft on instruments becomes second nature, until: you can change the gear and flap configurations without gaining or losing any altitude, your airspeed remains nailed where you want it, one minute of descent results in a loss of exactly 500 feet, one minute of climb results in a gain of exactly 500 feet, and the one-minute turns come out to exactly 180°.

Once you have mastered this basic pattern, you can make one change in it that will turn it into a procedure that at one time was part of all ATP flight tests. It was called the "canyon approach," and it was—and is—an excellent test of aircraft control.

The premise is that (referring back to FIG. 6-1), as the captain of an aircraft, you have been cleared for an approach to an airport located in a canyon. You reduce to approach airspeed in segment A. At the beginning of segment B you cross the initial approach fix (a radio beacon theoretically located on the rim of the canyon), lower gear and flaps, and descend to a Minimum Descent Altitude which is 500 feet below your cruising altitude.

Once down to Minimum Descent Altitude, you fly out the allotted time, which in this pattern is depicted as segment C (one minute at approach speed), and when you don't see the airport, you initiate the missed approach procedure. In this case, the missed approach procedure calls for an immediate 180-degree climbing turn, as depicted in segment D, which will take you back to your initial altitude. Naturally, the gear and flaps must be retracted during the wave-off.

The one change you have made to the original pattern you were practicing is that you no longer make that nice level turn at D as in the original problem. Instead, you have combined segments D and E into a climbing turn. Still, it's necessary to be at your initial altitude and the reciprocal heading as you complete the one-minute climbing turn.

If you are flying a multiengine aircraft, you should have the instructor pilot cut the inside engine (by retarding the throttle) as you begin the climb-out. With most light twins you won't be able to make the 500-FPM climb, but if you are really on the ball, you will get the turn timed correctly and also keep from descending below the Minimum Descent Altitude. This is not only a great instrument practice problem, but it sharpens your engine-out procedures as well.

PUTTING IT ALL TOGETHER

Another interesting sequence of maneuvers can be seen in FIG. 6-2. I have broken it down into 22 one-minute segments that will review every aspect of aircraft control under instruments with the exception of unusual attitudes.

In this series you will probably need to have the safety pilot review the procedure step-by-step as you go along, which is also good training for the day you will be flying in a two-pilot cockpit where the pilot not at the controls reviews the procedures for the person doing the flying.

I should note one thing here. There is nothing sacred about this series of patterns; you can always make up one of your own. As with the other pattern, fly this one visually at first to get an idea of what it's like. Then fly it on a full panel, and finally, with a partial panel. Try to be extremely precise with timing, as well as with the airspeeds, altitudes, and headings. Remember that each segment should be one minute in duration:

Segment A: Begin at 5000 feet AGL at cruise power and cruise speed. Use any heading, though it's easier if you start on a cardinal point (i.e., north, south, east, or west).

Segment B: While maintaining the heading and altitude, smoothly reduce your airspeed to approach speed.

Segment C: Begin a 500-FPM rate of descent, while still maintaining the original heading.

Segment D: Continue the 500-FPM rate of descent, and initiate a standard-rate 360-degree turn to the right.

Segment E: After 180 degrees of the turn, level off (you should now be at 4000 feet AGL) and maintain the approach airspeed. Continue the turn, and roll out on the initial heading.

Segment F: Reestablish a descent of 500 FPM.

Segment G: While continuing the descent, roll into a standard-rate 270-degree turn to the left, and after one minute, level off at 3000 feet AGL, maintaining approach airspeed.

Segment H: Continue the turn for 30 seconds, rolling out your initial heading plus 90°.

Fig. 6-2

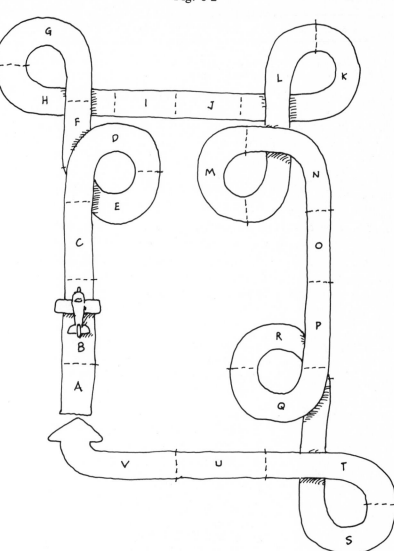

Segment I:	Accelerate to cruise airspeed. Maintain the new heading and an altitude of 3000 feet AGL.
Segment J:	Initiate a one-minute 500-FPM climb while maintaining the heading.
Segment K:	Continue the climb, and begin a standard-rate 270-degree turn to the left.

Segment L: After 180° of turn, continue the climbing turn for another 30 seconds (for a total of 90 seconds), and then, while maintaining the climb, roll into the first 90° of a standard-rate 360-degree turn to the right.

Segment M: Continue the climbing turn, leveling off at 5000 feet AGL.

Segment N: Continue to turn for 30 seconds (for a total of two minutes) while accelerating to cruise speed, finally rolling out on the reciprocal of the original heading in Segment A.

Segment O: Reduce power to approach airspeed.

Segment P: Initiate a 500-FPM descent, and if the aircraft has retractable gear, extend the gear.

Segment Q: While descending, begin a 360-degree standard-rate turn to the right, and extend approach flaps.

Segment R: Continue the descending right turn with gear and flaps extended. At the end of this second minute of the turn, you should once again be on the reciprocal of the initial heading and at 3500 feet AGL.

Segment S: Here you will initiate a climbing, 270-degree standard-rate left turn to simulate a missed approach, retracting the gear (if applicable) and flaps, while climbing at 500 FPM.

Segment T: Continue the climbing standard-rate left turn for 30 seconds (a total of 90 seconds), rolling out at your original heading plus 90°, all the while continuing the climb.

Segment U: Continue the climb, leveling off after one minute of straight flight. The altitude should once again be 5000 feet AGL.

Segment V: Establish cruise airspeed, then begin a 30-second, 90-degree, standard-rate turn to the right, rolling out in position to begin Segment A at the original altitude, heading, and airspeed.

This maneuver, properly executed, will go a long way towards preparing you to handle an aircraft with the precision necessary for instrument flight. During the procedure, you will have simulated all aspects of a normal instrument flight, including level flight; speed control; climbing, descending, and level turns; approach configurations; and missed approaches.

You can devise other patterns of your own, of course, but a pattern similar to the one depicted here will get all of the necessary maneuvers in without wandering all over the countryside.

VOR TRACKING AND TIME/DISTANCE PROBLEMS

You have one last area to work on before departing on your first cross-country instrument flight. This is a procedure that will cover VOR tracking, radial intercepts, and time-and-distance problems.

You can usually accomplish this problem successfully in one practice session using a single VOR facility. See FIG. 6-3.

To begin with, cross the VOR and proceed outbound on the 135-degree radial for a period of five minutes. Then, turn right to a heading of 270°. The problem now will be to intercept and track inbound on the 180-degree radial.

In addition, you will need to figure the time to the station from the point of intercept. This problem is primarily one of mental computation, devised to get your thought processes working independently of the motor processes that are actually flying the aircraft.

Once again, the pattern has been set up to keep you within a reasonable amount of airspace. You can set up any headings and intercepts you want, though the ones depicted here are easy to follow and will suffice to teach what you will need to know in actual instrument conditions.

A simple solution to a time/distance problem on an intercept is to position the aircraft 90° to the inbound radial. When you are 20° from the radial, begin timing yourself through the next 10° of bearing change, converting the time to seconds. Ten percent of the resulting time in seconds (just place the decimal point one digit in from the right) will provide the approximate time to the station in minutes. For example, if you have flown through 10° in two minutes (or 120 seconds), time to the station (in minutes) would be 10% of that, or 120 seconds × 10% = 12.0 minutes. Distance from the station would then be your ground speed (in NM per minute) times the time to the station. So, if you have a ground speed of 120 knots, or 2 NM per minute, you would be 24 NM from the station. Easy? You bet, but it seems much more difficult in a moving aircraft when you are trying to control it on instruments alone.

You can then add one other step to the problem. In order to allow adequate time to pin down the inbound course before entering the cone of confusion around the VOR, you should make it a practice to turn inbound only if you are more than three minutes from the station. This means that it must take more than 30 seconds to cross that 10° of bearing change that you time yourself through.

If you find that you are three minutes or less from the station, you should turn outbound 30° away from reciprocal of the inbound course, fly outbound for 1.5 minutes, make a standard-rate 180-degree turn (in the direction away from the station) back toward the course. Once you intercept the course, fly inbound to the station. Take another look at the left side of FIG. 6-3. You can see how this resembles a procedure turn. So, in addition to everything else, this pattern should also give you practice in procedure turns.

Returning to the explanation of the problem depicted in FIG. 6-3: you are heading 270°, which is 90° to your inbound course (which is the 180-degree radial of the VOR). To orientate the omni bearing indicator (OBI, or needle) properly, you should have it set to your inbound course, which will be 360° TO. In this example then, the OBI should be deflected to the left, showing that you have not reached the course.

Before everyone jumps on me for using the term *omni bearing indicator* instead of *course deviation indicator* (CDI), I prefer to use the term CDI in relation to flight directors, and OBI in relation to the simple VOR receiver. If you prefer the term CDI, feel free to substitute it whenever you see OBI.

In order to time yourself through 10° of bearing change, and still have time to make decisions as to whether to fly inbound or to fly a procedure turn first, you should back up the omni bearing *selector* (OBS) 20° from the inbound course. This means that, in this example, you should set it to 340° TO. Once again, the needle should be deflected to the left of the indicator.

Before long the needle will move off its peg. When it centers, you should check the clock, noting both the minute- and second-hand positions. Reset the OBS to 350° TO. When the needle centers again, take the time in seconds, and compute the time and distance. For the first 30 seconds of time from 340° TO to 350° TO, I find it useful to keep telling myself, "procedure turn." After 30 seconds have passed, if I have not yet made it through the 10-degree bearing change, I automatically change my thinking to, "direct inbound."

If you flew the initial outbound leg for five or six minutes, you should be more than three minutes from the station, and will make a right turn inbound when you get to the course. Naturally, after crossing the 350-degree course that was set on the OBS, you should immediately reset it to the desired inbound course of 360°. All this time, you should be maintaining the proper heading, airspeed, and altitude.

A strong wind will play havoc with this procedure as it may screw up your estimates, but for the most part they should work out pretty close.

Now, turn inbound, track to the VOR, and continue on the same course outbound for one minute. As you cross the VOR, you should make a simulated position report to ATC. Your new problem is to track inbound on the 270-degree radial.

In order to do this you must first put yourself on the proper side of the station; therefore, after flying the one-minute outbound leg from the station, you should turn left to a heading of 270° and fly outbound for one minute. Then turn south, which will be 90° to your inbound course again.

Once again, set the inbound course on the OBS. This time it will be 090° TO. Now, the OBI should be deflected to the right. If it is, reset the OBS to 110°

Fig. 6-3

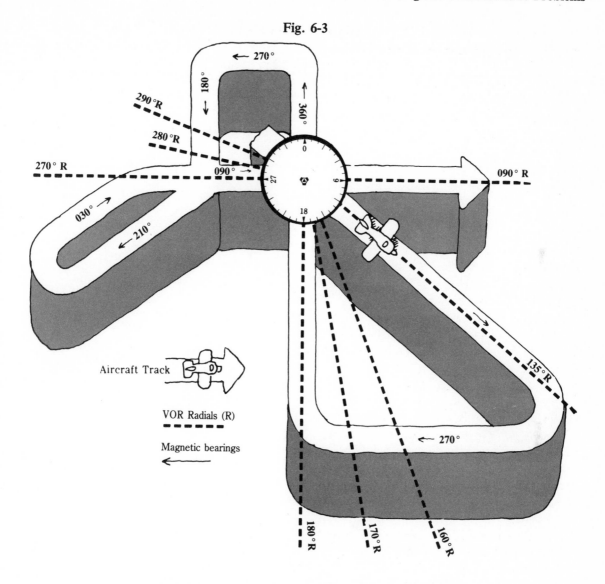

Aircraft Track

VOR Radials (R)
- - - - - - - -

Magnetic bearings
←

TO, which is 20° from your desired inbound track. When the needle centers, check the time and advance the OBS 10°, to 100° TO. In this case, assuming that your time is under 30 seconds—and it should be—you should fly a procedure turn as depicted, and while turning outbound, should once again set the inbound course on the OBS.

As you can see, you can set up many problems using this simple pattern, although, with the exception of the procedure turn, it may not be of much use on an actual IFR flight. Still, it is an excellent pattern for building up your mental prowess and your command of reciprocal bearings, while at the same time teaching you to fly the aircraft on instruments almost automatically.

Once you feel that you have mastered the instruments and are quite comfortable doing these problems, you will be ready for your first actual cross-country IFR flight.

7

Planning
the IFR Flight

PREFLIGHT PLANNING, TO MANY PEOPLE, MEANS NOTHING MORE THAN SCAN-
ning the charts, making a quick call to the weather or Flight Service people
to see if it's still VFR, a cursory glance at the aircraft with perhaps a perfunctory
kick at a tire, and then up, up, and away.

Instrument pilots cannot afford this degree of nonchalance. Murphy's well-
known law holds that, "Anything that can go wrong, will go wrong." When
we combine that with the fact that emergencies always seem to snowball, we tend
to become a little more careful, or at least we should.

At least 50 percent of effective instrument flying is psychological; thus, a
proper, careful, preflight procedure will put us in a mental condition to properly
handle the flight. In addition, this proper preflight procedure is required by the
FARs.

FAR 91.5 says:

> Each pilot in command shall, before beginning a flight, familia-
> rize himself with all available information concerning that flight. This
> information must include:
> (a) For a flight under IFR . . . weather reports and forecasts, fuel
> requirements, alternatives available if the planned flight cannot be com-
> pleted, and any known traffic delays of which he has been advised
> by ATC . . .

THE FLIGHT KIT

A fairly good place to begin this discussion is with the pilot's personal flight kit. Every instrument-rated pilot eventually puts together a flight kit that seems to work best for him or her. The items listed below make up a fairly comprehensive kit. As you gain more experience, you may want to add to it or subtract from it to suit your individual desires. You'll notice that I have recommended more than one of some of the items. These are inexpensive items that don't take up space or add much weight to your flight kit. Believe me—you'll be willing to pay a king's ransom should one fail or wear out in flight and you end up without a spare.

- ☐ Airway charts, SIDS, STARS, and approach plates for the section of the country you'll be flying in. For most light aircraft, the enroute low altitude charts will suffice for the airway charts.

- ☐ Sectional charts to cover the same area—and/or WAC charts, depending on the speed of your aircraft. These charts will better enable you to visualize the terrain you'll be flying over. There are many times when you'll get enough of a break in the clouds to catch a glimpse of the ground, and in many cases, the Sectional will enable you to confirm your position. There is one other use for the Sectional, which we'll talk about later.

- ☐ Two or more flashlights, with fresh spare batteries and extra bulbs, in case you suffer an electrical power failure at night. If you, like some other pilots, prefer to put a red lens on one of the flashlights, you'll have to remember that red lines and markings on your charts will be invisible under the red light.

- ☐ Two or more pens—felt-tips work best. They write heavily and dark enough to show up well in both dim lighting conditions and in turbulence, and they are excellent for copying clearances. Black is the best color for maximum visibility.

- ☐ Six or so sharpened pencils (#2 lead seems to be the best) for working up flight plans and other miscellaneous figuring. Dull points are difficult to write with, and to read later, so you should carry a small hand-held pencil sharpener, like you'd find in a child's pencil box. In fact, a child's pencil box is a great container for all of these small items. And don't forget a good eraser. The erasers on the pencils wear out a lot faster than the pencils do, so it's a good idea to have spares.

- ☐ One pocket computer, at least. There are many good computers on the market today; I happen to prefer the Jeppesen CR-2, which fits in a shirt pocket.

☐ Two (or more) plotters, one for sectional and WAC charts, and one for the IFR enroute charts. Remember, unlike the WAC or sectional charts, the enroute charts can be almost any scale. Always check the chart's scale so you will use the proper scale on the plotter.

☐ A pad or two of the latest FAA Flight Plan forms.

☐ Scratch pads or note paper. Here I find that the backsides of the small telephone message forms work just fine for clearances and miscellaneous figuring. They'll fit right in your shirt pocket along with your computer so they're always close at hand.

IFR AIRCRAFT REQUIREMENTS

Just as you need special charts, your aircraft will need special instrumentation for IFR flight. Part 91.33 lists what you need on board to operate in all environments. The instruments and equipment required for IFR flight are, in addition to those required for VFR flight, a two-way radio communications system and navigational equipment appropriate to the ground facilities to be used; gyroscopic rate-of-turn indicator; slip/skid indicator; sensitive altimeter; clock showing hours, minutes, and seconds with a sweep-second pointer or digital presentation; a generator of adequate capacity; artificial horizon (attitude indicator); directional gyro or equivalent; and for flight at or above 24,000 feet MSL, Distance Measuring Equipment (DME).

There are also special requirements for your VOR receivers. FAR 91.25 says this:

(a) No person may operate a civil aircraft under IFR using the VOR system of radio navigation unless the VOR equipment of that aircraft—

(1) Is maintained, checked, and inspected under an approved procedure; or

(2) Has been operationally checked within the preceding 30 days and was found to be within the limits of the permissible indicated bearing error . . .

These permissible errors are ±4° when using an FAA-operated or approved VOR test signal (VOT) or designated (usually by paint marks) surface VOR receiver checkpoint, or if dual VORs are checked against each other; and ±6° on on an approved in-flight check.

An aircraft logbook entry must be made for each VOR check. However, it is not necessary to have a mechanic do the check. You, the pilot, can do your own, but don't forget to make the logbook entry.

There are other required items for IFR flight, but they deal with such external things as lighting, and I won't bother with them in this discussion.

ICING AND THUNDERSTORM HAZARDS

Now, after ascertaining that both your aircraft and personal flight kit are in order, you should move to the weather briefing. After all, if the weather's too bad, you won't go. Remember, an instrument ticket is not a license to fly in any and all weather. Rather, it's proof that you've been taught to recognize what weather not to fly into, as well as what weather conditions you can handle.

For example, the regulations prevent you from flying into most icing conditions. FAR 91.209, which concerns large and turbine-powered multiengine aircraft, states:

(a) No pilot may take off in an airplane that has—

(1) Frost, snow, or ice adhering to any propeller, windshield, or power plant installation, or to an airspeed, altimeter, rate-of-climb, or flight attitude instrument system;

(2) Snow or ice adhering to the wings, or stabilizing or control surfaces; or

(3) Any frost adhering to the wings, or stabilizing or control surfaces, unless that frost has been polished to make it smooth.

(b) Except for an airplane that has ice protection provisions that meet the requirements in [a regulation setting forth anti-ice and deice requirements not applicable to most light aircraft], no pilot may fly—

(1) Under IFR into known or forecast moderate icing conditions . . .

Although these restrictions are specifically written to apply to large and turbine-powered multiengine aircraft, and there are no restrictions specifically written concerning light aircraft, it would be foolish to fly lightplanes where the heavies have been restricted (and it could be considered a violation of FAR 91.9—"Careless or Reckless Operation"—to do so).

Ice is one of the greatest hazards an airman can face, short of a wing falling off. It can add weight to the aircraft very quickly, which will increase the stalling speed. Additionally, it may build up to the point that the engine is no longer capable of carrying the load. It can build up in such a manner as to put the aircraft outside of CG limits, and, especially with rime ice, it builds in such a non-uniform shape as to completely destroy the lift of the wings. The worst icing conditions that you can encounter are freezing rain and freezing drizzle, both of which are capable of pulling you out of the sky in just a few minutes.

Though rime ice can form at temperatures as low as −40 °F (−40 °C), the very hazardous glaze or clear ice is usually confined to temperatures of 14–32 °F (−10° to 0 °C).

Check the weather carefully for reports of icing, and avoid flying into IFR conditions when the outside air temperature (OAT) is in the range of 10–32 °F. Find a different altitude—one that will result in a higher or lower OAT.

Even following these hints you will eventually find yourself in icing conditions, but it shouldn't be too hard to handle. One thing you must remember, however, is that ice does increase your stalling speed, so be prepared to land at a higher speed than normal should you have ice build-up on your aircraft.

One of the most insidious forms of icing is carburetor ice. If the humidity is high enough, this can form at any OAT from 14–70 °F. A functioning carburetor heat control will usually melt the ice, provided it is used in the early stages of formation. Pulling the carburetor heat out for a few minutes every 10 or 15 minutes will usually prevent major carburetor icing. The reason carburetor ice will form at high temperatures is that, as the intake air passes through the venturi of the carburetor, the air cools rapidly and any moisture in it can frost up the throat of the carburetor as well as the fuel nozzles. (I have had carburetor icing even over Hawaii.) This is why carburetor heat is pulled out on many aircraft when you close your throttle during power-off landings.

Another hazard to avoid like the plague is the thunderstorm. In addition to the icing hazard always associated with these awesome phenomena, you can be subjected to hail that can damage windshields and the leading edges of airfoils. They are also associated with severe wind shears that literally break an aircraft into pieces, and with microbursts that have forced high-powered jet aircraft into the ground.

The thunderstorms usually associated with fast-moving cold fronts can normally be seen and avoided, but if they're hidden (embedded) in the solid blanket of clouds associated with warm fronts, stationary fronts, or the warm side of occlusions, stay on the ground and fly another day.

AIRWAYS AND ALTITUDES

After checking the weather, you will have to check any NOTAMs that may apply to your flight, and, if you are flying into or out of large terminal areas, you will be looking for the possibility of preferred routes which have been established for the most orderly flow of traffic in and around those busy areas. These routes are listed in the back of the *Airport/Facility Directory (A/FD)*. The routes are either one-way or two-way.

Now, with all of this in mind, check your charts for a routing, using preferred routes if possible, that will avoid the thunderstorms and icing conditions. You may have still other restrictions to your choice of routes, such as altitude restrictions and obstructions that are beyond the operational limits of your aircraft.

It may be a good idea to review some of the terminology and definitions that you will run across. The lowest altitude you can ever fly on airways under instrument conditions will be determined from one of the following four restrictions as spelled out in the *Air Traffic Control Handbook*:

> MEA—Minimum En Route IFR Altitude. The lowest published altitude between radio fixes which assures acceptable navigational signal coverage and meets obstacle clearance requirements between those fixes. The MEA prescribed for a Federal Airway or segment thereof, area navigation low or high route, or other direct route, applies to the entire width of that airway, segment, or route between the radio fixes defining the airway, segment, or route.

> MCA—Minimum Crossing Altitude. The lowest altitude at certain fixes at which an aircraft must cross when preceding in the direction of a higher Minimum En Route IFR Altitude (MEA).

> MOCA—Minimum Obstruction Clearance Altitude. The lowest published altitude in effect between radio fixes on VOR airways, off-airway routes, or route segments, which meets obstacle clearance requirements for the entire route segment and which assures acceptable navigational signal coverage only within 25 statute miles of a VOR.

> MRA—Minimum Reception Altitude. The lowest altitude at which an intersection can be determined.

If a specific route lists both a MEA and a MOCA, the pilot may operate below the MEA down to, but not below, the MOCA, but only when within 25 statute miles of the VOR concerned. This can be helpful when, for example, you have to get a little lower to avoid, or to get out of, icing.

It is legal, and sometimes necessary, to operate off the airways. When the pilot decides to do so, the *ATC Handbook* states:

> Pilots are reminded that they are responsible for adhering to obstruction clearance requirements on those segments of direct routes that are outside of controlled airspace. The MEAs and other altitudes shown on low altitude IFR en route charts pertain to those route segments within controlled airspace, and those altitudes may not meet obstruction clearance criteria when operating off those routes. When planning a direct flight, check your Sectional or other VFR charts, too.

Aha, there's that other use of the sectional charts I mentioned earlier. They're a necessary part of your flight kit.

Another reason to be concerned about MEAs and MOCAs is that in some sections of the country you have to cross high terrain and may run into the need for supplemental oxygen which may not be on board. The regulations stipulate that all required crewmembers be on oxygen for all flight time exceeding 30 minutes that the aircraft is above 12,500 feet MSL cabin altitude, up to and including 14,000 feet MSL. For flight at cabin altitudes above 14,000 feet MSL they must be on oxygen for the entire period of time. In unpressurized aircraft, aircraft altitude and cabin pressure altitude are one and the same. Perhaps you will have to consider the alternative of roundabout routings if you do not carry oxygen.

When making up your tentative route, you should study the charts carefully to be familiar with all other routes that will be nearly parallel, as it is not unusual to be cleared for a routing other than what you file for—or to have your routing suddenly changed after becoming airborne.

FUEL AND ALTERNATE AIRPORT REQUIREMENTS

With all of this in mind, you can now prepare your flight plan. This should be done as accurately as possible, using all available wind and weather information. Even though you know that the conditions will seldom be exactly as forecast, especially at the lower altitudes, it's a lot easier to make small corrections in flight than major ones. Besides, you base your required fuel load on the information you get from the flight plan. In order to see exactly what's figured in, in the way of IFR fuel, take another look at the regulations. You can find the fuel requirements in FAR 91.23:

    (a)   . . . No person may operate a civil aircraft in IFR conditions unless it carries enough fuel (considering weather reports and forecasts, and weather conditions) to—

        (1) Complete the flight to the first airport of intended landing;

        (2) Fly from that airport to the alternate airport; and

        (3) Fly after that for 45 minutes at normal cruising speed . . .

    (b)   Paragraph (a) (2) of this section does not apply if—

        (1) Part 97 of this subchapter prescribes a standard instrument approach procedure for the first airport of intended landing; and

        (2) For at least 1 hour before and 1 hour after the estimated

time of arrival at the airport, the weather reports or forecasts or any combination of them, indicate—

    (i)   The ceiling will be at least 2000 feet above the airport elevation; and

    (ii)   Visibility will be at least 3 miles.

Although paragraph (b) may sound a little confusing at first, all it really means is that if the intended airport has an instrument approach procedure that has been approved, and if the weather is forecast to be VFR (actually, with the 2000-foot ceiling, a little higher than VFR), you won't need to file an alternate airport and your VFR fuel will suffice.

There is a built-in safety margin here if you look at it again. The fact that the field has an instrument approach should allow you to get in. The chances of the weather going from VFR all the way down to below IFR minimums, without being forecast to do so, is quite remote. On the other hand, if the weather is below VFR minimums, or forecast to go below them within the previously mentioned two-hour time period, you must file an alternate airport just in case the weather really goes down fast and closes your field.

Under IFR alternate airport weather minimums, FAR 91.83 tells us:

(c)   . . . Unless otherwise authorized by the Administrator, no person may include an alternate airport in an IFR flight plan unless current weather forecasts indicate that, at the estimated time of arrival at the alternate airport, the ceiling and visibility at that airport will be at or above the following alternate airport weather minimums:

    (1) If an instrument approach procedure has been published in Part 97 of this chapter for that airport, the alternate airport minimums specified in that procedure or, if none are so specified, the following minimums:

        (i)   Precision approach procedure: ceiling 600 feet and visibility 2 statute miles.

        (ii)   Non-precision approach procedure: ceiling 800 feet and visibility 2 statute miles.

    (2) If no instrument approach procedure has been published in Part 97 of this chapter for that airport, the ceiling and visibility minimums are those allowing descent from the MEA, approach, and landing, under basic VFR.

The alternate minimums are normally well above the primary landing minimums for the airport. This is another safety margin thrown in for you, because, if the weather at your intended airport goes below IFR minimums and you have to divert to the alternate, chances are that the weather will still be above landing minimums at the alternate airport. But, at the moment you divert, the alternate airport becomes your new airport of intended landing, and the published landing minimums are applicable for what is now your new destination, utilizing the facilities that are appropriate for the procedure.

Be aware that, in determining your alternate and fuel requirements, even if the forecast for your intended destination airport indicates that conditions will only be "occasionally" (or "chance of") below the minimums specified in 91.23 (b)(2) and 91.83(b), an alternate is still required.

Similarly, you may not select an alternate which is forecast to be "occasionally" (etc.) below the minimums in 91.83(c).

ATC advises that you file your flight plan at least 30 minutes prior to your time of departure. Otherwise, you can expect up to a 30-minute delay. If you file before you do your aircraft preflight, you should have your clearance in hand and be ready for your departure by the time you're finished with the preflight and the runup.

8

Departure Helpers

WELL, HERE YOU ARE, PERCHED EXPECTANTLY AT THE EDGE OF THE RUNWAY, awaiting your clearance. If this is like most small fields, you may have filed a flight plan something like this:

> IFR to Big Lake Airport via Lost Deer VOR, V16, V3, Fish, V22, Tuway intersection, V5, 8000 feet.

If you are departing from a typical large airport, you will find that the same clearance will be quite a bit more complicated, because many times ATC will add departure instructions. For example, if you filed this same flight plan from a large airport, you may receive a clearance something like:

> Speedy 50X is cleared to Big Lake Airport as filed, except, after take-off turn right to a heading of 150° until intercepting the 262-degree radial of Trout VOR, turn left via the 262-degree radial of Trout VOR until intercepting the 180-degree radial of Lost Deer VOR, direct. Maintain 2000 feet until intercepting the 262-degree radial of Trout VOR, then climb to and maintain 4000 feet to Lost Deer VOR, as filed, maintain 8000.

SIDs

You could have simplified the entire process by using a SID (Standard Instrument Departure). If you had used a SID in the flight plan above, you might receive a clearance such as:

> Speedy 50X is cleared to Big Lake Airport, Holiday 1 Departure, Fish
> Transition, as filed, maintain 8000 feet.

All of the rest of the complicated departure instructions would have been included in the SID itself.

SIDs, STARs (see Chapter 10), and other abbreviated clearances have been developed because of the need to put as many aircraft as possible into and through the ATC system. To accomplish this, it becomes necessary to keep the radio transmissions as brief as possible. Hence, the use of abbreviations like "as filed," and the use of SIDs and STARs. Another reason for these SIDs and such is to put them down on paper in such a manner as to simplify what otherwise could be a difficult clearance to copy, read back, understand, and comply with. In order for this to work, however, we, as pilots, have the responsibility to thoroughly understand the restrictions involved.

The *Jeppesen Airway Manual*, in its introduction section, has this to say about SIDs:

> Pilots of IFR civil aircraft operating from locations where SID procedures are effective may expect ATC clearances containing a SID. Use of a SID requires possession of at least the textual description of the SID. Pilots not desiring to use the SID are expected to advise ATC. Notification may be accomplished by filing "NO SID" in the remarks section of the filed flight plan or by the less desirable method of verbally advising ATC.

I can't see any reason to turn down a SID as long as you have the required textual portion in your possession and your aircraft can meet the various restrictions (which we'll talk about later). Turning it down will only make more work for everyone involved. If you file "NO SID," the only difference is that you will get the complete textual portion read to you, and you'll have to copy it down and read it back, which is sometimes very complicated and time-consuming. After all, ATC has devised the departure routings to expedite traffic and to give adequate separation between inbound and outbound flights, so it stands to reason that as long as you will be departing on that route anyway, you might as well make it easy on all concerned by having the SIDs in your possession and reviewing them before flight.

OBSTACLE CLEARANCE CONCERNS

It may be a good idea here to take a look at how the FAA devises obstacle clearance specifications. Jeppesen explains it this way:

Obstacle clearance is based on the aircraft climbing at 200 feet per nautical mile, crossing the end of the runway at 35 feet AGL, and climbing to 400 feet above the airport elevation before turning unless otherwise specified in the procedure. *[This is the basic obstacle clearance specification.]* A slope of 152 feet per mile, starting no higher than 35 feet above the departure end of the runway, is assessed for obstacles. A minimum of 48 feet of obstacle clearance is provided for each mile of flight. If no obstacles penetrate the 152 feet per mile slope, IFR departure procedures are not published. *[So far so good. If nothing is specified on the SID or in the takeoff section of the airport plan chart (more on that in Chapter 16) then all you need do is meet the above climb criteria.]* If obstacles penetrate the slope, obstacle avoidance procedures are specified. These procedures may be: a ceiling and visibility to allow the obstacles to be seen and avoided; a climb gradient greater than 200 feet per mile; detailed flight maneuvers; or a combination of the above. In extreme cases, IFR take-off may not be authorized for some runways. *[Unless you've got some really bad problems, any aircraft capable of IFR flight is able to meet the standard obstacle climb gradient.]*

Climb gradients are specified when required for obstacle clearance. Crossing restrictions in the SIDs may be established for traffic separation or obstacle clearance. When no gradient is specified, the pilot is expected to climb at least 200 feet per mile to MEA unless required to level off by a crossing restriction. *[Perhaps we should get our heads together here. We are so used to thinking in terms of climbing and descending so many feet per minute. These climb gradients are based on climbing so many feet per **mile**. To meet these restrictions, your rate of climb will be a function of airspeed. The faster you fly, the higher your rate of climb will have to be to meet the climb gradient.]* Climb gradients may be specified to an altitude/fix, above which the normal gradient applies. Some procedures require a climb in visual conditions to cross the airport (or an on-airport NAVAID) at or above an altitude. The specified ceiling and visibility minimums will be enough to allow the pilot to see and avoid obstacles near the airport. Obstacle avoidance is not guaranteed if the pilot maneuvers farther from the airport than the visibility minimum. *[This is a very important point. If you are given an IFR clearance with a two-mile visibility restriction, it is your responsibility to stay within two miles of the airport until above the ceiling specified in the same clearance. **You must remain in visual conditions to see and avoid any obstacles.**]* That segment of the procedure which requires the pilot to see and avoid obstacles ends when the aircraft crosses the specified point at the required altitude. Thereafter, standard obstacle protection is provided.

Take a look at an actual SID. FIG. 8-1 is the Great Swamp Six Departure (GRMP6.SBJ) from Morristown, New Jersey. You can see that it is labeled "SID" in the upper right hand corner so as not to be confused with an approach plate or a STAR (Standard Terminal Arrival Route). As a further identification aid, Jeppesen assigns SIDs the code number of 10-3 followed by an alphabetical suffix if there is more than one SID for the airport, as opposed to the code number 10-2 for STARs, and 10-1 for area charts.

As procedures are changed, ATC changes the numerical suffix of the SID. In this case, the Great Swamp Six departure has updated the Great Swamp Five departure, so you must make sure that you have the numerical suffix for the SID that is specified in your clearance.

At this point, I need to remind you that, by the time you read these words, many of the charts appearing in this book will be obsolete. *Do not attempt to use any chart in this book for actual navigation.* It is your responsibility to obtain the *current* charts for the routes you plan to fly.

The Jeppesen SID shows the SID both textually and pictorially so you can follow it more easily. Remember that you must have at least the textual portion in your possession.

The text of the SID is self-explanatory, giving headings and altitudes as well as the direction of all turns for each takeoff runway that you may use. If there is a runway at the airport that is not mentioned in the SID, you are not allowed to use it for an instrument takeoff when using that specified SID.

Following along with the Great Swamp Six SID, you can see that, after following the takeoff instructions for the runway you are using, you fly to the Solberg VORTAC, and then fly whatever transition that has been assigned. That will get you on your way in good shape. You can see that, on two of the runways, Rwy 12 and Rwy 23, you have to climb to a specified altitude *and* cross the airport boundary before being able to make your first turn. The other two departures require climbs to the northeast until 1700 feet before turning southeast.

An important thing to learn here, and something I think should be reiterated, is how much less radio congestion there is, and how much less chance of error in copying, reading back, and complying there will be when you receive a simple clearance using a SID. In this case you might get something such as:

> Speedy 50X is cleared to the Greater Pittsburgh Airport, Great Swamp Six departure, Philipsburg transition, then as filed, maintain 8000 feet.

Isn't this a lot better than the clearance you'd get if you didn't use the SID? Without the SID the same clearance would be:

> Wordy 20F is cleared to the Greater Pittsburgh airport as filed, maintain 8000 feet. After takeoff maintain runway heading until crossing the airport boundary and reaching 500 feet. Then turn left heading 210° until 2500 feet, then turn left heading 160° for radar vectors to the Solberg R-085 to Solberg VORTAC. Maintain 2500 feet. After crossing Solberg climb to 8000 feet on the Solberg R-280 and East Texas R-099 to East Texas VORTAC, then via . . .

NEW YORK Departure (R) 119.2

GREAT SWAMP SIX DEPARTURE (GRMP6.SBJ) (PILOT NAV)
(RADAR VECTORED)

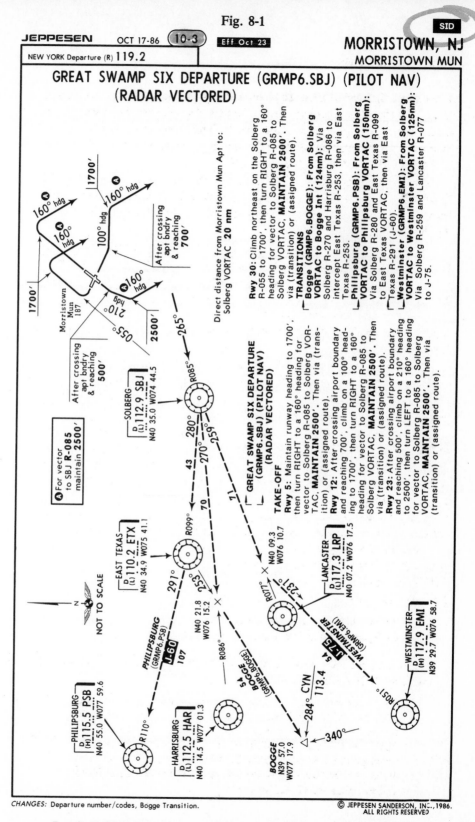

Direct distance from Morristown Mun Apt to:
Solberg VORTAC **20 nm**

Rwy 30: Climb northeast on the Solberg R-055 to 1700', then turn RIGHT to a 160° heading for vector to Solberg R-085 to Solberg VORTAC, **MAINTAIN 2500'**. Then via (transition) or (assigned route).
TRANSITIONS

Bogge (GRMP6.BOGGE): From Solberg VORTAC to Bogge Int (124nm): Via Solberg R-270 and Harrisburg R-086 to intercept East Texas R-253, then via East Texas R-253.

Phillipsburg (GRMP6.PSB): From Solberg VORTAC to Phillipsburg VORTAC (150nm): Via Solberg R-280 and East Texas R-099 to East Texas VORTAC, then via East Texas R-291 (J-60).

Westminster (GRMP6.EMI): From Solberg VORTAC to Westminster VORTAC (125nm): Via Solberg R-259 and Lancaster R-077 to J-75.

GREAT SWAMP SIX DEPARTURE
(GRMP6.SBJ) (PILOT NAV)
(RADAR VECTORED)

TAKE-OFF
Rwy 5: Maintain runway heading to 1700', then turn RIGHT to a 160° heading for vector to Solberg R-085 to Solberg VORTAC, **MAINTAIN 2500'**. Then via (transition) or (assigned route).
Rwy 12: After crossing airport boundary and reaching 700', climb on a 100° heading to 1700', then turn RIGHT to a 160° heading for vector to Solberg R-085 to Solberg VORTAC, **MAINTAIN 2500'**. Then via (transition) or (assigned route).
Rwy 23: After crossing airport boundary and reaching 500', climb on a 210° heading to 2500', then turn LEFT to a 160° heading for vector to Solberg R-085 to Solberg VORTAC, **MAINTAIN 2500'**. Then via (transition) or (assigned route).

NOT TO SCALE

AIRCRAFT PERFORMANCE RESTRICTIONS

You will not always be able to use a specific SID, however, due to operating limitations of your aircraft. An obvious example can be seen in the San Francisco, California SID 10-3 called the Dumbarton Two Departure (FIG. 8-2). Although this is not calculated for you on the chart, if you are taking off on Runway 10 L/R, the SID requires a rate of climb that will average out to 440 feet per mile or greater in order to cross the Woodside R-028/24 DME fix at or above 11,000 feet as that fix is only 25 miles from the airport. If you are heavy, have a strong tailwind, or have a low-performance aircraft, you may not be able to make it. If you are unable to comply with the requirements of a SID, you naturally cannot accept it, and most of the time you are the only one who knows the performance capabilities of your aircraft. ATC may give you a clearance utilizing a SID you can't conform with, and it's up to you to advise them of your capabilities.

I might as well explain what the Woodside R-028/24 DME fix is. Although it looks a little complicated at first, it is simply identification of the fix by giving the VOR involved (Woodside), the radial off of Woodside (028-degree radial), and the distance away from the VOR on that radial (24 DME). It really shouldn't be necessary to mention this, but as Murphy's Law is always lurking just around the corner, remember that the radial mentioned is just that—a radial—FROM the VOR.

In some cases it's quite obvious that the SID has been designed for high-performance aircraft. A good example of this is the 10-3G SID for San Francisco which is called the Shoreline Six Departure. It isn't necessary to show the actual SID to get my point across. The Melts Transition for this departure calls for crossing the Linden R-240/18 DME fix at or above 16,000 feet, crossing the Linden VORTAC at or above flight level (FL) 200 (around 20,000 feet—above 18,000 feet you set your altimeters to 29.92 inches and read the higher altitude as a flight level, which is the altimeter reading minus the last two zeros), and then crossing Melts Intersection at FL 230. Those last two requirements put all but transport and very-high-performance general aviation aircraft out of the picture.

Because of mountains to the west of SFO, there is also a note on the Shoreline Six Departure that says in part that when departing Runway 28 L/R, the weather conditions must be 2000-foot ceiling and three miles prevailing visibility with five miles to the west and northwest, so here you see some other type of obstruction clearance instructions.

Going back to FIG. 8-2, you also see a climb gradient chart laid out for you so that you can comply with the climb restrictions off Runway 19 L/R. The note tells you that you must climb at a minimum of 460 feet *per nautical mile* to 2400 feet. In the text for Runway 19 L/R departures you will note that you must turn LEFT as soon as practicable due to steeply rising terrain to 2000 feet immediately south of the airport.

Fig. 8-2

JEPPESEN   AUG 22-86 (10-3) **Eff Aug 28**   SAN FRANCISCO, CALIF.

SID

BAY Departure (R) NW-E **120.9** SE-W **135.1**   SAN FRANCISCO INT'L

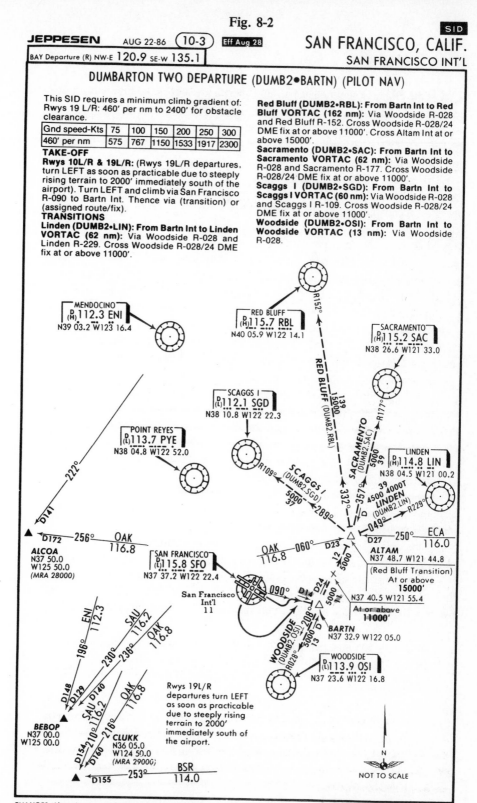

DUMBARTON TWO DEPARTURE (DUMB2•BARTN) (PILOT NAV)

This SID requires a minimum climb gradient of:
Rwys 19 L/R: 460' per nm to 2400' for obstacle clearance.

Gnd speed-Kts	75	100	150	200	250	300
460' per nm	575	767	1150	1533	1917	2300

TAKE-OFF

Rwys 10L/R & 19L/R: (Rwys 19L/R departures, turn LEFT as soon as practicable due to steeply rising terrain to 2000' immediately south of the airport). Turn LEFT and climb via San Francisco R-090 to Bartn Int. Thence via (transition) or (assigned route/fix).

TRANSITIONS

Linden (DUMB2•LIN): From Bartn Int to Linden VORTAC (62 nm): Via Woodside R-028 and Linden R-229. Cross Woodside R-028/24 DME fix at or above 11000'.

Red Bluff (DUMB2•RBL): From Bartn Int to Red Bluff VORTAC (162 nm): Via Woodside R-028 and Red Bluff R-152. Cross Woodside R-028/24 DME fix at or above 11000'. Cross Altam Int at or above 15000'.

Sacramento (DUMB2•SAC): From Bartn Int to Sacramento VORTAC (62 nm): Via Woodside R-028 and Sacramento R-177. Cross Woodside R-028/24 DME fix at or above 11000'.

Scaggs I (DUMB2•SGD): From Bartn Int to Scaggs I VORTAC (60 nm): Via Woodside R-028 and Scaggs I R-109. Cross Woodside R-028/24 DME fix at or above 11000'.

Woodside (DUMB2•OSI): From Bartn Int to Woodside VORTAC (13 nm): Via Woodside R-028.

(Reproduced with permission of Jeppesen Sanderson, Inc. NOT FOR USE IN NAVIGATION.)

On the climb gradient chart, ground speeds are across the top, and the required rates of climb are listed below. It would appear that many general aviation aircraft might be hard pressed to comply with the 460 feet-per-nautical-mile gradient required off Runways 19 L/R, especially with strong south winds dumping down off the mountains.

This points out again the need to study all of the information available before you file a flight plan. As a rule, the people at ATC have no concept of the operational capabilities of your aircraft. They are trying to help you out, and by trying to do so, they may issue a clearance that you have asked for. However, you could very well find yourself in the air, IFR, and unable to comply with the limitations of the SID, or some other part of the clearance. You have to study it all beforehand because you won't have much time once you're in the air.

If you are unable to comply with the requirements of one SID, you may still be able to find one that will be compatible with the operating capabilities of your aircraft. If you can't find one that you can use, or if you don't feel comfortable with any, simply file "NO SID" in the remarks section of your flight plan. It's really much easier for all concerned to use the SIDs. Remember the old saying, "A picture is worth a thousand words."

There's another phrase in your clearance that you need to look at: "cleared as filed." This is an abbreviation that is used by ATC when your route is essentially the same as what you filed. If only one small portion has been changed, you may get a complete readout, or you might receive, "Cleared as filed, *except* . . ." with a readout of only the portion that has been changed.

One very important point that must be emphasized here is that the cleared-as-filed clearance does not include the altitude filed for. Look back at the earlier examples in this chapter to see what I mean. The altitude must be given to you in addition to the cleared-as-filed portion.

If the original clearance has been substantially changed by you, your company, or ATC, you will definitely receive a full readout of your new clearance.

For an example of an abbreviated clearance with a slight change, suppose that you have filed to Pittsburgh from Morristown and have asked for a Great Swamp Six, J-60, etc., FL 180. You may get a clearance back that reads:

> Speedy 50X is cleared to the Greater Pittsburgh Airport, Great Swamp
> Six Departure, Philipsburg Transition, then as filed; maintain flight
> level 180, except, climb on runway heading to 2000 feet before turn-
> ing right to 260°.

In order to ensure the success of the program, as well as the accurate relaying of information, you should (1) include specific SID/Transitions and preferred routes in your flight plans whenever possible, (2) avoid making changes to a filed flight plan just prior to departure, and (3) most especially, *request route/altitude verification or clarification from ATC if any portion of the clearance is not clearly understood.* You should never be put in a position to have to say, "Well I thought you meant . . . "

FILING THE FLIGHT PLAN

In the preceding chapter, I mentioned filing your flight plan at least 30 minutes prior to your departure. This is to give ATC time to process the clearance and to fit it into the system. Once a flight plan has been filed, how do you go about getting your clearance?

This will depend on which type of airport you are operating from. You will normally find yourself in one of three situations:

- At an airport with a tower and a discrete Clearance Delivery frequency, you will simply call Clearance Delivery directly prior to calling Ground Control for taxi clearance. At airports where pre-taxi clearance procedures are in effect (as indicated in the *Airport/Facility Directory*), you will get your clearance not more than 10 minutes prior to taxi. At airports where this procedure is in effect, you will then know if you are to expect a delay prior even to starting your engines.

- At an airport with or without a tower or Flight Service Station, but at least within radio range of one of the above, you will get your clearance over the radio from whichever facility you are able to contact—the tower being the first choice. One exception to this rule is when you are unable to contact any of the above, but are able to work an ARTCC (Center) frequency, in which case you can call them directly.

- At an airport without any ATC facilities—and one from which you are unable to contact a control facility by radio when you are on the ground, you can take off in VFR conditions and pick up the IFR clearance once airborne (and still VFR) and within radio range of a facility. If you are unable to take off in VFR conditions, you will have to telephone the facility with which you filed your flight plan. They'll normally ask what time you expect to depart, and you will usually be given a clearance containing a "clearance void" time, which means that if you are not airborne by that time, your clearance will be voided and you will have to call for a new one. If something happens that makes it look as if you won't be able to make it off by the clearance void time, your best bet is to get on the horn again and ask for an extension of the void time. In any case, you must let ATC know within 30 minutes that you will not be able to comply. This will help prevent further delays as well as costly reroutes to other traffic that have been issued clearances based on your departure.

You should have a good working knowledge of all of the facilities and basic airways in the vicinity of your departure airport. This is because it isn't unusual to receive a change to your clearance shortly after becoming airborne. If you know the primary airways and the VOR frequencies, it will enable you to comply with the changes at once, double-checking the charts as time permits, rather than trying to fumble with the charts while still trying to get the gear up.

These course changes are especially prevalent in radar environments. When you will be given radar vectors, you will be advised of it prior to takeoff. You will normally be advised of the initial heading and the reasons for the vectors. By listening to the instructions you merely fly basic instrument maneuvers—climbs, turns, etc.—until you are established on course and told to, "resume normal navigation."

Sometimes, Departure Control will hand you off to a Center frequency where you will receive further vectors. You must not allow yourself to become too complacent when following these simple directions. You must still monitor your navigation receivers and be continuously aware of your position with respect to your requested route of flight, because you never know when your radios may decide to take a holiday and leave you with no air/ground communications.

LOSS OF RADIO COMMUNICATION

If you do lose radio contact, what will you do? We'll look into this subject much more deeply during our en route discussion in Chapter 10, but if it happens during the departure phase of your flight you will find yourself in one of three situations: (1) flying the clearance as received, in which case you keep right on complying with the clearance; (2) flying on an amended clearance; or (3) flying a radar vector.

In either case (2) or (3), you will have been issued instructions as to where your change of heading is taking you. In case (2), you may have been told:

> 50X, amendment to your clearance, now climb on the 030-degree radial until 8000 feet, and then turn left on course.

Should you lose communications capability while climbing through 3000 feet on the 030-degree radial, just comply with the clearance as it was given. Continue climbing to 8000 feet and then turn left to get on the flight planned route.

If you were on a westbound radar vector you may have been told something like:

> 50X, radar contact, turn left now, heading 240° to intercept the Spartan 276-degree radial.

If you were to lose communications then, you should turn further left to intercept the radial at a 90-degree angle in order to comply with Part 91.127(c)(1)(ii) which says:

> If being radar vectored, by the direct route from the point of radio failure to the fix, route, or airway specified in the vector clearance.

As you taxi to the active runway give the instruments a good check. Prior to taxiing, you should have set the directional gyro to the magnetic compass heading. Then as you make your turns while taxiing, you are able to check for proper movement of the DG.

The same thing holds true for your needle/ball, turn/slip, slip/skid indicator, or turn coordinator, whichever term is the vogue for this instrument at the time you read this (I prefer to call it the needle/ball). In any event, watch it as you're turning. The needle should deflect to the same direction the aircraft is turning.

Remember that the attitude indicator, needle/ball, and DG are all gyro-driven, and should have at least five minutes to come up to speed to prevent excessive precession and bearing wear.

COCKPIT ORGANIZATION

There's one thing that we have to talk about before you shove the throttle in and set off on your flight. You have to figure out what to do with all of the charts, flight plans, and assorted papers that are in the cockpit.

As time goes by, everyone develops his own method of cockpit organization. I'll tell you how I operate in a light aircraft—and why—and let you take it from there.

In the first place, although I have used several types of kneeboards, I have never found one that I have liked. Besides getting in the way of the yoke, they cause me to bend my head down more than I like to, and I hate to take a chance at getting my inner ear confused (vertigo) when I'm the only pilot on board.

So, I take the SIDs, STARs, approach plates, and airway charts that I am most likely to use, out of my flight kit. I have found that in most light aircraft they fit nicely in the corner formed by the windshield and the glareshield. Here they are both handy and out of my normal line of vision, and I don't have to bend my head down to look at them. The remainder of my flight kit is stowed near at hand should I need it, but out of my way. I keep my flight plan with my charts. Holding it against a chart or two gives me a stiff enough surface to write on so that I don't need a clipboard. If you do decide to use a clipboard, remember to keep the metal part of it away from your magnetic compass. This is the reason I don't even use a paper clip to hold my charts together.

My plotters stay in my flight kit because I should have no more use for them if I have done my preflight work properly. My computer fits in my shirt pocket, along with a felt-tip pen, a few sharp pencils, and one of those small telephone answering pads. As I said before, these are just the right size to jot your clearances on and still fit in your shirt pocket where they're always close at hand. When I get a new clearance I tear off the old sheet of paper and store it out of the way. It's a good idea to keep all of your clearances in the event any questions ever arise as to the conduct of your flight.

These procedures have worked just fine for me. As for yourself, you'll evolve a system of your own as time goes by, just as we all do.

9

Stay on Top
of Things

ONCE YOU ARE AIRBORNE AND NEAR THE LIMITS OF THE DEPARTURE CONTROL jurisdiction, you will be handed over to the appropriate air route traffic controller. Even though the departure controller has coordinated your handoff with the Center, there are three things the Center controller wants to know—who you are, what your altitude is, and what your final assigned altitude is. Proper radiotelephone techniques are covered in the *AIM* and the *ATC Handbook*, but some will be repeated here as there are far too many pilots flying today who don't use the correct phraseology and cause frequency congestion.

In the above case, your initial call to the Center would be something like:

> New York Center, Cessna One Seven Two Zero Zulu, out of 5000
> for 7000.

This says it all in just a few words. You have told him that you are on his frequency, who you are, what altitude you are passing through, and what altitude you are climbing to, which is the altitude you have been assigned. This is not necessarily your final altitude. Departure may have given you 7000 feet for some reason—usually because of other traffic—and before he's sure you are clear, he's handed you off to Center. In this case, you may call Center with the following terminology:

> New York Center, Cessna One Seven Two Zero Zulu, out of 5000
> for 7000—looking for 9000.

This has told the Center that you are going to level off at an intermediate altitude for some reason. Perhaps he doesn't know it, or perhaps Departure Control got busy and forgot to clear you out of it. In any case, it's only four additional words and it may save an entire exchange of transmissions later. You may find that the Center controller will clear you to your final altitude when he acknowledges your original call-up.

You'd be surprised how many people omit this information on their initial call; even seasoned airline captains are guilty of the omission. Many times I've heard, "Center, Air Carrier Six Sixteen, over."

Then Center has to come back with something like, "Roger, Air Carrier Six Sixteen, confirm you're climbing to assigned flight level of 250." This requires another response from the air carrier, which becomes a needless transmission.

Well, you have made your radio calls and have climbed to your cruising altitude where you have set up cruise power and cruise configuration. Now you can sit back and relax, right? Wrong. Your job is just beginning. There are a lot of things you still have to accomplish. For example, in addition to the basic aircraft control, you have your flight plans to keep up-to-date, reporting points to keep track of, communications, fuel management, and in-flight as well as destination weather changes to monitor and interpret.

I don't know what it is that makes perfectly good pilots grip the yoke and turn white knuckled when they enter a cloud, but they do. It's happened to me, and it will happen to you. Do we expect the plane to fly differently just because we can no longer see outside? Well, remember that the plane doesn't know the difference, so we must learn to relax. Don't grab the yoke in a death grip. Remember when your primary instructor tried to teach you how to differentiate control pressure from control displacement? He'd usually have you grip a pencil tightly, right? And then he'd apply pressure against it and ask you which way the pressure was being applied. If you were like I was, you couldn't tell him, proving that a gripping hand can't differentiate pressure.

The same thing holds true in instrument flight. If you're having a difficult time controlling the plane, remove one hand from the yoke and shake it a bit to get the blood circulating. This will allow the nerve endings to be sensitive to pressure again. Put your hand back on the yoke lightly, and do the same with your other hand. Then do the same thing with your feet. You'll notice quite a difference in the control of the aircraft and then, and only then, will you be able to properly trim the control pressures with the trim tabs.

"OK," you say, "so much for aircraft control, but what's this about flight plans? Didn't I use all the available information during flight planning to come up with an accurate flight plan?"

The answer, of course, is yes, you did use all available information when you made the flight plan, but weather conditions change and actual in-flight wind conditions are usually different from those forecast, especially at the lower altitudes. Therefore, keeping a running fix of your position and an accurate update on your ground speed will take up a lot of your time. You will also be working in-flight problems (mentally) to come up with a good wind correction angle so you will have an idea of the wind direction and velocity. This is a most important in-flight task.

ESTIMATING YOUR POSITION

Although you are under radar most of the time, there are still times when you won't be. When this happens, the controller will call you in the following manner:

Cessna 20Z, radar contact lost, what is your _____ estimate?

Normally the estimate he's asking for is to the next compulsory reporting point along your route of flight. This will be part of your flight plan unless you have had a route change since filing. If this is the case, or if the winds aloft have changed sufficiently from those forecast to change your ground speed, you will have to come up with a new estimated time from the last fix to the next reporting point. If all factors have remained the same, you will be able to read the estimate from your flight plan. In any case, the controller wants an estimated time as soon as you can possibly give it to him, as he has a lot of traffic to sequence through the area.

To keep him happy you may have to "guesstimate." You can do this easily and quite accurately by taking your indicated airspeed in knots and dividing it by 60 to come out to the nearest half-mile per minute. If you are indicating 120 knots, you will come out with a speed of two nautical miles per minute. If you are indicating 145 knots, you can use a speed of two-and-a-half miles per minute. This is really the speed for 150 knots, but it will be close enough.

If you have a strong headwind/tailwind factor, you can apply that as well. And if you are at an altitude above 5000 feet MSL, you will have to work in your true airspeed factor. These factors should be applied to indicated airspeed before dividing by 60. In any case, take the resulting miles-per-minute figure, divide it into the miles-to-go to your fix, add the result to the current time, and you will have a good estimate to start with. You can always update it later, but at least ATC will have something to work with.

How accurate is this system? Well, let's figure that the airway you are on has a midpoint of 40 miles. Take a look at FIG. 9-1.

The chart shows that, generally, the faster the plane, the more accuracy you will have (accuracy also improves with shorter distances), but you'd need an unusual wind condition, or an error in your true airspeed, to make much of an error in your guesstimates.

Indicated Airspeed (Knots)	NM/minute (rounded to nearest .5)		Est. Time to Reporting Point (to nearest minute)	Actual Time to Reporting Point (minutes)	Error (minutes)
90	1.5		27	26.7	.3
100	1.5		27	24.0	3.0
110	2.0		20	21.8	1.8
120	2.0		20	20.0	—
130	2.0		20	18.5	1.5
140	2.5		16	17.1	1.1
150	2.5		16	16.0	—
160	2.5		16	15.0	1.0
170	3.0		13	14.1	1.1
180	3.0	÷ 60 =	13	13.3	.3
190	3.0		13	12.6	.4
200	3.5		11	12	1.0
210	3.5		11	11.4	.4
220	3.5		11	10.9	.1
230	4.0		10	10.4	.4
240	4.0		10	10	—
250	4.0		10	9.6	.4
260	4.5		9	9.2	.2
270	4.5		9	8.9	.1
280	4.5		9	8.6	.4

Distance 40 NM ÷ ___ =

Fig. 9-1. *The accuracy of this estimation method increases with airspeed.*

The *AIM* says that you are allowed an error of ±3 minutes and that you must contact ATC and revise your estimated time to a reporting point if it becomes apparent that your previous estimate will be off by more than three minutes.

Because there is always the chance of radar failure and/or winds that are other than those forecast, you should work out ground speed as soon as possible after reaching cruising altitude.

As I've mentioned before, I feel very strongly about eliminating unnecessary head movements while flying on instruments, especially when I am the only pilot on board. (This is—as you remember—to decrease the possibility of suffering from vertigo, and these head movements tend to aggravate such a condition.) So, you should use as many mental tricks as you can in order to avoid the need to look around the cockpit for computers, calculators, and the like. At the same time, these tricks should maintain a high degree of accuracy.

If you have DME on board, it is a simple matter to figure ground speed. Many units have ground speed built in, but for those that don't, merely check the miles covered in one minute (measuring to the nearest half-mile) and use that. Estimates based on these figures will be well within limits.

With no DME on board, you will have to check ground speed between two fixes shown on the enroute chart. If no convenient fixes are shown, you can make your own by drawing radials from VORs that will cross the airway you are on. The closer the VORs are to you (as long as you are outside the cone of confusion), and the more perpendicular the radial is to the airway, the more accurate the results will be. In most of these cases, however, you will need your computer to work out the ground speed.

THE WEATHER'S ALWAYS CHANGING

Don't just work this out once and forget it, because the winds may change drastically as the flight progresses, especially during a frontal passage. Refigure or reconfirm your ground speed whenever time permits. You should always try to remain ahead of the aircraft.

How much these winds can vary from those forecast can be very surprising. I remember a flight from Burlington, Vermont, to Wilkes-Barre, Pennsylvania, one winter day some 25 years ago. I was flying a Cessna 205 without DME. The winds at my altitude, 6000 feet, were forecast to be light, about a 10-knot headwind component. These winds were just about as forecast on my outward flight, so I used them on my flight plan for my return flight to Pennsylvania and elected not to refuel, because I had more than my legal requirements on board, based on all contingencies.

I was to cross a fix shortly after reaching cruising altitude, and when I didn't get to it right away I became suspicious. I worked out a ground-speed estimate as soon as I could and came up with a 60-knot headwind component which left me with only a 65-knot ground speed. When I reported this to ATC they didn't believe me at first, although it was confirmed about 15 minutes later by a Mohawk Airlines flight. I had to make an unscheduled refueling stop in Albany, New York.

On the subject of changes in forecast weather, maybe we should take a look at how accurate a weather forecast should be. Here are a few figures from the National Weather Service:

- In a 12-hour forecast, a forecast of good weather (VFR) is more likely to be correct than an IFR forecast.

- Three to four hours in advance, there's an 80-percent chance of accuracy when forecasting conditions below VFR.

- The tendency is to forecast too little bad weather when distinct weather can be plotted.

- Surface visibility is difficult to forecast due to changes in snow or rainfall, fog density, and the like.

The following forecasts have a 75-percent chance of accuracy:

- Passage of warm fronts or slow-moving cold fronts, within ±2 hours, when forecast as much as 10 hours in advance

- Rapid lowering of ceiling below 1000 feet in pre-warm-front conditions, within ±200 feet and within ±4 hours

- Onset of a thunderstorm one or two hours in advance, if radar is available

- The time rain or snow will begin, within ±5 hours

By the same token, they cannot accurately predict:

- The time freezing rain will occur

- Location and occurrence of heavy icing

- Location and occurrence of a tornado

- Ceilings of 100 feet or zero

- Thunderstorms not yet formed

- Ice fog

It is up to the pilot-in-command to keep updated as to changes in weather conditions both on the proposed route of flight and at the destination and alternate airports. The easiest way to do this is to keep the volume up on the VOR receiver. Even though the identifier becomes monotonous, it will tell you that the station is still on the air, and you will automatically get the sequence, AIRMET, and SIGMET reports. Additionally, you may lose your communications receiver and not know it, and ATC may try to contact you through VOR voice.

I mentioned airframe and carburetor icing earlier. The most insidious of the two, in my opinion, is carburetor ice. After all, you can see the airframe begin to ice up and take precautionary measures, but you can't see inside the carburetor. Carburetor icing usually occurs at much higher outside air temperatures than airframe ice. Not only that, its adverse effects build up so gradually that you do not realize it. Therefore, at least once every 10 minutes, use the carburetor heat momentarily. When using it, pull the control all the way out. Partial carburetor heat can actually cause icing by heating up otherwise too-cold air to the icing temperature.

If ice has been building up inside the carburetor, the engine will run rough for awhile after the carburetor heat has been pulled out. You may have to work hard to maintain your airspeed and your altitude. Because carburetor ice builds faster during low power settings it may even build up as you taxi to the active runway. You should always experience a manifold-pressure or RPM drop when you check the carburetor heat, but if you experience unusual roughness as well, before you begin your takeoff roll, keep the carburetor heat on until the roughness goes away.

Carburetor ice is especially prevalent in areas of high outside air temperature, 50-80 °F, combined with high humidity. This is because, as the air flows through the carburetor venturi, the air cools, and its moisture condenses. As mentioned earlier, it is even a problem where I live in Hawaii.

If you are a victim of carburetor ice you will notice that you will have to add more and more throttle to maintain your cruising speed. This is why the first action you are taught in trying to find the cause of engine failure is to pull out the carburetor heat. By all means though, consult your aircraft operating manual about the use of carburetor heat in your engine.

Fuel-injected engines also experience icing in the intake system, although this is usually ice over the air cleaner. In this case the use of alternate air will usually clear up the problem, but again, consult your flight manual.

Other factors to consider are temperature and atmospheric pressure changes, both of which can cause erroneous altimeter readings. Pressure changes can be compensated for by resetting the altimeter whenever you are given an updated setting. Remember that the altimeter must be set to a station within 100 nautical miles. The old saying, "When moving from hot to cold or a high to a low, look out graveyard down below," still holds true. As the barometric pressure and/or temperature lowers, your altimeter will read higher than your actual altitude. These errors will be especially prevalent near mountains, which is why the regs require 2000 feet of ground clearance in mountainous areas.

When you got your weather briefing, if you remember, you looked at the past weather sequence reports as well as the current one. This was to give you an idea of the trend and the rate of change of the weather. As you cruise toward your destination, you will receive weather updates on the VOR voice and should be correlating them with the previous weather trend. If it appears that the weather is changing for the worse, then you should start directing your thinking toward diverting to your alternate. The sooner you make the actual decision to divert, the more fuel you will have to play with, and the more time you will have. If the weather at your intended destination is going down faster than forecast, then the same will probably hold true for the weather at your alternate.

AIRWAYS AND ALTITUDES

While you are cruising, you will also have to pay close attention to your position as far as the airway centerline is concerned. FAR 91.123 requires that you operate on the centerline of airways, and the only time you can deviate is if you deliberately turn before or after a turning fix to avoid flying outside the airway while in the turn. Most of us in general aviation aircraft won't have to worry about flying outside the airway in a turn. After all, it's eight miles wide (four miles each side of the centerline), but some high-performance, high-altitude, business aircraft must take this factor into consideration.

You can also deviate from the centerline to avoid heavy weather buildups, but only after first advising ATC of your intentions and receiving permission to deviate.

The FAA has established guidelines to use when you climb or descend. There are two basic climb or descent clearances.

If the controller includes the words ''at pilot's discretion'' in the clearance, he has offered you the option to begin climb or descent when you desire. You are also able to climb or descend at any rate desired, and even to level off at any intermediate altitude. The only restriction ATC applies to this clearance is that once you leave an altitude you cannot return to it. In other words, once you begin a descent, you must continue the descent (except for leveling off at an intermediate altitude). You may not climb again at any time. The same holds true for a climb. The only time you could vary your altitude by climbing, descending, and then climbing again, or vice versa, is when you have been given a ''block'' altitude.

If ATC does not add the words ''at pilot's discretion'' to the clearance, you should begin the maneuver promptly. ATC also expects you to climb or descend at what they call the ''optimum rate consistent with the operating characteristics of the aircraft.'' Continue the climb or descent at this optimum rate until 1000 feet before reaching the new altitude, and then attempt to climb or descend at a rate of 500 FPM. At any time you lose the ability to climb or descend at the rate of at least 500 FPM you should notify ATC.

The key phrase is the ''optimum rate'' for your aircraft. In an unpressurized aircraft any rate exceeding 700 FPM would not be practicable—especially on descent. A climb or descent at 400-500FPM would be best for passenger comfort. Naturally, in pressurized aircraft, you can climb or descend quite a bit faster than that.

The 500-FPM suggestion for the final 1000 feet of altitude change is to allow you to stabilize the climb/descent and to approach your assigned altitude at a slow enough rate to be able to level off without flying through the altitude.

Two other points concerning altitude changes: First, you are expected to initiate the change as soon as you acknowledge the clearance, unless it contains a restriction such as, ''after crossing . . . descend/climb to . . . .'' If, for some reason, the controller wants you to vacate your altitude immediately, he will add the word ''now'' to the clearance. Example:

Cessna 20Z, descend and maintain 4000. Begin descent now.

The second point is that if, for any reason, you have to level off at an intermediate altitude (say a passenger develops a bad earache), unless you are descending at pilot's discretion, you must notify ATC immediately.

VOR transmitters and airborne receivers have allowable errors. The farther you fly from the transmitter, the farther you'll be off course if you hold a constant heading. Remember that 1° of error equals 1 NM off course for each 60 NM you fly. If your airborne equipment error is 4°, and you fly an indicated centerline, when you get 60 miles from the VOR, you will be at the outside limit of the airway.

To prevent this from happening, ATC attempts to set the airways up so that aircraft are always within 45 miles of the transmitters. On long route segments, when the distance between the VORs is over 45 miles, specific changeover points (COPs) are indicated on the enroute charts by this symbol:

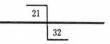

The numbers show the distance (in NM) to the COP from each of the two navigational VORs.

10

Radio Rhetoric and Holding Patterns

ONCE UPON A TIME, BEFORE RADAR COVERAGE WAS HEARD OF, RADIO COMmunications played a much greater role in the progress of an aircraft from point A to point B than they do today.

Two major types of radio contacts were initiated by the pilot back then. The first was merely a radio contact, such as when a plane was handed off from one controller to the next. The second was the position report that was given when the plane crossed a fix that required such a report.

Today, the use of radar has caused the position report to have almost become extinct. Because of this, pilots tend to become sloppy in the procedure. They have the same problem with flying ADF approaches and holding patterns, because these maneuvers are becoming more and more scarce in most parts of the country. Actually, this is the time when you should practice these things more.

The day will come when the Center's radar will be down and you will be forced to make these position reports. In order to cut down on radio frequency congestion, you should be well versed in their use.

Let's take a look at some of these basic communications procedures.

Earlier, I briefly discussed a radio contact when changing from Departure Control to Center. The same holds true whenever you change from any one controller to the next, be he Departure, another Center sector, or Approach. If you are in a radar environment, you will merely state whom you are calling, who you are, your altitude or flight level, and whether you're climbing, descending, or flying level. If you're climbing or descending, you must also add the assigned altitude or flight level you're flying to. Example:

> Cleveland Center, Cessna 1720Z, out of 5000 for 8000.

If you are not in a radar environment, and you do not have to give a *full* position report, your initial contact would include whom you're calling; who you are; your estimated time to your next compulsory reporting point; your altitude or flight level; whether you're climbing, descending, or in level flight; and again, if you're climbing or descending, the assigned altitude or flight level that you're climbing or descending to. Example:

> Cleveland Center, Cessna 1720Z estimating Big Lake intersection at one five [past the hour], level at 8000.

PROPER POSITION REPORTS

In a non-radar environment, a full position report would have to be made whenever you cross a compulsory reporting point. A compulsory reporting point is indicated on the enroute chart by a solid triangle.

If you were not in a radar environment and were told to make your frequency change when crossing a compulsory reporting point, your initial call, and all subsequent calls when crossing compulsory reporting points, would be simply whom you're calling, who you are, and where you are. Example:

> Cleveland Center, Cessna 1720Z, Big Lake intersection.

This will alert Center that a full position report will be forthcoming, and the controller will merely answer:

> Cessna 20Z, Cleveland Center, go ahead.

With this you will give your full position report which will consist of:

1. Who you are

P 2. Where you are (which will be the fix you just crossed)

T 3. The time you were there (in Universal Coordinated Time [UTC] based on a 24-hour clock)

A 4. Your altitude or flight level (and, if necessary, whether you're climbing or descending, and if you are, the assigned altitude or flight level you're climbing or descending to)

P 5. The estimated time you'll cross the next compulsory reporting point

T
P 6. The name of the next compulsory point following that estimated in #5

Naturally, if No. 5 or 6 is your clearance limit you will state that also.

Example: You were to contact Cleveland Center when crossing Big Lake intersection. You crossed it at 10 minutes after the hour, and you were climbing to a cruising altitude of 8000 feet. The next compulsory reporting point on your route is Frosty VOR, which is 40 miles ahead. Your ground speed has been averaging 120 knots. The next compulsory reporting point past Frosty VOR is Smokey intersection. Smokey intersection happens to be your clearance limit.

The initial contact would be the same as that shown above, but after Cleveland Center responds, you would give the remainder of your report:

> Cessna 20Z, Big Lake at two zero one zero, leaving five thousand to maintain eight thousand, estimating Frosty at three zero [if the hour is going to be the same hour, just like in the first part of the position report, you give only the minutes], Smokey next, clearance limit.

As you can see, this is a simple procedure that condenses a lot of information into just a few short words, but it requires a lot of practice to perform it properly and professionally, especially today when it's used so seldom.

Once back in radar contact, you will discontinue making the position reports unless you are informed that radar contact has been lost again, or that for some reason, radar service has been discontinued.

REQUIRED REPORTS TO ATC

There are additional reports that must be made to ATC or FSS without request. These reports are:

1. When leaving any previously assigned altitude or flight level for a newly assigned altitude or flight level;

2. When an altitude change will be made when you're operating "VFR on top;"

3. When unable to climb/descend at least 500 FPM;

4. When you have missed an approach, in which case you must request a specific action, such as clearance for another approach, or to your alternate, or perhaps to hold for awhile to try another approach when and if the weather improves. This would be the case if your visibility was restricted by one of a series of rain or snow showers, and you are trying to get in between them;

5. When your average true airspeed at cruise altitude varies by five percent or 10 knots (whichever is greater) from what you filed on your flight plan;

6. The time and altitude or flight level when reaching a holding fix or point to which you have been cleared;

7. When leaving any assigned holding fix or point;

8. When you lose any VOR, TACAN, ADF, LF, ILS, or air/ground communications capability;

9. When leaving the final approach fix (or outer marker) inbound on final approach; and

10. A corrected estimate whenever you realize that a previously submitted estimate is in error in excess of three minutes.

Nos. 9 and 10 above are only required when *not* in radar contact.

You must also report any weather conditions that have not been forecast and any other hazards to flight, including icing, snow, clear air turbulence, and even flocks of migrating birds.

MORE COMMUNICATION FAILURE PROCEDURES

The situation will become rather sticky though, if you suddenly lose your two-way communications capabilities. The regulations are set up to guide you as best they can in such a situation, even though emergencies rarely follow a set pattern, and it's hard to write a set of rules telling you how to handle them. The following has been set up as a guide, remembering that FAR 91.3, "Responsibility and Authority of the Pilot in Command," says:

(a) The pilot in command of an aircraft is directly responsible for, and is the final authority as to, the operation of that aircraft.

(b) In an emergency requiring immediate action, the pilot in command may deviate from any rule of this subpart or of Subpart B to the extent required to meet that emergency . . .

Unless you see fit to exercise your emergency authority as outlined above, FAR 91.127 sets up specific actions that you should follow if you lose your two-way communications capabilities.

As with many FAA rules, this section begins with the words, "Unless otherwise authorized by ATC, each pilot . . . shall comply with the rules of this section."

It goes on to say that if you are in VFR conditions, or if you encounter VFR conditions afterwards, you should continue VFR and land as soon as practicable.

If you do so, however, make sure you notify ATC as soon as possible that you are on the ground safely. If you're at a controlled airport, this is a simple trip to the tower, but if it's a non-controlled field, you'll have to find a phone.

If you are in IFR conditions, however, you should continue by specific routes and altitudes as follows:

- If you are already on an airway, you should fly the route as assigned in your last clearance.

- If you were being radar vectored to a route or fix, you should fly as directly as possible to the route or fix you were being vectored to. Of course, here you should be aware of obstacles, such as high mountains, that you were being vectored around.

- If you have been recleared during flight to a specific point, and have been told to expect further clearance via a specific route, fly the route you were told to expect.

- If you haven't been told to expect a specific routing, fly what you filed in your flight plan.

- Your altitude must be the highest of: the altitude last assigned by ATC, the altitude ATC has advised you to expect in a later clearance, or the minimum enroute altitude for each segment of the route.

A good example is the situation in FIG. 10-1. A pilot has been cleared via A, B, C, and D to E. While flying between A and B his assigned altitude is 6000 feet, and he is told to expect a clearance to 8000 feet at B. Prior to receiving the higher altitude assignment, he experiences two-way radio failure. The pilot would maintain 6000 feet to B, then climb to 8000 feet (the altitude he was advised to expect). He would maintain 8000 feet, then climb to 11,000 at C, or prior to C if necessary to comply with a Minimum Crossing Altitude at C. Upon reaching D, the pilot would descend to 8000 feet (even though the MEA is 7000), because 8000 is the highest of the altitude situations stated in the rule.

So far, everything's pretty straightforward, and although the actual wording of the FARs sometimes sounds complicated, if we sit and reason them out with an example or two, and try to see what the author had in mind, they tend to simplify themselves.

The only other problem to solve would be when to leave a clearance limit, and I'll quote from FAR 91.127(c)(3) for the answers to that:

    (i)   When the clearance limit is a fix from which an approach begins, commence descent or descent and approach as close as possible to the expect further clearance time if one has been received, or if one has not been received, as close as

Fig. 10-1

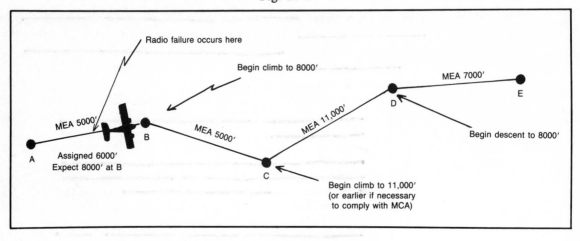

possible to the estimated time of arrival as calculated from the filed or amended (with ATC) estimated time en route.

(ii) If the clearance limit is not a fix from which an approach begins, leave the clearance limit at the expect further clearance time if one has been received, or if none has been received, upon arrival over the clearance limit, and proceed to a fix from which an approach begins and commence descent or descent and approach as close as possible to the estimated time of arrival as calculated from the filed or amended (with ATC) estimated time en route.

If you have not received holding instructions and are ahead of your flight plan ETA, you should hold at the fix so that you land as close to the ETA as possible. If there is more than one approach at your destination, make the approach of your choice (based on weather forecasts). ATC will have cleared the airspace on all of the approaches.

In the event you lose two-way communications, ATC will provide service on the basis that you are operating in accordance with the above rules. Naturally, during all of this, you will be monitoring the navaid voice facilities and will follow any instructions you may receive. You should try to establish radio contact on the last frequency over which you had two-way communications—which is why you should always write down each assigned frequency rather than just switch the radio to the new frequency.

Failing to make contact on the last frequency, you should try to make contact on FSS frequencies, and on 121.5 MHz. If you are transponder-equipped you should squawk code 7700 for one minute, followed by 7600 for 15 minutes, and repeat this procedure for the remainder of the flight.

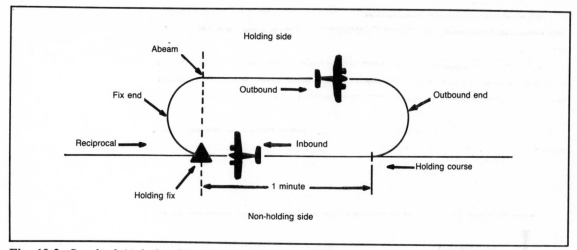

Fig. 10-2. *Standard (right-hand) holding pattern in no wind condition.*

THE HOLDING PATTERN

Back to normal flight operation. As you proceed along your way, ATC may find it necessary to slow you down, or stop you, to properly sequence all of the flights in the area. Because you cannot actually stop in midair, they will have you fly a racetrack flight path called a holding pattern, which serves the purpose. You will enter a holding pattern automatically if, when you come to a "clearance limit," you have received no further clearance.

Most holding patterns are depicted on the appropriate charts for the area. If you are required to hold at a fix where no pattern is depicted, you will receive the following information:

- The direction to hold in relation to the holding fix, in other words, north, northeast, east, etc.

- The fix itself

- The radial, course, magnetic bearing, or airway

- The length of the outbound leg, if the hold is based on DME distances

- Instructions to make the turns to the left, if the holding pattern is nonstandard

- The time to expect a further clearance

FIGURE 10-2 shows the terminology used in a standard (right turn) holding pattern. The maximum holding airspeeds are 175 knots IAS for prop-driven aircraft and 200 knots IAS for civil jets under 6000 feet. Civil jets are also restricted to 210 knots IAS between 6000 and 14,000 feet, and 230 knots IAS above 14,000 feet.

If an airspeed reduction is necessary to comply with these maximum speeds, you must begin the reduction within three minutes of your ETA over the holding fix.

Time your pattern so that the time of the inbound leg will be one minute if you are at or below 14,000 feet MSL. If you are above 14,000 feet, the inbound leg should be one and one-half minutes long. In order to establish this, you should fly the initial outbound leg for these durations, and then adjust the outbound leg time to get the proper inbound time. The timing is commenced abeam the fix. There may be times when ATC will designate a different inbound time, and if the holding fix is predicated on a DME distance, you don't worry about the time other than to note what the inbound and outbound times are so that you can cross the fix inbound at anytime specified by ATC.

Holding pattern turns should be made at the least bank angle of the following:

1. 3° per second;

2. 30-degree bank angle; or

3. 25-degree bank angle when using a flight director.

HOLDING PATTERN ENTRIES

The hardest thing for most pilots to figure out is how to enter a holding pattern. There are only three correct ways to enter a pattern, and you determine which one to use depending on your arrival heading with relation to the inbound leg.

As a guide, the FAA has established a line at 70° to the inbound leg on the holding side, and at 110° from the inbound leg on the non-holding side.

If you are entering the holding pattern from within this sector (Area 3 in FIG. 10-3), merely fly to the fix and turn outbound in the same direction as you are to hold; that means, turn right for right patterns and left for left patterns. This is termed a direct entry.

If you will enter from Area 1 in FIG. 10-3, you should cross the fix, make a turn opposite the direction of the holding turns, and then fly the first outbound leg on the non-holding side. At the end of the outbound leg, make another turn in the opposite direction of your holding turns, intercept the inbound leg, cross the fix, and enter the normal pattern. This is termed a parallel entry, or a parallel entry on the non-holding side.

Finally, if you are entering from Area 2 in FIG. 10-3, cross the fix and turn to fly a heading 30° to the outbound leg on the holding side. Fly this heading for one minute and then turn in the same direction as the holding turns to intercept the inbound leg. This is what is called a teardrop entry.

In all of these entries, you should make the necessary corrections to compensate for the known wind.

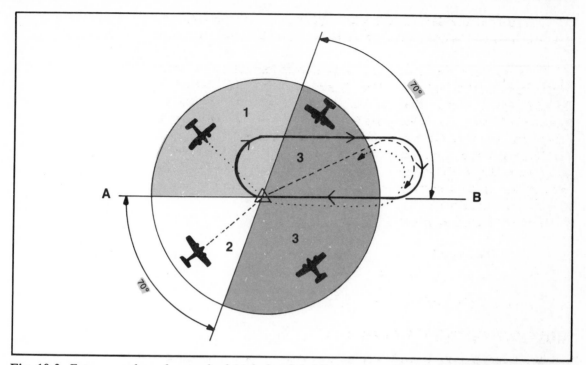

Fig. 10-3. *Entry procedures for standard (right-hand) holding pattern. Aircraft approaching from Zone 1 use a parallel entry. A teardrop entry is used from Zone 2. Aircraft in Zone 3 enter directly.*

Although reams have been written to explain how to know which entry to use, I have found that 90 percent of the time, the easiest entry to make from your position is the correct one.

If you're flying an aircraft with a full-faced DG, you might try this idea: Take a piece of thin, stiff, clear plastic, and a felt-tip pen. Trace FIG. 10-3, which depicts the entries for a standard right-hand holding pattern. Lay the line A-B over the face of the DG, with A on the inbound heading, B on its reciprocal, and the fix in the center, and read your entry directly from the pattern. For left-hand patterns, turn the plastic over. Simple? Try it.

STARs

As you near your destination, you may be cleared to use a STAR (Standard Instrument Arrival Route), which is:

> A preplanned instrument flight rule (IFR) air traffic control arrival procedure published for published for pilot use in graphic and/or textual form. STAR's provide transition from the en route structure to an outer fix or an instrument approach fix/approval waypoint in the terminal area.

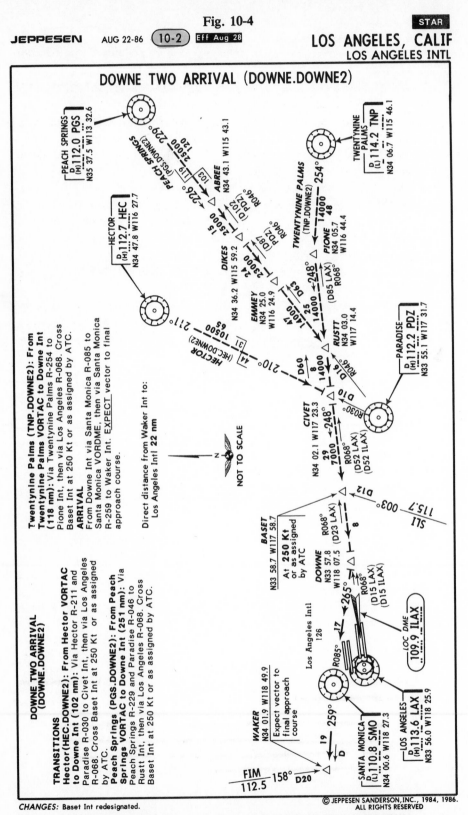

DOWNE TWO ARRIVAL (DOWNE.DOWNE2)

CHANGES: Baset Int redesignated.

(Reproduced with permission of Jeppesen Sanderson, Inc. NOT FOR USE IN NAVIGATION.)

STARs are usually made for airports in high-density areas, and like the SIDs that are used in departures, their main purpose is to simplify clearance procedures and cut down on radio frequency congestion. As with a SID, the pilot must have at least the textual description in his possession. The final decision to accept or reject a STAR rests with the pilot, and it simplifies matters a great deal if he makes the remark "NO STAR" in the remarks section of his flight plan if he doesn't want to avail himself of this aid.

FIGURE 10-4 shows the Downe Two Arrival to Los Angeles International Airport. The chart resembles a SID, except for the letters in the black box in the upper right corner and the "2" in the numerical listing (10-2) which is used for STARs. Remember, 10-1 is for area charts, 10-2 is for STARs, and 10-3 is for SIDs. If there are more than one of any of these for any one airport they will have a letter after the numeral, such as 10-2B, 10-2C, etc.

Again, this is a schematic, not to scale, but it does show, in pictorial form, the altitude restrictions en route for each transition to the approach and, in textual form, the exact routes to be flown. It also shows all runway restrictions that are pertinent.

11

The Art of Approach

IN THE OPINION OF MANY PILOTS, INSTRUMENT FLIGHT IS THE ULTIMATE TEST of an airman's skill. If this is so, then flying a good instrument approach has to be the epitome of the art.

Before we get into the actual approaches, let's take a look at some background information, basic concepts, and definitions of terms. Then I will elaborate on some pertinent regulations concerning instrument approaches.

To begin with, just why do we have instrument approach procedures? The *Air Traffic Control Handbook* puts it this way:

> Instrument approach procedures are designed so as to insure a safe descent from the en route environment to a point where a safe landing can be made.
>
> A pilot adhering to the altitudes, flight paths, and weather minimums depicted on the Instrument Approach Procedure (IAP) chart, or vectors and altitudes issued by the radar controller, is assured of terrain and obstruction clearance and runway or airport alignment during approach for landing.

Sounds simple, yes?

You say no.

Well, it really is. However, just like learning to take off and land, it requires patience, study, and practice. Like learning anything else, it is first necessary to establish a firm background to build upon. If, at this time, you are not proficient in straight-and-level flight, level turns, climbs and descents both straight ahead and while turning, slow flight, speed control, and emergency procedures—all under the hood—you're not ready for approach work. In addition to the maneuvers mentioned above, you should also be fairly proficient in flying airways, procedure turns, and holding patterns.

GETTING IT DOWN SAFELY

I suspect that you are asking, "Why? What's so different? Instruments are instruments."

It's simply that when you get on an approach, your mind will be so filled with procedures and figures that the control of the aircraft will have to be almost automatic. Not only that, but when you're on the approach, your margin of error becomes progressively smaller and smaller.

You can equate instrument flight with two cones lying on their sides with the large ends connected. The airports are at each small end, with one being your departure field and the other being your destination. When you lift off, you point your nose skyward and begin to climb. The higher you get, the larger your sphere of allowable error becomes. If your attention wavers, you can go to a full-needle-width deflection of the VOR before you get outside of the airway, which extends four miles each side of the centerline.

Sure, the regs say that you should be on the centerline, but if you drift off you are still in protected airspace. Also, if your altitude starts drifting off and you go up or down 300 feet, it's probably not dangerous, but it's poor airmanship and subject to a citation or a violation. Your chances of hitting something up there will be rare—unless someone else is also doing a sloppy job of holding an assigned altitude.

Now, you get on the approach and start down. Here your sphere of allowable error gets smaller each second. As you near your minimums, the allowable error becomes very small. At this point, a full deflection of the needle isn't four miles off, but the width of the airport environment, if you are on a VOR or NDB approach, and the width of the runway itself, on an ILS/MLS or localizer (LOC) approach. Tall structures can be found outside of this protected area, and running into one of them is not the right way to end a flight. Altitude becomes more critical down here also, and a 300-foot error could mean that you are suddenly very seriously dead.

I will assume that you're fairly good at your basic hood work, and that you practice from time to time with a safety pilot. You're ready to begin working on instrument approaches. But first, maybe you should know how the instrument approach procedure charts came about.

IN THE BEGINNING

Way back in 1930, a 23-year-old barnstormer by the name of Elroy B. "Jepp" Jeppesen was offered a job as an airmail captain for Boeing Air Transport Company, which is now known as United Air Lines. This promised a steadier income than that provided by his World War I surplus Jenny, so he took the job.

He was flying the rugged mountain terrain between Cheyenne and Salt Lake City. It was a dangerous route with or without navigational aids, which ranged from few to none. The route claimed many planes and pilots.

One day, Jepp bought a small 10-cent notebook and began jotting down all of the pertinent information regarding his routes. In addition to field lengths, obstructions, and altitudes, he even compiled a list of phone numbers of farmers along his route whom he could call for weather information. Some of this information would be very informative, while some might amount to no more than, "Well, I can see the barn through the snow." It was not unusual on his days off to find Jepp with a pocket altimeter, climbing mountains, trees, water tanks, and other obstructions to ascertain their correct heights.

Before long, pilots began talking both of his longevity and his "little black book," and he gave a few copies to his friends. The demand grew so great that he started publishing them in the cellar of his rooming house and selling copies to interested airmen. Business was so good that it was taking all of his time, so he tried to sell it to United Airlines for $5,000. The airline management turned the offer down, a move that ended up making Jepp a millionaire. He took an early retirement from United in 1954.

In 1957 he opened a facility in Frankfurt, Germany, due to the international demand, and in 1958 he opened an office in Washington D.C. to interface with the government. In 1961 he sold his publishing firm to Times/Mirror Publishing Company. In 1968 Times Mirror bought Sanderson Films, Inc., and in 1970 when Times Mirror took Sanderson Films to Denver, the two company names were merged into today's Jeppesen Sanderson, Inc.

Jepp's "little black book" has grown to volumes of charts and procedures that cover airways worldwide and approaches to more than 16,000 airports. Revisions are issued weekly. Jeppesen manuals are used by all U.S. commercial airlines and many foreign ones, as well as by a great majority of private and business pilots.

I am indebted to Jeppesen Sanderson, Inc. and to the Times/Mirror Publishing Company for the permission they have granted me to use excerpts from the firm's manuals and copies of "Jep" approach charts for our illustrations.

The government also publishes a set of charts, but because U.S. airlines all use "Jeps," and many instrument students have aspirations to fly for the airlines, I have elected to use the "Jeps" during these discussions. I will, however, devote a chapter to explaining the NOS charts so you will be aware of the similarities and differences between the two.

PRECISION AND NONPRECISION APPROACHES

There are two basic types of approach procedures—the precision approach and the nonprecision approach. There are numerous types of nonprecision approaches. Simply stated, the nonprecision approach is a standard instrument procedure that does not use an electronic glide slope. There are only three types of precision approaches—the Instrument Landing System (ILS), Microwave Landing System (MLS), and Precision Approach Radar (PAR) approaches. At this time the MLS is not yet fully operational, and the PAR approaches are few and far between—in fact, they are being phased out of the system.

For our discussion here, I will disregard the MLS as it will be quite a while before we find them in general use. I'll also disregard the actual flying of a PAR, because the ground controller "talks" the plane in, and about all the pilot can do is listen and do as he's told.

What components are necessary for an approach in order for it to be classified as an ILS? The ground components are a localizer, glide slope, outer marker and middle marker, and approach lights. If the procedures specify a visibility minimum based on Runway Visual Range (RVR), it will also need High Intensity Runway Lights (HIRL), Touchdown Zone Lighting (TDZL), Centerline Lighting (RCLS) and markings, and, naturally, the RVR transmissometers for that runway. Of course, before the pilot can accept an ILS approach, his aircraft must have the airborne equipment necessary to receive the ground components.

There are a few variations. The regulations do allow a compass locator or a precision radar to be substituted for the outer marker (OM) or middle marker (MM), and an airport surveillance radar (ASR) can usually be substituted for the outer marker.

All other approaches are nonprecision. These consist of the localizer, back course, VOR, NDB (ADF), and ASR approaches. The VOR and NDB (ADF) approaches are, in effect, designed to bring you down to the overall airport environment, while all of the others will bring you right down to the runway.

APPROACH MINIMUMS

One of the most important terms used in conjunction with the instrument approach procedure charts is "minimums." The minimums are comprised of two factors, the Minimum Descent Altitude (MDA) [or, in the case of a precision approach, the Decision Height (DH)], and visibility. Each type of approach has its own basic minimums. These are modified for different airports depending on many factors, including obstacle clearance and terrain.

Visibility is the factor that governs whether or not airliners can *initiate* the approach. When we speak of a field being closed due to weather, the visibility is lower than that allowed by the available approaches. (Under Part 91, you can start an approach regardless of visibility, as I'll discuss later. Prudent pilots, however, would not try to begin an approach when visibility is below minimums.)

The MDA or DH specified is merely the lowest altitude to which you can descend on the approach unless you have the runway environment in sight and are in a position to make a safe landing. If the airport is reporting a ceiling lower than the MDA/DH specified for the approach, you would still be allowed to commence the approach, although you would not normally expect to see the runway environment when you arrived at your minimums.

The minimums are modified further if certain navigational aids on the ground or in flight are inoperative. These changes are all spelled out on the instrument approach charts, but basically . . .

On ILS approaches, if the localizer is out, the approach is not authorized. If the glide slope is out, the DH increases as specified in the procedure. If the outer or middle marker is out, the DH is increased by 50 feet and the visibility increase will depend on your aircraft's approach category (discussed later in this chapter). On ILS and PAR approaches, if the ALS (Approach Light System) is out, the DH goes up by 50 feet and the visibility increases by ¼ mile. If the SSALSR (Simplified Short Approach Light System with RAIL) or MALSR (Medium Intensity Approach Light System with RAIL) is out, the DH for Categories A, B, and C increases by 50 feet and the visibility requirements go up by ¼ mile. RAIL, by the way, stands for Runway Alignment Indicator Lights, which are the sequenced flashing lights we see on Approach Light Systems, that many pilots have nicknamed "the rabbit," as they tend to run quickly toward the runway threshold.

If you are using an ILS with a visibility minimum of 1800 or 2000 feet RVR, the localizer and glide slope requirements are the same as above. But, if the outer or middle marker is out, you must increase the DH by 50 feet for all categories, and for Categories A, B, and C, the visibility goes up to ½ mile, while in Category D, it increases to ¾ mile. If the ALS is out, the DH goes up 50 feet and the visibility goes to ¾ mile. With the HIRL, TDZL, RCLS, or RVR out, there is no change in the DH, but the visibility goes to ½ mile. If only the RCLMs (Runway Centerline Markings) are missing, there is no visibility increase, but the DH will change according to the procedure.

In VOR, LOC, LDA (Localizer Type Directional Aid), and ASR, if the ALS, SSMALSR, or MALSR is out, the visibility increases ½ mile in Categories A, B, and C. It will increase ¼ mile in Categories A, B, and C if the SSALS, MALS, HIRL, or REIL (Runway End Identification Lights) is out.

In NDB (ADF) approaches, with the ALS, SSALSR or MALSR out, the visibility increases by ¼ mile in Categories A, B, and C.

I'm sure that by now you're thoroughly confused, but no one expects you to memorize this information. I only brought it up to show you that there are many times when the basic minimums may change, and you should be aware of them and know that you can find the new minimums in the appropriate blocks in the category/minimum section of the IAP chart that you'll be using.

AIRCRAFT CATEGORIES AND DESCENT MINIMUMS

I've been talking a lot about categories, so I guess it's a good time to take a look and see just what they are all about.

In order to make primary minimums as safe as possible, the FAA has established various categories based on aircraft approach speeds. Here are the actual definitions according to the *AIM* pilot/controller glossary:

> AIRCRAFT APPROACH CATEGORY—a grouping of aircraft based on a speed of 1.3 times the stall speed in the landing configuration at maximum gross landing weight. An aircraft shall fit in only one category. If it is necessary to maneuver at speeds in excess of the upper limit of a speed range for a category, the minimums for the next higher category should be used. For example, an aircraft which falls in Category A, but is circling to land at a speed in excess of 91 knots, should use the approach Category B minimums when circling to land. The categories are as follows:

> 1. Category A—Speed less than 91 knots.
>
> 2. Category B—Speed 91 knots or more, but less than 121 knots.
>
> 3. Category C—Speed 121 knots or more, but less than 141 knots.
>
> 4. Category D—Speed 141 knots or more, but less than 166 knots.
>
> 5. Category E—Speed 166 knots or more.

You'll notice the visibility requirements increase as the categories' speeds increase. That is because the turn radius is greater at the higher speeds and the plane will need more room—and consequently more visibility—to maneuver in.

As long as we're talking about definitions, we may as well define the descent minimums. There are two involved, the DH and the MDA.

> DECISION HEIGHT/DH—With respect to the operation of aircraft, means the height at which a decision must be made during an ILS, MLS, or PAR instrument approach to either continue the approach or to execute a missed approach.
> MINIMUM DESCENT ALTITUDE/MDA—The lowest altitude, expressed in feet above mean sea level, to which descent is authorized on final approach or during circle-to-land maneuvering in execution of a standard instrument approach procedure where no electronic glide slope is provided.

The DH is a "go/no-go" altitude, and you have absolutely no choice in the matter. If you can see enough of the runway environment when you reach the

DH to continue in and land *safely*, you do so. If you don't see the runway environment, you go around—*immediately*. Just what constitutes the runway environment is explained in FAR 91.116 below.

The MDA gives you a little more time to sort things out. With no electronic glide slope, you will hit the MDA at an uncertain distance from the runway. Once at the MDA, you fly out your time to the MAP (missed approach point). You may not descend below the MDA until you are in a position to make a normal approach to the runway. This is spelled out quite clearly in FAR 91.116, Takeoff And Landing Under IFR, which says in part:

(c) *Operation below DH or MDA.* Where a DH or MDA is applicable, no pilot may operate an aircraft . . . at any airport below the authorized MDA or continue an approach below the authorized DH unless—

(1) The aircraft is continuously in a position from which a descent to a landing on the intended runway can be made at a normal rate of descent using normal maneuvers . . . ;

(2) The flight visibility is not less than the visibility prescribed in the standard instrument approach procedure being used;

(3) . . . at least one of the following visual references for the intended runway is distinctly visible and identifiable to the pilot:

(i) The approach light system, except that the pilot may not descend below 100 feet above the touchdown zone elevation using the approach lights as a reference unless the red terminating bars or the red side row bars are also distinctly visible and identifiable.

(ii) The threshold.

(iii) The threshold markings.

(iv) The threshold lights.

(v) The runway end identifier lights.

(vi) The visual approach slope indicator.

(vii) The touchdown zone or touchdown zone markings.

(viii) The touchdown zone lights.

(ix) The runway or runway markings.

(x) The runway lights; and

(4) When the aircraft is on a straight-in nonprecision approach procedure which incorporates a visual descent point, the aircraft has reached the visual descent point, except where the aircraft is not equipped for or capable of establishing that point or a descent to the runway cannot be made using normal procedures or rates of descent if descent is delayed until reaching that point.

(d) *Landing.* No pilot operating an aircraft . . . may land that aircraft when the flight visibility is less than the visibility prescribed in the standard instrument approach procedure being used.

(e) *Missed approach procedures.* Each pilot operating an aircraft . . . shall immediately execute an appropriate missed approach procedure when either of the following conditions exist:

(1) Whenever the requirements of paragraph (c) of this section are not met at either of the following times:

(i) When the aircraft is being operated below MDA; or

(ii) Upon arrival at the missed approach point, including a DH where a DH is specified and its use is required, and at any time after that until touchdown.

(2) Whenever an identifiable part of the airport is not distinctly visible to the pilot during a circling maneuver at or above MDA, unless the inability to see an identifiable part of the airport results only from a normal bank of the aircraft during the circling approach.

That certainly spells things out clearly enough. Sometimes it may take a few readings to get it all set in your mind, but these are some of the most important things to remember about an instrument approach. Failure to comply with these paragraphs has cost a lot of lives and a lot of aircraft. We will spend more time with this section after we get into the actual approaches.

12

Mastering Minimums

BEFORE WE CONTINUE LEAFING THROUGH THE MANUALS, THERE ARE TWO GEN-
eral definitions I would like to review: visibility and visual approach.

VISIBILITY

Visibility on the ground is determined in one of two ways, by the human eye or by an instrument known as a transmissometer. Transmissometers are devices that measure the visibility by determining the amount of light that passes through the atmosphere.

The prevailing visibility is recorded by a trained observer at or near ground level. He looks at objects that are at known distances from his vantage point, such as trees, buildings, smokestacks, and mountains, as well as radio and TV broadcast antennas. At night the observer looks at lights in the same manner. Prevailing visibility is reported in miles and fractions of miles, and is defined as follows:

> Prevailing Visibility—The greatest horizontal visibility equaled or exceeded throughout at least half the horizon circle which need not necessarily be continuous.

There are two types of transmissometer-measured visibility:

> Runway Visibility Value/RVV—The visibility determined for a particular runway by a transmissometer. A meter provides a continu-

ous indication of the visibility (reported in miles or fractions of miles) for the runway. RVV is used in lieu of prevailing visibility in determining minimums for a particular runway.

Runway Visual Range/RVR—An instrumentally derived value, based on standard calibrations, that represents the horizontal distance a pilot will see down the runway from the approach end. It is based on the sighting of either high intensity runway lights or on the visual contrast of other targets whichever yields the greater visual range. RVR, in contrast to prevailing or runway visibility, is based on what a pilot in a moving aircraft should see looking down the runway. RVR is horizontal visual range, not slant visual range. It is based on the measurement of a transmissometer made near the touchdown point of the instrument runway and is reported in hundreds of feet. RVR is used in lieu of RVV and/or prevailing visibility in determining minimums for a particular runway.

A very important thing to note here is that both RVV and RVR values are for *specific* runways, and it is sometimes possible to make an approach to another runway when the prevailing visibility is higher. You will find this occurring at airports near the coast, where fog may roll in and cover only part of one runway—and that may be the runway with the transmissometer(s).

It's important for you to know that, because the RVR and the human visibility measurements are horizontal range, it may be more or less than what you'll see using slant range from the cockpit. Normally the visibility reported from the ground will be slightly better than what you'll find looking from the windshield on approach.

VISUAL APPROACH

At times, while under radar control, you may be cleared for a visual approach. You must be careful of this one. A visual approach is defined in the pilot/controller glossary as:

Visual Approach—An approach wherein an aircraft on an IFR flight plan, operating in VFR conditions under the control of an air traffic control facility and having an air traffic control authorization, may proceed to the airport of destination in VFR conditions.

The trap here is the phrase, "operating in VFR conditions." If you enter a cloud, or an area where the conditions revert to IMC (instrument meteorological conditions), you are in violation. So, it pays to look well ahead before you accept a visual approach. It is a useful tool, though, in helping you avoid long, drawn-out approaches, and it eases the burden on ATC. There is one other possible trap here. If you look in the *ATC Handbook* you'll find the visual approach amplified as:

a. When it will be operationally beneficial, ATC may authorize an aircraft to conduct a visual approach to an airport or to follow another aircraft when flight to, and landing at, the airport can be accomplished in VFR weather. The aircraft must have the airport or the identified preceding aircraft in sight before the clearance is issued. If the pilot has the airport in sight but cannot see the aircraft he is following, ATC may still clear the aircraft for a visual approach; however, ATC retains both separation and wake vortex separation responsibility. When visually following a preceding aircraft, acceptance of the visual approach clearance constitutes acceptance of pilot responsibility for maintaining a safe approach interval and adequate wake turbulence separation.

Perhaps we should consider an example: Approach Control is working four other aircraft. You are told that you are following a Hawaiian Air Lines L-1011 at 12 o'clock, six miles. You see traffic at your 12 o'clock position, or perhaps one o'clock, and it seems to be about the right distance. But, before you say, "Cessna 20Z has the L-1011," are you really sure that it's an L-1011? Is it really inbound? Is it a Hawaiian plane? Are there any clouds in the vicinity that may block it from your view before you land? You should only acknowledge the traffic if you can identify it positively—without a doubt in your mind—and be able to keep it in sight until you land. Remember, once you are cleared for a visual approach, and you accept it, you will be responsible for our own wake turbulence separation. You'll have to be careful with this one.

I think this is one of the most common mistakes of pilots with whom I fly. They seem to be in such a hurry to please ATC that they identify preceding aircraft—even at night—when there are a dozen other planes or lights around the airport area. A few years ago a DC-9 collided with a Cessna approaching San Diego airport, and one of the last sentences on the voice recorder of the DC-9 was that they had been looking at the wrong plane. Don't let this happen to you, no matter how big a hurry you are in to get to the field, and no matter how much you'd like to please ATC. *DON'T SAY YOU HAVE A PRECEDING AIRCRAFT IN SIGHT UNLESS YOU CAN IDENTIFY IT POSITIVELY.*

CONTACT APPROACH

In addition to the visual approach, there is one other time that you can deviate from the published approach procedure. Say that you are on an approach that has a 1½ mile minimum visibility requirement. The tower informs you that the visibility has just dropped to 1 mile. Also, suppose that you are below the base of the clouds and can see a highway below. You identify the highway and know that it runs alongside the runway.

Now, because the field has just dropped below minimums, you can either execute a missed approach when you reach the MAP, or you can ask for a contact approach. The *ATC Handbook* says that:

    a.   Pilots operating in accordance with an IFR flight plan, provided they are clear of clouds and have at least 1 mile flight visibility and can reasonably expect to continue to the destination airport in those conditions, may request ATC authorization for a contact approach.

    b.   Controllers may authorize a contact approach provided:

        (1) The contact approach is specifically requested by the pilot. ATC cannot initiate this approach.

        (2) The reported ground visibility at the destination airport is at least 1 statute mile.

        (3) The contact approach will be made to an airport having a standard or special instrument approach procedure.

        (4) Approved separation is applied between aircraft so cleared and between these aircraft and other IFR or special VFR aircraft.

    c.   A contact approach is an approach procedure that may be used by a pilot (with prior authorization from ATC) in lieu of conducting a standard or special IAP to an airport. It is not intended for use by a pilot on an IFR flight clearance to operate to an airport not having an authorized IAP. Nor is it intended for an aircraft to conduct an instrument approach to one airport and then, when "in the clear," to discontinue that approach and proceed to another airport. In the execution of a contact approach, the pilot assumes the responsibility for obstruction clearance. If radar service is being received, it will automatically terminate when the pilot is told to contact the tower.

You can see a tool here that can be very helpful to the instrument pilot. You must remember, though, that in order to execute a contact approach, you must be on an IFR flight plan, you can only use it to fly to your destination airport as filed on your flight plan, you cannot use it without ATC authorization, and you are fully responsible for obstruction clearance.

Many airports also have DF (direction finding) instrument procedures, but these are only for use when the pilot has declared a "distress" or "urgency" condition, such as would happen were you to lose your navigational capabilities.

STRAIGHT-IN AND CIRCLING MINIMUMS

You will find straight-in and/or circling minimums published for most runways. The circling minimums are always higher than the straight-in minimums. What constitutes a straight-in or circling approach presents a problem at times. For example, I have had a number of students ask me why a certain airport will have circling minimums when the final approach course is on the same heading as the runway. Once again we can go to the *ATC Handbook* for the answer:

b.   Straight-in minimums—Straight-in minimums are shown on IAP charts when the final approach course of the IAP is within 30 degrees of the runway alignment and a normal descent can be made from the IFR altitude shown on the IAPs to the runway surface. When either the normal rate of descent or the runway alignment factor of 30 degrees is exceeded, a straight-in minimum is not published and a circling minimum applies. The fact that a straight-in minimum is not published does not preclude the pilot from landing straight-in if he has the active runway in sight and has sufficient time to make a normal approach for landing. Under such conditions and when ATC has cleared him for landing on that runway, he is not expected to circle even though only circling minimums are published. If he desires to circle he should advise ATC. . .

d.   Circling Minimums—The circling minimums . . . provide adequate obstruction clearance and the pilot should not descend below the circling altitude until the aircraft is in a position to make final descent for landing . . .

(1) Maneuver the shortest path to the base or downwind leg, as appropriate, under minimum weather conditions. There is no restriction from passing over the airport or other runways.

(2) It should be recognized that many circling maneuvers may be made while VFR or other flying is in progress at the airport. Standard left turns or specific instructions from the controller for maneuvering must be considered when circling to land.

(3) At airports without a control tower, it may be desirable to fly over the airport to determine wind and turn indicators, and to observe other traffic . . .''

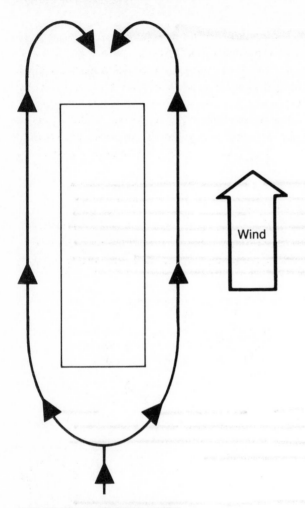

Fig. 12-1. *You are making an approach downwind and must circle to land into the wind. Once you sight the airport, you break right or left to make a standard downwind leg. This way you should never lose sight of the field.*

Wind

CIRCLING APPROACH

It is important to recognize that, if you sight the runway too late to make a normal descent to landing, you are required to circle. When circling, you may not descend below the circling altitude until you are in position to make a normal landing. This usually means when you turn final. A lot of good pilots have crashed while executing a circling approach because they went too low and hit one of the many obstructions found in the vicinity of most airports, or they developed vertigo when making a tight turn close to the ground, and stalled or spun in.

I remember watching a Convair 440 break out of the clouds years ago when I was living in the East. He was just over the end of a 6000-foot runway. The pilot, not wanting to take a wave-off, and being below circling minimums, tried to land. His descent was too steep and his airspeed was too high. He was using up way too much runway, and he was determined to get it on the ground, so he pushed the nose over. Halfway down the runway, his nosewheel hit and collapsed, and the aircraft slid to a stop about 50 feet from a 300-foot drop-off. Fortunately, no one was injured, but the aircraft suffered considerable damage, the field was closed for two days, and an 18-year veteran pilot lost a job. Instrument flying is no time to cut corners.

Look now at some examples of circling maneuvers (FIGS. 12-1 through 12-4).

In these maneuvers, the turns are executed using outside visual references and instruments. You should keep a close eye on your altitude, airspeed, and angle of bank.

RUNWAY NOT IN SIGHT

This brings us down to the missed approach. There are two situations in which a missed approach is mandatory. The first is when you reach the DH or MAP depicted on the IAP chart and do not have sufficient visual reference to complete

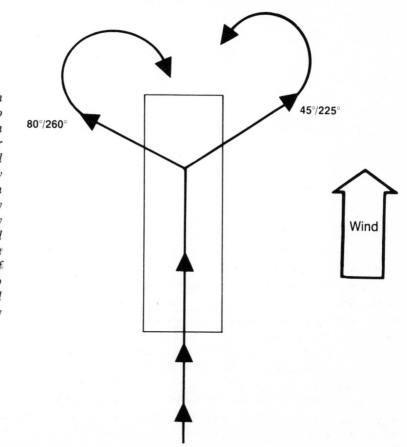

Fig. 12-2. *In this approach you either sight the field too late to maneuver as shown in FIG. 12-1, or the weather conditions along the normal downwind legs will not allow you the latitude to circle in that manner. In this case, fly directly down the runway (at the circling MDA), and upon reaching the approach end, execute any type of procedure turn that will keep you from losing visual reference with the runway (except when banking).*

80°/260°

45°/225°

Wind

the landing. The second is when you lose visual reference to the airport while executing a circling approach.

Whenever you make a missed approach, you must either comply with the published missed approach procedure as printed on the chart, or follow directions from ATC if they direct you to deviate from the published procedure. If you lose visual reference while executing a circling approach, initiate the missed approach by making a climbing turn toward the landing runway. Continue the turn until you are established on the proper missed approach procedure.

You should have noticed by now that, as I mentioned in Chapter 11, you'll be pretty busy flying the procedures, and the actual mechanics of flying the aircraft must be practically automatic.

It will be a good idea to practice the same maneuvers I suggested before (straight and level, climbs, and descents), all with and without turns, and at both normal speeds and slow or maneuvering speeds. This time, special emphasis should be placed on the proper use of trim.

Any time your plane is *established* in a new attitude, all possible control pressures should be relieved by proper trim. Remember, to use trim properly you

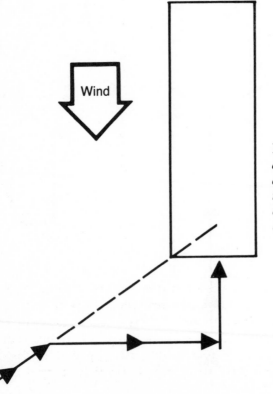

Fig. 12-3. *This shows your most desired break-off from a circling approach. You sight the runway in time to maneuver normally onto the extended centerline and execute a normal landing.*

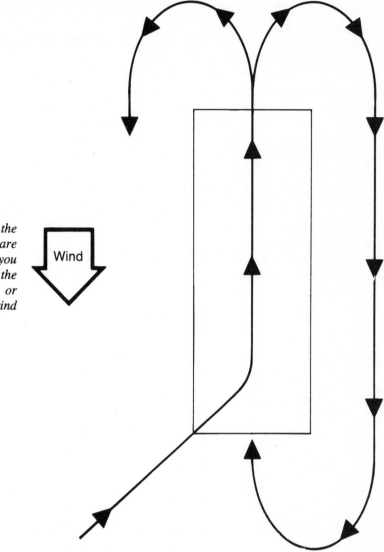

Fig. 12-4. *If you do not see the runway in time, but are approaching into the wind, you should fly down the runway to the departure end, and turn left or right to execute normal downwind and base legs.*

Wind

must first use control pressure to establish your new attitude. Then use the trim tabs so that the aircraft will maintain the required flight path practically "hands off". This will allow you time to take quick looks at approach plates, pick one up off the floor, or jot down a new clearance without the aircraft wandering around. It will also allow you to change attitudes quickly, such as going from descent to a missed approach climb without having to impart excessive pressures to the controls.

13

Enroute, Area, and SID/STAR Charts

L ET'S TURN OUR ATTENTION NOW TO THE ENROUTE CHARTS. IN THIS DISCUS-sion we'll only be working with Jeppesen charts. National Ocean Service (NOS) charts will be easy to transition to should you want to use them.

The low altitude (LO) charts in the continental United States and Canada are effective up to, but not including, 18,000 feet MSL. If you intend to fly higher than that you will need to use either the high (HI) or high/low (H/L) charts.

The LO and H/L Jeppesen charts have a unique feature that Jeppesen calls a "Zigdex." You know how much of a problem it is to fold and unfold large charts in the confined space of small cockpits. This is even more difficult when you are trying to control a plane under IFR conditions. Well, Jeppesen has found the answer.

If you look at the index map on the cover of the chart (FIG. 13-1), you will note a few gray squares and rectangles. These are found around some very large cities where the congestion is so bad that a lot of information has to be omitted. To solve this problem, Jeppesen has larger-scale area charts which should be used whenever you are flying into or out of these specific areas. The area charts are referenced on the enroute charts by a heavy dashed line with the identifier and location name. Many of the symbols that are found on the area charts are shown on the enroute charts in reduced scale so that pilots who are overflying the area can do so without having to open an area chart. But remember—if you are going to land or takeoff within that area, you need to use the area chart.

Also on the index map, you'll see that some of the major cities have been underlined. Now, on the back of the chart (FIG. 13-2), note that the upper edge has been trimmed off at an angle so that, when it is folded up, it zigzags back and forth like the switchbacks of a trail. Each of the underlined cities can be found on one of the folds. To find a specific area on the chart it is only necessary to open it up at the correct fold. From then on, all you have to do is open and close the folds like the pages in a book. It's a lot easier than trying to open and refold the entire chart.

Most altitudes are in feet above mean sea level (MSL), although some are in flight levels, in which case they will be noted as such.

En route communications are shown in two places on the chart—on the face of the chart itself and on the end folds (FIG. 13-2) for convenience when planning a flight. Except on the high altitude charts, the terminal communications are also shown in the tabulations on the end folds.

ROAD MAPS IN THE SKY

The charts are not all drawn to the same scale, so check the scale printed along the upper or side margin of the chart face before measuring anything on it. Jeppesen manufactures chart plotters that have a compass rose as well as all of the various scales marked on them. These plotters come in very handy when measuring off distances and bearings.

Let's take a look at some of the symbols to be found on the enroute chart. Radio identification and communications can be seen in FIG. 13-3.

All navaid facilities that form an airway or a route component are enclosed in shadow boxes. If they are not co-located, they are so noted in parentheses below the box. The name of the facility, its frequency, three-letter identification, and Morse code identifier are found inside the box, and if the facility has DME capability that is frequency-paired, a small "D" will be included preceding the frequency.

There are still quite a few TACAN stations operating throughout the country. Some of these have frequency pairing, which means that the VOR frequency is also the DME frequency. In this case, the frequency is shown with the three-letter ID. If it is not frequency-paired, the "ghost" VOR frequency will be shown in parentheses below the TACAN information.

To facilitate aircraft using area navigation such as Inertial Navigation System (INS) and OMEGA, the H/L and HI altitude charts also show the geographical coordinates below the code ID.

When landing aids perform en route functions, they are identified by round cornered boxes. As in the navaid shadow box, the frequency is provided in the box, as well as the DME if it is available and frequency-paired. These facilities include LOC, SDF, LDA, MLS, and KRM. Before we go on, I should define those that I haven't talked about in previous chapters. All of these definitions

Fig. 13-1

◄20 US (LO) JEPPESEN US (LO) 19 ►
1 INCH = 20 NM · 1 INCH = 20 NM

UNITED STATES
LOW ALTITUDE ENROUTE CHARTS

© JEPPESEN SANDERSON, INC., 1978, 1986. ALL RIGHTS RESERVED.

MEETS FAA REQUIREMENTS FOR AERONAUTICAL CHARTS

Within the continental U.S. & Canada, the airways shown on these charts are effective up to but not including 18,000' MSL. At 14,500' MSL and above, all airspace within the continental U.S. is controlled (Continental Control Area). Shaded blue areas shown on the face of enroute charts designate airspace that is uncontrolled. The U.S. Jet Route and Canadian High Level Airway Structures are superimposed to show their relationship with the low altitude airways. For operational detail of Jet Routes at or above 18,000' MSL, use US (HI) charts.

REVISION DATA

CHART US(LO)19 NOV 28-86 Numerous alternate airways redesig in the Marquette, Menominee, Traverse City and Saginaw, Mich areas. Airway bearings and Int formations revised from Iron Mountain, Mich VOR.

CHART US(LO)20 NOV 28-86 V-98 redesig Toronto, Ont VOR—Stirling VOR. V-104 redesig Ash, Ont VOR—Stirling VOR. V-496 revoked Coehill, Ont VOR—Kendl Int. Plattsburgh, NY VOR relocated, associated airways realigned thereto.

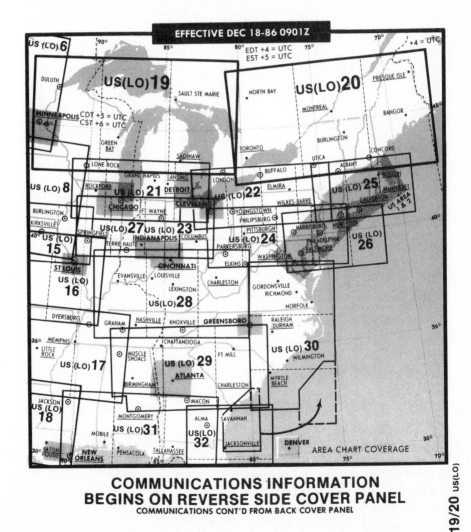

COMMUNICATIONS INFORMATION
BEGINS ON REVERSE SIDE COVER PANEL
COMMUNICATIONS CONT'D FROM BACK COVER PANEL

19/20 US(LO)

(Reproduced with permission of Jeppesen Sanderson, Inc. NOT FOR USE IN NAVIGATION.)

Fig. 13-2

1 MINNEAPOLIS	PRESQUE ISLE 6
2 GREEN BAY	MONTREAL 5
3 SAGINAW	TORONTO 4

◄ **19** US (LO)   COMMUNICATIONS   US (LO) **20** ►

BOLD NAME—Voice call. Light Names/Abbreviations—Identifying names/abbreviations not used in radio call. T—Transmit only. G—Guard only. *—Part-time operation. X—On-request. (R)—Radar Capability. R2 or R3—Stage II or III Radar for VFR. TCA 1 or TCA 2—Group I or Group II TCA for VFR. C—Clearance Delivery. **Cpt**—Clearance (Pre-taxi Proc). KDEN p6D—Charted location is shown by Area chart initials and/or by quarter panel number-letter combination. Common EMERGENCY 121.5 is not listed. Refer to Glossary and Abbreviations in Introduction pages for further explanations.

A .—	G ——.	M ——	S ...	Y —.——	5 .....
B —...	H	N —.	T —	Z ——..	6 —....
C —.—.	I ..	O ———	U ..—	1 .————	7 ——...
D —..	J .———	P .——.	V ...—	2 ..———	8 ———..
E .	K —.—	Q ——.—	W .——	3 ...——	9 ————.
F ..—.	L .—..	R .—.	X —..—	4 ....—	0 —————

ALBANY, N.Y.   p5C
Albany ATIS 120.45. **Albany App(R & ARSA)/ Dep(R & ARSA)** (Rwy 1-19 in use: 194°-011° 118.05, 011°-194° 125.0) (Rwy 10-28 in use: 275°-095° 118.05, 095°-275° 125.0) 124.7 127.15. **Twr** 119.5. **Gnd** 121.7. **C** 127.5.

ALMA, MICH.   p3C
Gratiot. **Saginaw** *App/*Dep 118.45.

ALPENA, MICH.   p3C
Phelps-Collins. **Collins** *App(R)/ *Dep(R) 134.8. *Twr 120.9 126.2. **Gnd** 121.9. Collins App/Twr op summers only, O/T **Wurtsmith** App/Dep 134.8 128.6.

ANOKA, MINN.   KMSP p1C
Gateway North Industrial. **Minneapolis App(R)/Dep(R)** 126.5.

APPLETON, WISC.   p2C
Outagamie. **Green Bay** *App(R)/ *Dep(R) 126.3. **Appleton** *Twr 119.6. **Gnd** 121.7.

AUBURN, MAINE   p6C
Auburn-Lewiston. **Portland** *App 125.5 124.05. *Dep 125.5. *Cpt 124.05.

AUGUSTA, MAINE   p6C
Augusta State. **Brunswick** *App/*Dep 128.35.

AUSTIN, MINN.   p1C
Austin. **Rochester App(R)/Dep(R)** 119.8.

BANGOR, MAINE   p6D
Bangor Int'l ATIS 125.6. **Bangor App(R&R3)/Dep(R&R3)** (335°-154° 124.5, 155°-334° 125.3). **Twr** 120.7. **Gnd** 121.9. **C** 121.9.

BAR HARBOR, MAINE   p6D
Hancock-Bar Harbor. **Bangor App(R)/ Dep(R)** 124.5. **C** 119.9.

BAY CITY, MICH.   p3C
Clements. **Saginaw** *App(R)/*Dep(R) 126.45.

GRIFFISS AFB, N.Y.   p5C
Griffiss AFB. **Griffiss App(R&R2)** 329°-157° 126.65, 158°-328° 118.5. **Dep(R&R2)** 120.9. **Twr** 126.2. GCA.

HARTFORD, WISC.   p2C
Hartford. **Milwaukee App(R)/Dep(R)** 124.75.

HIBBING, MINN.   p1A
Chisholm-Hibbing. **Duluth App(R)/ Dep(R)** 125.8.

HIGHGATE, VT.   p5D
Franklin. **Burlington App(R)/Dep(R)** 121.1 (East), 126.3 (West).

JUNEAU, WISC.   p2C
Dodge. **Madison** *App(R)/*Dep(R) 119.15.

K.I. SAWYER AFB, MICH.   p2A
K.I. Sawyer AFB. **Sawyer App(R&R2)** 119.1 116.3T. **Dep(R&R2)** 119.1. **Twr** 126.2 116.3T.

KITCHENER, ONT.   p4C
Waterloo-Guelph. **Waterloo** *Twr 126.0. **Gnd** 121.8. **Waterloo Broadcast** MF/10nm 126.0 when Twr inop.

LACONIA, N.H.   p6C
Laconia. **Manchester** *App(R)/*Dep(R) 127.35. **C** 119.85.

LA CROSSE, WISC.   p1D
La Crosse. *ATIS 124.95. **La Crosse** *Twr 124.3. **Gnd** 121.8. **La Crosse Rdo** (AAS) 124.3 121.8 when Twr inop.

LAKEVILLE, MINN.   KMSP
Airlake. **Minneapolis App(R)/Dep(R)** 125.0.

LEBANON, N.H.   p5D
Lebanon *ATIS 118.65. **Lebanon** *Twr 119.4. **Gnd** 121.6. **Lebanon Rdo** (AAS) 119.4 when Twr inop.

LINCOLN, MAINE   p6B
Lincoln. **Bangor App(R)/Dep(R)** 124.5.

PEASE AFB,   (NE CORR 1p3B) p6C
N.H.
Pease AFB **Pease App(R&R2)/Dep (R&R2)** 125.05. **Twr** 128.4.

PEMBROKE, ONT.   p4B
Pembroke. **Ottawa** *Tml Ctl(R) (Arr/ Dep) 135.2. **Petawawa** *Twr MF/5nm 122.8. **Pembroke UNICOM** MF/20nm 122.8 when Twr inop.

PITTSFIELD, MAINE   p6C
Pittsfield. **Bangor App** 125.3. **Dep** 126.85.

PLATTSBURGH, N.Y.   p5D
Clinton. **Burlington App(R)/Dep(R)** 121.1 (East), 126.3 (West). **C** 121.7. Plattsburgh AFB. **Burlington App (R)/Dep(R)** 121.1 (East), 126.3 (West). **Plattsburgh Twr** 126.2. **Gnd** 134.1. GCA.

PORTAGE, WISC.   p1D
Madison *App(R)/*Dep(R) 124.0 120.1.

PORTLAND, MAINE   p6C
Portland Int'l ATIS 119.05. **Portland** *App(R&R3)/*Dep(R&R3) (293°-111° 125.5, 112°-292° 119.75). *Twr 120.9. **Gnd** 121.9. **C** 121.65.

PRESQUE ISLE, MAINE   p6B
Northern Maine Regional. **Loring App(R)/Dep(R)** 124.7. **C** 121.6

PULASKI, WISC.   p2C
Carter. **Green Bay** *App(R) 119.4. *Dep(R) 126.55

QUEBEC, QUE.   p5B
Quebec ATIS 119.8(Eng), 128.3(Fr). **Quebec** *Arr(R)/*Dep(R) 127.85. **Twr** 120.3. **Gnd** 121.9.

ROCHESTER, MINN.   KMSP p1C
Rochester *ATIS 120.5. **Rochester** *App(R&R2)/*Dep(R&R2) (310°-129° 119.2, 130°-309° 119.8). *Twr 118.3. **Gnd** 121.9. **Rochester Rdo** (AAS) 118.3 when Twr inop.

ROCHESTER, N.H.   p6C

(Reproduced with permission of Jeppesen Sanderson, Inc. NOT FOR USE IN NAVIGATION.)

ENROUTE CHART LEGEND

NAVAID IDENTIFICATION

Navaid identification is given in shadow box when navaid is airway or route component, with frequency, identifier, and Morse Code. DME capability is indicated by a small "D" preceding the VOR frequency at frequency paired navaids. VOR and VOR-TAC navaid operational ranges are identified (when known) within the navaid box except on USA and Canada charts. (T) represents Terminal; (L) represents Low Altitude; and (H) represents High Altitude.

```
┌─ STOUT ─┐
│(H)114.1 STO│
└─ ·· ····· ─┘
```

Heavier shadow boxes are gradually replacing existing shadow boxes. There is no difference in meaning.

On HIGH/LOW altitude enroute charts, geographical coordinates (latitude and longitude) are shown for navaids forming high or all altitude airways and routes. On Area charts, geographical coordinates are shown when navaid is airway or route component.

```
┌─ KADENA ─┐
│D112.0 KAD│
└──────────┘
N26 22.4 E127 48.0
   335 KD
N26 20.0 E127 44.8
```

Some L/MF navaids are combined in the shadow box even though they are not part of the airway/route structure, except on US and CA charts. They are used for course guidance over lengthy route segments when airway/track is designated into a VOR.

```
┌─ BENBECULA ─┐
│D114.4 BEN│
└──────────┘
(Not Colocated)
```

When VOR and TAC/DME antennas are not colocated, a notation "Not Colocated" is shown below the navaid box.

MOODY
113.3 VAD
TAC-80

KENNEY
254 ENY

TAPTHONG
POINT
```
┌──────────┐
│(T)115.5 TH│
└──────────┘
```

LIPTON
TAC-88 LPT
(114.1)

GREAT
BARRINGTON
MASS 739
395 GBR

LOC
```
┌──────────┐
│ 108.7 IMBS │
└──────────┘
```

LAYTON

Off-airway navaids are unboxed on Low and High/Low charts. TACAN/DME channel is shown when VOR navaid has frequency paired DME capability. When an L/MF navaid performs an enroute function, the Morse Code of its identification letters are shown. (Off-airway VORs are boxed except on US and CA charts.)

When TACAN or DME are not frequency paired with the VOR, the TACAN is identified separately. The "Ghost" VOR frequency, shown in parentheses, enables civilian tuning of DME facility.

The navaid frequency and identification are located below the location name of the airport when the navaid name, location name, and airport name are the same.

LOC, SDF, LDA, MLS, and KRM navaids are identified by a round cornered box when they perform an enroute function. Frequency identification and Morse Code are provided. DME is included when navaid and DME are frequency paired.

Fan Marker name and code.

COMMUNICATIONS

RADIO FREQUENCIES

VHF frequencies for radio communications are included above NAVAID names, when voice is available through the NAVAID. These frequencies are also shown at other remoted locations. Radio Frequencies, which are in the 120 MHz range, are shown with the numbers "12" omitted; 122.2 is shown as 2.2, 122.35 as 2.35, etc. HF and LF frequencies are not abbreviated.

```
  2.2-2.45-5680
┌─ RIVER ─┐
│D114.6 RIV│
└── ·· ···· ─┘
```
River Radio transmits on 114.6 and transmits and receives on 122.2, 122.45 MHz and HF frequency 5680.

```
  2.1G-RIV
┌─ CANYON ─┐
│113.9 CNY│
└──────────┘
```
River Radio (RIV) guards (receives) on 122.1 and transmits through Canyon VOR on 113.9.

```
  2.6-RIV
┌─ DIAMOND ─┐
└──────────┘
      ⊙
```
River Radio transmits and receives on 122.6 located at Diamond. Small circle enclosing dot denotes remote communication site.

```
     ☎
  2.2-2.4
┌─ TAPEATS ─┐
│D112.2 TPT│
└──────────┘
```
Tapeats Radio transmits and receives on 122.2 and 122.4. Telephone symbol indicates additional frequencies in communications panel listed under Tapeats.

```
   HIWAS
 MIA WX-*2.0
┌─ MIAMI ─┐
│D115.9 MIA│
└──────────┘
N25 57.8 W080 27.6
```
HIWAS — Hazardous Inflight Weather Advisory Service. Broadcasts SIGMETS, AIRMETS and PIREPS continuously over VOR frequency.

```
  2.3-RIV
  2.6-PTM
┌─ PHANTOM ─┐
│ 364 PTM │
└──────────┘
```
River Radio transmits and receives at Phantom on 122.3. Additonally, Phantom Radio transmits and receives on 122.6.

```
  (RIVER FSS)
    LAVA
┌──────────┐
│D115.3 LVA│
└──────────┘
```
River Radio transmits through Lava VOR on 115.3, but is not capable of receiving transmissions through the VOR site.

```
2.2-2.6-3.6 (AAS)
 GRAND ARIZ
    1285
```
Grand Radio is located at the airport and transmits and receives on 122.2 and 122.6. Additionally, Grand Radio provides AAS (Airport Advisory Service) on 123.6.

```
   3.6 AAS
 NORTHSIDE
    390

U-2.8 MF/10 NM
 NORTHSIDE
    390

 3.6 ATF MOOSE
 NORTHSIDE
    390
```
Terminal Radio frequencies and service may be included over airport or location name. Radio call is included when different than airport or location name. Mandatory Frequencies (MF), Aerodrome Traffic Frequencies (ATF) or UNICOM (U) frequencies include contact distance when other than the standard 5 nm.

are from the Jeppesen chart glossary:

> Simplified Directional Facility (SDF)—a navaid "used for nonprecision instrument approaches. The final approach course may be offset from the runway, generally not more than three degrees, and the course may be wider than the localizer, resulting in a lower degree of accuracy." [The LDA and SDF approaches are almost the same, except for the accuracy and the fact that the LDA may be more than 3° off the runway heading.]

> Microwave Landing System (MLS)—"an instrument landing system operating in the microwave spectrum which provides lateral and vectored guidance to aircraft having compatible avionics equipment."

> KRM—"a system which provides three-axis position indication, similar to ILS," used in eastern Europe.

Flight Service Station (FSS) VHF frequencies in the United States and Canada will be found above the navaid names. Frequencies shown are usually all in the 120 MHz range and are shown with "12" omitted (e.g., 3.6 denotes 123.6 MHz).

Look at FIG. 13-3, in the five examples of how FSS River Radio operates. In the first example, you will see that River VOR is on frequency 114.6, with the identification RIV. It has DME and will transmit and receive on 122.2 and 122.45 MHz. It also transmits on 114.6 MHz. In addition it has two-way high-frequency communications capability on 5680 kHz.

As you continue your flight, you run across Canyon VOR on 113.9 MHz with the identifier CNY. Note that it does not have DME as there is no small "D" before the frequency. Also note that River Radio remotes through it, transmitting on the VOR frequency and receiving on 122.1 MHz. The letter "G" following the frequency 122.1 indicates that it guards (listens to) that frequency, but cannot transmit over it. The letters RIV following the "G" lets you know that you should use River Radio as the calling facility.

Sometimes you will find a Remote Communications Outlet, here shown as Diamond. This is not a VOR, hence no VOR frequency, identifier, or Morse code symbols, but you can see above the box that River Radio transmits and receives on 122.6 MHz and the location of the antenna is shown by the dot enclosed in the circle.

You might run across an L/MF facility such as Phantom (364 MHz PTM) that is used by both River Radio on 122.3 MHz and Phantom Radio on 122.6 MHz.

Finally, there are VORs which enable an FSS to transmit on the VOR frequency but which do not have any receiving capability. Such a situation is illustrated at Lava (115.3 MHz LVA).

The telephone symbol tells you that the facility has communications capabilities other than those shown on the chart. These will be found in the communications panel under the name of the facility.

Looking at FIG. 13-4, you will see that transcribed weather broadcasts are in-

Fig. 13-4

JUL 12-85   **INTRODUCTION**   **JEPPESEN**

ENROUTE CHART LEGEND
COMMUNICATIONS
(continued)

DEN WX-*2.0
DENVER
D 116.3 DEN
N39 51.6 W104 45.1

US "Enroute Flight Advisory Service". Ident of controlling station to call, using (name of station) FLIGHT WATCH on 122.0 MHz. Charted above VORs associated with controlling station and remoted outlets. Service is provided between 0600 and 2200 hours daily.

In all world areas, the telephone symbol indicates additional communications may be found in the communications tabulation after the associated NAVAID or location name. Telephone symbol does not necessarily mean that voice is available through the NAVAID.

VIRAC
RADIO

CRYSTAL
116.1 CRT

SECTOR 2
MANILA
CONTROL
119.3 126.1
128.2 130.1

Call and frequencies of Control Service for use within graphically portrayed Radio Frequency Sector Boundaries.

BELGRADE
WX
126.40

Plain language inflight weather station with name and frequency.

NASSAU
RADIO
E-CAR
124.2
5566 6537
8871 13344

Call and frequency of enroute service or control unit. SINGLE SIDE BAND capabilities are available unless specified otherwise.

TORONTO(R)
(LONDON)
119.4

Remote air/ground antenna for direct communications with control center. Center is named in large type and name of remote site is in parentheses below followed by appropriate VHF frequencies.

CHICAGO
(CEDAR RAPIDS)
121.4

NAVAID/COMMUNICATION DATA

(May be Shutdown)
(May be Test Only)
(May not be Comsnd)

Operational status at date of publication. Refer to Chart NOTAMS for current status, including substitute routes for VOR and VORTAC shutdowns.

(TWEB)
MAYBE
326 MBY

(TWEB) indicates continuous automatic weather broadcast is provided on the facility frequency.

(WX)
EAST BAY
362 EZB

Class SABH radio beacons of limited navigation suitability indicate their primary purpose of continuous automatic weather broadcast by (WX).

(R)

Enroute Radar capability. (All domestic U.S. centers are radar equipped so (R) is omitted from domestic U.S. center boxes.)

SAARBRUCKEN
343 SBN

Underline shown below navaid identifier, indicates Beat Frequency Oscillator (BFO) required to hear Morse Code identifier. Not shown on all series.

*

Asterisk indicates navaid operation or service not continuous.

H+04 & 15(1)

Marine beacon operation times. Transmission begins at 4 minutes past the hour and every 15 minutes thereafter in this illustration; other times will be indicated. Number in parentheses gives duration in minutes of transmission.

FOG:H+02 & 08

Facility operates in fog only at times indicated.

RESTRICTED AIRSPACE

Restricted airspace. The accompanying label indicates it as prohibited, restricted, danger, etc. See below.

On some charts prohibited areas are shown by a cross-hatch pattern.

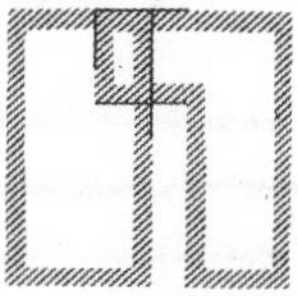

When restricted airspace areas overlap, a line is shown on the outer edge of each area through the area of overlap.

Training, Alert, Caution, and Military Operations Areas

CY(R)-4207 — Country identifier, designation in parens, and number
FL 450 — Upper Limit
GND — Lower Limit
SR-SS — Hours active
(MSP ARTCC) — Controlling Agency
(Limits may be tabulated)

●ED(R)-7
30000
GND

Dot indicates permanent activation on some chart series.

R-6001
24000
GND
(JAX ARTCC)

On USA charts K (indicating USA) and parens around the designating letter are omitted.

RESTRICTED AIRSPACE DESIGNATION

A-Alert
C-Caution
D-Danger
P-Prohibited
R-Restricted
T-Training
W-Warning
TRA-Temporary Reserved Airspace
MOA-Military Operations Area

Canadian Alert Area Suffixes
(A) Acrobatic
(H) Hang Gliding
(P) Parachute Dropping
(S) Soaring
(T) Training

(Reproduced with permission of Jeppesen Sanderson, Inc. NOT FOR USE IN NAVIGATION.)

dicated by the letters "TWEB" in parentheses over the name of the facility.

An asterisk (*) indicates that a facility's operation or service is not continuous.

As far as restricted airspace is concerned, it is important to recognize that the words and figures found near the restricted airspace block have a given order which will include the designation, both the upper and lower limits, the hours of operation, and the controlling agency. Many of them will have infrequent hours of operation and will list NOTAMs rather than days and times, so you should check the current NOTAMs to see if these areas will be activated during the time you plan to be near the area.

Airports are depicted similar to the way they are on any airway or aeronautical chart. The specific symbols can be seen in FIG. 13-5.

An airport not having a Jeppesen approach chart is designated by printing the airport name in both upper and lower case letters. The elevation shown below the name is in feet above mean sea level (MSL).

If an airport has a Jeppesen approach chart, the name of the location (by which it is indexed) is printed all in upper case letters. If the airport name is different from the location name the airport name will be printed in small type below the location name using both upper and lower case letters. This is useful information should you know the airport name and its approximate location, but not the actual listed name. In this case, look around the general area until you locate the airport name and note the chart designation name above it.

Now, look about halfway down the left side of the page (FIG. 13-5). Here you can see that there are three different symbols for reporting points. These are for compulsory reporting points, on-request reporting points, and low altitude compulsory reporting points.

With so much radar available to us these days, and its reliability as good as it is, we find fewer and fewer compulsory reporting points on the airways. Most of them are at the VORs, and even these are becoming fewer in number. The less we use things, though, the more we tend to forget them, so look at FIG. 13-5 again to refresh your memory.

If a holding pattern depicted on the chart is a DME holding pattern, the first number shown will be the DME distance of the fix (in relation to the DME facility upon which the holding pattern is predicated). The second number is the DME distance at the outbound limit. In the example shown, the fix is at 31 DME, the holding pattern is shown as utilizing nonstandard (left) turns, and you would turn inbound again at 39 miles DME.

If the length of the holding pattern is other than standard, the time (in minutes) will be printed in white numerals inside a dark diamond.

MINIMUM ALTITUDES, FIXES, AND REPORTING POINTS

Although we see many fixes that show a Minimum Reception Altitude (MRA), there are many parts of the country in which you can fly all your life and never

Fig. 13-5

ENROUTE CHART LEGEND
AIRPORTS

Civil   Military

○   ○   Airports

⚓   ⚓   Seaplane Base

Ⓗ   Ⓗ   Heliports

Andrews Co
3176
○   Airport not having a Jeppesen Instrument Approach Chart

(AAS)   AAS (Airport Advisory Service)

(AFIS)   AFIS (Aerodrome Flight Information Service)

NAME
642   Airport elevations are in feet AMSL.

RIVERSIDE
CALIF
816   Airport locations labeled in capital letters indicate a Jeppesen (Instrument) Approach Chart is published for that airport and is indexed by that name.

DENVER COLO
Jeffco
5654

CHARLOTTE NC
Douglas

Owens

When the airport name is different, it is shown following the approach chart indexing in small letters. Available terminal communications are provided in the COMMUNICATIONS tabulations. Airport is listed under the name in capital letters—Douglas Mun is listed under CHARLOTTE. When only the airport name is shown, the airport is listed under the airport name—Owens is listed under Owens Apt.

AIRWAY AND ROUTE COMPONENTS
AIRWAY AND ROUTES CENTER LINES

———————   Airway/Route

— — — —   Diversionary Route, Weekend Route (Europe)

▓▓▓▓▓▓   LF Airway (Canada & Alaska only)

▓▓▓▓▓▓   Overlying High Altitude Airway/Route

—[OTR]—   Oceanic Transition Route

AIRWAY FIXES

▲ ▲ ▲   Compulsory Reporting Point

△ △ △   On-Request Reporting Point

◣ ◣ ◣   Low Altitude Compulsory Reporting Point

The dot, formerly meaning VHF formation, is not significant and is being dropped except at navaid centers.

X   Mileage Break/Turning Point

Ⓜ Ⓜ   Meteorological report required (unless instructed otherwise), giving air temperature, wind, icing, turbulence, clouds and other significant weather. Report to controlling ground station, or station indicated.

Ⓜ RPMM
Ⓜ ABOVE FL 230

(D31/39)   Holding Pattern. DME figures, when provided, give the DME distance of the fix as the first figure followed by the outbound limit as the second figure.

②   Length of holding pattern in minutes when other than standard.

LIMON
V-8 7500 NW
(MRA 7000)   Fix name with Minimum Crossing Altitude (MCA) showing airway, altitude, and direction, and Minimum Reception Altitude (MRA).

△———095°→   LF bearings forming a fix are to the navaid.

△←—296°———   VHF radials forming a fix are from the navaid.

△←—296° BOR/116.8   VHF frequency and identifier included when off chart or remoted.

△ ABC :::/294 ——095°→   LF frequency, identifier and Morse Code included when off chart or remoted.

△——   Arrow along airway points from one of the navaids designating the reporting point. Other published radials may be used if they are greater than 30 degrees from the airway being used and are not beyond the COP.

△ D55/MA   Fix formed by 55 DME from MA navaid.

△ 10/D22   △ 12/D   "D" indicates DME fix and distance from the station that provides the DME mileage.

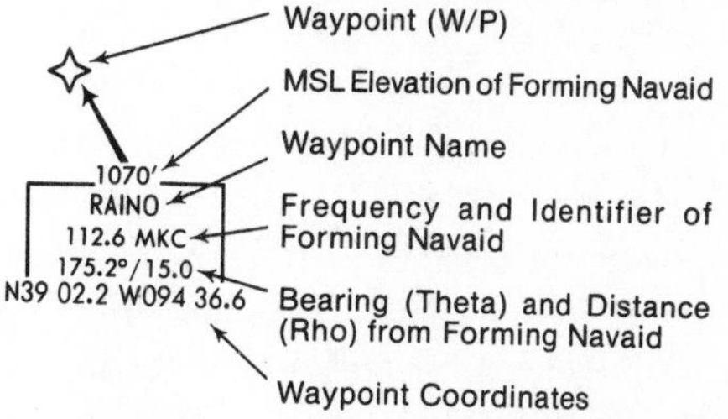

Waypoint (W/P)

MSL Elevation of Forming Navaid

◇   1070'
RAINO
112.6 MKC
175.2°/15.0
N39 02.2 W094 36.6

Waypoint Name

Frequency and Identifier of Forming Navaid

Bearing (Theta) and Distance (Rho) from Forming Navaid

Waypoint Coordinates

AIRWAY INFORMATION

V-168
J-71   Airway and route designators. Negative (white letters in blue) designators are used for distinction.

ADR-432
ATS
AWY-4
D   A-Amber. Some countries use the phonetic alphabet in lieu of "colored" designations, as Alpha in lieu of Amber, Golf in lieu of Green, etc.
ADR-Advisory Route
AR-Atlantic Route, Canada Alpha Route
ATS-Designated route without published identifier
AWY-Airway
B-Blue, Bravo
BR-Bahama Route, Canada Bravo Route

Direct Route

encounter a Minimum Crossing Altitude (MCA).

The pilot/controller glossary defines an MCA as:

> The lowest altitude at certain fixes at which an aircraft must cross when proceeding in the direction of a higher minimum en route IFR altitude (MEA).

FAR 91.119(b), which deals with minimum altitudes for IFR operations, says:

> (b) *Climb.* Climb to a higher minimum IFR altitude shall begin immediately after passing the point beyond which that minimum altitude applies, except that, when ground obstructions intervene, the point beyond which the higher minimum altitude applies shall be crossed at or above the applicable MCA.

So, you can see here that the reasoning for an MCA is that somewhere beyond the fix (and usually quite close to it), you will find some higher obstructions and you will want to be above them *before* you get into their territory.

In FIG. 13-5, LIMON intersection's MCA is explained. The symbol will first show the airway on which the MCA is applicable, the altitude of the MCA, and the direction of travel for which it is applicable. FIGURE 13-6 shows what LIMON might look like on a chart. Let's say that V-8 at LIMON is a NW/SE airway and you are eastbound on V-5, an E/W airway, planning to turn SE on V-8. In this case, the MCA would not apply to you. If, on the other hand, you were either westbound on V-5 and were planning to turn to the northwest, or northwest bound on V-8, the MCA would be in effect and would require you to cross the fix (LIMON) at or above the MCA.

Many fixes are formed by a VOR non-airway radial that crosses an airway. This sounds sort of confusing so take a look at the last symbol in the left-hand column of FIG. 13-5. In this case the airway, which has an on-request reporting point on it, could be oriented in any direction and is not illustrated. The 296-degree radial from the BOR VOR (on VHF frequency 116.8) is not part of any airway, but it helps to identify the on-request reporting point. The VOR itself is off to the right of the reporting point; once again, directions shown in regard to VORs are radials FROM, rather than bearings TO, the facility. Directions with regard to LF facilities, such as NDBs, are printed in green on the chart (as opposed to blue for VHF aids) and are bearings *to* the station.

If the fix is formed by a VOR radial or an LF bearing that is being remoted, or that is off the chart, the symbol will include not only the radial or bearing, but also the identifier of the VOR or LF facility above the line, and the frequency below the line. You can see both of these illustrated in the case of BOR as explained above, and by the LF facility ABC shown in the right-hand column.

Two on-request reporting point symbols are shown in the *right-hand* column of FIG. 13-5 (seven items down from the top). The numbers shown above the air-

Fig. 13-6

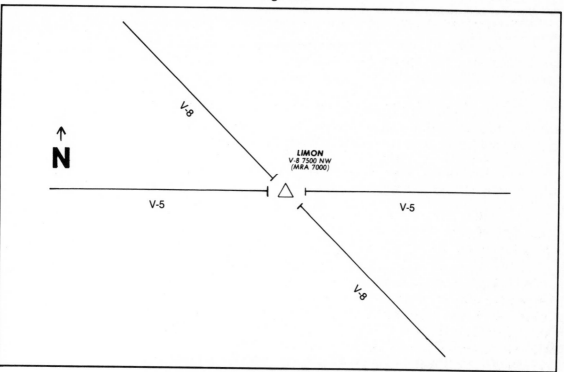

way running through these points indicate segment distances. The distance of the segment *between* the two on-request points is 10 miles. The distance between the right-hand reporting point and the next fix to the right (off the chart) is 12 miles. When you look below the course line, you see two more symbols. The one between the fixes is "D22" with a small arrow pointing to the left. This tells you that the left-hand fix (to which the arrow points) is 22 miles from the DME facility (off to the right). The symbol on the right, a "D" with an arrow, tells you that the DME distance (from the DME facility) to the right-hand reporting point is the same as the segment distance printed above the course line, in this case, 12 miles.

In the lower third of the right column in FIG. 13-5 you can see that airway and route designations are always shown in reverse (negative) type.

Turning to FIG. 13-7, look at some of the various ways we have of depicting Minimum Enroute IFR Altitudes (MEAs). MEA is defined as follows:

MINIMUM EN ROUTE IFR ALTITUDE/MEA—The lowest published altitude between radio fixes which assures acceptable navigational signal coverage and meets obstacle clearance requirements between those fixes. The MEA prescribed for a Federal airway or segment thereof, area navigation low or high route, or other direct route applies to the entire width of the airway, segment, or route between the radio fixes defining the airway, segment, or route.

In the United States, an MEA is depicted as either an altitude or flight level, and if a flight level, it will be designated with the letters "FL" preceding the numerals. At times, the MEA will be higher in one direction than in the other, in which case the altitudes will be shown with appropriate directional arrows.

A Minimum Obstruction Clearance Altitude (MOCA) is depicted with a "T" following the altitude, while a route Minimum Off-Route Altitude (MORA) is designated with a lower case "a" following the altitude.

What is the difference between the two? Let's start with the MOCA and the pilot/controller glossary description:

> MINIMUM OBSTRUCTION CLEARANCE ALTITUDE/ MOCA—The lowest published altitude in effect between radio fixes on VOR airways, off-airway routes, or route segments which meets obstacle clearance requirements for the entire route segment and which assures acceptable navigational signal coverage only within 25 statute (22 nautical) miles of a VOR.

This means that, if the route segment is over 50 statute miles long and you opt for the MOCA, you might not have proper VOR reception for part of your flight. So, in effect, the MOCA is almost a last-resort altitude.

The MORA is strictly a Jeppesen altitude. You won't find it in the ATC pilot/controller glossary. Jeppesen defines it this way:

> MINIMUM OFF-ROUTE ALTITUDE/MORA—This is an altitude derived by Jeppesen. The[route] MORA provides terrain and obstruction clearance within 10 NM of the route centerline (regardless of route width) and end fixes. A grid MORA altitude provides terrain and obstruction clearance within the section outlined by latitude and longitude lines. MORA values clear all terrain and obstructions by 1000' in areas where the highest terrain and obstructions are 5000' MSL or lower. MORA values clear all terrain and obstructions by 2000' in areas where the highest terrain and obstructions are 5000' MSL or higher. When a MORA is shown along a route as "unknown" or within a grid as "unsurveyed" a MORA is not shown due to incomplete or insufficient official source.

A broken section in the route indicates there is either a change in the MEA, MOCA, or route MORA. It is there primarily to show a change in MEA. This symbol will be omitted at a facility.

OTHER SYMBOLS

The total mileage between facilities is shown inside a six-sided polygon which is positioned along and parallel to the centerline of the airway. When two or more airways share the same course, the polygon has directional pointers indicating the airway to which the mileage applies.

If the changeover point (COP) for the navigational radio is other than at the midpoint of the leg or at the turning point on the route, it will be shown by a Z-like symbol crossing the airway (see FIG. 13-7, fourth item from the top right). The numeral on each side of this symbol shows the distance from the respective facility, at which point you should change the navigational radio's frequency. By doing so, you will be assured of adequate navigational reception along the entire route segment.

Now, take a look at the lower portion of the right-hand column in FIG. 13-7. This area shows the airway navaid/reporting point by-pass illustrations. These illustrations depict how routes are illustrated when they pass through facilities or intersections that are not required for that specific route. Locate the VOR symbol (second from the bottom). When a facility is used for a particular route, the route centerline ends at the outer circle of the facility symbol. It usually ends just short of the symbol, leaving enough room to show the outbound radial (as in the case of V-15). If the facility is not required, the airway centerline will be extended through the center of the symbol and no radial will be shown (as in the case of V-76). If a report is not required for one of the routes that pass through a reporting point, that route will be shown passing directly through the reporting point symbol, or the route will be shown as a semicircle so as not to fill in the center an open symbol.

FITTING ALL THE PIECES TOGETHER

Until now, we've been looking at individual symbols. Let's put them all together to see how they might look as part of a chart. Examine FIG. 13-8. At the top you will see latitude (horizontal) and longitude (vertical) tick marks along the chart edges. To help further, these ticks are shown as small crosses or plus marks along the face of the charts, indicating each half degree of latitude or longitude.

Look down the airway marked V-15W. First off, you can see that it's 42 miles to PASSE which is a compulsory reporting point when you are *not* in radar contact. PASSE requires a meteorological report as designated by the "M" within the circle preceding the name.

PASSE is formed by the intersection of V-15W and the 083-degree radial of the DVZ VOR which has a frequency of 117.4 MHz and lies somewhere off the left of the chart.

From the VOR at the top of the page to PASSE, the MEA is 5000 feet, as you can see by the numerals below the airway centerline. The small arrow just prior to PASSE points from the facility which designates the reporting point.

The perpendicular stubs crossing the airway on each side of the fix at PASSE indicate that the MEA is different on each side. Looking to the southeast of

PASSE, you will see that the MEA goes up to 6000 feet MSL. Notice the absence of those stubs at MACKS (over on V-15) where the MEA is 6000 feet MSL on both sides of the fix.

Moving along to the southeast of PASSE (which has an MRA of 6000 feet MSL, by the way), note that the distance from PASSE to the mileage break (indicated by the "X") is 31 nautical miles. The 105 within the six-sided figure tells you that it's a total of 105 nautical miles between the facilities on V-15W. The mileage segments to the break, 42 and 31, only add up to 73 nautical miles. The remaining 32-mile segment extends ESE from the mileage break to an NDB station along the route. The mileage break, then, also indicates a turn in the airway, in this case.

The shaded (screened) line running across the chart just above the mileage break symbol indicates that chart #2 overlaps this chart at that point.

As for the two airport symbols shown on the chart, you can determine that Jeppesen does not have any instrument approach procedure chart for Twiggy Airport because the airport name is in both upper and lower case. The field itself is 709 feet MSL. Jeppesen does provide an instrument approach chart for Vogt Municipal however. Vogt is at 1345 feet MSL, and the chart will be found listed under Waldo, Indiana.

The bearing to the NDB is the reciprocal of 255°, which is 075°. The MEA on this route segment is still 6000 feet MSL, while Jeppesen has included a Route MORA of 4000 feet MSL. The beacon itself is a compulsory reporting point.

The NDB is not only part of V-15W, but also helps to form V-15. The bearing *from* it on V-15 northbound is 315°. It is 42 nautical miles from the NDB to MACKS intersection, which has an MRA of 7000 feet MSL. MACKS is formed by V-15 and the 083-degree radial of DVZ VOR. The changeover point from the NDB to the unnamed VOR is 37 nautical miles northwest of the NDB and 52 nautical miles southeast of the VOR. The total distance between these facilities can be found by adding these two changeover point mileages together, adding up the three route segments (22, 25, and 42), or merely by reading the overall distance shown inside the six-sided figure (89).

You can also find a Maximum Authorized Altitude (MAA) symbol on this illustration. It's beneath the 6000-foot MEA below the V-15 airway identifier. The MAA (defined in the Glossary) on this airway is 13,000 feet.

Moving up now, past the MACKS on-request reporting point symbol, you will notice an arrow pointing from the VOR to the fix symbol with "D47" below it. This indicates that you can determine the fix by the DME distance from the facility to the fix, which is 47 nautical miles. You can also add the two segment distances of 22 and 25 nautical miles to arrive at the same figure.

Proceeding northwest from MACKS, note that the MEA of 6000 feet MSL is followed by "5000T", which is the MOCA between MACKS and LIMON. The stubs at LIMON indicate an MEA change similar to that at PASSE. Not only

Fig. 13-7

ENROUTE CHART LEGEND
AIRWAY INFORMATION (Continued)

DOM

D-(suffix) Advisory service only
DOM-Domestic Route. Use by foreign operators requires special authorization.
F-(suffix) Flight Information
G-Green, Golf
GR-Gulf Route
H or HL-High Level
J-Jet
L-(suffix) L/MF airway
NAT-Route associated with the North Atlantic Organized Track structure.
OTR-Oceanic Transition Route
PDR-Predetermined Route
R-Red, Romeo
R-(suffix) RNAV route
RR-Canada Romeo Route
SP-Supersonic RNAV route
U-Upper
UL-(prefix) RNAV route
V-Victor
V-(suffix) VOR airway
W-White, Whiskey

NAT

OTR

R-11

J888 R

UL-5

← **A 5**   One Way Airway

2500   MEA (Minimum Enroute Altitude), shown as altitude or flight level.

FL 40
3950 STD   Metric MEA converted to feet using standard altimeter setting.

13786T   *4202 mT*
13800a   *4300 ma*   On some chart series, altitudes are provided in both feet and meters. The letter "M" following an altitude in italic type is the metric altitude.

■■■   MEA is established with a gap in nav-signal coverage.

←**6500**
9000→   Directional MEAs as indicated.

1300T   MOCA (Minimum Obstruction Clearance Altitude).

1300a   Route MORA (Route Minimum Off-Route Altitude). See glossary.

MAA 25000
MAA FL 240   MAA (Maximum Authorized Altitude), shown as altitude or flight level.

┤ ├   MEA change, limit of MAA applicability or MAA change. Also MOCA or MORA change when MOCA or MORA is charted with no MEA. Symbol is omitted at navaid.

V 1 ... **V 3** ... **V 1-2**
V 2-3 ... 45
12 65 52 22 15 30 △   Mileages. Total mileage between navaids ◯ is positioned along respective airway centerline. Total mileage may have directional pointers ◇ when there are multiple airway designators. The pointers parallel the airway centerlines along which the mileage applies.

137°   VOR radial & route bearings (magnetic)

137°T   VOR Radial and route bearings (True in the Northern Domestic Airspace of Canada).

←**279°**   ADF bearings (inbound or outbound magnetic).

←**279°T**   ADF bearings (True from navaid in the Northern Domestic Airspace of Canada).

←**266°T**
086°T→   ADF bearings (True at track midpoint in the Northern Domestic Airspace of Canada).

21
32   The navigation frequency COP (changeover point) between two stations is indicated by mileages from the station to the point of change. Omitted when at midpoint or turning point.

E>   Means even thousands altitudes/flight levels are used in the direction of the arrow and odd thousands in the opposite direction. For application of this symbol above FL 290, the flight levels 310, 350, 390, etc. (left half of the cruising level rose) are considered even. The symbol is shown where altitude/flight level assignment is opposite that shown in the standard cruising altitude/flight level rose.

O>   Means odd thousands altitude/flight level per the above definition. "O" is used only on one way airways to show that odd altitude/flight level assignments apply.

E&O>   Means all altitudes, even and odd, are available in the direction indicated.

AIRWAY NAVAID/REPORTING POINT BY-PASS

When an airway passes over or turns at a navaid or reporting point, but the navaid is not to be utilized for course guidance and/or no report is required, the airway centerline passes around the symbol. In cases where a by-pass symbol cannot be used, an explanatory note is included.

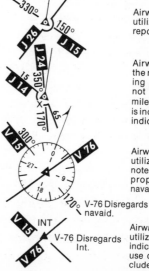

Airway J-26 does not utilize the navaid or reporting point.

Airway J-14 turns at the navaid or reporting point but does not utilize them. A mileage break "X" is included to further indicate a turn point.

Airway V-76 does not utilize the navaid. A note indicating the proper use of the navaid is included.

V-76 Disregards navaid.

V-76 Disregards Int.

Airway V-76 does not utilize the Int. A note indicating the proper use of the Int is included.

(Reproduced with permission of Jeppesen Sanderson, Inc. NOT FOR USE IN NAVIGATION.)

is 5000 feet MSL the MOCA between LIMON and MACKS, but it is also the MCA at LIMON when heading southeast, as indicated by the wording "V-15 5000 SE" found under the name LIMON.

Northwest of LIMON, you will see another arrow from the VOR with the letter "D" below it, indicating that the DME distance from the VOR to LIMON is the same as the segment distance of 22 miles. LIMON itself is formed by the airway V-15 (the 144-degree radial of the VOR) and the 051-degree bearing *to* a remote L/MF facility that uses the identifier RO and the frequency 346 kHz. The short line with the small arrow following the bearing, indicates that the L/MF facility is either remoted or off the right side of the chart.

Directional MEAs exist northwest of LIMON: 3000 feet MSL heading toward the VOR and 4000 feet MSL heading away from the VOR toward LIMON.

Now, let's continue our discussion of enroute charts by referring to FIG. 13-9.

A time zone boundary is indicated by a line of small green **T**'s. This is useful information because the time zones wander around the chart, and you'd hate to arrive somewhere thinking it was 4:30 P.M. only to find that you were in the wrong time zone and everything closed up half an hour ago because it's really 5:30.

The lateral limits of the TCAs are shown as a waffled pattern of light blue/gray.

Looking down the right-hand column, you will see that a small grid shows shorelines and latitude/longitude lines. You will notice the figures 62, 75± and 28 superimposed on the grids. This is Jeppesen's way of indicating the MORA for each section of the grid, or "Grid MORA." In this case, the left grid section has a MORA of 6200 feet MSL, the right section has a MORA of 2800 feet MSL, while the center section has a MORA which is *believed* not to exceed 7500 feet MSL, as depicted by the ±.

What this last part means is this: There are times when Jeppesen receives terrain height information where the values are given to them as plus or minus so many feet. In cases like this, Jeppesen will take the highest value and include it in the MORA with the plus/minus figure to indicate that it is not an exact altitude. Because they have used the highest elevation given to them, they are confident that the terrain does not enter the 1000- or 2000-foot clearance space that the MORA is trying to achieve.

Now look at the border information given at the bottom of the right-hand column. A name in the margin is the "next airway navaid to which the total mileage is given."

Among the examples illustrated, you will see both "18 to WIND" and "32 to DADE," with respective MEAs. Outside the margin, you will see CHEJU and TAIPEI, to indicate the next airway facility. The identifier and frequency of CHEJU indicate that the VOR designates an "on-chart reporting point, changeover point, or course change."

Fig. 13-8

ENROUTE CHART LEGEND

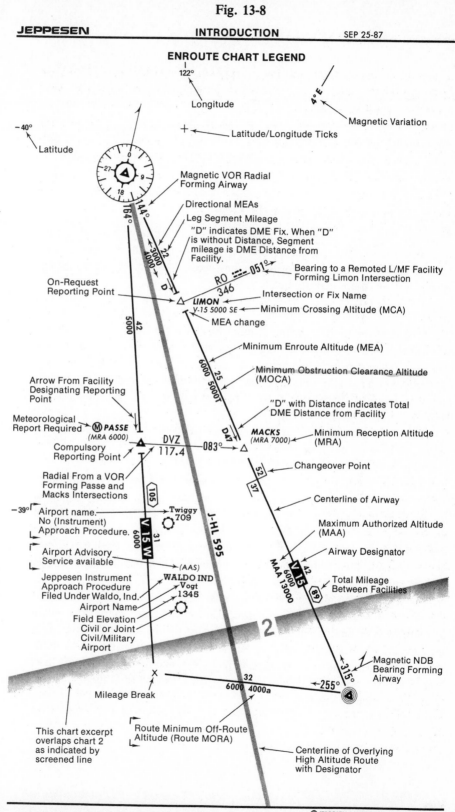

Longitude

Latitude/Longitude Ticks

Magnetic Variation

−40° Latitude

Magnetic VOR Radial Forming Airway

Directional MEAs

Leg Segment Mileage

"D" indicates DME Fix. When "D" is without Distance, Segment mileage is DME Distance from Facility.

Bearing to a Remoted L/MF Facility Forming Limon Intersection

On-Request Reporting Point

Intersection or Fix Name

Minimum Crossing Altitude (MCA)

MEA change

Minimum Enroute Altitude (MEA)

Minimum Obstruction Clearance Altitude (MOCA)

Arrow From Facility Designating Reporting Point

"D" with Distance indicates Total DME Distance from Facility

Meteorological Report Required

Minimum Reception Altitude (MRA)

Compulsory Reporting Point

Changeover Point

Radial From a VOR Forming Passe and Macks Intersections

Centerline of Airway

−39° Airport name. No (Instrument) Approach Procedure.

Maximum Authorized Altitude (MAA)

Airway Designator

Airport Advisory Service available

Jeppesen Instrument Approach Procedure Filed Under Waldo, Ind.

Total Mileage Between Facilities

Airport Name

Field Elevation Civil or Joint Civil/Military Airport

Mileage Break

Magnetic NDB Bearing Forming Airway

This chart excerpt overlaps chart 2 as indicated by screened line

Route Minimum Off-Route Altitude (Route MORA)

Centerline of Overlying High Altitude Route with Designator

(Reproduced with permission of Jeppesen Sanderson, Inc. NOT FOR USE IN NAVIGATION.)

In FIG. 13-10 you should note the second item on the left. Many times there is too much information to put on the chart; at least, it's not possible to put it directly alongside the symbol to which it is referring. Other times, the same information may apply to more than one area on the same chart. In these cases it will be indicated by a number or letter in reverse print; these are called "ball flags." When you see one or more of these symbols, you will find the information in a nearby box.

AREA CHARTS EASE CLUTTER

As mentioned earlier in this chapter, area charts are large-scale charts for high-density areas. By using them, pilots arriving or departing from airports within these areas will have all the information they need without cluttering up the enroute chart any more than it already is.

The lower section of FIG. 13-11 shows extra symbols that you find on the area charts.

First of all, there is a communications block for the major airports shown on each chart. Also, major airports are illustrated by airport symbols that show runways. If the departure and arrival routes are different, the departure route is indicated by a solid line with an arrow, while the approach route uses a dashed line with an arrow. If the arrival and departure routings are the same, a heavy solid line is used without the arrow.

The area chart acts as a sort of transition chart between the enroute and the approach charts by showing AMAs.

Aha—you ask, "What are AMAs?"

Area Minimum Altitudes (AMAs) are something like MORAs, except they are not depicted along routes or in latitude/longitude grids. Instead, a general layout of the terrain is depicted (bottom of FIG. 13-12). The different heights of the terrain are shown by gradient tints. The AMA is shown within the different tinted sections, or "envelopes," the same way that the Grid MORA is shown on the enroute charts, with the larger of the numerals depicting thousands of feet and the smaller numerals depicting hundreds of feet.

As in the MORA altitudes, values of 5000 feet or less allow for a 1000-foot obstruction clearance, while values above 5000 feet will clear obstructions within that area by 2000 feet. Sometimes the AMA value will be higher than the MEA for a specific area because the MEA is only for the terrain beneath the airway itself.

AMAs began appearing on charts in mid-1983, and by now the charts have been converted to this symbology, so the contour lines shown at the top of FIG. 13-12 are essentially obsolete.

Fig. 13-9

ENROUTE CHART LEGEND

BOUNDARIES

::::::::::::::::::::::::::   ADIZ, DEWIZ and CADIZ

•——————•   FIR, UIR, ARTCC or OCA boundary.

— · — · · — · —   International boundary.

┬─┬─┬─┬─┬─   Time zone boundary.

QNH
-o-o-o-o-o-o-o-o-o-   QNH/QNE-boundaries.
QNE

CONTROLLED AIRSPACE

Controlled airspace shown in white.

Uncontrolled airspace shown as a tint.

Controlled airway/route.

Uncontrolled airway or advisory route.

Control Area boundary within controlled airspace (CTA, TMA).

TCA (Terminal Control Area) Waffle screen shows lateral limits.

∪∩∪∩∪   Radio Frequency Sector Boundary.

•••••••••••   Boundaries within TMAs or CTAs defining different altitude limits.

U.S. control zone within which special VFR weather minimums for fixed wing aircraft are not authorized.

Control Zone or Aerodrome Traffic Zone (controlled).

Class C Control Zone.

Aerodrome Traffic Zone (no control). Aircraft broadcast intentions on standard enroute frequency, and listen on same, when within such zones.

Airport Radar Service Area (ARSA).

ALTITUDE LIMITS AND TYPES OF CONTROL

$\dfrac{4000}{\text{CTR, ATZ, TIZ}}$ CTR-Control Zone
ATZ-Aerodrome Traffic Zone
TIZ-Traffic Information Zone

$\dfrac{\text{FL 360}}{\text{UTA}}$ UTA-Upper Control Area

$\dfrac{\text{FL 70}}{4000}$ TMA   TMA-Terminal Control Area
OCTA-Oceanic Control Area

ORIENTATION

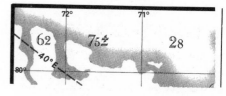

Grid shown at the intersection of units of latitude and longitude or by complete line.

Magnetic variation isogonic lines are indicated at the edge of the chart or are extended fully across the chart in a continuous dashed line.

Shorelines and large inland lakes are shown.

Grid Minimum Off-Route Altitude (Grid MORA) in hundreds of feet provides terrain and obstruction clearance within the section outlined by latitude and longitude lines. Grid MORA values followed by a ± are believed not to exceed the altitudes shown.

BORDER INFORMATION

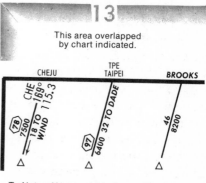

This area overlapped by chart indicated.

To Notes: Name outside the neatline is the next airway navaid to which the total mileage is given. Navaid identification is shown on all charts except the US and Canada/Alaska chart series. Reporting point name is shown when it is the airway termination.

To Notes: Name inside the neatline is the first reporting point outside the chart coverage to which the mileage and MEA are shown.

Airway lead information: The frequency and identifier of an off-chart navaid are shown when the navaid designates an on-chart reporting point, changeover point or course change.

Fig. 13-10

JEPPESEN   **INTRODUCTION**   SEP 14-84

ENROUTE CHART LEGEND
MISCELLANEOUS

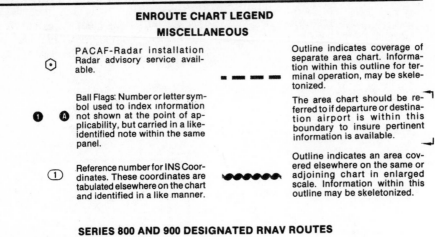

PACAF-Radar installation Radar advisory service available.

Ball Flags: Number or letter symbol used to index information not shown at the point of applicability, but carried in a like-identified note within the same panel.

Reference number for INS Coordinates. These coordinates are tabulated elsewhere on the chart and identified in a like manner.

Outline indicates coverage of separate area chart. Information within this outline for terminal operation, may be skeletonized.

The area chart should be referred to if departure or destination airport is within this boundary to insure pertinent information is available.

Outline indicates an area covered elsewhere on the same or adjoining chart in enlarged scale. Information within this outline may be skeletonized.

SERIES 800 AND 900 DESIGNATED RNAV ROUTES

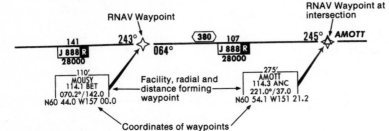

(Reproduced with permission of Jeppesen Sanderson, Inc. NOT FOR USE IN NAVIGATION.)

Fig. 13-11

ENROUTE CHART LEGEND
HIGH ALTITUDE CHARTS

The following legend, applicable to High Altitude Charts only, is in addition to the preceding legend. Many items in the preceding legend are also applicable to the High Altitude Charts.

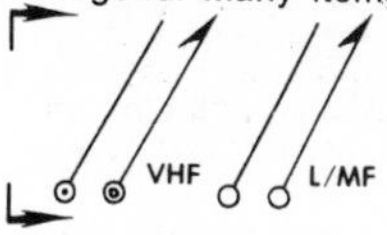

VHF, L/MF Navigational Facilities.

| UA 6 | Europe high level airway/route. |

| UB 5 | South America high level airway/route. |

ALAMOSA
ᴰ113.9 ALS
N37 20.9 W105 48.9

Geographical coordinates (latitude and longitude) of each facility are shown across the bottom of the facility box.

| A 97 | Pacific high level airway/route. |

| J 20-L | Japan Jet routes at and above FL 240. |

"L"
ATHENS
ᴰ109.6 AHN
N33 56.8 W083 19.5

The letter "L" indicates an L-class facility designated as usable in the High Altitude airspace. The letter "T" indicates a T-class facility. In areas of congestion, off-route facility geographical coordinates are shown in an alphabetical listing elsewhere on the chart.

| UG 4 | One-way airway/route. |

J 60
(1500-0300Z)

One-way preferred route 24 hours unless hours are indicated. Two-way during other hours.

J 11
J 11
VHF

Jet routes. The thin route centerline is used on United States and Canada-Alaska chart series in areas of congestion.

25000
FL 250

MEA (Minimum enroute altitude)—shown only when higher than floor of the high altitude structure.

HL 500
L/MF

Canada High Level airways.

HL 500

J-HL 500

USA-Canada border crossing route. J-500 within USA, HL-500 within Canada.

AREA CHARTS

The following legend, applicable to Area Charts only, is in addition to the preceding legends. Many items in the preceding legends are also applicable to the Area Charts.

⟵——————— Departure route.

⟵ - - - - - - - Arrival route.

▬▬▬▬▬▬ Arrival & Departure on same route.

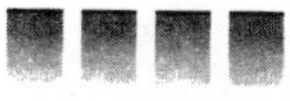

▮▮▮▮ Speed Limit Point-Speed restriction on shaded side of symbol.

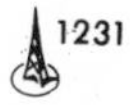

1231 Man-made obstruction having a height of 1000' or more above ground, with elevation above sea level. Shown on Area Charts without AMAs.

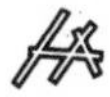

Airport diagram showing runways of major airports only.

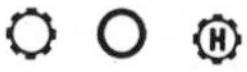

○ ○ ⓗ Other airports are shown by green symbols.

Communications frequencies for the major airports shown on an area chart are given in a block as illustrated below.

	App(R)	Dep(R)	Twr	Gnd	ATIS
Chicago-**Midway**	Chicago 119.35	Chicago 119.35	118.7	121.7 121.85 **C**	120.05
Chicago O'Hare Int'l	Chicago 119.0	Chicago (340°-159°) 125.0 (160°-219°) 127.4 (220°-339°) 125.4	(N) 118.1 (S) 120.75	121.9 121.6 **Cpt**	135.15

SIDs, STARs, ETC.

Before talking about approach charts, let's take a look at some of the specific symbols on the SID, STAR, and Profile Descent charts.

Notice in FIG. 13-13 that many of the symbols are the same as those found on enroute charts. The routes are shown as solid lines with arrows, while transition tracks use a dashed line. For the transition portion, the name and computer identification of the route are found above the track while the MEA and segment mileage are below it.

If a SID includes a heading, it will be shown with the letters "hdg" following the heading to be flown. Visual flight tracks are depicted by a series of short arrows.

FIGURE 13-14 shows various crossing restrictions and course guidance information. Profile Descent tracks are shown using heavy solid lines with arrows. (A Profile Descent is an uninterrupted descent from cruising altitude to initial approach.) Some of the fixes require airspeed and/or crossing altitude restrictions that may include minimum and/or maximum crossing altitudes.

Near the bottom of FIG. 13-14 you will see a SID climb gradient/climb rate table. If a SID does not have a published minimum climb gradient, you can assume that there are no terrain or obstacle problems. In this event, a minimum climb gradient of 152 feet per nautical mile should be flown to the MEA or assigned altitude, unless any climb reductions are necessary to comply with published restrictions.

If, however, there are obstacles or terrain that will penetrate the 40:1 slope that results from a climb of 152 feet per nautical mile, you will have a steeper climb gradient requirement shown on the chart.

Many times, Jeppesen will publish a climb gradient/climb rate table to help you calculate the necessary rate of climb for your aircraft. This is similar to the descent/time-conversion tables published at the bottom of the approach plates that I will discuss in a later chapter.

All you need to know is your actual ground speed in knots. Once you have that, just read your required rate of climb from the chart, interpolating as necessary. Using the chart in FIG. 13-14, for example, with a ground speed of 120 knots, you would need a rate of climb of approximately 660 feet per minute to give you a climb gradient of 330 feet per nautical mile. At 240 knots ground speed, your rate of climb would have to be 1320 feet per minute.

This is an important item to check, as there will be times when your aircraft won't be able to meet the requirement. And there will be times when, due to wind shears or other factors, you won't know until you are airborne that you can't make the necessary climb gradient. In such a case you will have to let ATC know immediately so they can vector you to a safe area.

Finally, at the very bottom of FIG. 13-14 you will find an example (self-explanatory) of a lost communications procedure block.

Fig. 13-12

ENROUTE CHART LEGEND
AREA CHARTS (Continued)

Area Charts that have terrain elevations in excess of 4,000 feet above the main airport may contain terrain information. Terrain is portrayed by either terrain contour lines with high point values or Area Minimum Altitude (AMA) envelopes with AMA values. The newer AMA application will gradually replace the earlier contour application starting with the June 3, 1983 revision. Differences are shown in the preceding legend.

TERRAIN CONTOURS

When charted, terrain contour values will be indicated together with the appropriate gradient tint in a contour legend box on the chart.

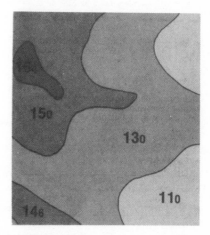

CONTOUR LEGEND

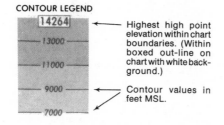

← Highest high point elevation within chart boundaries. (Within boxed out-line on chart with white background.)

← Contour values in feet MSL.

Gradient tint indicates terrain rise between two charted contours (i.e., 4000′-6000′).

When charted, high points may be either terrain or man-made obstructions. The high point value will be the MSL elevation of the highest point.

AREA MINIMUM ALTITUDE (AMA) ENVELOPES

When charted, AMA envelopes portray the general layout of terrain in comparison to the detailed layout of contour lines. Terrain rise between two charted envelope lines is indicated by gradient tints.

The area between each envelope line includes an AMA figure which represents the terrain and obstacle clearance altitude for the envelope area. AMA values clear all terrain and obstructions by 1000 feet in areas where the highest terrain and obstructions are 5000 feet MSL or lower. AMA values clear all terrain and obstructions by 2000 feet in areas where the highest terrain and obstructions are 5001 feet MSL or higher.

DME arcs and radials are included for relating position to AMA envelope.

NOTE: An MEA may be lower than an AMA because of locally lower terrain beneath an airway.

Fig. 13-13

JUL 12-85   **INTRODUCTION**   **JEPPESEN**

SID, STAR, AND PROFILE DESCENT LEGEND
GRAPHIC
(Charts are not drawn at a specific scale)

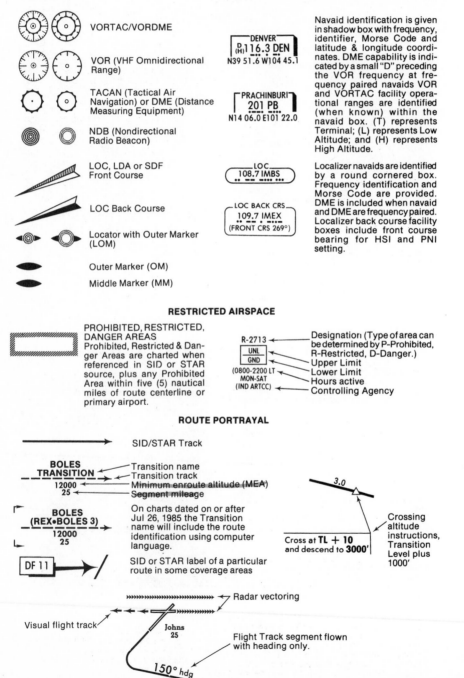

RADIO SYMBOLS

VORTAC/VORDME

VOR (VHF Omnidirectional Range)

TACAN (Tactical Air Navigation) or DME (Distance Measuring Equipment)

NDB (Nondirectional Radio Beacon)

LOC, LDA or SDF Front Course

LOC Back Course

Locator with Outer Marker (LOM)

Outer Marker (OM)

Middle Marker (MM)

RADIO IDENTIFICATION

DENVER
D(H) 116.3 DEN
N39 51.6 W104 45.1

PRACHINBURI
201 PB
N14 06.0 E101 22.0

LOC
108.7 IMBS

LOC BACK CRS
109.7 IMEX
(FRONT CRS 269°)

Navaid identification is given in shadow box with frequency, identifier, Morse Code and latitude & longitude coordinates. DME capability is indicated by a small "D" preceding the VOR frequency at frequency paired navaids VOR and VORTAC facility operational ranges are identified (when known) within the navaid box. (T) represents Terminal; (L) represents Low Altitude; and (H) represents High Altitude.

Localizer navaids are identified by a round cornered box. Frequency identification and Morse Code are provided. DME is included when navaid and DME are frequency paired. Localizer back course facility boxes include front course bearing for HSI and PNI setting.

RESTRICTED AIRSPACE

PROHIBITED, RESTRICTED, DANGER AREAS
Prohibited, Restricted & Danger Areas are charted when referenced in SID or STAR source, plus any Prohibited Area within five (5) nautical miles of route centerline or primary airport.

R-2713 ← Designation (Type of area can be determined by P-Prohibited, R-Restricted, D-Danger.)
UNL ← Upper Limit
GND ← Lower Limit
(0800-2200 LT ← Hours active
MON-SAT
(IND ARTCC) ← Controlling Agency

ROUTE PORTRAYAL

SID/STAR Track

BOLES
TRANSITION ← Transition name
← Transition track
12000 ← Minimum enroute altitude (MEA)
25 ← Segment mileage

BOLES
(REX•BOLES 3)
12000
25

On charts dated on or after Jul 26, 1985 the Transition name will include the route identification using computer language.

DF 11

SID or STAR label of a particular route in some coverage areas

3.0

Cross at **TL + 10** and descend to **3000'**

Crossing altitude instructions, Transition Level plus 1000'

Radar vectoring

Visual flight track

Johns
25

Flight Track segment flown with heading only.

150° hdg

Fig. 13-14

JEPPESEN   **INTRODUCTION**   FEB 8-85

SID, STAR AND PROFILE DESCENT LEGEND
GRAPHIC (Continued)
ROUTE PORTRAYAL (Continued)

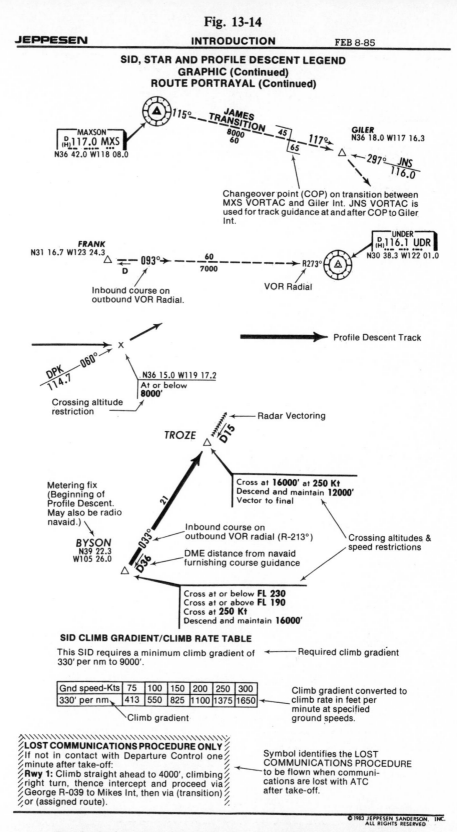

Changeover point (COP) on transition between MXS VORTAC and Giler Int. JNS VORTAC is used for track guidance at and after COP to Giler Int.

Inbound course on outbound VOR Radial.

VOR Radial

Profile Descent Track

Crossing altitude restriction

Radar Vectoring

Metering fix (Beginning of Profile Descent. May also be radio navaid.)

Inbound course on outbound VOR radial (R-213°)

DME distance from navaid furnishing course guidance

Cross at **16000'** at **250 Kt**
Descend and maintain **12000'**
Vector to final

Crossing altitudes & speed restrictions

Cross at or below **FL 230**
Cross at or above **FL 190**
Cross at **250 Kt**
Descend and maintain **16000'**

SID CLIMB GRADIENT/CLIMB RATE TABLE

This SID requires a minimum climb gradient of 330' per nm to 9000'.   Required climb gradient

Gnd speed-Kts	75	100	150	200	250	300
330' per nm	413	550	825	1100	1375	1650

Climb gradient

Climb gradient converted to climb rate in feet per minute at specified ground speeds.

LOST COMMUNICATIONS PROCEDURE ONLY
If not in contact with Departure Control one minute after take-off:
Rwy 1: Climb straight ahead to 4000', climbing right turn, thence intercept and proceed via George R-039 to Mikes Int, then via (transition) or (assigned route).

Symbol identifies the LOST COMMUNICATIONS PROCEDURE to be flown when communications are lost with ATC after take-off.

(Reproduced with permission of Jeppesen Sanderson, Inc. NOT FOR USE IN NAVIGATION.)

14

Approach Charts:
The Plan View

A N AIRPORT WITH A PUBLISHED INSTRUMENT APPROACH CAN HAVE ONE AP-
proach, or it can have ten or more. Each approach is depicted individually,
with very few exceptions (such as an NDB or LOC approach which may be combined with an ILS when they both use the same routing).

The first approach to the airport is printed on the first page of the series;
the plan view of the airport, as well as airport data and the takeoff and alternate
minimums, are usually printed on the reverse side of that first page. The remainder
of the approach chart pages for that airport will normally have approaches on
both sides of the page.

FIGURE 14-1 shows the general format for both the approach chart and the
airport chart. It explains that for many major airport charts published after October 1986, the airport chart may precede the first approach chart. In this case
they are numbered 10-9, 10-9A, 10-9B, etc. This has been done because some
airport layouts have become so very complex that even veteran pilots get lost
without detailed information—information that won't fit on just one page.

Each approach chart is a storehouse of information. Like the enroute chart,
it is vitally important that you take the time to familiarize yourself with the chart
legend so you can derive the necessary information from the charts. And you
must review this information periodically. Remember, these approach charts are
designed to lead you down the rosy approach path to the airport or its runways.
Often times, they will allow you to thread the needle between mountains, an-

tenna farms, or high-rise buildings when forward visibility is down to bare minimums.

Then, if you get to your missed approach point and still can't see the runway, the charts will lead you safely through the missed approach—but only if you understand and follow the approach and missed approach exactly.

Look at FIG. 14-2, and see what you can learn from the chart's heading.

First of all, you should check the calendar date against the chart *effective* date. You don't want to use a chart before it becomes effective. Why would you have a new chart before an effective date? Well, if a very important change is scheduled in a procedure, the cartographers will issue the charts early enough to assure that all subscribers receive their copies in time to note the change. Additionally, all revisions are Friday dated, and changes effective after the printing date will be shown with an effective date noted. If the chart does not have an effective date shown, it is current and effective when received.

FILING THE CHARTS

The number circled to the right of the chart issue date is the chart index number. The first digit represents the airport. If there are two or more airports in the same vicinity, the chart makers will make one of them #1, another #2, and so on. Assignment of these numbers is purely discretionary.

The second digit will tell you the type of approach, or the type of chart. The third digit merely sets up a filing order for charts of the same type at the same airport. For example, many airports will have more than one ILS or VOR approach. In the case of VOR approaches, they will be numbered 13-1, 13-2, 13-3, 13-4, and so on.

In the case of ILS approaches, the indexing is further broken down; 11-1 would be a CAT I approach to a specific runway, and 11-1A would be the CAT II and CAT IIIA approaches to the same runway.

The charts that have a zero (0) for the second digit are for SIDs, STARs, area charts, etc. In these cases the third digit is used to designate the type of charts, and the suffix will be the filing index. For example, the area chart itself is a 10-1, the TCA chart is a 10-1T, STARs are 10-2 (suffixed by A, B, C, etc.), SIDs are 10-3 (also suffixed by letters), noise abatement charts are 10-4, taxi charts are 10-5, and the newest charts of all, the airport charts and their attendant pages, are 10-9 (again with letter suffixes).

Let's say that you are looking at the approaches to John Q Airport and note an approach numbered 13-2 but can't find a 13-1. Well, don't panic. There may not be a 13-1. Perhaps the procedure was abandoned, or perhaps ATC is planning on developing a 13-1 in the future.

The best way to double-check is to save your last check sheet and the revision notes from that last check sheet to the present time. The check sheet is a listing of all of the pages in your manuals. Check off any page you may be miss-

Fig. 14-1

APPROACH CHART LEGEND

Approach charts are graphic illustrations of instrument approach procedures prescribed by the governing authority. All charts meet FAA requirements for aeronautical charts. The following legend pages briefly explain symbology used on approach charts throughout the world. *Not all items apply to all locations.* The approach chart is divided into specific areas of information as illustrated below.

FORMATS

The first approach procedure published for an airport has the procedure chart published on the front side with the airport chart on the back side. On charts dated on or after Oct 24-86, on major airports, the airport chart may preceed the first approach procedure. These locations will have expanded airport information that may occupy more than one side. When an airport has more than one published approach procedure, they are shown front and back on additional sheets. Blank pages will indicate "INTENTIONALLY LEFT BLANK".

APPROACH PROCEDURE CHART FORMAT

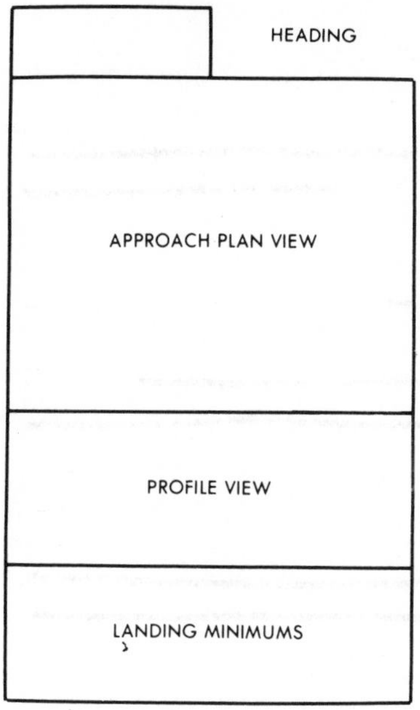

    HEADING

APPROACH PLAN VIEW

PROFILE VIEW

LANDING MINIMUMS

AIRPORT CHART FORMAT

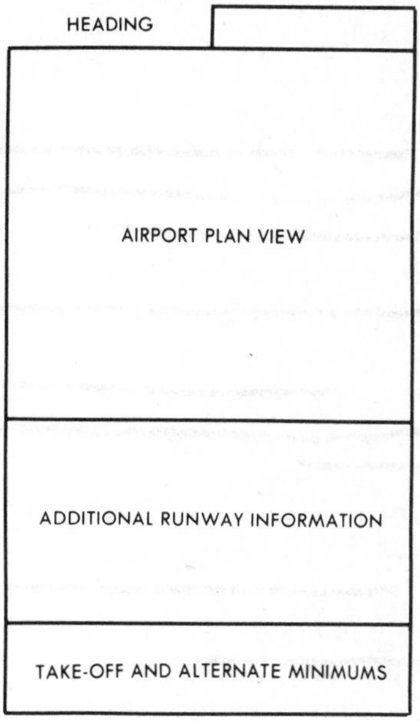

HEADING

AIRPORT PLAN VIEW

ADDITIONAL RUNWAY INFORMATION

TAKE-OFF AND ALTERNATE MINIMUMS

ing. When you get a new check sheet, keep it and throw away all the old check sheets and revision notices. That way you always have something to refer back to. If the check sheet doesn't list a 13-1 for that airport, chances are there isn't one. If you are still in doubt, go through the revision notices to see if one was issued in the meantime. Most of the time Jeppesen will leave a blank page in that spot anyway, with a note on it that the page has been left blank deliberately.

What if your check sheet does list a 13-1? Well, again, go over the revision notices to see if you were supposed to have destroyed it in the meantime. If your search indicates that you should have a 13-1 and you still can't find it, just drop a note to Jeppesen and get a replacement by return mail.

Now, take a look at the big circle under the chart effective date. This is the MSA (Minimum Safe Altitude) circle.

The MSA is set up to give you a 1000-foot obstacle clearance within 25 nautical miles from a specific navigational facility. This facility is identified outside the circle on the lower right side. If, for any reason, the radius of the MSA circle is other than 25 nautical miles, it will be so noted.

If the circle is broken up into different sectors (sectors are defined as inbound magnetic bearings so you can tell the sector you are in directly from your compass), the altitudes then become known as Minimum Sector Altitudes. They are designed for obstruction clearance only and will not always give you navigational reception. In fact, Jeppesen's glossary states that, " . . . this altitude is for EMERGENCY USE ONLY and does not necessarily guarantee NAVAID reception." (Emphasis is Jeppesen's.) Another important thing to remember is that, because the center of the circle is located at a navigational facility that the approach procedure is predicated upon, the MSA is not necessarily a 25-NM dius around the *airport*.

The last column to the right in the heading lists the geographical location of the airport, and under that, the airport name. The charts are filed alphabetically, by geographical location.

The procedure identification is listed below the airport name and here is another area where caution must prevail. Some airports have many approaches, so it becomes necessary to identify each of them individually. But, if you're bouncing around in some gigantic thunderstorm, or if you're tired and in a hurry to get on the ground, you may just hear, "cleared for the VOR DME . . . approach." The airport may have a number of VOR DME approaches, and you may, in haste, turn to the VOR DME Rwy 20 chart when you were cleared for the VOR DME-A approach. So, it behooves you to be sure of the approach you have been cleared for. One way to help is to always read back the approach clearance for confirmation.

If the approach has a letter suffix, such as VOR-A, or VOR DME-A, or DME-B, it means that the approach will not meet the criteria for straight-in minimums, and is therefore a circling approach.

APPROACH CHART LEGEND
HEADING

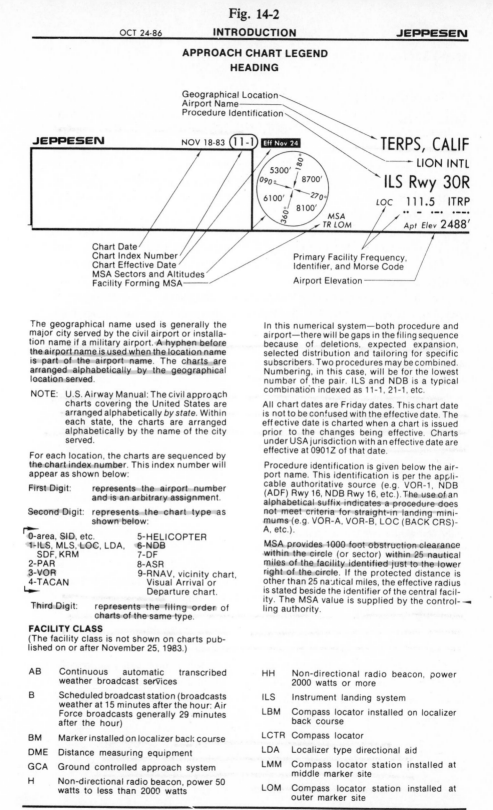

The geographical name used is generally the major city served by the civil airport or installation name if a military airport. A hyphen before the airport name is used when the location name is part of the airport name. The charts are arranged alphabetically by the geographical location served.

NOTE: U.S. Airway Manual: The civil approach charts covering the United States are arranged alphabetically *by state*. Within each state, the charts are arranged alphabetically by the name of the city served.

For each location, the charts are sequenced by the chart index number. This index number will appear as shown below:

First Digit: represents the airport number and is an arbitrary assignment.

Second Digit: represents the chart type as shown below:

0-area, SID, etc.	5-HELICOPTER
1-ILS, MLS, LOC, LDA, SDF, KRM	6-NDB
2-PAR	7-DF
3-VOR	8-ASR
4-TACAN	9-RNAV, vicinity chart, Visual Arrival or Departure chart.

Third Digit: represents the filing order of charts of the same type.

FACILITY CLASS
(The facility class is not shown on charts published on or after November 25, 1983.)

AB   Continuous automatic transcribed weather broadcast services

B   Scheduled broadcast station (broadcasts weather at 15 minutes after the hour: Air Force broadcasts generally 29 minutes after the hour)

BM   Marker installed on localizer back course

DME   Distance measuring equipment

GCA   Ground controlled approach system

H   Non-directional radio beacon, power 50 watts to less than 2000 watts

In this numerical system—both procedure and airport—there will be gaps in the filing sequence because of deletions, expected expansion, selected distribution and tailoring for specific subscribers. Two procedures may be combined. Numbering, in this case, will be for the lowest number of the pair. ILS and NDB is a typical combination indexed as 11-1, 21-1, etc.

All chart dates are Friday dates. This chart date is not to be confused with the effective date. The effective date is charted when a chart is issued prior to the changes being effective. Charts under USA jurisdiction with an effective date are effective at 0901Z of that date.

Procedure identification is given below the airport name. This identification is per the applicable authoritative source (e.g. VOR-1, NDB (ADF) Rwy 16, NDB Rwy 16, etc.). The use of an alphabetical suffix indicates a procedure does not meet criteria for straight-in landing minimums (e.g. VOR-A, VOR-B, LOC (BACK CRS)-A, etc.).

MSA provides 1000 foot obstruction clearance within the circle (or sector) within 25 nautical miles of the facility identified just to the lower right of the circle. If the protected distance is other than 25 nautical miles, the effective radius is stated beside the identifier of the central facility. The MSA value is supplied by the controlling authority.

HH   Non-directional radio beacon, power 2000 watts or more

ILS   Instrument landing system

LBM   Compass locator installed on localizer back course

LCTR   Compass locator

LDA   Localizer type directional aid

LMM   Compass locator station installed at middle marker site

LOM   Compass locator station installed at outer marker site

(Reproduced with permission of Jeppesen Sanderson, Inc. NOT FOR USE IN NAVIGATION.)

The primary facility frequency, the identifier, and the Morse code dots and dashes fall in below the procedure identification, followed by other pertinent information such as, "Ops not continuous." The airport elevation is shown in feet above sea level (MSL).

In the upper left corner of the approach charts (FIG. 14-3) is the arrival air/ground communications data, listed systematically in the sequence you would be using it on approach: the ATIS frequency, then the Approach, Tower, and Ground Control frequencies.

For a while, prior to October 1984, Jeppesen was only putting the Approach Control frequency on the first chart at a location. On all other charts for that location you would find a note directing you to the first chart for that frequency. This saved time in making revisions, because many times every chart at a location had to be reissued when only a frequency was changed, but the hassle of having to leaf back and forth in the approach charts prompted the change back to the original method of putting the frequencies on each chart.

Transition altitudes (where aircraft operating in flight levels change back to altitudes), as well as other pertinent altimeter setting information, are shown in the lower part of the communications box.

Jeppesen uses a three-letter code that you will find in the communications section. "G" means that the frequency is guarded (listened to) only, "T" means that ATC only uses that frequency to transmit, and "X" tells you the frequency is available upon request.

THE BIRD'S-EYE VIEW

Jeppesen defines the plan view at the top of FIG. 14-4. In effect the plan view is a bird's-eye view of the approach with the flight path drawn in (looking like what you would *like* to see on the tracing paper after you get out of a simulator).

The plan view gives you a tremendous amount of information, and you must understand each and every symbol if you want to go about your job in a safe, professional manner. Many of the symbols require little or no thought, but some of them could use a little more explanation. For example, if you find the symbol for an offset localizer, you will have to make some sort of turn to the landing runway when you get down to minimums, and because of this, your minimums will be higher than they would be for a straight-in ILS.

Notes on the page will provide such information as how many degrees the localizer is offset from the runway heading, as well as how far from the threshold the approach course crosses the runway centerline. These offset localizers are usually LDAs, which are defined in the glossary:

> LOCALIZER TYPE DIRECTIONAL AID (LDA)—A NAVAID, used for nonprecision instrument approaches with utility and accuracy comparable to a localizer but which is not a part of a complete ILS and is not aligned with the runway.

Fig. 14-3

JEPPESEN INTRODUCTION OCT 24-86

APPROACH CHART LEGEND
HEADING (continued)

FACILITY CLASS (continued)

MH	Non-directional radio beacon, power less than 50 watts	VOR	VHF omni-directional range
		VORTAC	Co-located VOR and TACAN
MLS	Microwave landing system	W	Without voice facility
SDF	Simplified directional facility	Z	VHF location marker at radio station
TAC	In combination with class for other facilities, standard distance measuring feature of full TACAN		

COMMUNICATION AND ALTIMETER SETTING DATA

Communications for "arrivals" are given in normal sequence of use as shown below. See Airport Chart Legend, Introduction page 116, for other communications.

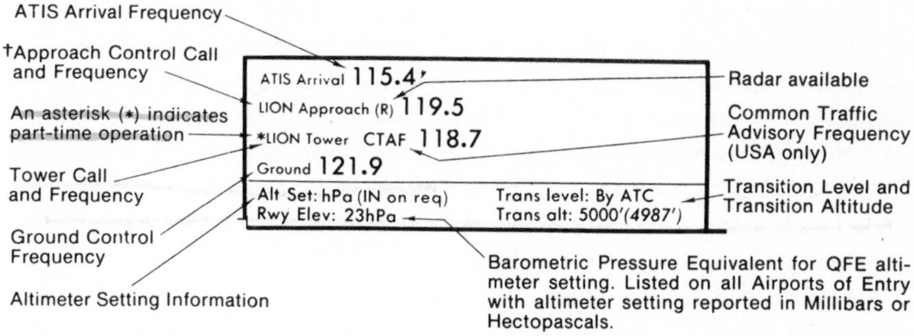

ATIS Arrival Frequency

†Approach Control Call and Frequency

An asterisk (*) indicates part-time operation

Tower Call and Frequency

Ground Control Frequency

Altimeter Setting Information

ATIS Arrival 115.4'	
LION Approach (R) 119.5	
*LION Tower CTAF 118.7	
Ground 121.9	
Alt Set: hPa (IN on req)	Trans level: By ATC
Rwy Elev: 23hPa	Trans alt: 5000'(4987')

Radar available

Common Traffic Advisory Frequency (USA only)

Transition Level and Transition Altitude

Barometric Pressure Equivalent for QFE altimeter setting. Listed on all Airports of Entry with altimeter setting reported in Millibars or Hectopascals.

<u>ON CHARTS DATED ON OR AFTER AUG 31-84</u>

Transition level and transition altitude are listed on the bottom line of the communications and altimeter setting data box. Transition level and transition altitude will not be charted when the altimeter setting boundary is portrayed on the respective enroute chart unless published on respective procedure source document by the governing authority.

Trans level: FL 60 — The transition level (QNE) is the lowest level of flight using standard altimeter setting (29.92 inches of mercury or 1013.2 millibars or 1013.2 hectopascals.)

Trans alt: 5000'(4987') — The transition altitude (QNH) is the altitude at and below which local pressure setting must be used.

Altimeter setting units are listed on the bottom line of communications data box.

†On charts dated prior to OCT 26-84, the approach control frequency is listed only on the first approach chart at a location. A cross reference note on subsequent approach charts directs you to the first approach chart for the proper frequency.

Barometric Pressure Equivalent in millibars or hectopascals enables aircraft operators who use QFE altimeter setting for landing to establish the QFE altimeter setting by subtracting the hectopascal or millibar equivalent from the reported QNH altimeter setting. The value shown is the barometric pressure equivalent for the height reference datum for straight in landing. The height reference datum will be the runway threshold elevation (Rwy), airport elevation (Apt), or the runway touchdown elevation (TDZ), as applicable.

Letter designations behind a frequency indicate operation as follows:

G-guards only
T-transmits only
X-on request

Bearings defining frequency sectors are clockwise outbound
(e.g. 270° to 090° would be north of the airport.)

An example of the notes mentioned above can be seen on the Honolulu, Hawaii, LDA DME Rwy 26L approach. This note states:

Use IEPC LDA DME when on LOC course. Localizer course offset from landing runway by 45 degrees. Final approach course crosses runway centerline 8100′ from threshold.

So, you see here that even though you have a 45-degree cut to make to get lined up with the runway, you have over a mile and a half to accomplish it. The minimum visibility for this approach is two miles, so even though the course change is over 30°, the two-mile visibility gives you enough time to line up with the centerline so the approach is considered a straight-in.

Under bearing symbols, you see that bearings are magnetic courses unless the letter T is after the course direction, in which case it will be a true course. You will find true courses in the Far North.

Looking a little farther down, note that the symbol for EWD in the example also shows the Morse code identifier and the explanation for this information: "charted on the VOR radial/NDB radial when forming facility is outside of planview." You saw the same thing on the enroute charts, remember?

Take a look at the upper left-hand column of FIG. 14-5. Prior to November 25, 1983, the position fixes were depicted by both name and an open circle. After that date, Jeppesen began using filled and open triangles, as are used on enroute charts. If there are alternate means of identifying a fix these means will be specified, such as in the example, where the fix can be either the outer marker or 6.2 DME. The note here also reveals that if you so request, you can substitute ASR for the outer marker. Due to its increased precision, you can ask for PAR to substitute for both the outer and the middle markers.

TRANSITIONING FOR THE APPROACH

Moving on to the approach transition (formerly called the terminal route) information, the nautical mileage is shown above the course line, the minimum altitude is shown below the line, and the magnetic course is depicted on the line. Sometimes, the route is merely a heading (rather than a bearing to or from a facility) in which case "hdg" will follow the magnetic course symbol.

One of the most misunderstood symbols is "NoPT". Some pilots will say this means that you are not required to make a procedure turn, while others will say that procedure turns are not authorized. I have heard pilots argue both points, and they are both half-right. The procedure turn is not required, nor is it authorized without ATC clearance. These procedures have been set up to speed the flow of traffic. Our airspace is getting too congested to have aircraft wandering

Fig. 14-4

APPROACH CHART LEGEND
APPROACH PLAN VIEW

The plan view is a graphic picture of the approach, usually presented at a scale of 1 in= 5 NM. On charts published prior to November 25, 1983, scales that differ from 1in = 5 NM are noted at the bottom edge of the page. On charts published on or after November 25, 1983, the scale is stated along the left edge of the plan view. Latitude and longitude are shown in 10 minute increments on the plan view neatline. Symbols used in the plan view are shown below.

NAVAIDS

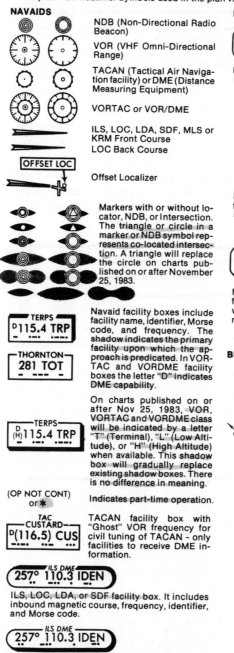

NDB (Non-Directional Radio Beacon)

VOR (VHF Omni-Directional Range)

TACAN (Tactical Air Navigation facility) or DME (Distance Measuring Equipment)

VORTAC or VOR/DME

ILS, LOC, LDA, SDF, MLS or KRM Front Course
LOC Back Course

OFFSET LOC — Offset Localizer

Markers with or without locator, NDB, or Intersection. The triangle or circle in a marker or NDB symbol represents co-located intersection. A triangle will replace the circle on charts published on or after November 25, 1983.

Navaid facility boxes include facility name, identifier, Morse code, and frequency. The shadow indicates the primary facility upon which the approach is predicated. In VORTAC and VORDME facility boxes the letter "D" indicates DME capability.

On charts published on or after Nov 25, 1983, VOR, VORTAC and VORDME class will be indicated by a letter "T" (Terminal), "L" (Low Altitude), or "H" (High Altitude) when available. This shadow box will gradually replace existing shadow boxes. There is no difference in meaning.

(OP NOT CONT) or ✳ — Indicates part-time operation.

TACAN facility box with "Ghost" VOR frequency for civil tuning of TACAN - only facilities to receive DME information.

ILS, LOC, LDA, or SDF facility box. It includes inbound magnetic course, frequency, identifier, and Morse code.

This shadow box will gradually replace existing shadow boxes. There is no difference in meaning.

NAVAIDS (continued)

Localizer Back Course facility box. Front course included for HSI and PNI setting.

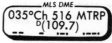

RNAV Waypoint information below Navaid facility box. RNAV Waypoint information is shown when it is an authorized substitution.

MLS facility box including inbound magnetic final approach course, MLS channel, identifier with Morse code and VHF "Ghost" frequency for manually tuning DME.

BEARINGS

106°→ Magnetic course

106°T→ True course

VOR cross radials and NDB bearings forming a position fix are "from" a VOR and "to" an NDB.
Morse code ident is charted on VOR radial/NDB radial when forming facility is outside of planview.

around procedure turns that take two minutes (minimum) to complete, or as much as five minutes if you fly the published procedure.

The procedure turn is merely designed to allow you to reverse direction so you will be on the inbound course. It also gives you some time to get down to your initial approach altitude.

You find the "NoPT" on DME arc approaches, straight-in approaches, and various approach transitions depicted on the charts, which also show procedure turns from overhead approaches. This is to help differentiate the various initial approaches and let you use the same charts, should the terminal radar fail.

With more and more aircraft being compressed into our airspace, more and more routes seem to crop up on enroute and approach charts. At times, these routings result in a mess of lines crisscrossing the charts, intermixed with numbers and symbols. It is important to understand such subtle things as the differences in the widths of the lines, for example, or in the position of the numbers in relation to the lines, so that you will have a full understanding of what the charts are trying to tell you.

The approach transitions are tracks that are defined by courses, minimum altitudes, and fixes; they are designed to bring you from the initial approach fix (IAF) to the final approach fix (FAF). The mileage figures shown on these transitions are only between the fixes shown on the transition. They are not the mileage to the airport.

Again, this is obvious while you are sitting in your easy chair under a no-stress condition, but it is possible to misread or misunderstand it while you're bouncing around in a rainstorm with flickering panel lights on a dark night, especially if you've been going for 14 or 16 hours.

On the bottom of the left-hand column you can see how Jep insets a dog leg route with an off-chart turn. It is important to note that these insets are not to scale; also, the dog leg turn fixes are not charted on enroute and area charts.

Look at the triangular-shaped transition halfway down the right-hand column. Here you see a route from STOUT (STO) to TOWER. The route goes via PLANT intersection. Transition routes are depicted in heavy lines; they are the routes you *must* fly. You are not authorized to fly the 275-degree course from STO to TOWER, because this light line with a small arrow only shows a cross radial which helps to form the fix. You are only assured obstacle clearance when you are on the published route. The heavy line from STO to PLANT ends in a light line which indicates both an approach transition and a cross radial.

In the next diagram below, you see two IAFs leading to an approach. HANDS is located by two cross radials, one from STO and the other from MLS. Both facilities are off the chart as indicated by the complete identification of them. There is a dog leg 4.1 miles SE of HANDS. From the dog leg it is another 2.5 miles to JOHNS which is identified by the 090-degree course and the 200-degree cross radial from STO.

Fig. 14-5

JEPPESEN   INTRODUCTION   OCT 24-86

APPROACH CHART LEGEND
APPROACH PLAN VIEW (continued)

POSITION FIXES

On charts dated prior to November 25, 1983, position fixes are portrayed by an open circle. O

On charts dated on or after November 25, 1983, position fixes are portrayed by a triangle. △▲

On charts dated on or after August 31, 1984 the DME value will be portrayed as D10.0. When fix and co-located navaid name are the same, only the navaid name is displayed.

Allowable substitutions for identifying a fix are noted in the planview. At the pilots request, where ATC can provide the service, ASR may be substituted for the OM. In addition, PAR may be substituted for OM and MM.

APPROACH TRANSITIONS

NM distance and minimum altitude between fixes and/or navaids.

Route without facility guidance.

Route without minimum altitude. Altitude to be assigned by ATC.

(IAF)   Initial Approach Fix

(IF)   Intermediate Approach Fix

NoPT   No procedure turn, Race track pattern or any other type of course reversal procedure required or authorized without ATC clearance.

❶   Flag notes -see applicable reference notes elsewhere on the plan view.

Crossing altitude and descent instructions.

Approach transition inset. (Dog leg route, with off-chart turn). Also provided when route originates at an off-chart intersection designated only for approach use—such fixes are not charted on enroute and area charts.

APPROACH TRANSITIONS (continued)

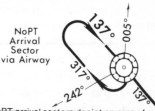

NoPT Arrival Sector via Airway

NoPT arrival sectors depict an area of approach transition routing to an approach fix. No procedure turn is required nor authorized without ATC clearance when an arrival course is within the charted sector and on an established airway radial to the fix.

Approach transition track, distance, and altitude from a defined fix is illustrated below.

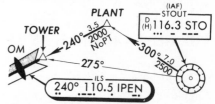

Note that the routes from STO to Plant to Tower are approach transitions, whereas the STO R-275° is not an approach transition. The STO R-275° has a small arrowhead and is a cross radial forming Tower. The STO R-300° has a large and small arrowhead indicating both an approach transition and a cross radial forming Plant. Plant and Tower are also formed by the IPEN localizer course.

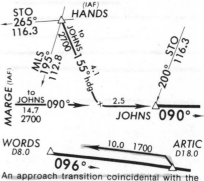

An approach transition coincidental with the approach procedure flight track is charted offset from the flight track for clarity.

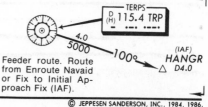

Feeder route. Route from Enroute Navaid or Fix to Initial Approach Fix (IAF).

The second IAF is off the chart to the left. The IAF in this case is known as MARGE, and it is 14.7 miles to JOHNS as noted below the transition course line. There is also a minimum altitude of 2700 feet shown on this section of the transition.

Because the approach procedure flight track is portrayed by a bold line, it would be difficult to show the approach transition segment when the segment coincides with the approach procedure track. The answer is to draw the approach transition alongside the approach path line. The line signifying the approach transition will jut out from a fix and terminate in a heavy arrow pointing parallel to the approach path, as in the WORDS-ARTIC example in FIG. 14-5.

If you look at the upper left-hand column of FIG. 14-6 you will see how the approach transitions are depicted using DME arcs. The DME distance is shown alongside the arc itself, in this case 18 DME. The minimum altitude is shown just inside the arc.

THE REST OF THE WAY IN

An interesting example of an approach procedure flight track is shown near the bottom of the left-hand column. It shows a holding pattern designed to lose altitude over an NDB, after which the outbound leg of the approach procedure is a 105-degree magnetic course, followed by a left turn to a 270-degree magnetic course inbound. Once inbound, the series of small arrowheads indicate that the remainder of the approach is a *visual* flight track.

In the right-hand column you will see procedure turns and course reversals. Four are illustrated here. The upper one is a schematic of a procedure that you could call the "generic" procedure turn. Remember that this is just a schematic and need not be followed exactly. The same is true of the 80°/260° turn that is shown. All you are required to do in these two cases is to make your reversal on the same side of the approach course as depicted, and to stay within the protected airspace at or above the minimum altitude.

The next two course reversals, the teardrop and the holding pattern, however, must be adhered to as published. This is an important point to remember.

ODDS AND ENDS

Moving on to FIG. 14-7, as far as the missed approach is concerned, about all that is pictured on the chart is a heavy dashed line with a heavy arrowhead which shows the initial maneuvering course. The remainder of the procedure is written out in text form and can be found below the approach profile diagram.

Remember that if you are forced to execute a missed approach out of a circling approach, your initial climbing turn must be made toward the landing runway. Then continue the turn until you are established on the missed approach course. The missed approach fix inset, shown near the top of the left-hand column,

APPROACH CHART LEGEND
APPROACH PLAN VIEW (continued)

APPROACH TRANSITIONS (continued)

Approach transitions via DME arcs are illustrated below with distance from facility, direction of flight, start and termination points of the arc. DME arc approach transitions may be started from any airway or authorized direct route which intercepts the arc. Lead radials may be provided as an advisory point for turning to the final approach course. DME arc altitude is maintained until final.

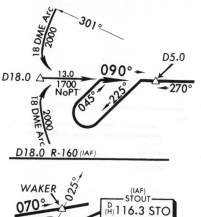

Approach transitions may be described under the originating navaid with course, distance, altitude, and terminating point.

APPROACH PROCEDURE FLIGHT TRACK

The approach procedure flight track is portrayed by a bold line. This track begins in the plan view at the same location where the profile begins.

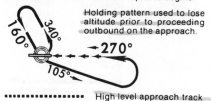

Holding pattern used to lose altitude prior to proceeding outbound on the approach.

●●●●●●●●●●●●●● High level approach track

➤➤➤➤➤➤➤ Visual flight track

PROCEDURE TURNS-COURSE REVERSALS

Schematic portrayal of procedure turn

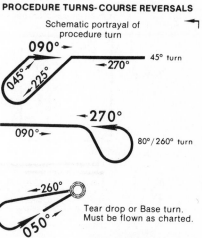

45° turn

80°/260° turn

Tear drop or Base turn. Must be flown as charted.

Holding pattern or Racetrack pattern. When used in lieu of procedure turn, must be flown as charted unless radar vectored.

When a procedure turn, Holding pattern, Racetrack pattern, Teardrop or Base turn is not portrayed, they are not authorized.

ALTITUDES

2300′	All altitudes in the plan view are "MINIMUM" altitudes unless specifically labeled otherwise. Altitudes are above mean sea level in feet. May be abbreviated "MIM."
MANDATORY 2400′	Mandatory altitudes are labeled "MANDATORY" and mean at the fix or glide slope intercept.
MAXIMUM 1900′	Maximum altitudes are labeled "MAXIMUM." May be abbreviated "MAX."
RECOMMENDED 2000′	Recommended altitudes are labeled "RECOMMENDED."

APPROACH CHART LEGEND
APPROACH PLAN VIEW (continued)

MISSED APPROACH

 Initial maneuvering course for missed approach. Details of the missed approach are specified below the profile diagram.

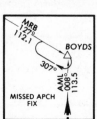

Missed approach fix inset.

HOLDING PATTERN

Holding pattern not part of the approach procedure. DME figures, when provided, give the DME distance of the fix as the first figure followed by the outbound limit as the second figure. 3000 indicates the minimum holding altitude, (MHA).

Length of holding pattern in minutes when other than standard

Indicates procedure for leaving the holding pattern.

AIRPORTS

IFR airports in the area and VFR airports underlying the final approach are depicted.

⊿	Airport to which the approach is designed
○	Nearby Military airport
⬡	Nearby Civil or joint use Military airport
(H) Ⓗ	Heliport
⊛	Civil Seaplane Base
⊕	Military Seaplane Base
✿	Airport with light beacon
⊗	Abandoned or closed airport

A reference circle, 5 statute miles in radius, is centered on the airport to emphasize obstructions and other information close to the airport.

AIRSPACE

R-2402	Restricted airspace (Refer to the enroute chart for limitations.)
SC(P)-23	

ORIENTATION DETAILS

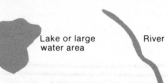

Lake or large water area   River

OBSTRUCTIONS

1. All obstructions are not charted.
   a. In areas of congestion, when a number of obstructions are in close proximity of one another, only the highest of the obstructions is charted.
   b. Obstructions below 50' above the airport elevation within the airport reference circle and those below 100' above the airport elevation outside of the airport reference circle are not charted.

2. The black dot (●) for obstructions is used to locate-
   a. Those which are 50' to 99' above the airport elevation within the airport reference circle.
   b. Those which are 100' to 499' above the airport elevation outside of the airport reference circle.

3. Pictorial symbols for obstructions are used, if identifiable, or an unknown obstruction symbol, if not identifiable, to locate-
   a. Those which are 100' or higher above the airport elevation within the airport reference circle.
   b. Those which are 500' or higher above the airport elevation outside of the airport reference circle.

4. Minimum altitudes of the instrument approach procedure provide prescribed clearances of terrain and structures beneath the flight path.

All heights are shown above Mean Sea Level (MSL).

⚓⚓⚓⚓⚓⚓	Tower, stack, tank, water tower, building, church. Center of circular base is true position.
—T———T—	Power and pole line
1500' ☀	Terrain
★	Aeronautical beacon/light (Includes airport/aerodrome/ identification beacons or hazard beacon/flashing obstruction light.)
1600' ⋀	Structure unknown
5280' ◆	Highest obstruction in the charted area
502' ●	Not identified
±	Doubtful accuracy

is depicted on charts when the missed approach fix is at a location outside the chart boundaries.

As a VFR pilot, you are conditioned to the color-coded sectional charts on which you can visualize what the en route terrain will look like just by looking at the topographical color on the chart. As you transition from VFR to IFR flying, you have to reevaluate the information available on the charts you will be using. As an IFR pilot, you will require even more information from charts, but color coding it would make other information too hard to find and hard to read. Although the airport chart shows more ground detail, about all you will get from the approach plate plan view is the type of airport, large masses of water, restricted areas, specific obstructions that may come up into your airspace, and a five-statute-mile-radius circle drawn around the airport.

Take a look at the bottom of the left-hand column to see what I mean. The five-mile "reference" circle is to "emphasize obstructions and other information close to the airport." This circle and the water areas are shown in a light gray.

Carefully study what is said concerning obstructions. In the first place, not all of the obstructions will be charted. If there are a number of obstructions close to each other, such as a group (or "farm") of radio antennas, only the highest one will be depicted.

Obstructions below 50 feet above the elevation of the airport that are within the five-mile airport reference circle, and those below 100 feet above the airport elevation outside the circle, will not be indicated.

"Why is that?" you ask. Well, it's to avoid clutter on the chart for one thing; and for another, you aren't supposed to descend that low anyway, so they shouldn't really concern you.

Obstructions between 50 and 99 feet above the surface of the airport within the airport reference circle, and between 100 and 499 feet outside the circle, are depicted by a black dot. The chances of you deliberately being that low in those areas, are practically nil. Higher obstructions are charted using symbols as shown on FIG. 14-7. It's important to know what these symbols represent. They will help you to visualize the area even without a color code.

Remember, as long as you are on the prescribed approach course at or above the minimum allowable altitude, you won't have any problems with obstructions.

15

Approach Charts: The Profile View

T HE PROFILE VIEW OF THE APPROACH CHART IS DESCRIBED OFFICIALLY AS THE "vertical cross section of the plan view." It is as if you are watching the aircraft descend while you are standing off to the side of the approach path. While the plan view depicts your flight path over the ground, the profile view shows the aircraft's altitude above the surface, and is, therefore, a most critical tool for the instrument pilot.

Taking a look at FIG. 15-1, you see three types of nonprecision approach profiles. Above them you will note a relatively new Jeppesen feature—a table of recommended altitudes/heights at various DME fixes. This table is designed to allow for a constant rate of descent; however, the altitude/heights are only *recommended* figures, and the minimums depicted in the profile view still apply. Also, you won't find this table on all nonprecision approaches, although I am sure Jeppesen will add them to more and more as the charts are updated.

Finally, regarding the tables, they do not always read from left to right as most other tables do. They are orientated to read in the same direction as the profile is depicted.

NONPRECISION APPROACHES

Take a look at the uppermost approach depicted on FIG. 15-1. Here you have the standard nonprecision approach that includes an overhead approach, an outbound leg, a procedure turn, and an inbound leg. You begin by passing over the

VOR and proceeding outbound on the 280-degree radial. Notice a group of numbers to the left of the VOR. These numbers represent, and define the limits of, the procedure turn. In this case, the procedure turn must be completed within 10 nautical miles of the VOR, the fix that the turn is predicated upon. Remember, the protected airspace begins at the fix where the outbound track begins, not necessarily from the final approach fix, unless they are co-located. Also, the turn *must be completed* within the distance specified.

The large number above the line (1200′) is the minimum altitude for the procedure turn, and the smaller number in parentheses below the line (1126′) is the height in feet above the TDZE (Touchdown Zone Elevation), the runway end, or the airport.

The most complete definition of the TDZE is in the pilot/controller glossary:

> TOUCHDOWN ZONE ELEVATION/TDZE—The highest elevation in the first 3000 feet of the landing surface. TDZE is indicated on the instrument approach procedure chart when straight-in landing minimums are authorized.

For more on the TDZE look ahead at the second symbol down from the top left on FIG. 15-4. Here you will learn that the number shown in parentheses (1200′) is the:

> Height in feet above airport, runway end, or TDZ elevation. Height is measured from airport elevation unless TDZE or runway end elevation is noted at the airport symbol.

The airport symbol referred to is the heavy horizontal bar on the ground reference line (which is the third symbol down from the top left of FIG. 15-4, as well as that shown in the right side of the two top illustrations in FIG. 15-1).

Going back to the nonprecision approach mentioned above, you will see that, after completing the procedure turn and inbound on the 280-degree radial (equivalent to a magnetic course of 100°, or 100° TO on your VOR), you are allowed to descend a little lower, in this case down to 1000 feet MSL (926 feet above the TDZE), until reaching the FAF.

INBOUND FROM THE FAF

The FAF is identified by a Maltese Cross symbol on the profile view. It is described in the chart glossary:

> FINAL APPROACH FIX (FAF)—The designated fix from or over which the final approach (IFR) to an airport is executed. The FAF identifies the beginning of the final approach segment of the instrument approach . . . FAF is charted only when specified by official source.

Fig. 15-1

APPROACH CHART LEGEND
PROFILE VIEW

The top of the profile view on certain *non-precision* approaches contains a table of *recommended* altitudes/heights at various DME fixes to allow a constant rate of descent. The altitudes/heights are *recommended* only; minimum altitudes in the profile view apply. The table is sequenced in the same direction as the profile is portrayed.

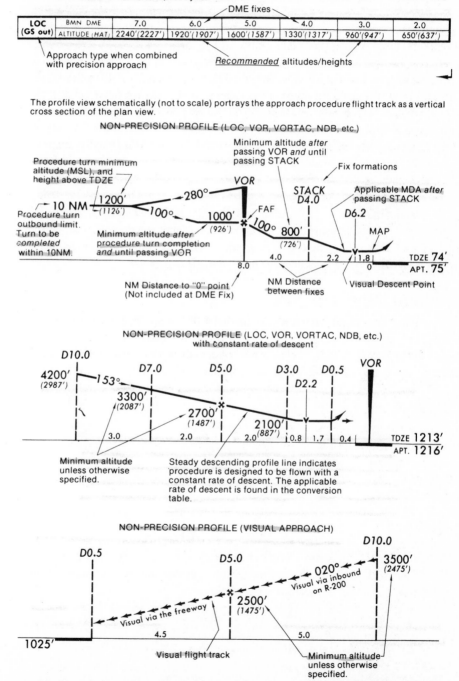

LOC (GS out)	BMN DME	7.0	6.0	5.0	4.0	3.0	2.0
	ALTITUDE (HAT)	2240'(2227')	1920'(1907')	1600'(1587')	1330'(1317')	960'(947')	650'(637')

DME fixes

Approach type when combined with precision approach

Recommended altitudes/heights

The profile view schematically (not to scale) portrays the approach procedure flight track as a vertical cross section of the plan view.

NON-PRECISION PROFILE (LOC, VOR, VORTAC, NDB, etc.)

Minimum altitude *after* passing VOR *and* until passing STACK

Fix formations

Procedure turn minimum altitude (MSL), and height above TDZE

VOR

STACK D4.0

Applicable MDA *after* passing STACK

10 NM — 1200' (1126')

280°

D6.2

Procedure turn outbound limit. Turn to be *completed* within 10NM.

100°

1000' (926')

FAF

100° 800' (726')

MAP

Minimum altitude *after* procedure turn completion *and* until passing VOR

8.0

4.0

2.2

1.8

0

TDZE 74'
APT. 75'

NM Distance to "0" point (Not included at DME Fix)

NM Distance between fixes

Visual Descent Point

NON-PRECISION PROFILE (LOC, VOR, VORTAC, NDB, etc.) with constant rate of descent

D10.0

4200' (2987')

153°

D7.0

D5.0

D3.0

D0.5

VOR

3300' (2087')

2700' (1487')

2100' (887')

D2.2

TDZE 1213'
APT. 1216'

3.0

2.0

2.0

0.8

1.7

0.4

Minimum altitude unless otherwise specified.

Steady descending profile line indicates procedure is designed to be flown with a constant rate of descent. The applicable rate of descent is found in the conversion table.

NON-PRECISION PROFILE (VISUAL APPROACH)

D0.5

D5.0

D10.0

020°
Visual via inbound on R-200

3500' (2475')

2500' (1475')

Visual via the freeway

1025'

4.5

5.0

Visual flight track

Minimum altitude unless otherwise specified.

(Reproduced with permission of Jeppesen Sanderson, Inc. NOT FOR USE IN NAVIGATION.)

Inbound past the FAF (in this case, the VOR), your course to the runway will be the 100-degree radial of the VOR (100° FROM on your VOR receiver). The numeral 8.0 under the VOR symbol and below the ground reference line indicates the distance, in nautical miles, between that point and the "0" point (in this case, the runway threshold). The zero point can be shown under middle markers, inner markers, or other points as well. It is not shown when a DME fix is at the same location. As an example, there is no mileage shown under the ground reference line at STACK. Indicated by D4.0, STACK is 4.0 miles DME from the VOR (which, in this case, is also the FAF). On the other hand, look at the center illustration on FIG. 15-2 and you will see, under the letters LOM (outer compass locator), a DME distance of 5.8 from MTN, while the 4.7 is below the ground reference line. Similar data is printed for the LMM (middle compass locator). The reason for this is that the DME to the markers is measured from a geographical point other than the "0" point whereas the numerals beneath the ground reference line show the distance to the "0" point at the runway threshold.

Continuing with FIG. 15-1, after you pass the FAF inbound you will use a step-down descent, descending first to 800 feet MSL until you pass STACK, which is a fix 4.0 DME along the 100-degree radial on the final approach course. Once past STACK you can continue down to your MDA.

VISUALIZING THE VDP

Above the ground reference line you find 4.0 between the FAF and STACK, 2.2 between STACK and the "V" symbol, and 1.8 between the "V" symbol and the runway threshold. These are the segment distances between these points, all of which add up to the 8.0 miles from the FAF to the "0" point.

The "V" symbol is the Visual Descent Point (VDP) which is described in the chart glossary:

> VISUAL DESCENT POINT/VDP—A defined point on the final approach course of a non-precision straight-in approach procedure from which normal descent from the MDA to the runway touchdown point may be commenced, provided the approach threshold of that runway, or approach lights, or other markings identifiable with the approach end of that runway are clearly visible to the pilot.

In other words, you are not to go below the MDA until you are past the VDP. When flying VFR it's also a good idea to stay at or above the MDA until the VDP; this will give you a mental picture of what the runway environment will look like under real-life instrument conditions.

To save the trouble of having to add up all of the segment distances, the distance from the applicable facility, in this case D6.2, is included above the descent profile line.

In the center illustration of FIG. 15-1 you will see a nonprecision profile using a steady rate of descent. You can find the rate of descent in the conversion table (which is discussed later), but the minimum altitudes shown at the various points of the approach still apply. In this example, the VOR is on the airport surface, and the missed approach point is 0.4 miles from the runway threshold. The small arrow pointing toward the runway indicates that the rest of the approach (from the MAP in this case) must be flown visually.

At times, you will find a nonprecision profile utilizing a visual approach as illustrated at the bottom of FIG. 15-1, but this is self-explanatory.

PRECISION APPROACHES CUT A FINE LINE

Once you get into precision approaches you find some additional symbols. Take a look at the top illustration in FIG. 15-2 to see what I mean.

The first difference you will see is between the procedure turn information and the FAF. Here, the descent profile has been split into two different lines, one solid and one dashed.

Many airports will use locator beacons in conjunction with the outer marker. Sometimes this beacon will be incorporated into an NDB approach and the dashed line will signify the descent profile for the NDB approach. At other times the glide slope may malfunction, either your airborne equipment or the ground equipment, in which case the ILS will revert to a LOC approach and again the dashed line will signify the profile flight path.

Why do you see two different altitudes (1800' and 1400') inbound after the procedure turn? Because the entry to each type of approach is based on different thinking. Without glide slope or DME information, you are never really sure where you are along the ground track; unless, of course, you are crossing one of the fixes. So, you want to get down as low as you can, as soon as you can, so you will be sure to be at your MDA before arriving at the MAP. On the other hand, when you do have the glide path information, you'll usually want to have the aircraft stabilized on the glide slope as soon as possible—certainly prior to crossing the LOM inbound.

The nonprecision FAF, as indicated by the Maltese cross, is the LOM in this illustration. However, the FAF for precision approaches is always the published glide slope intercept point, which in this case is reached prior to the LOM (unless ATC has authorized a lower-than-normal glide slope interception altitude). The inbound ILS course of 043° is illustrated inside the localizer symbol, and the glide slope altitude of 1689 feet (1615 above TDZE) at the LOM is under the two-dash Morse code identifier of the LOM.

To illustrate these points further, you can see that, from the glide path intercept point, which is slightly before crossing the FAF, to the DH, an aircraft on an ILS approach will continue down a steady descent path. However, an aircraft flying the localizer or NDB approach will descend to 1400 feet MSL before crossing the FAF. Then it will descend to the MDA, level off, and maintain the MDA until it reaches the MAP.

Again, note the distances from fixes to the ''0'' point listed below the ground reference line. The 4.2 above the line is the distance between the LOM and the MM.

DH, MAP, AND OTHER ACRONYMS

Look now at the differences in altitudes and geographical positions between the DH and the MAP.

In the first place, you should understand that the DH is the altitude at which you will be when you arrive at the MAP on an ILS approach, *if* you are properly on the glide slope.

On the other hand, on a nonprecision approach, when you reach the MDA you are allowed to fly out the *time* to the MAP before initiating the missed approach procedure. In this case, you will not be allowed to descend as low as if you were on an ILS, due to a lack of precision either in altitude, azimuth, or both. After all, if you are timing your approach, your actual ground position can vary slightly from the charted MAP, and if you don't get down to your MDA before reaching the MAP, you will still have to break off the approach if you don't have the runway environment in sight. The higher minimum altitude gives you adequate obstruction clearance, compensating for the lack of precision.

You may find other notes placed in the profile view. One found in this illustration is the TCH (Threshold Crossing Height), which in this case is 58 feet. You will only find this listed on precision approaches as it signifies the height at which the glide slope crosses the threshold. On some charts its placement may lead you to believe that it refers to the nonprecision approach path that it appears to be attached to, but remember, that it is the threshold crossing height *for the glide slope*.

If the Obstruction Clearance Altitude (OCA) is lower than the charted DH or MDA it will be listed as shown in the illustration. In this case it is depicted (even though it is the same as the DH) because it is definitely lower than the MDA.

The center profile of FIG. 15-2 shows a descending turn in combination with the procedure turn. The procedure turn is to be started after flying outbound for a specific time (in this case, one minute). It also shows an LMM rather than just the MM shown in the upper illustration.

CAT II AND CAT IIIA

Well, here are the granddaddys of all instrument approaches. You may fly your entire career and never get into equipment that will allow you to fly down to these minimums—as low as zero/zero on a CAT IIIC. Still, you should be aware of how they are portrayed.

Fig. 15-2
JEPPESEN **INTRODUCTION** OCT 24-86

APPROACH CHART LEGEND
PROFILE VIEW (continued)

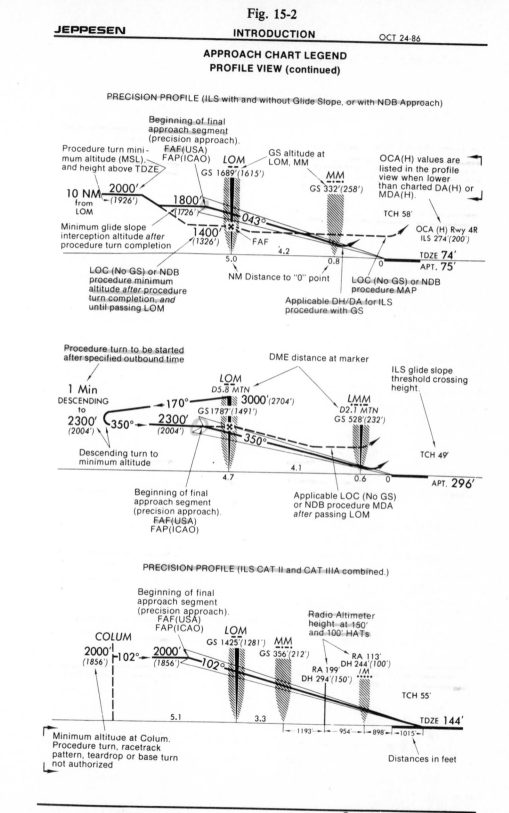

PRECISION PROFILE (ILS with and without Glide Slope, or with NDB Approach)

Beginning of final approach segment (precision approach). FAF(USA) FAP(ICAO)

Procedure turn minimum altitude (MSL), and height above TDZE

GS altitude at LOM, MM

OCA(H) values are listed in the profile view when lower than charted DA(H) or MDA(H).

LOM GS 1689'(1615')

MM GS 332'(258')

10 NM from LOM
2000' (1926')
1800' (1726')
043°
1400' (1326') FAF

Minimum glide slope interception altitude *after* procedure turn completion

TCH 58'

OCA (H) Rwy 4R ILS 274'(200')

TDZE 74'
APT. 75'

5.0   4.2   0.8   0

LOC (No GS) or NDB procedure minimum altitude *after* procedure turn completion, *and* until passing LOM

NM Distance to "0" point

LOC (No GS) or NDB procedure MAP

Applicable DH/DA for ILS procedure with GS

Procedure turn to be started after specified outbound time

DME distance at marker

ILS glide slope threshold crossing height.

1 Min DESCENDING to 2300' (2004')
350°
170°
2300' (2004')

LOM D5.8 MTN
3000'(2704')
GS 1787'(1491')
350°

LMM D2.1 MTN
GS 528'(232')

Descending turn to minimum altitude

TCH 49'

4.7   4.1   0.6   0

APT. 296'

Beginning of final approach segment (precision approach). FAF(USA) FAP(ICAO)

Applicable LOC (No GS) or NDB procedure MDA *after* passing LOM

PRECISION PROFILE (ILS CAT II and CAT IIIA combined.)

Beginning of final approach segment (precision approach). FAF(USA) FAP(ICAO)

Radio Altimeter height at 150' and 100' HATs

COLUM
2000' (1856')
102°
2000' (1856')
102°

LOM GS 1425'(1281')
MM GS 356'(212')

RA 199' DH 294'(150')
RA 113' DH 244'(100')
IM

TCH 55'

5.1   3.3

TDZE 144'

1193' 954' 898' 1015'

Minimum altitude at Colum. Procedure turn, racetrack pattern, teardrop or base turn not authorized

Distances in feet

APPROACH CHART LEGEND
PROFILE VIEW (continued)

MISSED APPROACH

The missed approach text is located immediately below the profile diagram.

MISSED APPROACH POINT (MAP)

Precision approaches (using glide slope): Immediately upon reaching the Decision Height (DH) while descending on the glide slope and continued descent cannot be controlled by visual reference.

Non-precision approaches (no glide slope): Upon reaching the Missed Approach Point (MAP). A table at the lower left corner of the chart will specify the MAP and, if applicable, a time at various speeds from fix to MAP. When times are not shown, a timed approach is Not Authorized. Where a DME Fix is portrayed in addition to a distance, the DME Fix may be used for determining the MAP for DME equipped aircraft. The runway threshold and MAP often coincide.

SYMBOLS

ON CHARTS DATED PRIOR TO AUG. 31, 1984

| Altimeter Setting In **MILLIBARS** |

This note informs pilots of the local mode of setting altimeters to current pressure (inches of mercury, millibars, hectopascals or millimeters of mercury. One millibar = one hectopascal.) In the U.S.A., the altimeter setting is given in inches of mercury. In some countries the altimeter setting is given as a QFE value for millibars or millimeters of mercury.

TRANS LEVEL: FL 40

The transition level (QNE) is the lowest level of flight using standard altimeter setting (29.92 inches of mercury or 1013.2 millibars or 1013.2 hectopascals.)

TRANS ALT: 3000' (2926')

The transition altitude (QNH) is the altitude at and below which local pressure setting must be used.

TRANS LEVEL and **TRANS ALT** will not be charted when the altimeter setting boundary is portrayed on the respective enroute chart unless published on the respective procedure source document by the governing authority.

OCL Rwy 04R
274'(200')   Obstruction Clearance Limit

OCA (H) Rwy 26
720'(263')   Obstruction Clearance Altitude (Height)

On charts dated on or after OCT 24, 1986 OCA(H) values are in the profile view only when lower than charted DA(H) or MDA(H).

TCH   Threshold Crossing Height

LAKE   Fan marker with name or ILS marker with marker code and, when appropriate, glide slope crossing altitude above sea level and above TDZE, runway end or airport elevation.

SYMBOLS (continued)

VOR   VOR, DF, NDB, or Waypoint labeled only as to facility depicted. "Z" indicates VHF location markers.

LOM   Marker and NDB co-located (LOM, LMM)

VOR   VOR, not used for course guidance, by-passed during final approach, and used solely to provide DME fixes both before and after its passage. -or- Facility used solely for start of outbound procedure track, with procedure turn or course reversal and final approach inbound to another facility.

Named fix formed by VOR radial or NDB bearing, or DME, or radar.

| REDOE R-269 SLI or 020° OS or 5.8 DME | REDOE D5.8 |

ON CHARTS DATED ON OR AFTER AUG. 31, 1984

All allowable substitutions for identifying a fix are noted in the planview. Only DME values will be displayed in the profile. Note: ILS DME should *not* be used to determine position over middle marker, runway threshold or runway touchdown point unless specified on the approach chart.

✖   Final Approach Fix (FAF) (If specified by state source)

D2.0   Visual Descent Point (VDP) (If specified by state source)

Approach procedure flight track

Approach procedure flight track of non-precision approach (LOC, No GS, NDB, or VOR) when charted in same profile with precision approach.

High level approach track

Visual flight track (One or more arrows)

2300'   All altitudes in the profile view are "MINIMUM" altitudes unless specifically labeled otherwise. Altitudes are above mean sea level in feet. May be abbreviated "MIM."

MANDATORY **2400'**   Mandatory altitudes are labeled "MANDATORY" and mean at the fix or glide slope intercept.

MAXIMUM **1900'**   Maximum altitudes are labeled "MAXIMUM". May be abbreviated "MAX".

In the first place, these are straight-in approaches in which neither procedure turns, base turns, nor any other turn is authorized. Your aircraft has to be specially equipped and certified, and *you* have to be certified as well. The beginning of the approach is just like any other ILS, but look at where the descent ends. That's right—1015 feet down the runway. It flies you right to the ground.

The letters RA appear twice, once at the inner marker (IM) not used in normal ILS approaches, and again at a point between the MM and the IM. The numbers shown after the RA are for the radio altimeter height above the ground at those points. Those points are at 150 and 100 feet above touchdown or HAT (Height Above Touchdown).

If that's the case, why don't the radio altimeters read 150 and 100 at these points? That's because radio altimeters read directly off the ground. They tell you the height of the aircraft above the ground, and the ground at any given distance from the runway is very seldom the same elevation as the runway itself. In the first instance the radio altimeter would read 199 feet, so the ground is 49 feet below the touchdown elevation. In the second instance the radio altimeter would read 113 feet, so the ground there is 13 feet lower than the touchdown zone.

To see how much more accuracy is involved once you get to approaches below normal ILS minimums, note that the distances between the MM, the 150-foot HAT point, the IM (which is the 100-foot HAT in this instance), the threshold, and the touchdown point *are all measured in feet, not miles.*

You can get an uncluttered look at some of the profile symbols by looking at FIG. 15-3. Here you see the VDP, the FAF, the visual flight track path, and others.

MISSED APPROACH

If you remember the format used on approach charts, the heading information is at the top of the page. This is followed by the approach plan view. Under that is the profile view, and finally, at the bottom of the page are the landing minimums.

The missed approach procedures are written out below the profile view, just before the landing minimums. The missed approach is a very critical area of the approach. Here you are at a minimum altitude, tooling along in the dark (so to speak) with your aircraft all dirtied up and ready to land. If you can't see the airport when you get to the MAP, it's time to get back up in the ozone where you will be safe. But in order to clean up, climb, and miss all of the buildings, trees, poles, mountains, and the like, the missed approach must be executed in an orderly fashion.

When reviewing your approach plates prior to filing your flight plan, you also reviewed the missed approach procedure. When there are two pilots in the plane, it's a good idea for the one not flying to read the missed approach procedure aloud after passing the FAF inbound.

When there is only one pilot on board, I find it useful to copy the missed approach procedure in advance on a small file card—or on one of those pages from the telephone answering pad—and tape it to the glare shield where I can see it without having to take my hands off the controls. I put the initial turn and altitude information in large capital letters so they'll catch my eye (naturally, when taping the card up it has to be placed where it won't block the instruments from view). Remember, when the time comes to execute the missed approach, you will be pretty busy applying power, retracting the gear and flaps, transitioning from a descent to a climb regime, turning, resetting navigational radios, and reporting to the proper control facility, so you won't have time to scan a page in the manual for the procedure—*and you definitely don't want to rely on your memory.*

The upper part of FIG. 15-4 presents a few more symbols that may be of interest. You have already reviewed the procedure turn symbol. The upper right-hand symbol shows a holding pattern used in lieu of a procedure turn. Here you see the inbound and outbound bearings as well as the time of the inbound leg and the minimum altitude. Below this symbol note the words "Procedure based on 120 KT IAS." This indicates that if you have a faster aircraft you will have to shorten all times to remain within the protected airspace.

LANDING MINIMUMS

Landing minimums are presented in a standard format table depending on the type of approach. To simplify the understanding of these minimums, the only information shown in each table will be those items that specifically affect that particular approach.

Take a look at the "FORMAT FOR COMBINED ILS AND NDB," found on the bottom of FIG. 15-4. The letters A, B, C, and D running down the left-hand border of the format signify the aircraft approach categories.

The table is broken up into various blocks. The DH or MDA will be shown in the upper part of the table, while the visibility requirements necessary to initiate the approach will be shown in the blocks below.

Although the explanation of these tables can be seen in FIG. 15-6, I'll discuss some of the points here.

The format shown in FIG. 15-4 is just an illustration. The headings used on the actual charts may be somewhat different, depending on what lights and auxiliary systems are available on a particular approach. Furthermore, the delineations of the various blocks will depend on many factors, like the airport itself, the surrounding terrain, or aircraft performance, for instance.

The lowest minimums listed in any format will be found on the left side of the chart. Less-desirable minimums are shown in descending order to the right. In this case, note that all minimums to the left of the vertical double line are predicated on straight-in approaches. The minimums to the right side of the double line are for circling approaches.

Fig. 15-4

JEPPESEN **INTRODUCTION** OCT 24-86

APPROACH CHART LEGEND
PROFILE VIEW (continued)

SYMBOLS (continued)

RECOMMENDED
2000'

Recommend altitudes are labeled "RECOMMENDED."

(1200')

Height in feet above airport, runway end, or TDZ elevation. Height is measured from airport elevation unless TDZE or runway end elevation is noted at the airport symbol.

TDZE **74'**
APT. **75'**

Touchdown Zone Elevation. (Runway End or Threshold Elevation when labeled RWY.)

Official Airport Elevation

Procedure turn minimum altitude (MSL)

10 NM **1200'** *(1126')*

Height above TDZE, runway end, or airport.

Procedure turn outbound limit. When the outbound procedure track is depicted in the profile view, the turn limit is from the fix where the outbound track begins. The turn must be completed within the specified distance.

Combined procedure turn (course reversals) and NoPT procedure flight tracks

CHIPS
3000' *(2780')*

10 NM
3000' *(2780')*

270°

090°   090°

NoPT procedure flight track

Flight tracks when procedure turn is used

Minimum altitude at fix.

1 Min **080° ← 260°** **2000'** *(1900')*

Holding pattern used in lieu of procedure turn with holding limit, outbound and inbound bearings, and minimum altitude.

Procedure based on 120 KT TAS.

When airspeeds are indicated in profile note, higher airspeeds require shortened times to assure remaining in the protected area.

4920' STD

QNE altitude (standard altimeter setting) converted from meters. This appears only where official profile altitude in meters is above transition level.

Radar required.

Radar vectoring is required when it is the only approved method for providing a procedure entry and/or for identifying a terminal fix.

CH or HC   Critical height

120°   Glide Slope with inbound magnetic course of Localizer.

Glide Slope, Glide path intercept is the Final Approach Fix (FAF USA),Final Approach Point (FAP ICAO) for precision approaches. The glide slope symbol starts at the FAF/FAP

035°   MLS glide path with inbound magnetic final approach course.

Begin missed approach (pull up)

LANDING MINIMUMS

PRESENTATION

Landing minimums are presented for each category of aircraft in a format subdivided to show the minimums required for conditions that can affect minimums. Only the appropriate subdivisions pertinent to the approach are included. The following are illustrations of typical minimum table formats used on Jeppesen charts.

Publication of minimums does not constitute authority for their use by all operators. Each individual operator must obtain appropriate approval for their use. (Special printing to provide other minimums suitable to a particular operator can be arranged.)

FORMAT FOR COMBINED ILS AND NDB

			STRAIGHT-IN LANDING RWY						CIRCLE-TO-LAND	
			ILS			LOC (GS out)		NDB		
	FULL	TDZ or CL out	ALS out	MM out		MM out	ALS out	ALS out		MDA
A									A	
B									B	
C									C	
D									D	
Gnd speed-Kts		70	90	100	120	140	160			
GS										

First, look at the straight-in minimums. Start at the vertical line going down from the "ILS." This line tells you that the DH is different on each side of the line. In other words, it will be lower for the first three columns than it will be with the MM out. This is not always the case, so it pays to read the format carefully on each chart you are using.

Whenever you see a horizontal line, it will tell you that visibility minimums are different above and below the line. These differences are not always the same for each category in each situation, so you should check the landing minimums for the approach charts you're using very carefully. This statement cannot be repeated too often.

Several other formats, shown in FIG. 15-5, are included here for comparison. Many of the formats include conversions tables. These tables are useful for a couple of reasons, but to give it more meaning, let's look at the examples shown in FIG 15-7 where some numbers have been plugged in.

The obvious time to use this table is when you are flying an approach that uses time/speed to determine the MAP. It's also a good backup for any approach in which it can be utilized, especially nonprecision approaches. On precision approaches it gives you a fairly good estimate of the rate of descent you'll need to stay on the glide slope. If you maintain this rate of descent, yet find yourself deviating from the glide slope, you might be experiencing wind shear. Sometimes this will be your first indication that a wind shear exists.

The conversion table at the top left of FIG. 15-7 is for a precision approach. The upper line is ground speed in knots. This means that you will have to convert from statute miles per hour, unless your airspeed indicator is calibrated in knots, and then add or subtract the known or estimated headwind or tailwind components. Naturally, you will have to interpolate, but that should be no major problem. The second line shows the glide slope angle—in this case it's 2.50°—as well as what your rate of descent should be, based on your estimated ground speed, to stay on the glide slope.

The bottom line gives the amount of time (in minutes and seconds) from the nonprecision FAF to the MAP, useful for timed localizer approaches when the glide slope is out of service. In the example, it shows that the distance from the LOM to the MAP is 2.6 nautical miles, and the time ranges from 2 minutes and 14 seconds to just 59 seconds, depending on your ground speed.

In the nonprecision approach table on the right, the glide slope line is omitted. The distance from the VOR to the MAP is 3.9 miles. The rest is self-explanatory.

If the time/speed table is missing, it means that you are unable to determine the MAP by time. In such a case, a timed approach is not authorized.

Fig. 15-5

APPROACH CHART LEGEND
LANDING MINIMUMS (continued)

Format for ILS CAT II

STRAIGHT-IN LANDING RWY								
CAT II ILS								
RA DH							RA DH	
Gnd speed · Kts	70	90	100	120	140	160		
GS								

The left column lists the lowest available CAT II minimum, normally DH 100, visibility RVR 12 (350m). The right column lists the CAT II minimum applicable when certain airborne equipment is out of service or when pilot and operator requirements preclude the use of lower minimum. This minimum is normally DH 150, visibility RVR 16 (500m).

Format for combined ILS CAT II and ILS CAT IIIA.

STRAIGHT-IN LANDING RWY								
CAT IIIA ILS						CAT II ILS		
						RA DH	RA DH	
Gnd speed · Kts	70	90	100	120	140	160		
GS								

Format for VOR or NDB. "Ceiling required" is included only when a ceiling is required by a country's governing authority.

STRAIGHT-IN LANDING RWY							CEILING REQUIRED CIRCLE-TO-LAND	
MDA								
	CEILING-VISIBILITY						MDA CEIL-VIS	
A							A	
B							B	
C							C	
D							D	
Gnd speed-Kts	70	90	100	120	140	160		
GS								

Fig. 15-6

JEPPESEN   **INTRODUCTION**   OCT 24-86

APPROACH CHART LEGEND
LANDING MINIMUMS (continued)

Definitions of terms and abbreviations in minimum formats.

A, B, C, D	Aircraft categories (See Chart Glossary)
AZ (GP out)	Azimuth (Glide path out) on MLS approach.
All Non Skd	All Non Scheduled. These minimums apply for Mexico ILS approaches only.
ALS out	Approach lights out of service
CAT I ILS	CAT I ILS approach
CAT II ILS	CAT II ILS approach
CAT IIIA ILS	CAT IIIA ILS approach
CEILING REQUIRED	Indicates that a ceiling is required for landing.
CIRCLE-TO-LAND	Circling landing minimums applicable for all runways
DA	Decision Altitude - MSL altitude
DA(H)	Decision Altitude (Height)
DH	Decision Height - MSL altitude
FULL	All components of ILS are operating (LOC, GS, OM (or FAF), MM and approach lights).
HIRL out	High Intensity Runway Lights out of service
ILS	ILS approach
LOC (GS out)	Localizer approach (ILS without GS)
MDA	Minimum Descent Altitude - MSL altitude
MDA(H)	Minimum Descent Altitude (Height)
MM out	MM out of service and no legal substitutions available
MLS	MLS approach
NA	Not authorized
NDB	NDB approach
ODALS out	ODAL approach lights out of service
RA	Radio Altimeter (height above ground)
RAIL out	RAIL portion of approach lights out of service
RMS	RMS approach
STRAIGHT-IN LANDING RWY	Runway for which charted minimums apply
TDZ or CL out	Touchdown Zone lights or centerline lights out of service
( )	Numbers in parentheses represent Height Above Touchdown (HAT) or Height Above Threshold or Height Above Airport (HAA)

LANDING APPROACH CONDITIONS

The fact that straight-in minimums are not published does not preclude the pilot from landing straight-in, using published circling minimums, if he has the straight-in runway in sight in sufficient time to make a normal approach for landing. Under such conditions, and when Air Traffic Control has cleared him for landing on that runway, he is not expected to circle even though straight-in minimums are not published. If he desires to circle, he should advise ATC.

Circle-to-land minimums for each category of aircraft apply to all operators with the following two exceptions for Air Carriers that hold USA Federal Aviation Administration Operations Specifications:

1. B-727 Air Carrier jets must use minimums specified for D aircraft.
2. B-747, DC-10, and L-1011 Air Carrier jets are required to use 1000 (HAA)-3 when published minimums are lower.

Conditions affecting DH, MDA, or visibility are provided in column headings of the minimum table on each chart.

The most advantageous condition, with the lowest possible minimum, is presented in the first column at the left, followed by columns of less favorable conditions labeled to show the landing aid or light system out of service. WHEN TWO OR MORE COMPONENTS ARE OUT, THE HIGHEST APPLICABLE CHARTED MINIMUM SHOULD BE USED.

Column headings for ILS minimums include all installed lights and components *that affect minimums.* When the glide slope of an ILS is "out" the column heading is identified as a localizer approach with glide slope out-"LOC (GS out)".

Except for ILS minimums, installed lights and components *that do not affect minimums* are omitted from approach condition headings. Thus when there is no "ALS out" or Component out (i.e. "MM out") column charted minimums will not change when the approach lights or component is reported out of service.

When lights or navaids are not installed, column headings naming them are omitted from all charts.

Altimeter setting requirements or other special conditions may alter the sequence of the minimums. A review of all notes or minimum box titles should always be made.

SIDESTEP INOPERATIVE COMPONENTS

For a runway identified as sidestep, such as SIDESTEP RWY 24L:
Inoperative light components shown in Rwy 24L column are those for the lights installed on *Rwy 24L, not* the lights for Rwy 24R.

VISIBILITY

Visibility for any approach condition is shown below the condition in a band for each aircraft category. Visibility is shown alone, or in addition to RVR. When a governing authority specifies

APPROACH CHART LEGEND
LANDING MINIMUMS (continued)

CONVERSION TABLE

At the bottom of the approach chart page, there is a conversion table as shown below.

Gnd speed · Kts		70	90	100	120	140	160
GS	2.50°	315	405	450	539	629	719
LOM to MAP	2.6	2:14	1:44	1:34	1:18	1:07	0:59

Gnd speed · Kts	70	90	100	120	140	160
VOR to MAP 3.9	3:21	2:36	2:20	1:57	1:40	1:28

The speed table relates aircraft approach speeds to the rate of descent for the ILS glide slope (descent in feet per minute). For non-precision approaches it relates speed to the distance shown from the final approach fix (FAF) or other specified fix to the missed approach point (MAP).

Some missed approach points are calculated on a time/speed basis after completion of the procedure turn inbound on final approach. The absence to a time/speed table means the MAP cannot be determined by time and a timed approach is Not Authorized.

Gnd speed · Kts	70	90	100	120	140	160
Descent rate D7.0 to D3.0	466	600	667	800	934	1067
MAP at 1.5 DME						

ON CHARTS DATED ON OR AFTER APR 20-84

Non-precision approaches designed to be flown at a constant rate of descent have a rate of descent provided in the conversion table. The conversion table specifies a rate of descent that allows arrival at minimum altitudes shown in the profile view. The descent rate is a recommended rate only. Minimum altitudes shown in the profile view apply.

Gnd speed · Kts		70	90	100	120	140	160
Rwy 5, 23, PAR GS	2.50°	315	405	450	539	629	719
Rwy 30 PAR GS	2.55°	321	413	458	550	642	733

On PAR charts:
Speed table with rates of descent on PAR glide slope is provided.

ON CHARTS DATED ON OR AFTER AUG 31, 1984

Gnd speed Kts		70	90	100	120	140	160
ILS GS	2.50°	315	405	450	539	629	719
LOC Descent Gradient 5.2%		377	484	538	646	753	861
MAP at MM							

When provided by the state, a non-precision descent gradient is provided with a descent table in feet per minute.

Gnd speed · Kts	70	90	100	120	140	160
Glide path Angle 3.00°	377	484	538	646	753	861
FAF to MAP 5.1	4:22	3:24	3:04	2:33	2:11	1:55

On MLS charts the Glide path angle authorized for the procedure and rate of descent table is provided.

Amendment number of a procedure. An amendment number increase generally indicates a procedure change.

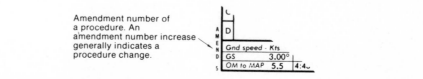

16

Airport Charts

THE AIRPORT CHART IS NORMALLY FOUND ON THE REVERSE SIDE OF THE FIRST approach chart for the airport. As I mentioned in Chapter 14, though, some of the airports are becoming so large and complex that it is necessary to produce even larger charts of the airport, the taxiways, and in some cases, the gate locations at the terminals.

To refresh your mind as to the general format, look back once again at FIG. 14-1. The airport chart format is on the right side of the page and is made up of four sections just like the approach chart. The upper portion is the heading, the next one down is the airport plan view, below that you will see the runway data, and finally, at the bottom of the page, you find the take-off and alternate minimums for that airport.

Now, take a look at a sample heading in FIG. 16-1. The location and airport name in this example are on the left side of the heading. The latitude and longitude are listed directly under the airport name; these coordinates are shown for the Airport Reference Point (ARP), when one is charted at the airport. Otherwise, the source of the coordinates will be shown. In the example you will also see that the airport is 7.7 miles from the TRP VOR.

The ICAO or U.S. airport identifier is printed in bold type just to the left of the chart index number.

The communications block is divided into two sections. The left side pertains primarily to frequencies used on the ground, while the right side is for frequencies used in flight. The frequencies are listed in the order that you will use them during your departure. First you find ATIS, then below that the Clearance Delivery, Ground, and Tower frequencies. The Departure Control frequencies and the VOR test frequency, if applicable, are found on the right side of the block.

NEW SYMBOLS

You will find some symbols new to you on the airport plan view. To help understand them, take a look at FIGS. 16-2, 16-3A, and 16-3B.

As on the approach chart, the symbols on the airport plan are all in white/black and shades of gray. This reduces the amount of detail that can be shown, so many symbols are used. Basically, paved runways are black, unpaved runways are white, and taxiways and ramps are gray. Permanently closed taxiways are shown by gray X's.

The runway numbers are all magnetic unless they are followed by a "T" to indicate that they are true headings. True headings are only found in the Far North. Most runways today have their magnetic heading shown in smaller numbers below the runway number as seen in the second example down in the left-hand column of FIG. 16-2. A "W" will follow the runway number if it is a seaplane operating area or a water runway.

Let's begin examining the Milwaukee airport chart by glancing at the communications block on FIG. 16-3A first, to see how Milwaukee breaks up its Departure Control frequencies, depending on which runway is in use, and which way you'll be turning after takeoff.

THE AIRPORT AS SEEN FROM THE AIR

On the airport plan view, you can see that Runways 25L, 31, 19R and 13 all have displaced landing thresholds as indicated by the white crossbar placed across the runway.

The ARP (airport reference point, where the latitude and longitude coordinates are measured) can be seen just to the west of the midpoint of Runway 1L/19R. The legend in the right-hand column of FIG. 16-2 tells you that, if the ARP is located on a runway, the position will be indicated by an arrow from the letters ARP and the symbol will be omitted.

Every runway at Milwaukee, has the elevation of both ends marked on the chart. If this information is omitted the information is not available.

Taxiways are identified alphabetically, e.g., G, M, DD. And the Milwaukee chart indicates a taxiway under construction between Taxiways G and K.

ADDITIONAL RUNWAY INFORMATION

The only lights shown on the airport plan view are approach lights and beacons, and while the approach lights are "normally shown to scale in a recogniza-

Fig. 16-1

APPROACH CHART LEGEND
AIRPORT CHART FORMAT

The airport chart appears only on the back side of the first approach chart. It contains information pertaining to the airport, air/ground communications, take-off, alternate minimums, and special landing minimums.

HEADING

Geographic name, airport name, latitude and longitude, elevation, magnetic variation, location identifier, index number, revision date and communications are given at the top of the page as illustrated below. All communications for departing the airport are listed in order of use. On charts dated on or after June 9, 1983, the designated Common Traffic Advisory Frequency (CTAF) is shown for U.S. public airports without a control tower or where the tower is part-time. UNICOM, when available, is charted when other local communication capabilities are not available.

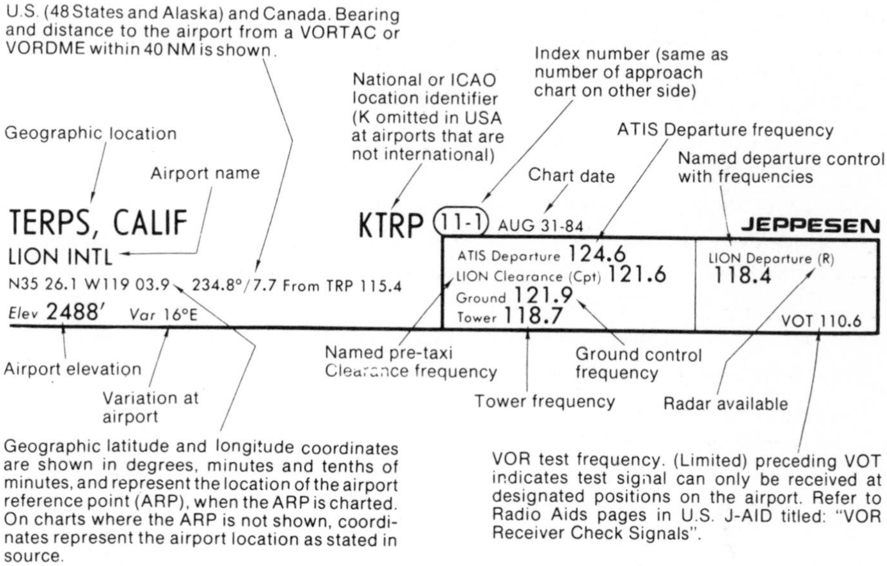
U.S. (48 States and Alaska) and Canada. Bearing and distance to the airport from a VORTAC or VORDME within 40 NM is shown.
National or ICAO location identifier (K omitted in USA at airports that are not international)
Index number (same as number of approach chart on other side)
Geographic location
Airport name
ATIS Departure frequency
Named departure control with frequencies
Chart date
TERPS, CALIF
LION INTL
N35 26.1 W119 03.9 234.8°/7.7 From TRP 115.4
Elev 2488' Var 16°E
KTRP
11-1
AUG 31-84
JEPPESEN
ATIS Departure 124.6
LION Clearance (Cpt) 121.6
Ground 121.9
Tower 118.7
LION Departure (R) 118.4
VOT 110.6
Airport elevation
Variation at airport
Named pre-taxi Clearance frequency
Tower frequency
Ground control frequency
Radar available
Geographic latitude and longitude coordinates are shown in degrees, minutes and tenths of minutes, and represent the location of the airport reference point (ARP), when the ARP is charted. On charts where the ARP is not shown, coordinates represent the airport location as stated in source.
VOR test frequency. (Limited) preceding VOT indicates test signal can only be received at designated positions on the airport. Refer to Radio Aids pages in U.S. J-AID titled: "VOR Receiver Check Signals".

(Reproduced with permission of Jeppesen Sanderson, Inc. NOT FOR USE IN NAVIGATION.)

ble form,'' the easiest way to determine what type of system(s) is installed is to read the information in the ''Additional Runway Information'' table which is often located below the airport plan view. In Milwaukee's case, however, this table appears on the reverse side of the plan view (FIG. 16-3B).

For a complete listing of the abbreviations and an example of an ''Additional Runway Information'' table, take a look at FIG. 16-4. This example shows the wealth of information you can derive from this one small block. The definitions of the abbreviations are quite straightforward, but there are a few that may benefit from discussion. ''CL,'' for example, means centerline lights. If it is shown by itself, it means that these lights are arranged in what is considered to be a standard configuration. In the standard configuration, you will find that the centerline lights are white from the approach end of the runway until 3000 feet from the departure end. From that point until 1000 feet from the departure end, you will see alternating red and white lights. All of the centerline lights in the final 1000 feet are red. These are a tremendous help during low visibility conditions. Some airports use all white centerline lights, and in that case, the symbol will be ''CL (white).'' If the centerline lights are in a nonstandard configuration, and the configuration is not known, the symbol is ''CL (non-std).''

If the nonstandard configuration is known, it will be specified in the symbol. Look at the example shown in FIG. 16-4. You will see ''CL (50W, 20R & W, 20R),'' which means that the first 5000 feet from the approach end are white, the next 2000 feet are red and white, and the last 2000 feet are red.

You should remember, though, that we're talking about centerline lights, right in the center of the runway, not the runway edge lights. Some people get the two confused. It is also important to fix the configuration of the lights in your mind. It would be very embarrassing to be rolling out fast, expecting red and white alternating lights and then red lights at the end of the runway, only to be on a runway that has all white lights.

WHAT YOU SEE AIN'T ALWAYS WHAT YOU GET

Look again at the ''Additional Runway Information'' table on FIG. 16-4, and find the columns listing the usable lengths for the runways. These are set up for three conditions: landing beyond the threshold, landing beyond the glide slope, and takeoff.

You will not see anything in the landing-beyond-the-threshold column unless the runway has a displaced threshold. Then, the figure shown is the effective length of the runway from the displaced threshold to the departure end.

For the usable length when landing beyond the glide slope, the figure is taken from a point abeam the glide slope transmitter to the departure end of the runway. For a runway using PAR, it is from the point of the theoretical glide path/runway intersection to the departure end of the runway.

APPROACH CHART LEGEND
AIRPORT PLAN VIEW

SYMBOLS

Physical feature symbols used on the airport chart are illustrated below.

Symbol	Description	Symbol	Description
●━(27)	Runway number is magnetic unless followed by T for true in the far north.	▲	Helicopter landing pad
●━(27)₂₆₇°	Runway number and (when known) magnetic direction, unless followed by T for true in the far north.	⊕ ARP	Airport Reference Point. Off-runway. Center of cross positioned at exact location.
☐☐ (27W)	Seaplane operating area, or water runway.	ARP ━↑	Airport Reference Point. Located on runway centerline. Arrow points to exact location.
▬	Paved runway	▷	RVR measuring site, may have identifying letter or number.
☐	Unpaved runway	✪	Airport/Aerodrome/ Identification beacon.
▨	Pierced steel planking (PSP)	⌒	Railroad
≡≡≡	Seaplane operating area or water runway. Dash lines indicate operating area.	-T——-T-	Pole line
▬▮	Displaced landing threshold	⸸	Lighted pole
◄▬····	Approach lights extending to displaced landing threshold	≡ — ≡	Marsh, rice paddies and mud flats
▬▲	Unidirectional Arrester Gear	⌒	Road
▬▲	Bidirectional Arrester Gear	⸍⸍	Bluff
▬	Jet Barrier	⸍⸍	Reef
▬✕	Closed runway	⸂⸃⸄	Trees
▬☐	Stopway or overrun	☌	Cone
➤ ≡≡	Area under construction	✈	Tee
▬☐	Runway shoulder (when readily noticeable)	◁	Tetrahedron
✕╱✕ A B	Taxiway and apron	▮ ■ ▲	Buildings
✕ ✕ ✕ ✕ ✕	Permanently closed taxiway	▨	Large building

```
Feet  0    1000  2000  3000  4000  5000
      |⊢⊢⊢|⊢⊢⊢|⊢⊢⊢|⊢⊢⊢|⊢⊢⊢|
Meters  0       500      1000      1500
```
Bar Scale

No differentiation between types of surface for ramps, taxiways, closed runways, closed taxiways, runway shoulders, and areas other than runways are shown. Stopways and overruns are shown regardless of surface with the length when known. Stopway and overrun lengths are not included in runway lengths.

ADDITIONAL INFORMATION

Runway end elevations are shown on the airport diagram if source is available.

Approach lights and beacons are the only lighting symbolized on the airport diagram. Approach lights are normally shown to scale in a recognizable form. For approach light symbols see page 121.

A representative selection of obstructions known to Jeppesen is depicted. The elevation of obstructions depicted is above mean sea level (MSL).

Latitude and longitude ticks at tenths of a minute interval are charted around some plan view neat lines.

On charts dated on or after May 9, 1986, a schematic of the Low Level Wind Shear Alert System (LLWAS) is displayed on the airport planview. Each schematic provides the abbreviated name and relative position of each sensor.

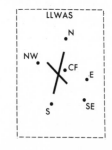

Glance again now at FIG. 16-3B and take a look at the data for Runway 1L/19R in the ''Additional Runway Information'' table. Although the runway is shown on the plan view as being 9690 feet long, the displaced threshold on 19R reduces its effective length to 8915 feet when landing beyond the threshold. Wouldn't it be embarrassing if you figured your weight and balance for landing on a 9690-foot runway by just taking a cursory glance at the plan view without looking at the additional information?

There is no reduction in usable length for landing beyond the threshold in the other direction (Runway 1L), so that box is left blank. Because glide slope angles are set up to effect touchdown somewhere between 750 and 1500 feet from the threshold, you will see that for landing beyond the glide slope, Runway 1L has a usable length of 8439 feet, and Runway 19R has a usable length of 7861 feet. Runway 25L restricts you to 7338 feet when landing beyond the threshold, and Runways 13 and 31 restrict you to 5137 and 5344 feet, respectively, when landing beyond the threshold.

Although takeoff usable lengths are not listed for any of the runways at Milwaukee, had they been, they would have been measured from the point the takeoff roll commences to the end of the pavement that is usable for takeoff.

The note ''Turbojet NA'' in that column indicates that Runway 1R is not available for jet departures. At times, there are also other restrictions for a runway. These are indicated by ❶, ❷, ❸, etc. Milwaukee is a good example of this. The reasoning behind some of the restrictions, besides sounding confusing at first, is hard to understand at times. To tax your brains a bit, take a look at the restrictions concerning Runway 13/31, and see if you can figure out why some of them came about.

TAKEOFF MINIMUMS

The last section of the airport chart is the takeoff and alternate minimums table. This block is explained quite well in FIG. 16-5.

The block may be broken down into two main sections, takeoff minimums and alternate minimums. Or the takeoff minimum block may appear above the alternate minimum block, as in Milwaukee's case, depending on the amount of information printed.

The takeoff minimum block is further divided into an air carrier section and a general section. You can see at the top of FIG. 16-5 that takeoff minimums apply only to Part 121, 123, 129, and 135 operators, but Part 91 operators would be wise to heed them.

Study FIG. 16-5 very carefully. There's a lot of good information included. Look at the ❶ preceding ''TAKE-OFF'' in the heading. If you look down below to where the note is explained, you can see that it says, ''Rwy 4: 300′ ceiling - 1 required or charted minimums with a minimum climb of 290′/NM to 1000′.''

Fig. 16-3A

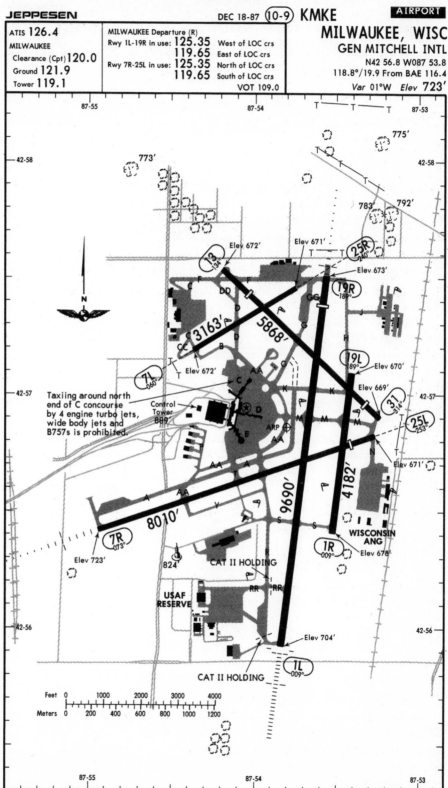

GENERAL
Low level wind shear alert system.

ADDITIONAL RUNWAY INFORMATION

RWY				USABLE LENGTHS — LANDING BEYOND —		TAKE-OFF	WIDTH
				Threshold	Glide Slope		
1R ❶ 19L	MIRL					Turbojet NA	150'

❶ Closed to all but CAT I aircraft 2200-0600 when parallel runway available.

RWY				Threshold	Glide Slope	TAKE-OFF	WIDTH
1L	HIRL CL ALSF-I TDZ	grooved	RVR		8439'		200'
19R	HIRL CL MALSR	grooved	RVR	8915'	7861'		
7R	HIRL SSALR	grooved	RVR		6836'		150'
25L	HIRL REIL VASI-L	grooved		7338'			
7L ❷	MIRL VASI-L (angle 3.1°)						100'
25R	MIRL VASI-L (angle 3.5°)						

❷ Closed to all jet aircraft and aircraft over 12,500 lbs.

RWY		Threshold	WIDTH
13 ❸	MIRL VASI-L	5137'	150'
31	MIRL VASI-R	5344'	

❸ Turbojets-Prior permission required.
Closed 2200-0600 except to lightweight single engine aircraft.

TAKE-OFF

	Rwys 1L, 19R			Rwys 1R, 13, 19L, 25R, 25L, 31		Rwy 7L			Rwy 7R		
CL & RCLM any RVR out, other two req						With Mim climb of 264'/NM to 900'		Other	With Mim climb of 299'/NM to 1100'		Other
		Forward Vis Ref	STD	Forward Vis Ref	STD	Forward Vis Ref	STD		Forward Vis Ref	STD	
1 & 2 Eng	TDZ RVR 6	RVR 16 or ¼	❶RVR 50 or 1	¼	1	¼	1	300-1	RVR 16 or ¼	❸RVR 50 or 1	300-1
	Mid RVR 6										
3 & 4 Eng	Rollout RVR 6		❷RVR 24 or ½		½		½			RVR 24 or ½	

❶ FAR 135: Rwy 1L, RVR 18; Rwy 19R, RVR 24.   ❸ FAR 135: RVR 24.
❷ FAR 135: Rwy 1L, RVR 18.

FOR FILING AS ALTERNATE

	Precision	Non-Precision	NDB Rwy 7R
A			
B	600-2	800-2	NA
C			
D			

CHANGES: Usable lengths.

AMEND 4

Fig. 16-4

JEPPESEN　　　　　　**INTRODUCTION**　　　OCT 24-86

APPROACH CHART LEGEND
ADDITIONAL RUNWAY INFORMATION (continued)

RWY	ADDITIONAL RUNWAY INFORMATION			USABLE LENGTHS LANDING BEYOND		TAKE-OFF	WIDTH
				Threshold	Glide Slope		
4R	HIRL CL ALSF-I TDZ	grooved	RVR				150'
22L	HIRL CL	grooved	RVR		6641'		
4L	HIRL CL HIALS SFL					NA	150'
22R							
7	RL VASI (angle 2.4°, TCH 10')						200'
25							
13	HIRL CL VASI LDIN			11,972			150'
31	HIRL CL SSALR VASI (non-std) HST-H			11,252			

RUNWAY LIGHTS-ABBREVIATIONS

RL--Runway Edge Lights

HIRL--High Intensity Runway Edge Lights

MIRL--Medium Intensity Runway Edge Lights

REIL--Runway End Identifier Lights
(threshold strobe)
TDZ--Touchdown Zone Lights

HST-H-High Speed Taxiway turn-off with green centerline lights H indicates taxiway identification.

CL--Standard centerline light configuration
White lights then alternating red & white lights between 3000' and 1000' from

runway end and red lights for the last 1000'.
-or-
Exact configuration is not known.
Known non-standard configurations are stated as listed below

CL (white)--all lights are white full length of runway.

CL(non-std)--non standard, configuration unknown

CL(50W, 20R & W, 20R)--non standard, configuration known--first 5000' white lights; next 2000' alternating red & white lights; last 2000' red lights.

APPROACH LIGHTS-ABBREVIATIONS

ALS--Approach Light System

HIALS--High Intensity Approach Light System

MIALS--Medium Intensity Approach Light System

SFL--Sequenced Flashing Lights

F--Condenser-Discharge Sequential Flashing Lights/Sequenced Flashing Lights

ALSF-I--Approach Light System with Sequenced Flashing Lights

ALSF-II--Approach Light System with Sequenced Flashing Lights and Red Side Row Lights the last 1000 feet.

SSALF--Simplified Short Approach Light System with Sequenced Flashing Lights

SALSF--Short Approach Light System with Sequenced Flashing Lights

MALSF--Medium Intensity Approach Light System with Sequenced Flashing Lights

RAIL--Runway Alignment Indicator Lights (Sequenced Flashing Lights which are installed only in combination with other light systems)

SSALR--Simplified Short Approach Light System with Runway Alignment Indicator Lights

MALSR--Medium Intensity Approach Light System with Runway Alignment Indicator Lights

SALS--Short Approach Light System

SSALS--Simplified Short Approach Light System

MALS--Medium Intensity Approach Light System

LDIN--Sequenced Flashing Lead-in Lights

ODALS--Omni-Directional Approach Light System

VASI--visual approach slope indicator (L or R indicates left or right side of runway only)

AVASI--abbreviated visual approach slope indicator (L or R indicates left or right side of runway only)

VASI (3 BAR)--visual approach slope indicator for high cockpit aircraft (L or R indicates left or right side of runway only)

T-VASI--Tee visual approach slope indicator

AT-VASI--abbreviated Tee visual approach slope indicator (L or R indicates left or right side of runway only)

VASI (Non-Std)--visual approach slope indicator when known to be non-standard

VASI--VASI/AVASI/NON-STD angles are shown when known to be less than 2.5° or more than 3.0°. T-VASI/AT-VASI angles are shown at all times. VASI (3-bar) descent angles are shown when other than upwind angle 3.25°, downwind angle 3.00°.

PAPI--Precision Approach Path Indicator (L or R indicates left or right side of runway only)

TCH--Threshold crossing height. Height of the effective visual glide path over the threshold.

MEHT--Minimum Eye Height over Threshold. Lowest height over the threshold of the visual on glide path indication.

MEHT or TCH is shown (on charts dated MAR 30-84 or later) when less than 60 feet for the upwind bar of a 3-bar VASI system or less than 25 feet for all other systems including PAPI.

(Reproduced with permission of Jeppesen Sanderson, Inc. NOT FOR USE IN NAVIGATION.)

Fig. 16-5
OCT 24-86 **INTRODUCTION** **JEPPESEN**

APPROACH CHART LEGEND
TAKE-OFF AND ALTERNATE MINIMUMS (continued)

U.S. FORMAT FOR CHARTS DATED PRIOR TO NOV 12-82

Take-off restrictions, including ceiling and visibility requirements, and IFR departure procedures apply to FAR 121, 123, 129 and 135 operators.

When indicated, an option of two take-off minimums may be authorized for a take-off runway; either a ceiling and visibility or the visibility shown in a column in the minimums format when a minimum climb rate can be achieved by the operator. On runways where an option is specified, the term "charted minimums" refers to the columnized take-off visibility authorized for that runway and operator.

EXAMPLE: Rwy 4, FAR 121 operators have the option of 300 ceiling-1, or the charted minimums of RVR 16 or ¼ with minimum climb of 290'/NM to 1000'.

For take-off minimums lower than RVR 16 or ¼ only the runways as specified above the column will be authorized.

Standard minimums will be shown in the column titled "GENERAL" and apply to all runways except where indicated for runways that require minimums higher than standard, or lower than standard minimums are authorized.

Standard take-off minimums for FAR 121, 123, 125, 129 and 135 operators.

Restrictions in this column, if any, apply to all operators.

Reminder for take-off alternate requirement.

Footnotes in this column apply to 135 operators.

Approaches with electronic glide slope.

LOC, VOR, etc. approaches.

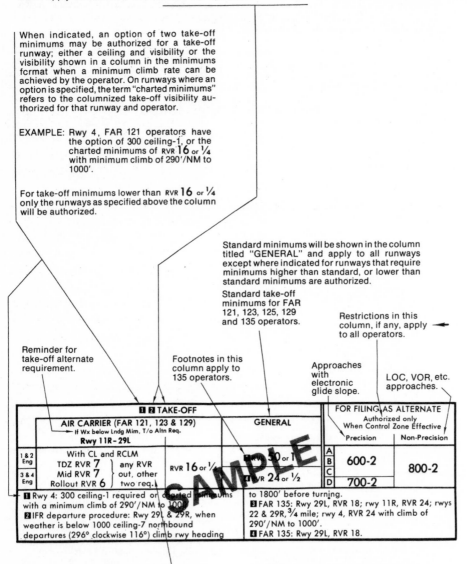

Where only two transmissometers are installed, the touchdown and rollout RVRs are required and are controlling. If three transmissometers are installed, all are controlling and the failure of any one transmissometer not affect operations provided the remaining two RVR values are at or above appropriate minimums.

NA charted in the take-off column indicates *Not Authorized for take-off during IFR conditions.* NA charted in the alternate column indicates *IFR minimums not authorized for alternate use.*

This means that you need at least a ceiling of 300 feet *and* a visibility of 1 mile to take off. It gives you the option of using the charted minimums for takeoff, but only if your aircraft can climb at a rate of at least 290 feet per nautical mile until you reach 1000 feet. That would indicate obstructions somewhere in the initial part of the climb. These options are explained more in the notes on the upper left-hand side of FIG. 16-5.

The takeoff minimums under "Air Carrier" are broken down into two sections. The left section applies to Rwy 11R-29L only, while the section on the right applies to the rest of the runways. There is also a note immediately under the "Air Carrier" heading which says that if the weather is below landing minimums, those operators must have a *takeoff alternate* filed. A takeoff alternate is a safety precaution in the event of an emergency after the takeoff. It ensures that the airliner will be able to land at another airport if the weather at the departure airport is below landing minimums at the time of departure.

The "General" column has some notes in it, and they apply to Part 135 operators, while the "Air Carrier" columns apply to Part 121, 123, and 129 operators as specified.

Not all airports are equipped with transmissometers, in which case the takeoff minimums are expressed in miles or fractions thereof. Where there is a transmissometer, the takeoff minimums may sound somewhat confusing.

Notice in the example that, if Runway 11R-29L has both the centerline lights and the runway centerline markings, plus two out of three of the transmissometers operating, you can get down to your lowest takeoff minimums. The required RVR for each of the transmissometers is listed to the left.

Now look back at Milwaukee and see how many options are available depending on the runway and the equipment in use. Some day you will run across instances where the takeoff minimums are *higher* than many of the landing minimums, due to obstructions. So, read the notes on the applicable airport charts very carefully.

ALTERNATE MINIMUMS

The alternate minimums block is very straightforward. For one example, take a look at FIG. 16-6. This column is divided into two sections. The section on the left indicates that you can only use the precision approach or the localizer to Runway 2, or the localizer DME back course to Runway 20, if the airport has the listed minimums. In addition, these approaches are only authorized when the Control Zone is effective.

You can use the minimums for the VOR approaches listed to the right (VOR Rwy 2, VOR Rwy 20, VOR DME-A, or VOR DME Rwy 20), or the NDB approach to Rwy 20, at any time—provided that you have approved weather service.

What is approved weather service? Well, the weather bureau will suffice when it is operating, but when it is closed you will be out of luck unless you happen to fly for a commuter or an air carrier that has its own approved weather people.

EXPANDED AIRPORT CHARTS

I talked earlier about the new expanded airport charts that are coming out for some of the major airports. Take a look at those that have been produced for LAX—Los Angeles International (FIGS. 16-7 through 16-10).

FIGURE 16-7, in its original form, is actually a fold-out chart to show the complexity of LAX. There are cargo buildings, terminals, and outbuildings scattered all over the field, and the taxiways are quite complex. Another interesting thing about LAX is that there are three different tower frequencies shown in the communications block.

The "Additional Runway Information" section as well as the takeoff and landing minimum blocks are shown on the reverse side of the airport chart (FIG. 16-8).

The terminal area (gates and taxiways), Imperial Cargo Complex, and West Pads, with their attendant taxiways, are complex enough that an additional chart (FIG. 16-9) has been created just to illustrate those specific areas of the airport.

FIGURE 16-10 lists the latitude and longitude coordinates of every gate, for the benefit of those aircraft using area navigation equipment.

So you can see that, as terminals and airspace become more and more congested, the charts change to keep pace. You must keep up with these rapid changes.

Hopefully, by now you have learned the importance of studying all of the information available to you on Jeppesen charts, as well as in the explanatory pages. In the next chapter we'll take a look at the NOS charts to see how they compare.

Fig. 16-6

KAHULUI

N20 54.1 W156 26.0

Elev 53'   Var 11°E

*ATIS 124.6	*MAUI Departure (R)
MAUI Clearance 120.6	120.2
Ground 121.9	
*Tower CTAF 118.7	
UNICOM 122.95	

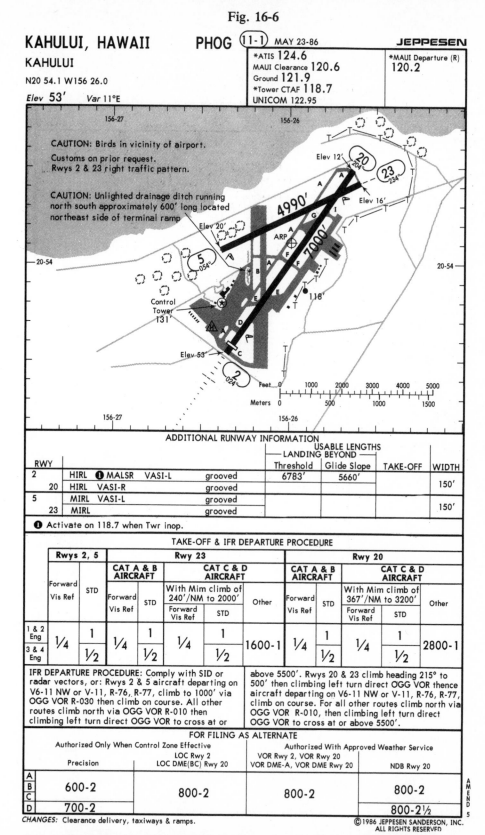

CAUTION: Birds in vicinity of airport.

Customs on prior request.
Rwys 2 & 23 right traffic pattern.

CAUTION: Unlighted drainage ditch running north south approximately 600' long located northeast side of terminal ramp

ARP ⊕

Control Tower 131'

Elev 20'
Elev 53'
Elev 12'
Elev 16'
118'
4990'
7000'

5 — 054°
20 — 204°
23 — 234°
2 — 024°

| Feet | 0 | 1000 | 2000 | 3000 | 4000 | 5000 |
| Meters | 0 | | 500 | 1000 | | 1500 |

ADDITIONAL RUNWAY INFORMATION

RWY					USABLE LENGTHS — LANDING BEYOND Threshold	Glide Slope	TAKE-OFF	WIDTH
2	HIRL	❶ MALSR	VASI-L	grooved	6783'	5660'		
20	HIRL	VASI-R		grooved				150'
5	MIRL	VASI-L		grooved				
23	MIRL			grooved				150'

❶ Activate on 118.7 when Twr inop.

TAKE-OFF & IFR DEPARTURE PROCEDURE

	Rwys 2, 5		Rwy 23				Rwy 20			
			CAT A & B AIRCRAFT		CAT C & D AIRCRAFT		CAT A & B AIRCRAFT		CAT C & D AIRCRAFT	
	Forward Vis Ref	STD	Forward Vis Ref	STD	With Mim climb of 240'/NM to 2000'	Other	Forward Vis Ref	STD	With Mim climb of 367'/NM to 3200'	Other
					Forward Vis Ref / STD				Forward Vis Ref / STD	
1 & 2 Eng	1/4	1	1/4	1	1/4 / 1	1600-1	1/4	1	1/4 / 1	2800-1
3 & 4 Eng		1/2		1/2	/ 1/2			1/2	/ 1/2	

IFR DEPARTURE PROCEDURE: Comply with SID or radar vectors, or: Rwys 2 & 5 aircraft departing on V6-11 NW or V-11, R-76, R-77, climb to 1000' via OGG VOR R-030 then climb on course. All other routes climb north via OGG VOR R-010 then climbing left turn direct OGG VOR to cross at or above 5500'. Rwys 20 & 23 climb heading 215° to 500' then climbing left turn direct OGG VOR thence aircraft departing on V6-11 NW or V-11, R-76, R-77, climb on course. For all other routes climb north via OGG VOR R-010, then climbing left turn direct OGG VOR to cross at or above 5500'.

FOR FILING AS ALTERNATE

	Authorized Only When Control Zone Effective Precision	LOC Rwy 2 LOC DME(BC) Rwy 20	Authorized With Approved Weather Service VOR Rwy 2, VOR Rwy 20 VOR DME-A, VOR DME Rwy 20	NDB Rwy 20
A B C	600-2	800-2	800-2	800-2
D	700-2			800-2½

AMEND 5

CHANGES: Clearance delivery, taxiways & ramps.

Fig. 16-7

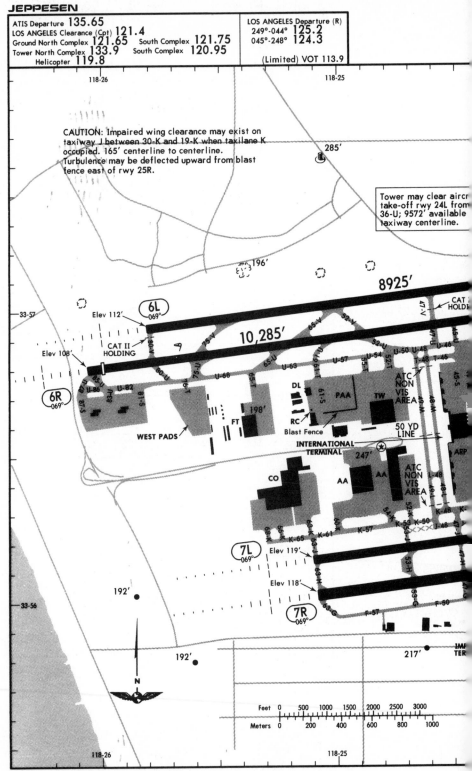

JEPPESEN

ATIS Departure 135.65
LOS ANGELES Clearance (Cpt) 121.4
Ground North Complex 121.65   South Complex 121.75
Tower North Complex 133.9   South Complex 120.95
Helicopter 119.8

LOS ANGELES Departure (R)
249°-044° 125.2
045°-248° 124.3

(Limited) VOT 113.9

118-26   118-25

CAUTION: Impaired wing clearance may exist on taxiway J between 30-K and 19-K when taxilane K occupied. 165' centerline to centerline. Turbulence may be deflected upward from blast fence east of rwy 25R.

285'

Tower may clear aircr take-off rwy 24L from 36-U; 9572' available taxiway centerline.

196'

8925'

6L 069°

Elev 112'

CAT HOLDI

47-V

33-57

CAT II HOLDING

10,285'

Elev 108'

6R 069°

U-82

U-68   U-57

DL

PAA

TW

ATC NON VIS AREA

48

198'

FT

RC

Blast Fence

50 YD LINE

WEST PADS

INTERNATIONAL TERMINAL

247'

CO

AA   AA

ATC NON VIS AREA

K-65   K-61   K-57

7L 069°   Elev 119'

192'

Elev 118'

7R 069°

33-56

192'

217'

N

Feet 0   500   1000   1500   2000   2500   3000
Meters 0   200   400   600   800   1000

118-26   118-25

182

CHANGES: Helicopter frequency, runway 25L lights.

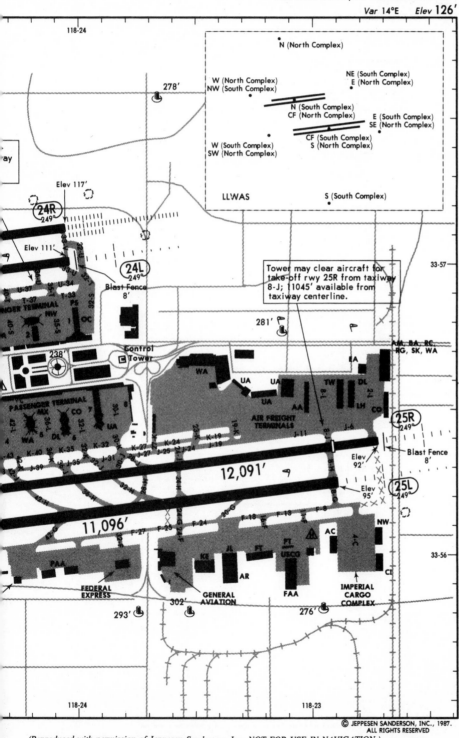

LOS ANGELES, CALIF
LOS ANGELES INTL

LAX 113.6-On Airport   N33 56.6 W118 24.4

Var 14°E   Elev **126'**

118-24

N (North Complex)

278'

NE (South Complex)
E (North Complex)

W (North Complex)
NW (South Complex)

N (South Complex)
CF (North Complex)

E (South Complex)
SE (North Complex)

W (South Complex)
SW (North Complex)

CF (South Complex)
S (North Complex)

LLWAS

S (South Complex)

Elev 117'

24R
249°

33-57

Elev 111'

24L
249°

Blast Fence
8'

Tower may clear aircraft for
take-off rwy 25R from taxiway
8-J; 11045' available from
taxiway centerline.

281'

AA, BA, RC
RG, SK, WA

Control
Tower

238'

EA

WA

UA   UA

PASSENGER TERMINAL

UA   AA

TW   DL

LH   CO

AIR FREIGHT
TERMINALS

J-11   J-6

25R
249°

Blast Fence
8'

Elev
92'

12,091'

Elev
95'

25L
249°

11,096'

NW

AC

4-C

33-56

PAA

FT
USCG

CI

FEDERAL
EXPRESS

302'

GENERAL
AVIATION

AR

FAA

IMPERIAL
CARGO
COMPLEX

293'

276'

118-24

118-23

(Reproduced with permission of Jeppesen Sanderson, Inc. NOT FOR USE IN NAVIGATION.)

GENERAL
Taxiway closures throughout the airport. Consult current NOTAMs.
Birds in vicinity of airport.

ADDITIONAL RUNWAY INFORMATION

RWY				USABLE LENGTHS LANDING BEYOND Threshold	Glide Slope	TAKE-OFF	WIDTH
6R	HIRL CL MALSR VASI (3 bar)-L	grooved	RVR	9964'	9128'		150'
24L	HIRL MALSR		RVR		9259'		
6L	HIRL CL MALSR VASI (3 bar)-L	grooved	RVR		7920'		150'
24R	HIRL CL ❶ALSF-II TDZ		RVR		7899'		

❶ Operates as SSALR during VFR conditions.

RWY				Threshold	Glide Slope	TAKE-OFF	WIDTH
7R	HIRL CL MALSR VASI-L	grooved	RVR		10,022'		200'
25L	HIRL CL ❷SSALR TDZ		RVR		10,094'		

❷ ALSF-II system when weather below CAT-I limits.

RWY				Threshold	Glide Slope	TAKE-OFF	WIDTH
7L	HIRL CL MALSR VASI-L	grooved	RVR		11,017'		150'
25R	HIRL CL MALSR		RVR	11,129'	10,091'		

TAKE-OFF

	CL & RCLM any RVR out, other two req.	Rwys 6L, 7L, 7R, 24R, 25L, 25R Forward Vis Ref	STD	Rwys 6R, 24L Forward Vis Ref	STD
1 & 2 Eng	TDZ RVR **6**	RVR **16** or ¼	RVR **50** or 1	RVR **16** or ¼	RVR **50** or 1
	Mid RVR **6**				
3 & 4 Eng	Rollout RVR **6**		RVR **24** or ½		RVR **24** or ½

IFR DEPARTURE PROCEDURE

Comply with SID or radar vectors, or: Rwys 6L/R,
7L/R climb to 2000' heading 070°, then turn right
direct SLI VOR. Rwys 24L/R, 25L/R climb to 3000'
heading 250°, then turn left direct SLI VOR.

FOR FILING AS ALTERNATE

	Precision	Non-Precision
A B C D	600-2	800-2

CHANGES: Lighting, runway 6R usable length.

Fig. 16-9

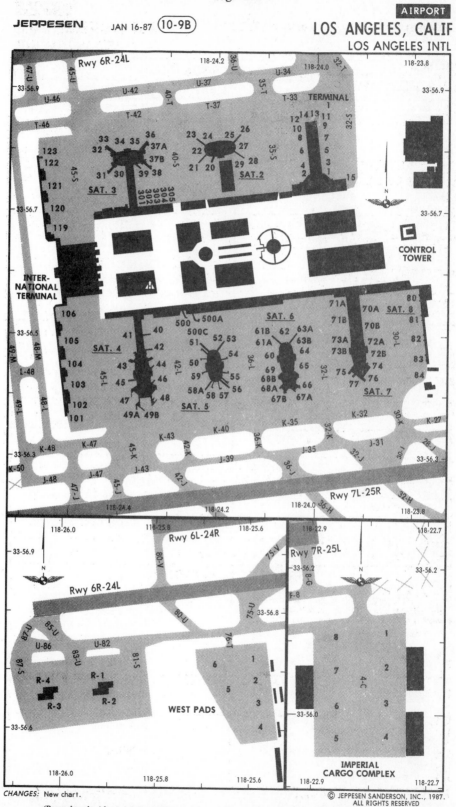

JEPPESEN   JAN 16-87 (10-9B)

LOS ANGELES, CALIF
LOS ANGELES INTL

CHANGES: New chart.

(Reproduced with permission of Jeppesen Sanderson, Inc. NOT FOR USE IN NAVIGATION.)

Fig. 16-10

AIRPORT

JEPPESEN JAN 16-87 (10-9C)

LOS ANGELES, CALIF
LOS ANGELES INTL

PARKING BAY COORDINATES

BAY No.	COORDINATES
Imperial Cargo Complex	
1,2	N33 56.1 W118 22.8
3,4	N33 56.0 W118 22.8
5,6	N33 56.0 W118 22.9
7,8	N33 56.1 W118 22.9
International Terminal	
101 thru 104	N33 56.4 W118 24.5
105,106	N33 56.5 W118 24.5
119 thru 121	N33 56.7 W118 24.5
122,123	N33 56.8 W118 24.5
Passenger Terminal	
Terminal 1	
1 thru 10	N33 56.8 W118 24.0
11 thru 14	N33 56.9 W118 24.0
15	N33 56.8 W118 23.9
Satellite 2	
20	N33 56.8 W118 24.2
21	N33 56.8 W118 24.3
22	N33 56.8 W118 24.2
23	N33 56.8 W118 24.3
24,25	N33 56.8 W118 24.2
26 thru 28	N33 56.8 W118 24.1
29	N33 56.8 W118 24.2
Satellite 3	
30 thru 35	N33 56.8 W118 24.4
36 thru 38	N33 56.8 W118 24.3
39	N33 56.8 W118 24.4
301	N33 56.7 W118 24.4
302 thru 305	N33 56.7 W118 24.3
Satellite 4	
40	N33 56.5 W118 24.3
41	N33 56.5 W118 24.4
42	N33 56.5 W118 24.3
43	N33 56.4 W118 24.4
44	N33 56.4 W118 24.3
45	N33 56.4 W118 24.4
46	N33 56.4 W118 24.3
47	N33 56.4 W118 24.4

BAY No.	COORDINATES
Satellite 4 (Cont'd)	
48	N33 56.4 W118 24.3
49A	N33 56.4 W118 24.4
49B	N33 56.4 W118 24.3
Satellite 5	
50 thru 54	N33 56.5 W118 24.2
55 thru 59	N33 56.4 W118 24.2
500	N33 56.5 W118 24.3
500A,500C	N33 56.5 W118 24.2
Satellite 6	
60 thru 62	N33 56.5 W118 24.1
63A thru 64	N33 56.5 W118 24.0
65 thru 67A	N33 56.4 W118 24.0
67B thru 69	N33 56.4 W118 24.1
Satellite 7	
70A,70B	N33 56.5 W118 23.9
71A	N33 56.6 W118 24.0
71B	N33 56.5 W118 24.0
72A,72B	N33 56.5 W118 23.9
73A,73B	N33 56.5 W118 24.0
74	N33 56.5 W118 23.9
75 thru 77	N33 56.4 W118 23.9
Satellite 8	
80	N33 56.6 W118 23.8
81 thru 83	N33 56.5 W118 23.8
84	N33 56.4 W118 23.8
West Pads	
1,2	N33 56.7 W118 25.6
3,4	N33 56.6 W118 25.6
5	N33 56.7 W118 25.6
6	N33 56.7 W118 25.7
R-1	N33 56.7 W118 25.9
R-2	N33 56.6 W118 25.9
R-3	N33 56.6 W118 26.0
R-4	N33 56.7 W118 26.0

CHANGES: New chart.

17

NOS
Approach Charts

THERE ARE NO HARD AND FAST RULES FOR CARTOGRAPHERS TO FOLLOW WHEN producing approach plates as long as all necessary information is presented. Many pilots think that the National Ocean Service (NOS) charts are confusing because they cram a lot of information on one sheet of paper. Others say the NOS charts are much better than the Jeppesen products because NOS charts give you all the information you need on one piece of paper without making you turn pages to discover items such as the airport diagram. This all boils down to personal choice, which will depend, to an extent, on what you used while you were learning.

The NOS charts come in bound volumes that are updated every 56 days, with a Change Notice volume issued on the 28th day. It is possible, though, to get them in either a spiral ring-type or loose-leaf style, held together by metal clips. These versions are available through the Air Chart Company in Venice, California, operated by the world famous unlimited air racer, Howie Keefe, who for many years owned and flew the clipped-wing P-51 *Miss America*. Howie also offers an interesting approach to chart updates that saves a lot of time and can be applied to both NOS and Jeppesen charts.

General information and abbreviations for NOS charts appear near the front of the volume and tell you that distances are in nautical miles (NM), except for the visibility which will be in statute miles (SM), and that the RVR will be in hundreds of feet. The ceilings shown will be in feet above the airport elevation, and the radials, bearings, headings, and courses are magnetic.

The approaches themselves are arranged by airport name, and then, if the airport has more than one approach, they are listed with the NDB approach first, followed by ILS, LOC, LOC/DME, VOR, VOR/DME, and RNAV approaches.

ILS BY NOS

FIGURE 17-1 shows the ILS approach for Runway 9L at Opa Locka, Florida. The upper-left and lower-left corners of the chart identify the specific approach (in this case, ILS RWY 9L) in bold letters. The upper-right and lower-right corners identify the airport's name in upper case letters and its geographical location in smaller upper case letters. The three-letter identifier follows the airport name. In the center of the lower margin (called the trailer) you will find the latitude and longitude coordinates.

The plan view comprises the upper two-thirds of the plate. The profile view is below the plan view on the left. The minimums information is below the profile view, followed by any notes. The airport diagram is located below the plan view on the right side of the plate (large airports will have a separate airport chart), including any appropriate notes, and the distance and time from the FAF to the MAP is under the airport diagram, when applicable. So, you can see that there is a great deal of information on one side of an approach plate. But some of it is difficult for an old or tired pair of eyes to read, and the pulp paper it's printed on doesn't make it any easier. If I were using these plates, I would make a magnifying glass part of my flight kit.

You should be aware of the large circle on the plan view. In FIG. 17-1 this circle depicts a 10-nautical-mile radius. It is not necessarily drawn around the airport, but rather around the facility upon which the Minimum Sector Altitudes (MSAs) are predicated. And although it is usually of 10-NM radius, it can vary. So check the radius when you look at the chart. The radius can be found along the edge of the circle. The airport may not even be within the circle, as in the case of FIG. 17-1, where the 10-mile ring just barely chops across some of the runways.

I mentioned MSAs. Take a look at the bottom-left portion of the plan view and you will see the ones for Opa Locka. The data above the circle tell you that the facility the MSA is predicated on is, in this case, the Miami (MIA) VOR, and the radius is 25 NM. Note that, in the northwest sector, from a bearing to the VOR of 040° (220-degree radial) through a bearing of 180 degrees (360-degree radial) the MSA is 1500 feet MSL. The MSA for the rest of the circle is 2500 feet MSL.

The radio frequencies you will use on approach are listed in the upper-left corner of the plan view. With the exception of the ATIS frequency, these are listed in the order that you will use them, beginning with Approach Control and continuing down through Ground Control. Any note concerning the airport, in

Fig. 17-1

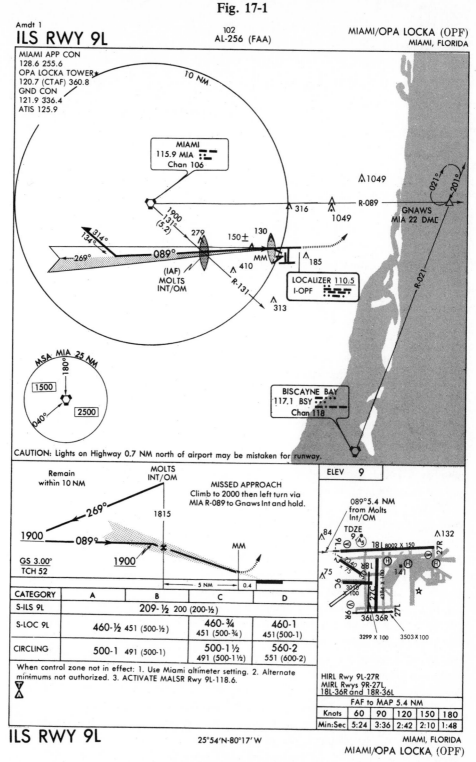

Amdt 1
ILS RWY 9L

102
AL-256 (FAA)

MIAMI/OPA LOCKA (OPF)
MIAMI, FLORIDA

MIAMI APP CON
128.6 255.6
OPA LOCKA TOWER★
120.7 (CTAF) 360.8
GND CON
121.9 336.4
ATIS 125.9

MIAMI
115.9 MIA
Chan 106

10 NM

∧1049
R-089
∧ 316
∧ 1049
GNAWS
MIA 22 DME

021°
201°

1900
131°
(3.2)
279
314°
134°
269°
089°
150±
130
MM
410
R-131
∧ 185
∧ 313
(IAF)
MOLTS
INT/OM

LOCALIZER 110.5
I-OPF

R-021

MSA: MIA 25 NM
1500
180°
040°
2500

BISCAYNE BAY
117.1 BSY
Chan 118

CAUTION: Lights on Highway 0.7 NM north of airport may be mistaken for runway.

MOLTS
INT/OM
Remain
within 10 NM

MISSED APPROACH
Climb to 2000 then left turn via
MIA R-089 to Gnaws Int and hold.

ELEV 9

269°
1815
1900
089°
1900
MM

GS 3.00°
TCH 52

5 NM
0.4

089° 5.4 NM
from Molts
Int/OM

TDZE
9
∧84
∧132
18L 8002 X 150
27R
18R
141
9C
3016
X 100
27C
75
9R
36L 36R
27L
3299 X 100
3503 X 100

CATEGORY	A	B	C	D
S-ILS 9L	209-½ 200 (200-½)			
S-LOC 9L	460-½ 451 (500-½)		460-¾ 451 (500-¾)	460-1 451 (500-1)
CIRCLING	500-1 491 (500-1)		500-1½ 491 (500-1½)	560-2 551 (600-2)

When control zone not in effect: 1. Use Miami altimeter setting. 2. Alternate
minimums not authorized. 3. ACTIVATE MALSR Rwy 9L-118.6.

HIRL Rwy 9L-27R
MIRL Rwys 9R-27L,
18L-36R and 18R-36L

FAF to MAP 5.4 NM					
Knots	60	90	120	150	180
Min:Sec	5:24	3:36	2:42	2:10	1:48

ILS RWY 9L

25°54'N-80°17'W

MIAMI, FLORIDA
MIAMI/OPA LOCKA (OPF)

(NOT FOR USE IN NAVIGATION)

this case the note about the highway lights, is printed near the bottom of the plan view.

Missed approach instructions are printed in the profile view as are any procedure turn instructions. In the case of an ILS, both the glide slope angle and the Threshold Crossing Height of the glide slope are indicated in the profile view section.

Notes concerning displaced thresholds and lighting are included with the airport diagram. On approaches other than ILS and LOC, a helpful arrow indicates the direction from which you will be approaching the airport.

Look at the minimums table of the approach plate. Notice the categories listed along the top, and the various approaches listed down the left side. In this case, the approach minimums are for straight-in approaches (ILS and LOC) to Runway 9L, and for circling approaches to the airport.

A LOT OF PAGE TURNING

In the next section of the approach plate you will find information that doesn't fit anywhere else. In the case of Opa Locka you find both a ''T'' and an ''A'' in reverse type, set within black triangles. The ''T'' indicates that the takeoff minimums are not standard, or there are published departure procedures, or both. The ''A'' indicates that the alternate minimums are not standard. In either or both cases, you must turn to the list of tabulated data for airports, in the front of the booklet.

There is only so much room on one 5″×8″ piece of paper; it's virtually impossible to include everything on one plate. As a result, NOS charts show non-standard takeoff and landing minimums on pages other than the approach chart.

When you open the approach chart book, you find the explanatory pages. Although they are laid out quite logically, they still require you to do a lot of page turning. The explanation of the approach categories is quite straightforward, especially regarding how you must change your category to a higher one if you are flying a circling approach in which your aircraft will be maneuvering in a configuration that increases the stall speed.

You will find the Landing Minima Format at the bottom of FIG. 17-2 (as a tribute to NOS, I'll use the word ''minima'' for awhile!). It is different enough from the Jeppesen format to justify an explanation.

While Jeppesen puts the categories in a vertical column and breaks up the horizontal row to show the various minima for inoperative-component approaches, NOS charts list the categories horizontally, then show the various approaches in columns. In the case of an ILS approach, if the glide slope is inoperative, you only look down to the next line to find the minima for the LOC approach. Notice that, in FIG. 17-2, the minima for the ILS and LOC are for straight-in approaches, signified by the ''S''. If you use the ILS or LOC to reach the airport, but plan to circle to land, find the minima on the bottom line, labeled ''CIRCLING''.

Fig. 17-2

INSTRUMENT APPROACH PROCEDURES EXPLANATION OF TERMS

The United States Standard for Terminal Instrument Procedures (TERPS) is the approved criteria for formulating instrument approach procedures.

AIRCRAFT APPROACH CATEGORIES

Speeds are based on 1.3 times the stall speed in the landing configuration at maximum gross landing weight. An aircraft shall fit in only one category. If it is necessary to maneuver at speeds in excess of the upper limit of a speed range for a category, the minimums for the next higher category should be used. For example, an aircraft which falls in Category A, but is circling to land at a speed in excess of 91 knots, should use the approach Category B minimums when circling to land. See following category limits:

MANEUVERING TABLE

Approach Category	A	B	C	D	E
Speed (Knots)	0-90	91-120	121-140	141-165	Abv 165

RVR/Meteorological Visibility Comparable Values

The following table shall be used for converting RVR to meteorlogical visibility when RVR is not reported for the runway of intended operation. Adjustment of landing minima may be required – see Inoperative Components Table.

RVR (feet)	Visibility (statute miles)	RVR (feet)	Visibility (statute miles)
1600	$\frac{1}{4}$	4500	$\frac{7}{8}$
2400	$\frac{1}{2}$	5000	1
3200	$\frac{5}{8}$	6000	$1\frac{1}{4}$
4000	$\frac{3}{4}$		

LANDING MINIMA FORMAT

In this example airport elevation is 1179, and runway touchdown zone elevation is 1152.

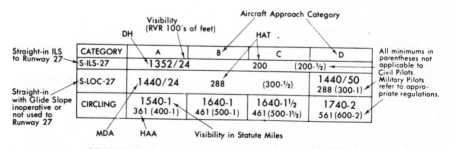

CORRECTIONS, COMMENTS AND/OR PROCUREMENT

Forward Corrections and Comments to:

National Ocean Service
Aeronautical Chart Branch N/CG31
6010 Executive Blvd. Rockville, Md. 20852
Tel: (301) 443-8077

Procure from:

National Ocean Service
Distribution Branch N/CG33
Riverdale, Md. 20737
Tel: (301) 436-6993

(NOT FOR USE IN NAVIGATION)

Unlike the Jeppesen charts, with the NOS versions, if you have inoperative components on your approach, you are obliged to turn to another page to see what changes you must make to your minima (FIG. 17-3). Although this format is fairly easy to understand, you would be hard pressed to find the correct page if you were already on your approach when something decided to quit. In fact, unless you had a copilot on board who could do the research for you, you would probably have to execute a missed approach until you got everything straightened out. With the Jeppesen chart, you could glance at the bottom of the page and make the necessary adjustments to the MDA more efficiently. This is an important point, particularly when making an approach to an alternate, when you're low on fuel, or if you are going into a busy field and a miss would put you way back in a long daisy chain.

Also noteworthy in FIG. 17-3 is the caution that reads:

> This table may be amended by notes on the approach chart. Such notes
> apply only to the particular approach category(ies) as stated.

Some amendments are indicated by a cross that appears in the type-of-approach block, with the appropriate note below, as you see in FIG. 17-4. The note increases the required visibility to RVR 5000 for Category D aircraft conducting straight-in localizer approaches to Miami International's Runway 9L when the middle marker is inoperative. At other times, these changes will be indicated by an asterisk. You may even find some increases listed in the notes with no asterisk, cross, or other indication. So, once again, you have to read *everything* on every chart.

BASIC TAKEOFF AND ALTERNATE MINIMA

The basic regulations that apply to minima are FAR 91.116(f) and 91.83(c). In effect, these regulations set up standard takeoff and alternate minima. For takeoff, these require 1-SM visibility for airplanes with one or two engines, and ½-SM visibility for those with more than two engines, except for Part 91 operators, as explained earlier.

To meet standard alternate minima, you need a 600-foot ceiling and 2-SM visibility for precision (ILS and PAR) approaches and an 800-foot ceiling with 2-SM visibility for nonprecision approaches. In the Jeppesen format, all of this information, including any nonstandard requirements, is listed under the takeoff and alternate minimum formats which are found on each airport chart.

The NOS charts present this information in a different manner. NOS lists takeoff and alternate minima in the front of the booklet. These pages (FIGS. 17-5 through 17-8) spell out the standard minima, as mentioned above, and then list each airport that has minima different from standard. To find out if the airport you are operating at has nonstandard minima, you need only look at the note

Fig. 17-3

Instrument Approach Procedures (Charts)
INOPERATIVE COMPONENTS OR VISUAL AIDS TABLE

Landing minimums published on instrument approach procedure charts are based upon full operation of all components and visual aids associated with the particular instrument approach chart being used. Higher minimums are required with inoperative components or visual aids as indicated below. If more than one component is inoperative, each minimum is raised to the highest minimum required by any single component that is inoperative. ILS glide slope inoperative minimums are published on instrument approach charts as localizer minimums. This table may be amended by notes on the approach chart. Such notes apply only to the particular approach category(ies) as stated. See legend page for description of components indicated below.

(1) ILS, MLS, and PAR

Inoperative Component or Aid	Approach Category	Increase DH	Increase Visibility
MM*	ABC	50 feet	None
MM*	D	50 feet	¼ mile
ALSF 1 & 2, MALSR, & SSALR	ABCD	None	¼ mile

*Not applicable to PAR

(2) ILS with visibility minimum of 1,800 or 2,000 RVR.

MM	ABC	50 feet	To 2400 RVR
MM	D	50 feet	To 4000 RVR
ALSF 1 & 2, MALSR, & SSALR	ABCD	None	To 4000 RVR
TDZL, RCLS	ABCD	None	To 2400 RVR
RVR	ABCD	None	To ½ mile

(3) VOR, VOR/DME, VORTAC, VOR (TAC), VOR/DME (TAC), LOC, LOC/DME, LDA, LDA/DME, SDF, SDF/DME, RNAV, and ASR

Inoperative Visual Aid	Approach Category	Increase MDA	Increase Visibility
ALSF 1 & 2, MALSR, & SSALR	ABCD	None	½ mile
SSALS, MALS & ODALS	ABC	None	¼ mile

(4) NDB

ALSF 1 & 2, MALSR, & SSALR	C	None	½ mile
	ABD	None	¼ mile
MALS, SSALS, ODALS	ABC	None	¼ mile

(NOT FOR USE IN NAVIGATION)

Fig. 17-4

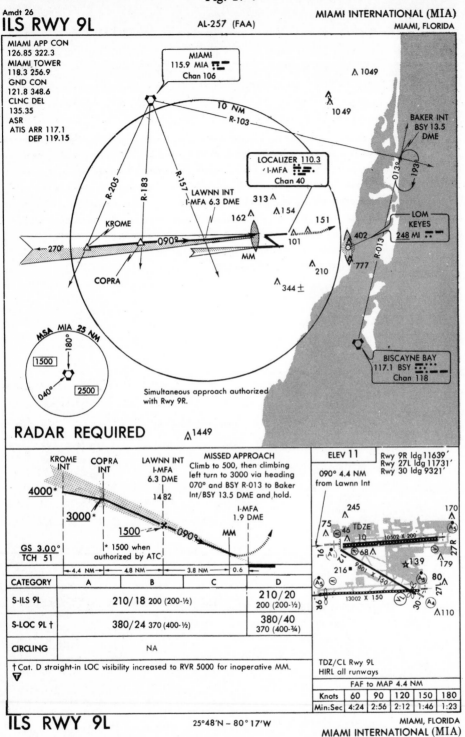

Amdt 26

ILS RWY 9L

AL-257 (FAA)

MIAMI INTERNATIONAL (MIA)
MIAMI, FLORIDA

MIAMI APP CON
126.85 322.3
MIAMI TOWER
118.3 256.9
GND CON
121.8 348.6
CLNC DEL
135.35
ASR
ATIS ARR 117.1
DEP 119.15

MIAMI
115.9 MIA
Chan 106

10 NM
R-103

BAKER INT
BSY 13.5
DME

LOCALIZER 110.3
I-MFA
Chan 40

LAWNN INT
I-MFA 6.3 DME

LOM
KEYES
248 MI

KROME

COPRA

MM

BISCAYNE BAY
117.1 BSY
Chan 118

MSA MIA 25 NM
1500 — 180° — 2500
040°

Simultaneous approach authorized
with Rwy 9R.

RADAR REQUIRED

	KROME INT	COPRA INT	LAWNN INT I-MFA 6.3 DME	I-MFA 1.9 DME
	4000*	3000*	1482	
			1500	MM

MISSED APPROACH
Climb to 500, then climbing
left turn to 3000 via heading
070° and BSY R-013 to Baker
Int/BSY 13.5 DME and hold.

GS 3.00°
TCH 51

* 1500 when
authorized by ATC

090°

	4.4 NM	4.8 NM	3.8 NM	0.6

CATEGORY	A	B	C	D
S-ILS 9L	210/18 200 (200-½)			210/20 200 (200-½)
S-LOC 9L †	380/24 370 (400-½)			380/40 370 (400-¾)
CIRCLING	NA			

† Cat. D straight-in LOC visibility increased to RVR 5000 for inoperative MM.

ELEV 11

090° 4.4 NM
from Lawnn Int

Rwy 9R ldg 11639'
Rwy 27L ldg 11731'
Rwy 30 ldg 9321'

TDZ/CL Rwy 9L
HIRL all runways

FAF to MAP 4.4 NM				
Knots	60	90	120	150	180
Min:Sec	4:24	2:56	2:12	1:46	1:23

ILS RWY 9L

25°48'N – 80°17'W

MIAMI, FLORIDA
MIAMI INTERNATIONAL (MIA)

(NOT FOR USE IN NAVIGATION)

section of the individual approach chart. There you will find a white "T" in an inverted black triangle if the takeoff minima are nonstandard, and a white "A" in a black triangle if the alternate minima are nonstandard. Then turn to the appropriate page in the front of the book and check out the differences, or you can just look up the airports in these pages to begin with. In either case, it amounts to a lot of page turning or trying to memorize the standard minima, which leads to errors. The less you commit to memory the better off you are.

As with all minima, the takeoff and alternate minima are based on obstacle clearance and aircraft performance. You will see, for example, that although there are no ceiling requirements in the standard takeoff minima, you might have them in nonstandard situations, such as seen in FIGS. 17-5 through 17-8.

In the note section for Albert Whitted Airport in St. Petersburg, Florida (FIG. 17-9), you will find a note that tells you:

> When control zone not effective the following applies: 1. Use Tampa, FL altimeter setting. 2. Increase all MDAs 40 feet. 3. Alternate minimums not authorized.

The note goes on to say that you need ADF, DME, or RADAR for this approach. Looking below the table you find the symbols that tell you that nonstandard takeoff and alternate minima are specified for this airport, so look at the tabulations in the front of the book.

FIGURE 17-5 lists the standard alternate minimums at the top of the page. Then look down at "ALBERT WHITTED" and find that you get an answer like you'd find in the Yellow Pages—"SEE ST. PETERSBURG, FL." So, you turn to St. Petersburg on the next page (FIG. 17-6), where you see that Whitted is not authorized for use as an alternate airport via the VOR Rwy 18 approach when the control zone is not effective.

Then look up the nonstandard takeoff minimums (FIG. 17-7). Once again you have the standard minimums spelled out at the top of the page, and you have to turn the page to FIG. 17-8 to find the note for ALBERT WHITTED airport. You see that, for Runways 6, 18, 24, and 36 (in other words, all of the runways), all takeoffs require both a ceiling of 200 feet and visibility of one mile.

Look at some of the other nonstandard takeoff and landing minimums on these pages to review some of the differences you will experience in instrument flying. Next time you look through a complete set of approach charts, whether they be Jeppesen or NOS, see if you can find the possible reasons for the variations.

PICKING A CHART APART

Let's now look further at the Albert Whitted approach chart (FIG. 17-9). The procedure turn for this approach is a holding pattern over the St. Petersburg VOR-

TAC, which is also the IAF for the airport. The holding pattern, when depicted in lieu of a procedure turn, is mandatory except when radar vectors are being provided.

Note that the holding pattern is shown in both the plan and profile views. The inbound leg of the holding pattern should be one minute in duration.

The distance from the IAF to the FAF is 5 NM. The FAF is PINEL intersection which can be identified in three ways: it's 5 DME from St. Petersburg VOR (PIE), it's on the 073-degree bearing to PICNY (an outer compass locator for another approach), or it can be identified by a radar fix. (Now you can see why ADF, DME, or radar is required for this approach.) From PINEL to the MAP is another 3.9 NM, or 8.9 DME from the VOR. Under the airport diagram you can see a table which you can use to estimate time from the FAF to the MAP. Remember, the speed you want to use is your *ground speed in knots*.

An arrow runs from the upper part of the airport diagram down toward Runway 18. The note on it reads "158 degrees 3.9 NM from Pinel Int." This helps you visualize the path your aircraft will fly on the approach.

AIRPORT LIGHTING

In the airport diagram in FIG. 17-10 you see a "V" within a circle alongside the numerals for Runways 36L/18R, 9/27, and 18L, and "V$_L$" in a circle next to Runway 36R. Looking at the bottom-right of FIG. 17-11 you find that these letters indicate that the runways are equipped with VASI (Visual Approach Slope Indicators.) The "V" is for the two-bar VASI that most of us are familiar with, which provides approach slope guidance for most aircraft. The "V$_L$" indicates a three-bar VASI, which uses an upper bar to provide a higher Threshold Crossing Height to accommodate long-bodied or jumbo aircraft.

In the two-bar system, if both upper and lower bars are white you are too high; if they're both red, you're too low. With red on top and white on the bottom, you're on the glide slope.

Three-bar systems are to give large aircraft adequate gear clearance when crossing the threshold. Those of us flying light aircraft, and even carriers flying other than wide- or long-bodies, can use the lower pair of light bars. Larger aircraft use the upper pair. If you've ever seen a wide-bodied jet on approach and have noticed how high the pilot sits above the landing gear, you can see why the third bar is there. His main gear are 50 feet lower than his eyes, so when following the standard VASI, there would be too great a chance of landing short.

In FIG. 17-10 you can see the "A1", "A3", and "A5" inside circles on the airport diagram. These are symbols representing various approach light systems, which are illustrated on FIG. 17-11. The dot at the top of those circles tells you that the runway also has sequence flashing lights.

You can find the instructions for activating the pilot radio-controlled airport lighting systems at the front of the approach plate book. If you are flying to a

Fig. 17-5

INSTRUMENT APPROACH PROCEDURES (CHARTS)

⚠ IFR ALTERNATE MINIMUMS
(NOT APPLICABLE TO USA/USN/USAF)

Standard alternate minimums for nonprecision approaches are 800-2 (NDB, VOR, LOC, TACAN, LDA, VORTAC, VOR/DME or ASR); for precision approaches 600-2 (ILS or PAR). Airports within this geographical area that require alternate minimums other than standard or alternate minimums with restrictions are listed below. NA - means alternate minimums are not authorized due to unmonitored facility or absence of weather reporting service. Civil pilots see FAR 91. USA/USN/USAF pilots refer to appropriate regulations.

NAME	ALTERNATE MINIMUMS	NAME	ALTERNATE MINIMUMS
ALBERT WHITTED — SEE ST. PETERSBURG, FL		FT. MYERS, FL	
		SOUTHWEST FLORIDA REGIONAL ...	NDB Rwy 6
ALEXANDER HAMILTON — SEE CHRISTIANSTED, ST. CROIX, VI			ILS Rwy 6*
			VOR Rwy 24
			RADAR-1
CHARLOTTE AMALIE, ST. THOMAS, VI		*ILS, Category E 700-2¼; LOC, Category E 800-2¼	
CYRIL E KING	VOR-A, 1200-3	NA when control tower closed.	
	ILS Rwy 9*		
*ILS, LOC 1200-3		GAINESVILLE REGIONAL, FL	
			VOR-A*
CHRISTIANSTED, ST. CROIX, VI		*Category C, 800-2¼; Category D, 800-2½.	
ALEXANDER HAMILTON	NDB Rwy 9, 1200-3		
	VOR Rwy 27*	KEY WEST INTL, FL	
*Non-DME equipped aircraft 900-3.			NDB-A
			VOR-B
CYRIL E KING — SEE CHARLOTTE AMALIE, ST. THOMAS, VI			RADAR-1
		NA when Key West FSS is closed.	
DAYTONA BEACH REGIONAL, FL		LAKELAND MUNI, FL	
	VOR Rwy 16		NDB Rwy 5
Category D, 800-2¼			ILS Rwy 5
			VOR Rwy 13
FLORENCE CITY-COUNTY, SC			VOR Rwy 27†
	NDB Rwy 9*	†Categories C, D, 800-2½	
	ILS Rwy 9†	NA when control zone not in effect.	
*Category D 800-2¼			
†ILS Categories A, B, C, 700-2; Category D 700-2¼; LOC Category D 800-2¼		LUIS MUNOZ MARIN INTL — SEE SAN JUAN, PR	
		MARATHON FLIGHT STRIP, FL	
FT. LAUDERDALE, FL			NDB Rwy 7
FT. LAUDERDALE EXECUTIVE	RNAV Rwy 8	NA when local altimeter and weather not available.	
	NDB Rwy 8*		
	ILS Rwy 8†	MAYAGUEZ, PR	
NA when control zone not in effect.			VOR Rwy 9
*Category D, 800-2¼		Categories A, B, C, 900-2½	
†ILS, Category D, 700-2			
FT. LAUDERDALE-HOLLYWOOD INTL			
	ILS Rwy 9L, 700-2		
	ILS Rwy 27R*		
*ILS, 700-2			

SE-3

Fig. 17-6

NAME	ALTERNATE MINIMUMS	NAME	ALTERNATE MINIMUMS

MERCEDITA — SEE PONCE, PR

MIAMI, FL
OPA LOCKA
                RNAV Rwy 9L
                VOR Rwy 9L
                ILS Rwy 9L
  NA when control zone not effective.

  TAMIAMI . . . . ILS Rwy 9R
  ILS, Category D, 700-2

OPA LOCKA — SEE MIAMI, FL

ORLANDO EXECUTIVE, FL
                VOR Rwy 13
  VOR only Category D, 800-2 ¼ .

PALM BEACH INTERNATIONAL — SEE
WEST PALM BEACH, FL

PANAMA CITY-BAY COUNTY, FL
                RADAR-1
             VOR or TACAN-A
          VOR or TACAN Rwy 14
          VOR or TACAN Rwy 32
  †ILS, Category D, 700-2
  NA when control zone not in effect except for
  operators with approved weather reporting
  service.

PENSACOLA REGIONAL, FL
                RADAR-1
  NA when control tower closed.

POMPANO BEACH AIRPARK, FL
                VOR Rwy 14
  NA when control zone not in effect.

PONCE, PR
  MERCEDITA . . . . VOR Rwy 30, 900-2 ¾
  NA when control tower closed.

ST. PETERSBURG, FL
  ALBERT WHITTED . . . . VOR Rwy 18
  NA when control zone not effective.

  ST. PETERSBURG-CLEARWATER INTL
                ILS Rwy 17L
  ILS, LOC, Category E, 1000-3

SAN JUAN, PR
  LUIS MUNOZ MARIN INTL . . . . ILS Rwy 10
  ILS Category E, 700-2 ¼ ; LOC Category E,
  800-2 ¼

SANFORD, FL
                NDB Rwy 9
                RNAV Rwy 9
                ILS Rwy 9
  NA when control zone not in effect.

SARASOTA-BRADENTON, FL
                NDB Rwy 32
                ILS Rwy 32
                VOR Rwy 14
                VOR Rwy 22
           VOR Rwy 32, 900-2 ¾
                RADAR-1
                ILS Rwy 14
  NA when control zone not in effect

SOUTHWEST FLORIDA REGIONAL — SEE
FT. MYERS, FL

SPACE CENTER EXECUTIVE — SEE
TITUSVILLE, FL

TALLAHASSEE MUNI, FL
                ILS Rwy 27L†
                ILS Rwy 36*
  †ILS Categories A, B, C, 700-2, Category D,
  700-2 ¼
  †LOC, Category D, 800-2 ¼
  *NA when control tower closed.

TAMIAMI — SEE MIAMI, FL

TAMPA INTL, FL
                ILS Rwy 36L
  ILS, LOC, Category E, 1000-3.

TITUSVILLE, FL
  SPACE CENTER EXECUTIVE
                NDB Rwy 18
                ILS Rwy 36†
  NA when control zone not effective.
  †ILS, 700-2.

WEST PALM BEACH, FL
  PALM BEACH INTERNATIONAL . . . . . ILS Rwy 9L*
                VOR Rwy 13†
  *ILS Category D, 700-2.
  †Category C, 800-2 ¼ ; Category
  D, 800-2 ½

SE-3

(NOT FOR USE IN NAVIGATION)

Fig. 17-7

INSTRUMENT APPROACH PROCEDURES (CHARTS)
▼IFR TAKE-OFF MINIMUMS AND DEPARTURE PROCEDURES
Civil Airports and Selected Military Airports

CIVIL USERS: FAR 91 prescribes take-off rules and establishes take-off minimums as follows:
(1) Aircraft having two engines or less – one statute mile. (2) Aircraft having more than two engines – one-half statute mile.

MILITARY USERS: Special IFR departure procedures, not published as Standard Instrument Departure (SIDs), and civil take-off minima are included below and are established to assist pilots in obstruction avoidance. Refer to appropriate service directives for take-off minimums.

Airports with IFR take-off minimums other than standard are listed below. Departure procedures and/or ceiling visibility minimums are established to assist pilots conducting IFR flight in avoiding obstructions during climb to the minimum enroute altitude. Take-off minimums and departures apply to all runways unless otherwise specified. Altitudes, unless otherwise indicated, are minimum altitudes in feet MSL.

NAME	TAKE-OFF MINIMUMS	NAME	TAKE-OFF MINIMUMS

ALBERT WHITTED — SEE ST. PETERSBURG, FL

ALEXANDER HAMILTON — SEE CHRISTIANSTED, ST. CROIX, VI

BUNNELL, FL
FLAGLER COUNTY
IFR DEPARTURE PROCEDURE: Rwy 29, aircraft departing on a course between 270° clockwise to 360° climb on heading 270° to 1300' before proceeding on course.

CHARLOTTE AMALIE, ST. THOMAS, VI
CYRIL E KING .... Rwy 9, 400-1
IFR DEPARTURE PROCEDURES: Rwy 9, immediate climbing right turn to heading 120°. Continue climb to 2000 before turning north. Rwy 27, climb runway heading to 2000 before turning north.

CHRISTIANSTED, ST. CROIX, VI
ALEXANDER HAMILTON .... Rwy 9, 300-1
IFR DEPARTURE PROCEDURE: Rwy 27, climb runway heading to 1100 before turning right.

CRAIG MUNI — SEE JACKSONVILLE, FL

CYRIL E KING — SEE CHARLOTTE AMALIE, ST. THOMAS, VI

DAYTONA BEACH REGIONAL, FL
Rwys 6R, 16, 24L/34, 300-1

DELAND MUNI/SIDNEY H. TAYLOR FIELD, FL
IFR DEPARTURE PROCEDURE: Rwys 5, 8, 12, 26, 30, 36, aircraft proceeding on a course between 120° CW to 260°, fly runway heading to 1800. Rwy 18, aircraft proceeding on a course between 120° CW to 260°, fly heading 120° to 1800. Rwy 23, aircraft proceeding on a course between 120° CW to 260°, fly heading 260° to 1800.

DESTIN-FT. WALTON BEACH, FL
IFR DEPARTURE PROCEDURE: Rwy 14, climb runway heading to 400 before making turn.

FLAGLER COUNTY — SEE BUNNELL, FL

FORT LAUDERDALE, FL
FT. LAUDERDALE-EXECUTIVE
IFR DEPARTURE PROCEDURE: Rwy 8, fly runway heading to 300 feet before turning north. Rwy 26, fly runway heading to 500 feet before turning south.

FORT LAUDERDALE-HOLLYWOOD INTL
Rwys 13, 27L, 300-1
IFR DEPARTURE PROCEDURE: Rwys 9L/R, climb runway heading to 500 before turning.

FORT MYERS, FL
PAGE FIELD .... Rwy 31, 300-1*
*or standard with minimum climb of 280 feet per NM to 300'.

FORT PIERCE, FL
ST. LUCIE COUNTY INTL .... Rwy 18, 600-1*
Rwy 36, 600-1†
*or standard with minimum climb of 300' per NM to 600 or turn right heading 270° to 600 before proceeding on course.
†or standard with minimum climb of 250' per NM to 600.
IFR DEPARTURE PROCEDURE: Rwy 14 climb runway heading to 600 before turning right.

ISLA GRANDE — SEE SAN JUAN, PR

JACKSONVILLE, FL
CRAIG MUNI .... Rwy 22, 1100-2*
*or standard with specified departure.
IFR DEPARTURE PROCEDURE: Rwy 22 minimum climb of 290' per NM to 1100 required or climb straight ahead to 500 then left or right turn of at least 045° to 1100 before proceeding on course.

KEY WEST INTL, FL
IFR DEPARTURE PROCEDURE: Rwy 9, climb runway heading to 200 before turning north. Rwy 27, climb runway heading to 200 before turning south.

SE-3

Fig. 17-8

NAME	TAKE-OFF MINIMUMS	NAME	TAKE-OFF MINIMUMS

KISSIMMEE MUNI, FL
Rwy 6, 300-1

LUIS MUNOZ MARIN INTL — SEE
SAN JUAN, PR

MARCO ISLAND, FL
IFR DEPARTURE PROCEDURE: Rwy 35, aircraft proceeding on a course between 270° clockwise to 030° fly heading 030° to 1000' before proceeding on course.

MAYAGUEZ, PR
Rwy 9, 700-1*
*or standard with a minimum climb of 350' per NM to 2300.
IFR DEPARTURE PROCEDURE: Rwys 9 and 27, climb on R-259 within 10 NM to cross MAZ VOR/DME at or above 2500 Northbound and Southbound RTE-1 and Northeast bound G-3.

MERCEDITA — SEE PONCE, PR

MIAMI, FL
MIAMI INTL . . . . Rwy 9L, 800-1*
Rwy 9R, 800-1†
Rwy 12, 800-1‡
*or standard with minimum climb of 220' per NM to 1100 or climb runway heading to 1100 before turning right.
†or standard with minimum climb of 220' per NM to 1100 or comply with RADAR vectors.
‡or standard with minimum climb of 220' per NM to 1100 or climb runway heading to 1100 before turning left.

OPA LOCKA
Rwys 9R, 9C, 12, 18R, 27L, 27C, 30, 36L, NA.

TAMIAMI
IFR DEPARTURE PROCEDURE: All Rwys climb runway heading to 1400' before turning south.

NASA SHUTTLE LANDING FACILITY — SEE
TITUSVILLE, FL

NEW SMYRNA BEACH, FL
Rwys 2, 6, 300-1

OPA LOCKA — SEE MIAMI, FL

PAGE FIELD — SEE FT. MYERS, FL

PAHOKEE, FL
PALM BEACH COUNTY GLADES
Rwy 7, 35, 400-1
Rwy 17, 300-1

PALM BEACH COUNTY GLADES — SEE
PAHOKEE, FL

PERRY-FOLEY, FL
IFR DEPARTURE PROCEDURE: Rwys 6, 12, 30, 36, climb on runway heading to 800 before turning.

PETER O. KNIGHT — SEE TAMPA, FL

POMPANO BEACH AIRPARK, FL
Rwy 14, 400-1

PONCE, PR
MERCEDITA . . . . Rwy 30, 500-1
IFR DEPARTURE PROCEDURES: Rwy 30 immediate climbing left turn to 2100 direct PSE VOR/DME. Climb in holding pattern to 2700 for Route 9, 3500 for Route 11 before departing PSE VOR/DME. Rwy 12 climb runway heading direct PSE VOR/DME continue climb on R-130 to 2100 with right turn direct PSE VOR/DME. Climb in holding pattern to 2700 for Route 9, 3500 for Route 11 before departing PSE VOR/DME.

ST. LUCIE COUNTY INTL — SEE
FORT PIERCE, FL

ST. PETERSBURG, FL
ALBERT WHITTED . . . . . . Rwys 6, 18, 24, 36, 200-1

SAN JUAN, PR
ISLA GRANDE . . . . Rwy 9, 400-1
Over 2 eng . . . . NA

LUIS MUNOZ MARIN INTL
Rwy 8, ¾ mile**
Rwy 10, ½ mile**
Rwys 26, 28, 300-1*
*or standard with a minimum climb of 450' per NM to 1000.
IFR DEPARTURE PROCEDURE: SE bound (120° CW 165°) minimum climb of 365' per NM to 4200' or climb to 2900' before entering this sector.
**(FAR 135).

SE-3

Fig. 17-9

Amdt 5

VOR RWY 18

AL-613 (FAA)

ST. PETERSBURG/ALBERT WHITTED (SPG)
ST. PETERSBURG, FLORIDA

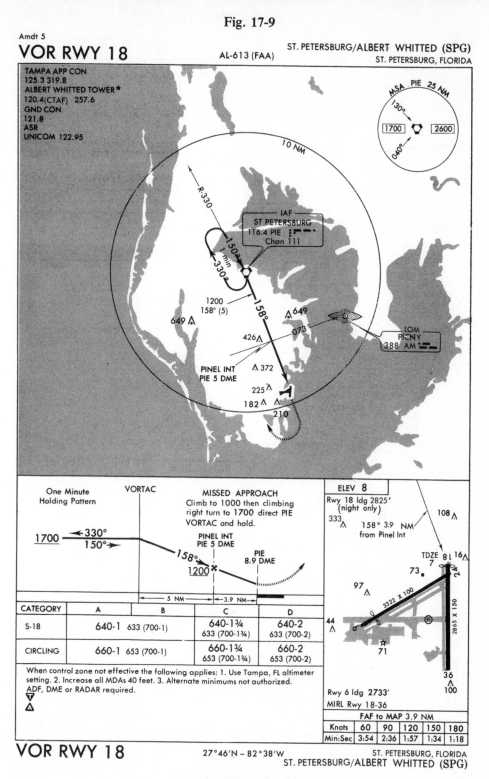

TAMPA APP CON
125.3 319.8
ALBERT WHITTED TOWER ★
120.4(CTAF) 257.6
GND CON
121.8
ASR
UNICOM 122.95

MSA PIE 25 NM
130°
1700   2600
040°

10 NM

R-330

IAF
ST PETERSBURG
116.4 PIE ⋮⋮⋮
Chan 111

1 50°
330°
1 min

1200
158° (5)

158°

649 ∧

073°

426 ∧

LOM
PICNY
388 AM ⋮⋮⋮

PINEL INT
PIE 5 DME

∧ 372

225 ∧

182 ∧

210

649 ∧

One Minute Holding Pattern   **VORTAC**

MISSED APPROACH
Climb to 1000 then climbing right turn to 1700 direct PIE VORTAC and hold.

1700 ←330°
150°→

PINEL INT
PIE 5 DME

158°

1200 ✕

PIE
8.9 DME

|← 5 NM →|← 3.9 NM →|

CATEGORY	A	B	C	D
S-18	640-1 633 (700-1)		640-1¾ 633 (700-1¾)	640-2 633 (700-2)
CIRCLING	660-1 653 (700-1)		660-1¾ 653 (700-1¾)	660-2 653 (700-2)

When control zone not effective the following applies: 1. Use Tampa, FL altimeter setting. 2. Increase all MDAs 40 feet. 3. Alternate minimums not authorized.
ADF, DME or RADAR required.
▽
△

ELEV 8

Rwy 18 ldg 2825'
(night only)

333 ∧

108 ∧

158° 3.9 NM
from Pinel Int

TDZE 8

16 ∧

73.

97 ∧

3322 X 100

44 ∧

(H)

★ 71

36
∧
100

Rwy 6 ldg 2733'
MIRL Rwy 18-36

FAF to MAP 3.9 NM					
Knots	60	90	120	150	180
Min:Sec	3:54	2:36	1:57	1:34	1:18

VOR RWY 18

27°46'N – 82°38'W

ST. PETERSBURG, FLORIDA
ST. PETERSBURG/ALBERT WHITTED (SPG)

(NOT FOR USE IN NAVIGATION)

201

Fig. 17-10

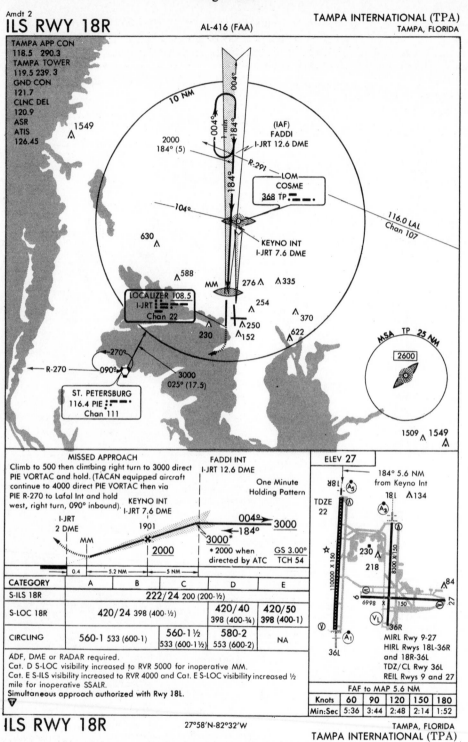

Fig. 17-10

Amdt 2
ILS RWY 18R   AL-416 (FAA)   TAMPA INTERNATIONAL (TPA)
TAMPA, FLORIDA

TAMPA APP CON 118.5 290.3
TAMPA TOWER 119.5 239.3
GND CON 121.7
CLNC DEL 120.9
ASR
ATIS 126.45

(IAF) FADDI I-JRT 12.6 DME

LOM COSME 368 TP

116.0 LAL Chan 107

KEYNO INT I-JRT 7.6 DME

LOCALIZER 108.5 I-JRT Chan 22

MSA TP 25 NM — 2600

ST. PETERSBURG 116.4 PIE Chan 111

MISSED APPROACH
Climb to 500 then climbing right turn to 3000 direct PIE VORTAC and hold. (TACAN equipped aircraft continue to 4000 direct PIE VORTAC then via PIE R-270 to Lafal Int and hold west, right turn, 090° inbound).

FADDI INT I-JRT 12.6 DME — One Minute Holding Pattern

KEYNO INT I-JRT 7.6 DME

GS 3.00° TCH 54

ELEV 27 — TDZE 22

FAF to MAP 5.6 NM

CATEGORY	A	B	C	D	E
S-ILS 18R	222/24 200 (200-½)				
S-LOC 18R	420/24 398 (400-½)			420/40 398 (400-¾)	420/50 398 (400-1)
CIRCLING	560-1 533 (600-1)		560-1½ 533 (600-1½)	580-2 553 (600-2)	NA

ADF, DME or RADAR required.
Cat. D S-LOC visibility increased to RVR 5000 for inoperative MM.
Cat. E S-ILS visibility increased to RVR 4000 and Cat. E S-LOC visibility increased ½ mile for inoperative SSALR.
Simultaneous approach authorized with Rwy 18L.

Knots	60	90	120	150	180
Min:Sec	5:36	3:44	2:48	2:14	1:52

ILS RWY 18R   27°58'N-82°32'W   TAMPA, FLORIDA
TAMPA INTERNATIONAL (TPA)

(NOT FOR USE IN NAVIGATION)

202

Fig. 17-11

LEGEND
INSTRUMENT APPROACH PROCEDURES (CHARTS)
APPROACH LIGHTING SYSTEMS – UNITED STATES

Each approach lighting system indicated on Airport Diagrams will bear a system identification indicated in legend.

A dot " • " portrayed with approach lighting letter identifier indicates sequenced flashing lights (F) installed with the approach lighting system e.g. (A₁)

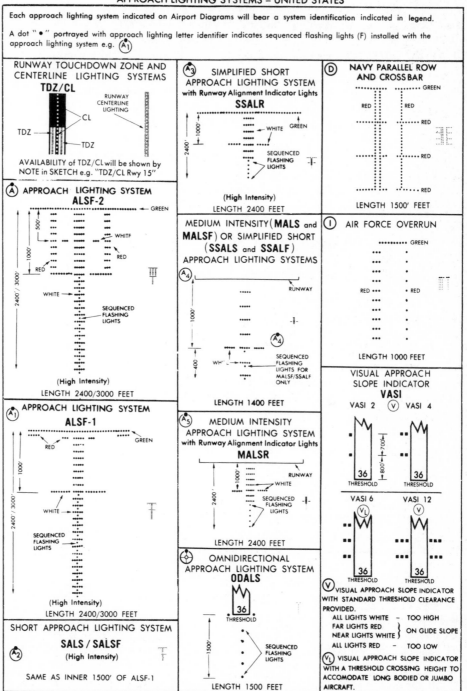

RUNWAY TOUCHDOWN ZONE AND CENTERLINE LIGHTING SYSTEMS

TDZ/CL

AVAILABILITY of TDZ/CL will be shown by NOTE in SKETCH e.g. "TDZ/CL Rwy 15"

(A) APPROACH LIGHTING SYSTEM
ALSF-2

(High Intensity)
LENGTH 2400/3000 FEET

(A₁) APPROACH LIGHTING SYSTEM
ALSF-1

(High Intensity)
LENGTH 2400/3000 FEET

SHORT APPROACH LIGHTING SYSTEM

SALS / SALSF
(High Intensity)

SAME AS INNER 1500' OF ALSF-1

(A₃) SIMPLIFIED SHORT APPROACH LIGHTING SYSTEM
with Runway Alignment Indicator Lights
SSALR

(High Intensity)
LENGTH 2400 FEET

MEDIUM INTENSITY (**MALS** and **MALSF**) OR SIMPLIFIED SHORT (**SSALS** and **SSALF**) APPROACH LIGHTING SYSTEMS

LENGTH 1400 FEET

(A₅) MEDIUM INTENSITY APPROACH LIGHTING SYSTEM
with Runway Alignment Indicator Lights
MALSR

LENGTH 2400 FEET

OMNIDIRECTIONAL APPROACH LIGHTING SYSTEM
ODALS

LENGTH 1500 FEET

(D) NAVY PARALLEL ROW AND CROSS BAR

LENGTH 1500' FEET

(I) AIR FORCE OVERRUN

LENGTH 1000 FEET

VISUAL APPROACH SLOPE INDICATOR
VASI

VASI 2   (V)   VASI 4

VASI 6   VASI 12

(V) VISUAL APPROACH SLOPE INDICATOR WITH STANDARD THRESHOLD CLEARANCE PROVIDED.

ALL LIGHTS WHITE – TOO HIGH
FAR LIGHTS RED   } ON GLIDE SLOPE
NEAR LIGHTS WHITE
ALL LIGHTS RED – TOO LOW

(VL) VISUAL APPROACH SLOPE INDICATOR WITH A THRESHOLD CROSSING HEIGHT TO ACCOMODATE LONG BODIED OR JUMBO AIRCRAFT.

(NOT FOR USE IN NAVIGATION)

field with such a system, you will find the information in the notes area of the approach plate. In FIG. 17-12, the VOR/DME-A chart for Lake City, Florida, it reads, "ACTIVATE Rwy 10 and 28 MIRL and VASI—122.7"—which simply means that the radio-controlled lighting system is activated on 122.7 and that, when activated, it will control the Medium Intensity Runway Lights and the VASI on Runways 10/28. To operate the system, tune your transmitter to 122.7, and key the mike five times within five seconds. This will turn on the medium intensity lights.

At some airports, if you were to key the mike seven times within five seconds, that would activate the highest intensity lights available, while three keys in five seconds would activate the lowest intensity lights available. By checking your approach plates you can determine the highest intensity lights available and key the mike to bring them up to that intensity initially. This will allow you to pick up the lights at the greatest distance, which is especially useful in low visibility conditions or around strange airports. Then, as you get closer, and the bright lights begin to bother you, use the keying technique to lower their intensity.

NOS PROCEDURE TURNS

An approach procedure begins at the IAF. From this point on, the procedure track will be indicated by a heavy line with arrowheads indicating the proper direction to be flown. These, and other symbols used on the plan view, can be seen in FIG. 17-13. You can follow this track on a DME arc to an ILS approach to Orlando Executive Airport (FIG. 17-14).

Seen in the upper left-hand column of FIG. 17-13, the procedure turn is indicated by a half an arrowhead as well as the inbound and outbound magnetic courses.

About midway down the left-hand column, note three different holding patterns. The dark, heavy line indicates a holding pattern that is being used in lieu of a procedure turn. The second type, with a finer line, indicates a normal arrival holding pattern. The third type, shorter and finer still, depicts a holding pattern used in conjunction with a missed approach, as you can see in FIG. 17-14 at OVIDO.

For some reason, the NOS charts don't have any plan view symbol for the teardrop procedure turn, but they do indicate it on the profile view. The upper left-hand diagram on FIG. 17-15 signifies a teardrop procedure turn, and you can see how it differs from the profile of a normal procedure turn. The teardrop has a continuous line, while the normal procedure turn shows a break at the outbound end.

In the normal procedure turn illustration at the top center of FIG. 17-15, the procedure turn altitude is 2400 feet as depicted by the numeral above the line,

Fig. 17-12

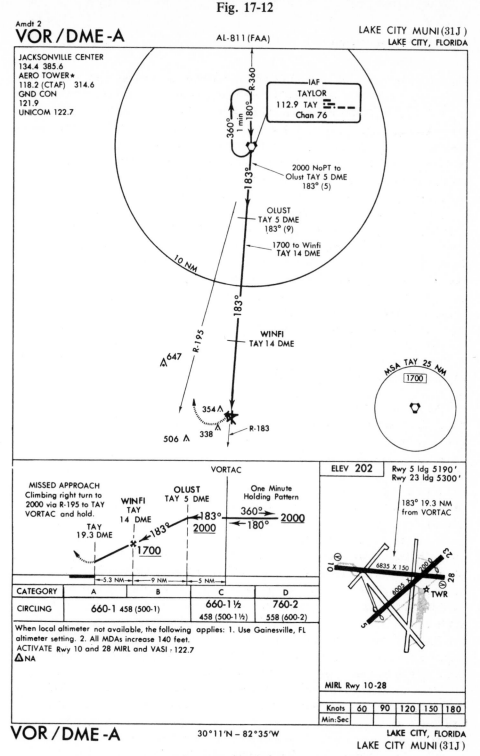

VOR/DME-A

AL-811 (FAA)

LAKE CITY MUNI (31J)
LAKE CITY, FLORIDA

JACKSONVILLE CENTER
134.4 385.6
AERO TOWER★
118.2 (CTAF) 314.6
GND CON
121.9
UNICOM 122.7

IAF
TAYLOR
112.9 TAY
Chan 76

R-360
360° 1 min
180°
183°

2000 NoPT to
Olust TAY 5 DME
183° (5)

OLUST
TAY 5 DME
183° (9)

1700 to Winfi
TAY 14 DME

10 NM

183°

R-195

647

WINFI
TAY 14 DME

MSA TAY 25 NM
1700

354
338
506
R-183

MISSED APPROACH
Climbing right turn to
2000 via R-195 to TAY
VORTAC and hold.

VORTAC

One Minute
Holding Pattern

ELEV 202

Rwy 5 ldg 5190'
Rwy 23 ldg 5300'

OLUST
TAY 5 DME
183°
2000

360°
180°
2000

183° 19.3 NM
from VORTAC

WINFI
TAY
14 DME

183°

TAY
19.3 DME

1700

6835 X 150

6005 X 150

TWR

| 5.3 NM | 9 NM | 5 NM |

CATEGORY	A	B	C	D
CIRCLING	660-1 458 (500-1)		660-1½ 458 (500-1½)	760-2 558 (600-2)

When local altimeter not available, the following applies: 1. Use Gainesville, FL
altimeter setting. 2. All MDAs increase 140 feet.
ACTIVATE Rwy 10 and 28 MIRL and VASI : 122.7
⚠ NA

MIRL Rwy 10-28

Knots	60	90	120	150	180
Min:Sec					

VOR/DME-A

30°11'N – 82°35'W

LAKE CITY, FLORIDA
LAKE CITY MUNI (31J)

(NOT FOR USE IN NAVIGATION)

near the break in the procedure turn track. You will see the same numeral below and to the right, with a "lightning bolt" pointing to the inbound leg just prior to the LOM. If you look down at the "PROFILE SYMBOLS" in the lower right-hand column of the page, you can see that this symbol indicates the glide slope intercept, which is always the FAF on precision approaches.

Note the small "2156" above the Maltese cross symbol. This indicates the glide slope altitude at the outer marker. The outer marker is the FAF when the glide slope is out. This is a good checkpoint when flying an ILS approach to let you know you are not on a false glide slope.

So you can see that, in this case, you should intercept the glide slope at 2400 feet, *prior* to reaching the LOM, then descend on the glide slope, arriving at the LOM when your altimeter reads about 2156 feet.

Now, look at the altitudes depicted in the bottom center of FIG. 17-15. These are self-explanatory, but you should make sure that you understand them. Basically, the line drawn over, under, or over *and* under a numeral, indicates a barrier you should not penetrate. Therefore, if the altitude has lines at both top and bottom it is a mandatory altitude. If the line is above the altitude it says that you must stay at or below that altitude—it is a maximum altitude. A line beneath the altitude indicates a minimum altitude, and if there are no lines, the altitude is merely recommended.

CLIMB AND DESCENT GRADIENTS

I mentioned previously that the glide slope intercept altitude will give you a clue as to whether or not you are on the true glide slope. Another check would be to determine what your rate of descent *should* be. You know your indicated approach speed, and when you get the ATIS or the numbers from Approach Control, you can apply the correction to your airspeed to find out your approximate ground speed on approach. Then you look at the symbol at the bottom of the profile view to determine the glide slope angle for the airport. In both the example shown in FIG. 17-15 and the actual approach in FIG. 17-14, the glide slope angle is 3.0°. Taking this angle and your ground speed in knots, you can look at the rate-of-descent table in FIG. 17-16 and determine that the rate of descent for a ground speed of, say, 120 knots, should be 635 feet per minute. Use this recommended rate to also check for wind shear during the approach. If you need to descend at too great a rate you are probably experiencing a tailwind; too low a rate would indicate a headwind.

The introductory pages also contain tables to help determine the rate of climb necessary to meet certain airport or runway climb gradient restrictions (FIG. 17-17).

This chapter was included to give you some insight into the layout of NOS charts. Comparing these to the Jeppesen charts should help you decide which type you prefer. Whichever type you decide upon, remember that the legends

Fig. 17-13

LEGEND
INSTRUMENT APPROACH PROCEDURES (CHARTS)

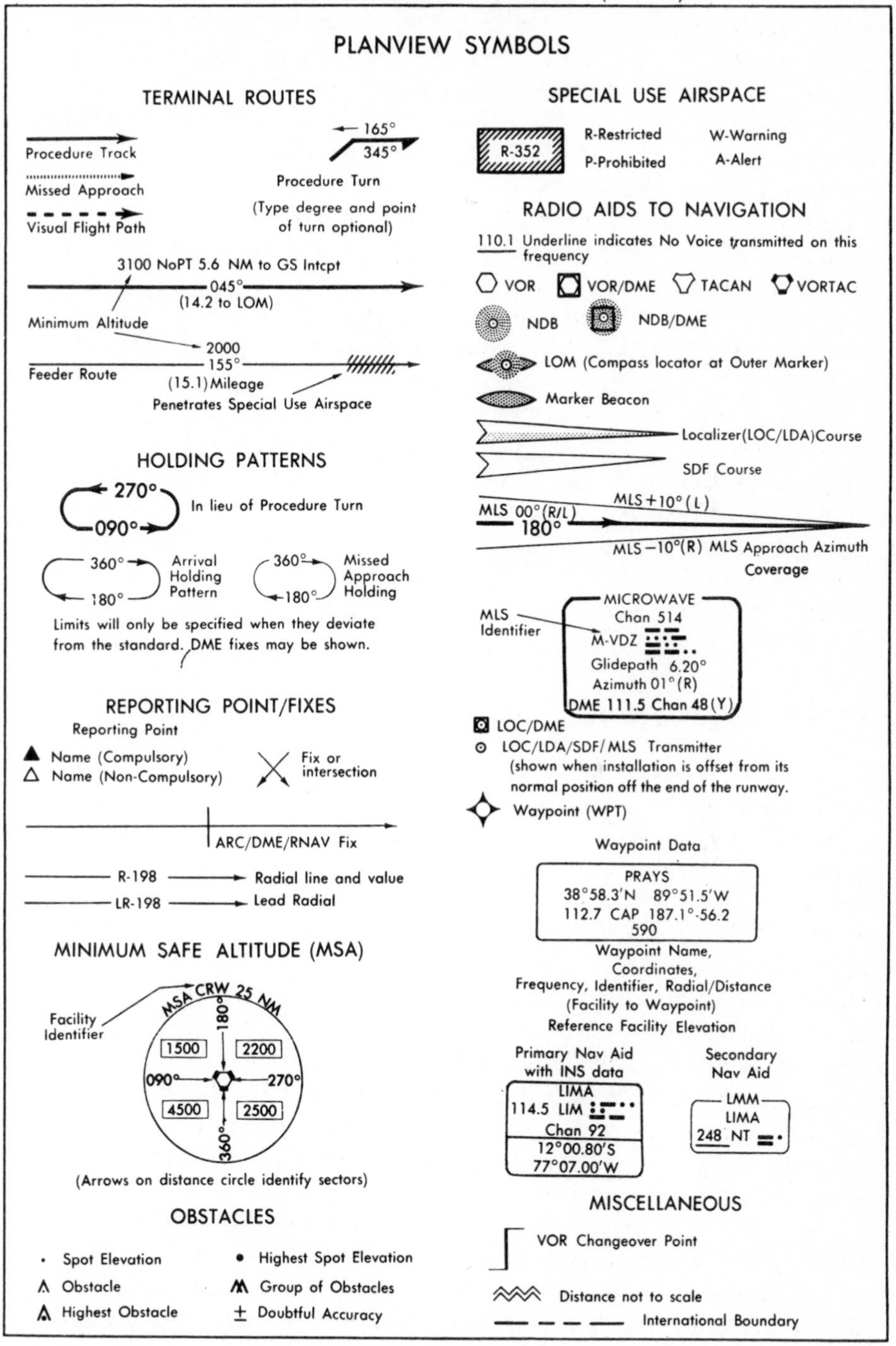

PLANVIEW SYMBOLS

TERMINAL ROUTES

Procedure Track

Missed Approach

Visual Flight Path

← 165°
345°
Procedure Turn
(Type degree and point
of turn optional)

3100 NoPT 5.6 NM to GS Intcpt
045°
(14.2 to LOM)
Minimum Altitude

2000
155°
(15.1) Mileage
Feeder Route
Penetrates Special Use Airspace

HOLDING PATTERNS

← 270°
090°
In lieu of Procedure Turn

360°
180°
Arrival
Holding
Pattern

360°
180°
Missed
Approach
Holding

Limits will only be specified when they deviate
from the standard. DME fixes may be shown.

REPORTING POINT/FIXES

Reporting Point

▲ Name (Compulsory)
△ Name (Non-Compulsory)

✕ Fix or
intersection

ARC/DME/RNAV Fix

R-198 → Radial line and value

LR-198 → Lead Radial

MINIMUM SAFE ALTITUDE (MSA)

MSA CRW 25 NM
180°
Facility
Identifier
1500 2200
090°   270°
4500 2500
360°

(Arrows on distance circle identify sectors)

OBSTACLES

· Spot Elevation
∧ Obstacle
⩘ Highest Obstacle

● Highest Spot Elevation
⋏⋏ Group of Obstacles
± Doubtful Accuracy

SPECIAL USE AIRSPACE

R-352
R-Restricted   W-Warning
P-Prohibited   A-Alert

RADIO AIDS TO NAVIGATION

110.1 Underline indicates No Voice transmitted on this
frequency

⬡ VOR   ▢ VOR/DME   ▽ TACAN   ⬡ VORTAC

NDB   NDB/DME

LOM (Compass locator at Outer Marker)

Marker Beacon

Localizer(LOC/LDA)Course

SDF Course

MLS 00°(R/L)   MLS +10°(L)
180°
MLS −10°(R) MLS Approach Azimuth
Coverage

MLS
Identifier
MICROWAVE
Chan 514
M-VDZ
Glidepath 6.20°
Azimuth 01°(R)
DME 111.5 Chan 48(Y)

▣ LOC/DME
⊙ LOC/LDA/SDF/MLS Transmitter
(shown when installation is offset from its
normal position off the end of the runway.

◆ Waypoint (WPT)

Waypoint Data

PRAYS
38°58.3'N   89°51.5'W
112.7 CAP 187.1°-56.2
590

Waypoint Name,
Coordinates,
Frequency, Identifier, Radial/Distance
(Facility to Waypoint)
Reference Facility Elevation

Primary Nav Aid
with INS data

LIMA
114.5 LIM
Chan 92
12°00.80'S
77°07.00'W

Secondary
Nav Aid

LMM
LIMA
248 NT

MISCELLANEOUS

⌐ VOR Changeover Point

〰〰 Distance not to scale

— — — — International Boundary

Fig. 17-14

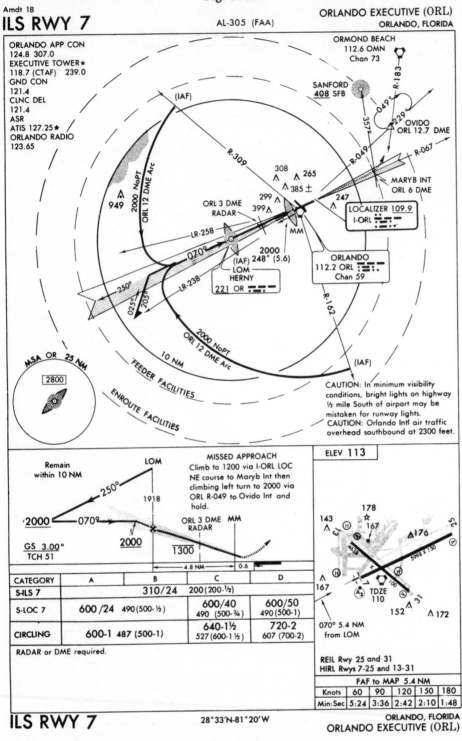

Amdt 18

ILS RWY 7

AL-305 (FAA)

ORLANDO EXECUTIVE (ORL)
ORLANDO, FLORIDA

ORLANDO APP CON
124.8 307.0
EXECUTIVE TOWER★
118.7 (CTAF) 239.0
GND CON
121.4
CLNC DEL
121.4
ASR
ATIS 127.25★
ORLANDO RADIO
123.65

LOCALIZER 109.9
I-ORL

ORLANDO
112.2 ORL
Chan 59

ORMOND BEACH
112.6 OMN
Chan 73

SANFORD
408 SFB

OVIDO
ORL 12.7 DME

MARYB INT
ORL 6 DME

CAUTION: In minimum visibility conditions, bright lights on highway ½ mile South of airport may be mistaken for runway lights.
CAUTION: Orlando Intl air traffic overhead southbound at 2300 feet.

MSA OR 25 NM
2800

FEEDER FACILITIES
ENROUTE FACILITIES

Remain within 10 NM

LOM

MISSED APPROACH
Climb to 1200 via I-ORL LOC NE course to Maryb Int then climbing left turn to 2000 via ORL R-049 to Ovido Int and hold.

ELEV 113

GS 3.00°
TCH 51

ORL 3 DME RADAR

MM

4.8 NM   0.6

REIL Rwy 25 and 31
HIRL Rwys 7-25 and 13-31

CATEGORY	A	B	C	D
S-ILS 7		310/24 200(200-½)		
S-LOC 7	600/24 490(500-½)		600/40 490(500-¾)	600/50 490(500-1)
CIRCLING	600-1 487(500-1)		640-1½ 527(600-1½)	720-2 607(700-2)

RADAR or DME required.

070° 5.4 NM from LOM

FAF to MAP 5.4 NM					
Knots	60	90	120	150	180
Min:Sec	5:24	3:36	2:42	2:10	1:48

ILS RWY 7

28°33'N-81°20'W

ORLANDO, FLORIDA
ORLANDO EXECUTIVE (ORL)

(NOT FOR USE IN NAVIGATION)

Fig. 17-15

LEGEND
INSTRUMENT APPROACH PROCEDURES (CHARTS)

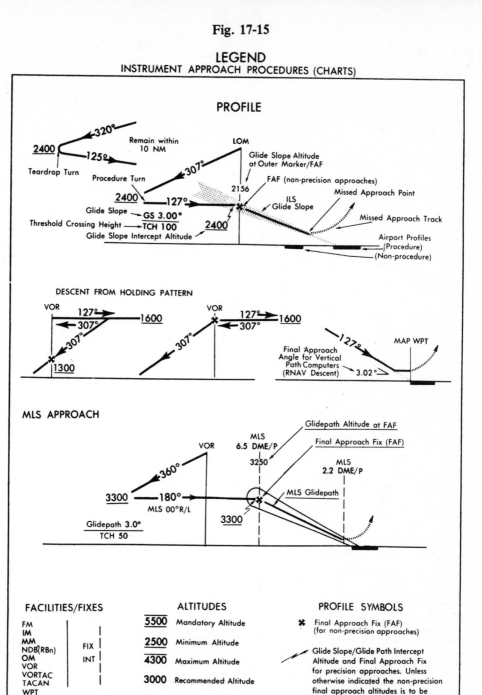

(NOT FOR USE IN NAVIGATION)

Fig. 17-16

INSTRUMENT APPROACH PROCEDURE CHARTS
RATE OF DESCENT TABLE
(ft. per min.)

A rate of descent table is provided for use in planning and executing precision descents under known or approximate ground speed conditions. It will be especially useful for approaches when the localizer only is used for course guidance. A best speed, power, attitude combination can be programmed which will result in a stable glide rate and attitude favorable for executing a landing if minimums exist upon breakout. Care should always be exercised so that the minimum descent altitude and missed approach point are not exceeded.

ANGLE OF DESCENT (degrees and tenths)	GROUND SPEED (knots)										
	30	45	60	75	90	105	120	135	150	165	180
2.0	105	160	210	265	320	370	425	475	530	585	635
2.5	130	200	265	330	395	465	530	595	665	730	795
3.0	160	240	320	395	480	555	635	715	795	875	955
3.5	185	280	370	465	555	650	740	835	925	1020	1110
4.0	210	315	425	530	635	740	845	955	1060	1165	1270
4.5	240	355	475	595	715	835	955	1075	1190	1310	1430
5.0	265	395	530	660	795	925	1060	1190	1325	1455	1590
5.5	290	435	580	730	875	1020	1165	1310	1455	1600	1745
6.0	315	475	635	795	955	1110	1270	1430	1590	1745	1905
6.5	345	515	690	860	1030	1205	1375	1550	1720	1890	2065
7.0	370	555	740	925	1110	1295	1480	1665	1850	2035	2220
7.5	395	595	795	990	1190	1390	1585	1785	1985	2180	2380
8.0	425	635	845	1055	1270	1480	1690	1905	2115	2325	2540
8.5	450	675	900	1120	1345	1570	1795	2020	2245	2470	2695
9.0	475	715	950	1190	1425	1665	1900	2140	2375	2615	2855
9.5	500	750	1005	1255	1505	1755	2005	2255	2510	2760	3010
10.0	530	790	1055	1320	1585	1845	2110	2375	2640	2900	3165
10.5	555	830	1105	1385	1660	1940	2215	2490	2770	3045	3320
11.0	580	870	1160	1450	1740	2030	2320	2610	2900	3190	3480
11.5	605	910	1210	1515	1820	2120	2425	2725	3030	3335	3635
12.0	630	945	1260	1575	1890	2205	2520	2835	3150	3465	3780

(NOT FOR USE IN NAVIGATION)

Fig. 17-17

INSTRUMENT TAKEOFF PROCEDURE CHARTS
RATE OF CLIMB TABLE
(ft. per min.)

A rate of climb table is provided for use in planning and executing takeoff procedures under known or approximate ground speed conditions.

REQUIRED CLIMB RATE (ft. per NM)	GROUND SPEED (KNOTS)						
	30	60	80	90	100	120	140
200	100	200	267	300	333	400	467
250	125	250	333	375	417	500	583
300	150	300	400	450	500	600	700
350	175	350	467	525	583	700	816
400	200	400	533	600	667	800	933
450	225	450	600	675	750	900	1050
500	250	500	667	750	833	1000	1167
550	275	550	733	825	917	1100	1283
600	300	600	800	900	1000	1200	1400
650	325	650	867	975	1083	1300	1516
700	350	700	933	1050	1167	1400	1633

REQUIRED CLIMB RATE (ft. per NM)	GROUND SPEED (KNOTS)					
	150	180	210	240	270	300
200	500	600	700	800	900	1000
250	625	750	875	1000	1125	1250
300	750	900	1050	1200	1350	1500
350	875	1050	1225	1400	1575	1750
400	1000	1200	1400	1600	1700	2000
450	1125	1350	1575	1800	2025	2250
500	1250	1500	1750	2000	2250	2500
550	1375	1650	1925	2200	2475	2750
600	1500	1800	2100	2400	2700	3000
650	1625	1950	2275	2600	2925	3250
700	1750	2100	2450	2800	3150	3500

(NOT FOR USE IN NAVIGATION)

and explanatory pages should be reviewed periodically. Each time you review, you will run across symbols or explanations that you have forgotten. Remember, pilots never know enough. One of the marks of a professional pilot is that he or she is willing to open the manuals to review procedures, even when there isn't a check flight coming up or a cloud in the sky.

18

VOR Approaches

Rᴇᴛᴜʀɴɪɴɢ ᴛᴏ ᴛʜᴇ ᴊᴇᴘᴘᴇꜱᴇɴ ᴄʜᴀʀᴛꜱ, ʏᴏᴜ ᴡɪʟʟ ɴᴏᴡ ʙᴇ ʟᴏᴏᴋɪɴɢ ᴏᴠᴇʀ ꜱᴏᴍᴇ actual approach plates, and I'll talk you through the approaches. I'll try to make my explanations general enough to work in any aircraft; however, when I speak of flying at your approach airspeed you will have to realize that this is good for learning and practice, but if you are at a busy airport in actual IFR conditions, and flying an aircraft with an approach speed of less than 120 knots, you may have to fly up to your V_a speed so as not to force that 747 or L-1011 behind you into a holding pattern.

Before we go too far, here are a few helpful hints for IFR flight:

- Always keep the volume of your navigational radio high enough to hear the identifier. Although this is a very distracting sound in some situations, it will let you know at once if the facility goes off the air. It will also give ATC a way of communicating with you if you lose your communications capabilities and are not aware of it.

- Use every navigational aid you have on board. Have them all tuned and identified. This way, if one fails, you will have an immediate backup.

- Once cleared for an approach, get a final check on the weather. It may have gone down below your particular minimums, and the controller may be too busy to notice. Remember that you will be the one left holding the bag if you land below the authorized minimums for your aircraft. This last check on the weather will also give you some idea of what you can expect to see when you break out.

- In order to establish a consistent pattern for setting up your VOR radios in a single-pilot cockpit, *try* to use your #1 VOR for the course you are actually flying. Set the #2 VOR to indicate intersections, turning points, lead-in radials, missed approaches, or for the next course you will be flying. Once reaching the new course point, fly using the #2 VOR as your reference until you are able to reset your #1 VOR to the new course. This procedure may not always be practicable, however, especially on a series of short approach segments, as you'll be able to see in the some of the sample approaches throughout the remainder of this book.

EXECUTING A VOR APPROACH

Let's plan a simple IFR flight to Kaunakakai Airport on the island of Molokai in Hawaii.

By looking at the upper right corner of the approach plate (FIG. 18-1), you can see that Kaunakakai has a VOR approach based on the Molokai VOR (116.1) with the identifier MKK. In the upper left you also note that it is controlled by Molokai Tower on 125.7, but that the tower operation is not continuous, as indicated by the asterisk and "CTAF"—Common Traffic Advisory Frequency. The tower frequency is used as the CTAF when the tower is closed.

The airport elevation is 454 feet MSL, and a quick glance at the plan view reveals that the airport is in a bowl, surrounded by hills ranging from 612 feet one mile north, to 1459 feet (the highest elevation on the plate), which is the hilltop on which the VOR is located, to the west of the field.

Without even looking in the minimums block you know that this is not a straight-in approach because of the suffix "A" after the approach type (VOR-A). Still, by looking at the inbound course you see that the final approach course is well within 30° to Runway 5, which should qualify for straight-in minimums. "Aha," you say, remembering our earlier discussions. "Here's one of those approaches requiring a steeper-than-normal descent angle." That, plus the surrounding high terrain, necessitates the high circling minimums.

Turn the chart over to the back and take a look at the airport diagram (FIG. 18-2). There are two runways. The main one, 5/23, is 4494 feet long, and the shorter one, 17/35, is 3118 feet long. Hills, and power lines (not shown on the chart), on the approach ends of Runways 17 and 23 necessitate the displaced thresholds shown by the white blocks across the runways. The "Additional Runway Information" table shows that, landing on Runway 17, the effective runway length is reduced to 2692 feet. Usable landing length of Runway 23 is 3901 feet. Both runways are 100 feet wide, Runway 5/23 has Medium Intensity

Fig. 18-1

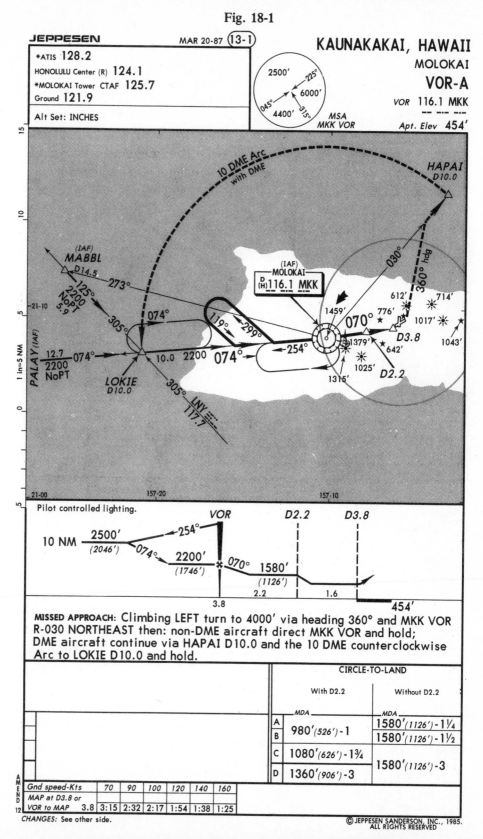

Fig. 18-2

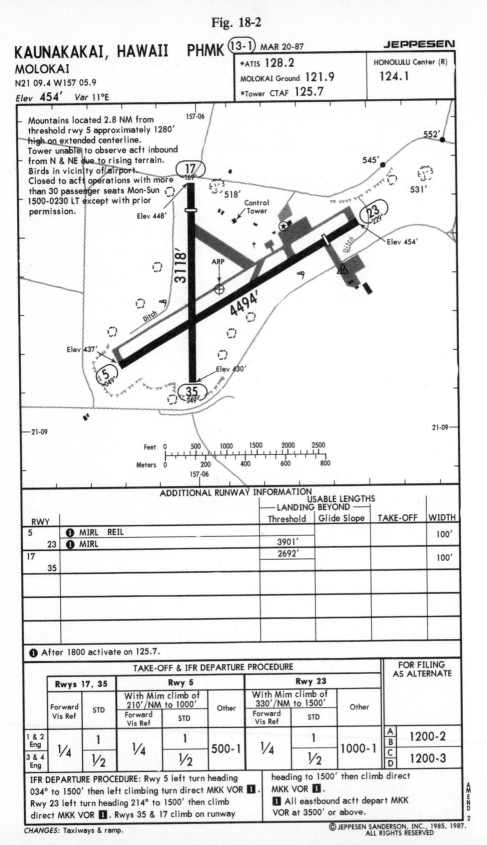

KAUNAKAKAI, HAWAII PHMK (13-1) MAR 20-87 JEPPESEN
MOLOKAI
N21 09.4 W157 05.9
Elev 454'   Var 11°E

*ATIS 128.2	HONOLULU Center (R)
MOLOKAI Ground 121.9	124.1
*Tower CTAF 125.7	

Mountains located 2.8 NM from threshold rwy 5 approximately 1280' high on extended centerline.
Tower unable to observe acft inbound from N & NE due to rising terrain.
Birds in vicinity of airport.
Closed to acft operations with more than 30 passenger seats Mon-Sun 1500-0230 LT except with prior permission.

17 169° Elev 448'
23 229° Elev 454'
5 049° Elev 437'
35 349° Elev 430'

Control Tower
ARP
3118'
4494'
Ditch
Ditch

552'
545'
531'
518'

Feet 0 500 1000 1500 2000 2500
Meters 0 200 400 600 800

ADDITIONAL RUNWAY INFORMATION

		USABLE LENGTHS LANDING BEYOND			
RWY		Threshold	Glide Slope	TAKE-OFF	WIDTH
5	❶ MIRL REIL				100'
23	❶ MIRL	3901'			
17		2692'			100'
35					

❶ After 1800 activate on 125.7.

TAKE-OFF & IFR DEPARTURE PROCEDURE

	Rwys 17, 35		Rwy 5			Rwy 23			FOR FILING AS ALTERNATE	
			With Mim climb of 210'/NM to 1000'		Other	With Mim climb of 330'/NM to 1500'		Other		
	Forward Vis Ref	STD	Forward Vis Ref	STD		Forward Vis Ref	STD			
1 & 2 Eng	1/4	1	1/4	1	500-1	1/4	1	1000-1	A / B	1200-2
3 & 4 Eng		1/2		1/2			1/2		C / D	1200-3

IFR DEPARTURE PROCEDURE: Rwy 5 left turn heading 034° to 1500' then left climbing turn direct MKK VOR ❶. Rwy 23 left turn heading 214° to 1500' then climb direct MKK VOR ❶. Rwys 35 & 17 climb on runway heading to 1500' then climb direct MKK VOR ❶.

❶ All eastbound acft depart MKK VOR at 3500' or above.

AMEND 2

CHANGES: Taxiways & ramp.

Runway Lights, and the approach end to Runway 5 has REIL. These lights are pilot-actuated after 1800 local time, as can be seen in the note at the bottom of the table. (More on this in Chapter 20.)

Some interesting notes are found along the upper-left side of the airport plan view, specifically, the one about the 1280-foot mountain located 2.8 NM (northeast) from the threshold of Runway 5 on the extended centerline. That explains the IFR departure procedure (at the bottom of the chart) requiring all eastbound aircraft to depart the MKK VOR at 3500 feet or above.

There are some interesting climb gradient restrictions in the takeoff minimums block also. Those aircraft taking off on Runway 5 can reduce the visibility minimum below one mile provided they have a 500-foot ceiling and can climb at 210 feet per nautical mile to 1000 feet, while aircraft departing Runway 23 can go with a visibility less than one mile if they have a 1000-foot ceiling, and can climb at 330 feet per nautical mile to 1500 feet.

The profile view on the approach chart (FIG. 18-1) shows a step-down altitude from the final approach fix to the 2.2 DME, and then down to the final minimums. Notice that if you cannot identify the 2.2 DME (e.g., if you are not DME equipped), you cannot descend any lower than the initial step-down altitude of 1580 feet MSL.

I mentioned earlier that the airport is in a "bowl" surrounded by higher terrain. A good indication of just how close this terrain is to the field can be seen by the 280-foot increase in the MDA between Category C (1080 feet) and Category D aircraft (1360 feet).

Now, let's set up two hypothetical approaches to Molokai. One from Maui (from the east), and the other from Honolulu (from the west).

APPROACHING FROM THE EAST

From Maui you will be westbound as you approach the VOR. You should double-check that both of your VOR receivers are tuned to the MKK VOR (check the Morse code identifier). Then set the #2 OBS to the outbound course of 254°, check your DME, and ask for the current weather. After making sure that the DME is operating, take a quick look at the chart to confirm your minimums. If you are in most light aircraft you will look under Category A. As you have an operating DME, you can use the lowest minimums. You must have one mile visibility, and you will be able to descend to an MDA of 980 feet after you cross the 2.2 DME inbound.

The field is reporting a zero-wind condition (for a change!), so your ground speed will be the same as your approach speed, which is around 100 knots. Glance at the conversion chart under the minimums table, and find that, at a ground speed of 100 knots, it will take two minutes and 17 seconds to fly from the FAF at the VOR to your MAP.

As you approach the VOR, slow to approach speed and complete your descent and in-range checklists. Crossing the VOR, track outbound on the 254-degree radial (already dialed in to #2) and begin your descent. The profile view shows that you must complete your procedure turn within 10 nautical miles, that your initial turn will be made to the northwest, and that the minimum procedure turn altitude is 2500 feet MSL (2046 feet above the airport elevation).

Even though you know you can make any type of course reversal you choose on this particular approach (as long as you remain on the north side of the course, at or above the procedure turn minimum altitude), you decide to use the standard procedure turn as depicted, because it will give you a little more time to get all squared away for the approach.

After you turn right to a heading of 299°, fly outbound for one minute. During this time descend and maintain 2500 feet. After the one-minute outbound leg, make a standard-rate 180-degree turn to the left, rolling out on a heading of 119°. While waiting to intercept the inbound course, you can set your #1 OBS to 074°. At the same time, set the #2 OBS to 070°, which will be your final approach track after you cross the MKK VOR, which is the FAF. As the #1 needle centers, indicating that you have intercepted the course, turn inbound. Once you are established on the inbound course (and not before), you can continue your descent to 2200 feet MSL.

As you fly inbound to the VOR, you want to get the airway bracketed to within 10°, because once you are past the FAF you don't want to have to turn more than 5° to stay on course.

How do you tie down a course this close? Well, it becomes a matter of concentration and setting up tighter and tighter brackets. The ultimate goal is to find the correct heading to properly compensate for the wind drift. When you turn inbound, you first turn to the published inbound heading. One of three things will happen. You will either stay on course, drift to the right, or drift to the left. If you drift right or left you will have to correct for the drift. If you are to the right of your course, make an immediate turn of 10° to the left of the published inbound course and *hold* that heading. Again, one of three things will happen. The needle (OBI) will stay where it is, telling you that you have turned just enough to correct for the wind; it can continue drifting to the left, telling you that you have not turned far enough to compensate for the wind; or it will start back toward center indicating that you have overcorrected for the wind.

If you have not corrected enough, you will turn another 10° to the left and watch what happens. Again, you will have one of the same three results.

When your correction is enough to stop the drift of the needle, you will turn an additional 10° to start it back toward the center.

When the needle centers, remove 5° of the last correction and *hold* this new heading. From then on, a 10-degree correction (really a five-degree if you are sharp) to either side of this new heading should be enough to bring you back on course. You would have a good idea of the initial correction necessary if you had properly tied down your *outbound* course between the VOR and the procedure turn, but if you had other problems and never got around to working out a wind correction angle, the procedure mentioned above will get you on course in a short time. Remember, though, that this has to be accomplished before you get into the cone of confusion around the VOR.

APPROACHING FROM THE WEST

Let's suspend this approach from Maui and join up with it later. In the meantime, let's see how it would go up to this point if you had departed from Honolulu.

After leaving Honolulu International Airport you would have been routed to either of two IAFs. One is MABBL intersection, which is the intersection of the MKK 273-degree radial and the Lanai (LNY) 305-degree radial. The other is PALAY intersection which is 12.7 miles southwest of LOKIE on the MKK 254-degree radial.

At either point, you reset both of the navigational radios. I would set the #1 VOR to MKK, tune and identify it, and set the OBS to 074° TO. This will provide a double-check on LOKIE intersection, which is 10 DME west of the MKK VOR on the 254-degree radial, and/or the intersection of the two radials. Naturally, if you are approaching from MABBL, you would fly the #2 VOR (tuned to LNY) until reaching LOKIE, while if coming in from PALAY, you would track in on #1.

As in the approach from Maui, now would be a good time to get the current weather and check your minimums. When you are cleared for the approach you will begin your descent to 2200 feet MSL. The note on both transition courses says you can descend to 2200 feet. It also says that you will not make a procedure turn (NoPT). By the time you reach LOKIE you should have completed the descent and in-range checklists, your airspeed should be down to approach speed, and you should have the wind correction angle pretty well worked out.

Now, I may be confusing you when I speak of approach speed. A complex aircraft would normally still be in the clean configuration at this point, so the approach speed would be higher than when you lower the landing gear and flaps. If you are used to differentiating between this segment and the final approach segment by calling the speed "maneuvering speed" in this part of the approach, and "approach speed" in the final approach, be my guest—just as long as you recognize that, for our purposes here, we are referring to the same thing.

At LOKIE intersection reset your #2 radio to MKK, identify it, and set the OBS to 070°, which again will be your final approach course after crossing the FAF at MKK VOR. Review the approach and missed approach procedures, and tie down the inbound heading to determine your approximate wind correction angle.

INBOUND FROM THE FAF

Now we're back to the point where we left the approach from Maui, and from this point on, both approaches will be the same.

When you cross the FAF, simultaneously check your time, lower the gear if you have retractable gear, extend approach flaps, initiate a descent of about 1000 feet per minute, set the #1 VOR's OBS to 070° FROM, turn to intercept the 070-degree radial, call the controlling facility to report passing the FAF inbound and leaving your altitude, and complete the pre-landing checklist. This sounds like a lot, so let's take the items one at a time.

In this approach your time check is important. If you have a DME failure, you can still fly-out your time to the MAP, even though you will have to use a higher MDA. It will also give you a fairly good cross-check as to how well your descent is progressing. A stopwatch mounted on the instrument panel or the yoke would be best, but if none is available, you can always use a wristwatch with a sweep-second hand. If it has a stopwatch function, so much the better.

Depending on the type of aircraft, lower the gear and select approach flaps. This is a simple matter of moving two handles or switches, depending on the aircraft. If you control the attitude properly, most planes will end up descending at close to 1000 FPM at approach airspeed just by adding the drag. Power changes should be very slight. A rate of descent of 450 FPM is sufficient on this approach, but most pilots, and I'm one of them, would rather descend a little faster, get to the MDA sooner, and fly out the time, than take a chance on hitting an unexpected updraft, or be distracted for a moment, and not get down in time.

Because you have so many things to do at practically the same time, it wouldn't be too much of a problem if you took a little longer to get the #1 radio set up because you could track on the #2 VOR for awhile. In this case, there's a heading difference of only four degrees and it will take the omnis 10 seconds or more to settle down after passing the VOR.

Turning to intercept the 070-degree radial is no big thing. Again, it's only a change of four degrees and a little rudder pressure alone will yaw you that far, without hardly dipping a wing.

Under radar, your radio report of crossing the FAF inbound is not *required*, unless requested by the controller, but is a good idea nevertheless. And like any radio report, it is only made after you have the aircraft well under control and have started the descent. I have seen student pilots so anxious to get the radio report out of the way that they give it immediately upon crossing the FAF. Some have even flown to the MAP without ever starting a descent because other aircraft were on the frequency and they couldn't get their report in. Remember, the aircraft doesn't stop in space while you're waiting to talk. *FLY THE PLANE FIRST. Talk later.*

Finally, complete the pre-landing checklist. If the controller is busy talking to someone else you can even finish this before talking to him.

All of this time you have been subconsciously flying the aircraft. You are past the FAF so you don't want to turn any more than 5° in either direction to stay on course. Remember that you are flying a VOR circling approach, the object of which is to position you so that, when you break out, you will see the airport environment. If you are scanning properly you should be able to hold your heading pretty well. With most aircraft, it's easier to just use rudder pressure to yaw it left or right a few degrees. It won't be a coordinated turn, but it can—and should—be smooth.

Once you get to 1580 feet, level off until you get to 2.2 DME, and then re-establish your descent to the MDA of 980 feet. (If you do not have DME, you must not descend below 1580 feet.)

If you break out early, you may be able to make a straight-in landing, but if you don't make visual contact until you fly out the time, you will be more than 500 feet above the field and will have to circle to land. Remember to maintain the MDA until you're in a position to make a normal descent to the runway.

FIELD NOT IN SIGHT

If you don't see the field before your time runs out (at the MAP), or if you lose sight of it while circling, you will have to execute the missed approach. The procedure at MKK is to make a climbing left turn, heading 360°, to 4000 feet. Maintain that heading until intercepting the MKK 030-degree radial, then track outbound on that radial (which means that once you're established on a heading of 360° and are in a positive climb, you will re-tune the #1 OBS to 030° FROM) while climbing to 4000 feet MSL.

Then, if you are not DME-equipped, turn directly back to the MKK VOR (you can turn right or left). As you turn you should be re-tuning the #1 OBS to 210° TO, and as you fly toward the VOR you should re-tune the #2 OBS to 074°, as this will be your inbound track to the VOR *after you are established in the holding pattern*. When you get to the VOR, hold there using the standard right-hand holding pattern as depicted in the plan view.

Remember the holding pattern entry procedures I talked about back in our holding pattern discussion? Make a teardrop entry in this case; your initial outbound heading after crossing the VOR will be 224°.

Now, looking back at the missed approach procedure, if you are DME-equipped, make the initial part of the missed approach the same as if you did not have a DME, climbing to 4000 feet outbound on the MKK 030-degree radial until you get to HAPAI, which is at 10 DME. From here, fly the 10-DME arc to LOKIE intersection, and hold there.

How would you enter the hold at LOKIE? Well, you must cross LOKIE to enter it, and if you are right on the arc when you cross LOKIE, the easiest pattern entry would be to turn to the left (toward the VOR on the non-holding side), fly for one minute, turn to the left again to track outbound on the MKK 254-degree radial to LOKIE, and then begin standard right turns to fly the holding pattern as depicted. More will be said about flying DME arcs in Chapter 19.

In order to accomplish the missed approach, apply takeoff power, retract the gear, and retract the flaps to the normal takeoff position. As soon as the aircraft attains normal climb speed, begin your climb. When you reach sufficient airspeed, retract flaps fully and set climb power. If you are flying an aircraft with sufficient power to climb with the gear extended, it is a good procedure to establish a positive rate of climb before retracting the gear.

While doing all of this you will be reporting to the controller that you are executing a missed approach. It saves time if you can also relay your intentions to him as that is the first question he will come back with if you don't tell him on your initial contact.

While on the approach itself, and during the en route portion of the flight, you should have been evaluating the conditions and your options. If the weather is reported as down, and it is expected to remain that way, you might decide to take a look, and if you can't get in, you'll ask for a clearance to your alternate. If you miss the approach because of a sudden rain or snow squall, or a shower that's passing over the field, you will probably either ask to initiate another approach at once, or perhaps hold for a few minutes to allow conditions to improve. In any case, the decision is yours to make, and you should have some plan of action in your mind.

In training, almost all of your approaches, except the final one of the session, will terminate in a missed approach. Just as you constantly think of an aborted takeoff while on the takeoff roll (until you're past the rejection speed or point), on an instrument approach you should be thinking missed approach until you are actually flaring-out to land.

Perhaps now you are beginning to realize why so much emphasis is put on practicing the basic instrument maneuvers until you can fly the plane without thinking about it. As you can see here, you have too much else on your mind when you actually start the approach.

19

DME Approaches

BEFORE WE GET INTO DME APPROACHES, LET'S TAKE A LOOK AT THE APPROACH to the Waimea-Kohala Airport, FIG. 19-1. There are some interesting aspects to this approach.

Start by looking at the airport information at the top of the page. You can see here that the airport elevation is 2671 feet MSL. You also see that it has a Control Zone that does not operate continuously. When the Zone is effective you will transmit to Honolulu Radio on 122.1, and receive on the Kamuela VOR (MUE) frequency of 113.3. There is a note in the communications section telling you that, when the Control Zone is not effective, the procedure is not authorized except for operators with approved weather reporting service. Basically, this refers to air carriers and commuters. I mentioned this in Chapter 16, and we'll get into it again in Chapter 21.

Notice that the Minimum Sector Altitudes are quite high. If you are approaching from the north, between inbound headings of 045° through 255°, the MSA is 6600 feet. For headings of 255° through 045°, it goes up to 14,800 feet with the MUE VOR as the center of the sector diagram. It looks as though you will be best off staying on the centerline of this approach.

Looking at the airport diagram (FIG. 19-2), you can see that the airport has a single runway, 4/22, and that it is 5200 feet long and 100 feet wide with no displaced thresholds.

The "Additional Runway Information" block shows that both runways have Medium Intensity Runway Lights and VASIs. The VASI for Runway 4 is to the right side of the runway, while the VASI for Runway 22 is to the left. All of these lights are pilot-controlled, as can be determined from the notes.

LEAD-IN RADIALS

A glance back at the plan view shows that if you are approaching from the UPP VOR, you will have to make a 120-degree turn to the left to get on the final approach course. Because of this, you have a lead-in radial, the MUE 244-degree radial. It crosses the UPP 174-degree radial, forming MURPH intersection. You have a dogleg from MURPH, beginning the approach transition with a minimum altitude of 4000 feet.

The note says that the dogleg allows no procedure turn. The distance from MURPH to the mileage break is 2.0 miles via the 156-degree heading (although in actual practice you will find that it is really one continuous turn from MURPH to the inbound course), and the distance from the mileage break to PUAKO intersection, which is the FAF, is another 6.0 miles.

HOLDING PATTERN IN LIEU OF PROCEDURE TURN

You have two other ways of reaching the FAF. Either straight-in from JASON intersection, or by flying an overhead approach from the MUE VOR, which uses a holding pattern for a course reversal at PUAKO. If you are flying an overhead approach you can see from the outbound approach transition that outbound minimum altitude is 6000 feet on the 234-degree radial, and that it is 5.9 miles to PUAKO. In this case, when you cross the PUAKO intersection outbound, PUAKO is the IAF.

The turns in the holding pattern will be to the right, with an inbound course of 054°, and you will be using a teardrop entry with an initial course of 204° when entering the holding pattern. The minimum altitude in the holding pattern is 4000 feet MSL, and the inbound legs should be one minute in length. As a backup to the DME you should tune the #2 OBS to the 152-degree radial of UPP for a check on PUAKO.

You will note that the ground rises rapidly to the north. Two miles north is a 3449-foot obstruction; 3½ miles northwest is a 4596-foot obstacle; and at only 6 miles out is a 5505-foot obstruction. That's why you can find a note in the "Circle-To-Land" section that says that you are not authorized to circle northwest of the airport. Also note that the terrain rises to 8773 feet just 11 miles southeast of the field and the highest point on the chart is 11,347 feet MSL.

The missed approach procedure calls for a climbing right turn to 4000 feet via the 234-degree radial of MUE VOR, with holding back at PUAKO.

Fig. 19-1

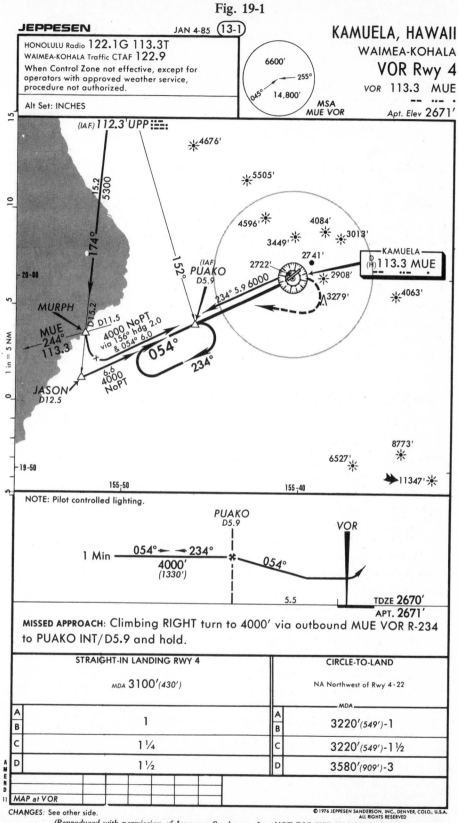

JEPPESEN   JAN 4-85 (13-1)

KAMUELA, HAWAII
WAIMEA-KOHALA
VOR Rwy 4
VOR 113.3 MUE
-- ..-- .
Apt. Elev 2671'

HONOLULU Radio 122.1G 113.3T
WAIMEA-KOHALA Traffic CTAF 122.9
When Control Zone not effective, except for
operators with approved weather service,
procedure not authorized.

Alt Set: INCHES

6600'
045° — 255°
14,800'
MSA
MUE VOR

(IAF.) 112.3' UPP

*4676'
*5505'
4596' *
4084' *
3449' *
*3013'
KAMUELA
(H) 113.3 MUE
-- ..-- .
15.2
5300
174°
152°
(IAF)
PUAKO
D5.9
234° 5.9 6000
2722'
2741'
*2908'
*4063'
MURPH
D15.2
MUE
244°
113.3
D11.5
4000 NoPT
via 156° hdg 2.0
& 054° 6.0
054°
234°
3279'
JASON
D12.5
6.6
4000
NoPT

8773'
*
6527'
*
*11347'

NOTE: Pilot controlled lighting.

PUAKO
D5.9
VOR
1 Min   054° — 234°
4000'
(1330')
054°
5.5
TDZE 2670'
APT. 2671'

MISSED APPROACH: Climbing RIGHT turn to 4000' via outbound MUE VOR R-234
to PUAKO INT/D5.9 and hold.

STRAIGHT-IN LANDING RWY 4			CIRCLE-TO-LAND	
MDA 3100'(430')			NA Northwest of Rwy 4-22	
			MDA	
A			A	3220'(549')-1
B	1		B	3220'(549')-1
C	1¼		C	3220'(549')-1½
D	1½		D	3580'(909')-3

AMEND
11 MAP at VOR

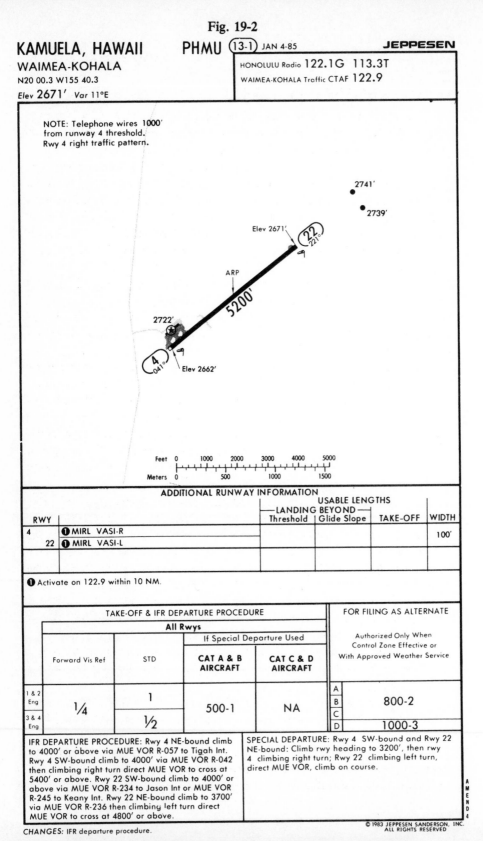

Fig. 19-2

WAIMEA-KOHALA

N20 00.3 W155 40.3

Elev 2671' *Var* 11°E

HONOLULU Radio 122.1G 113.3T

WAIMEA-KOHALA Traffic CTAF 122.9

NOTE: Telephone wires 1000' from runway 4 threshold. Rwy 4 right traffic pattern.

2741'

2739'

Elev 2671'

22
221°

ARP

5200'

2722'

4
041°

Elev 2662'

| Feet | 0 | 1000 | 2000 | 3000 | 4000 | 5000 |
| Meters | 0 | | 500 | 1000 | 1500 | |

ADDITIONAL RUNWAY INFORMATION

RWY		USABLE LENGTHS			WIDTH
		LANDING BEYOND			
		Threshold	Glide Slope	TAKE-OFF	
4	❶ MIRL VASI-R				100'
22	❶ MIRL VASI-L				

❶ Activate on 122.9 within 10 NM.

TAKE-OFF & IFR DEPARTURE PROCEDURE

		All Rwys			FOR FILING AS ALTERNATE
			If Special Departure Used		Authorized Only When Control Zone Effective or With Approved Weather Service
	Forward Vis Ref	STD	CAT A & B AIRCRAFT	CAT C & D AIRCRAFT	
1 & 2 Eng	1/4	1	500-1	NA	A / B 800-2
3 & 4 Eng		1/2			C / D 1000-3

IFR DEPARTURE PROCEDURE: Rwy 4 NE-bound climb to 4000' or above via MUE VOR R-057 to Tigah Int. Rwy 4 SW-bound climb to 4000' via MUE VOR R-042 then climbing right turn direct MUE VOR to cross at 5400' or above. Rwy 22 SW-bound climb to 4000' or above via MUE VOR R-234 to Jason Int or MUE VOR R-245 to Keany Int. Rwy 22 NE-bound climb to 3700' via MUE VOR R-236 then climbing left turn direct MUE VOR to cross at 4800' or above.

SPECIAL DEPARTURE: Rwy 4 SW-bound and Rwy 22 NE-bound: Climb rwy heading to 3200', then rwy 4 climbing right turn; Rwy 22 climbing left turn, direct MUE VOR, climb on course.

CHANGES: IFR departure procedure.

A M E N D 4

USING THE LEAD-IN RADIAL

Let's take a quick run-through of the approach to see how you will use the lead-in radial. The UPP VOR is the IAF on this routing, and you will be proceeding southward on the 174-degree radial and descending to the MEA of 5300 feet. You would naturally have your #1 VOR tuned to the UPP VOR (and identified) because you will be tracking it outbound. You have 15.2 miles to fly from the VOR to MURPH intersection, so there is plenty of time to take care of the checklists and to get the latest weather. Tune to and identify the MUE VOR on your #2 VOR. In this case, to identify MURPH, set the OBS at 064° TO, as this will put the needle on the right side of the scale, giving you a better picture of what's happening.

As you grind out those last few miles to MURPH, recheck the approach plate. Your minimums for the straight-in approach are pretty much the same for all aircraft. All aircraft can descend to 430 feet above the TDZE. The visibility for your Category A airplane is 1 mile, although it increases to as high as 1½ miles for Category D aircraft.

Here, as at Molokai, the high-speed aircraft take a beating in the circle-to-land minimums due to their increased radius of turn. Although the visibility increases ½ mile between Category A/B and Category C aircraft, the MDA remains the same. But moving up to Category D aircraft the MDA jumps 360 feet and the visibility increases by another 1½ miles. Perhaps now you can begin to understand the whys and wherefores behind all of these somewhat confusing figures.

There aren't any figures in the conversion box for a timed run from the VOR to the MAP because, in this case, the VOR *is* the MAP.

The #2 OBI (or CDI, if you prefer) is coming off the peg now, so bring your airspeed down to the clean configuration approach speed, tune the #1 VOR to MUE, identify it, and set the OBS to 054° TO. By now, the #2 needle has centered, and the #1 is coming off the peg, so start your turn to the left and begin descent to 4000 feet MSL. By the time you are about ready to roll out on the 156-degree heading, the #1 needle is almost centered, so continue your turn to 054° and begin tracking inbound to PUAKO. While turning, you should have been re-tuning your #2 VOR to the UPP VOR, checking the identifier, and setting the OBS to 152° FROM, so that you can identify PUAKO intersection to check against your DME. Inbound to the runway, PUAKO becomes the FAF. (How do you know? The FAF for a nonprecision approach is indicated only by the Maltese cross symbol in the profile view.)

The approach plate shows a total of 8.0 miles (2.0 + 6.0) from MURPH intersection to PUAKO, so you have plenty of time to lose those 1300 feet from 5300 feet to 4000 feet. During this period of time, you should go over the checklist and set the approach flaps. Crossing PUAKO, lower the gear, complete the pre-landing checklist, call-in to report the FAF inbound, and fly on down to your MDA of 3100 feet MSL.

After passing PUAKO, it's a good idea to reset your #2 VOR to MUE, and set the missed approach course (234°) on the OBS. This way, in the event of a missed approach, you won't have to be changing the radios while getting the power up and cleaning up the plane. Another thing to remember is that you will be at 3100 feet MSL, so more than likely, you won't be getting full performance from the aircraft when you apply the power, unless it's equipped with turbocharged engines.

ON TO HILO

There are many approaches to the General Lyman Airport in Hilo, Hawaii, but here you will only concern yourself with two of them, the VOR DME Rwy 26 (FIG. 19-3) and the VOR DME-A (FIG. 19-4).

Hilo is a controlled field with a part-time tower. The approach plates tell you that the tower frequency is 118.1. The field has radar and an Approach Control that operates on 119.7 Mhz. When the tower is not operating, use Honolulu Center on 126.6 and give your position reports in the blind on 118.1. Ground Control is 121.9.

The Minimum Sector Altitudes here are 1500 feet MSL between a 165-degree inbound heading, east to a 290-degree inbound heading; 5100 feet MSL from the 290-degree inbound heading, south to a 020-degree inbound heading, and then 14,800 feet MSL from the 020-degree inbound heading, west to a 165-degree inbound heading.

Note here that the circle-to-land MDAs are the same for both approaches even though the VOR DME-A increases the visibility requirements for Category A and B aircraft by ¼ mile. The VOR DME Rwy 26 plate shows a straight-in approach. The VOR DME-A, although it is a straight approach to the airport area, requires a circling approach to the runway (due to the angle between the final approach segment and the landing runway. Both approaches, as indicated in their names, require a DME receiver.

IT'S YOUR DECISION

The approach plate for the VOR DME 26 gives two possible initial approach segments: the 11-mile DME arc and the overhead approach. The FAF is VEWES intersection (as denoted by the Maltese cross), which is 5.0 DME from the ITO VOR on the 079-degree radial. VEWES can also be identified by the intersection of the 184-degree bearing to POA NDB and the 079-degree radial of ITO. VEWES intersection is also the missed approach holding fix for both approach plates, although the missed approach procedure is somewhat different in each case. The VOR DME Rwy 26 approach uses a climbing *right* turn in the missed approach, while you must make a climbing *left* turn if you miss on the VOR DME-A approach, proving again that it's necessary to double-check each and every procedure. Also notice that Hilo uses a non-standard left turn holding pattern.

228

Fig. 19-3

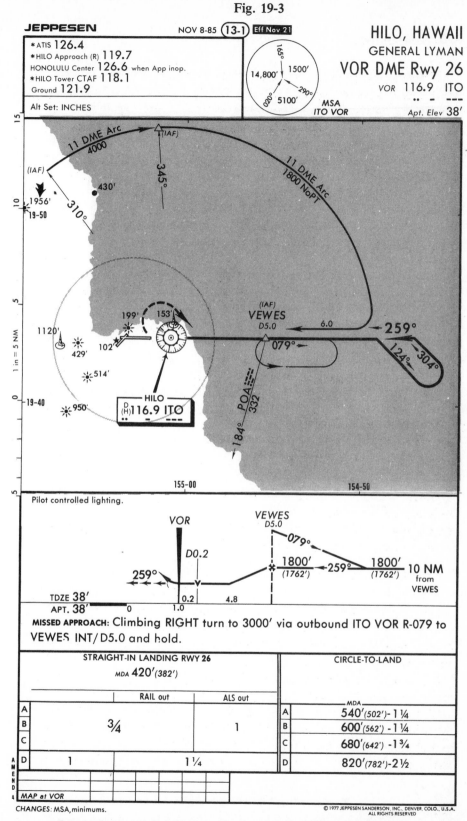

DME Approaches

Let's assume you are approaching from the northwest on the ITO 325-degree radial (145° TO on your #1 VOR). You have completed your descent checklist and have been cleared for the VOR DME-A approach. You are 20 miles out at 4000 feet when you get the weather. The tower reports 500 feet scattered, estimated 600 feet broken, 1000 feet overcast, with 1½ miles visibility in light rain showers. Visibility to the south is lower and a heavier rain shower is approaching from the south. Wind is from the southwest at 5 knots.

Under Part 91, you may *start* an instrument approach *regardless* of the reported ceiling and visibility. But you may not go below the MDA (or DH) and land unless (1) the *flight* visibility meets the applicable minimums shown on your chart, (2) you have the runway environment in sight, and (3) you can make a normal descent to landing.

Take a look at your minimums. You can try either approach, but you have been cleared for the VOR DME-A approach, which will be faster than the VOR DME Rwy 26 (flying the arc is very time-consuming). With the low ceiling and the rain showers, however, you ask to use the VOR DME Rwy 26 arc approach instead.

Why?

Well, take a look at the plan view on the VOR DME-A approach. If you have to fly it to the minimums, you must initiate a missed approach one mile DME before reaching the VOR. The only time you can continue to the VOR (i.e., follow the short arrows as shown in the profile view) is when you have visual reference with the *runway* environment and can continue to the runway by visual reference. You have to establish this reference prior to reaching the MAP, and the rain showers might be just bad enough to obscure your vision. Remember, the tower is reporting *ground* visibility, and what you will see outside the aircraft windshield is often much less than that. Also, you have to realize that, even if you do have visual reference prior to the MAP, you will still have to make a 114-degree turn to Runway 26 while close to the ground, and in rain showers to boot. And don't forget those heavier showers approaching the field from the southwest. Sure, the VOR DME-A might be possible—and it is more expedient—but it's easier and safer to fly the arc approach. My father always used to tell me that sometimes the long way around is the shortest way home. In the case of the arc approach, you can get a mile closer to the field because the MAP is at the VOR, which is only a mile from the threshold. In addition, should the approaching rain showers lower the ceiling, you will be able to use the straight-in MDA of 420 feet MSL off of the arc, along with the lower ¾-mile visibility.

If the weather conditions were better, say 1500 feet broken with two miles visibility and scattered rain showers, I'd be more inclined to take the VOR DME-A, and then only if I'd been there before and was familiar with the terrain and the ground reference points.

Fig. 19-4

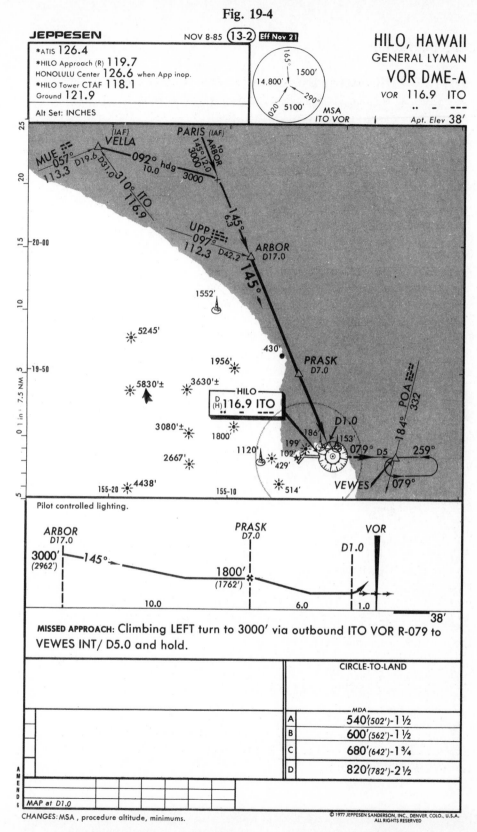

JEPPESEN   NOV 8-85 (13-2) [Eff Nov 21]

*ATIS 126.4
*HILO Approach (R) 119.7
HONOLULU Center 126.6 when App inop.
*HILO Tower CTAF 118.1
Ground 121.9

Alt Set: INCHES

HILO, HAWAII
GENERAL LYMAN
VOR DME-A
VOR 116.9 ITO
•• – ---
Apt. Elev 38'

MSA
ITO VOR
165° 1500'
14,800'
020 5100' 290°

Pilot controlled lighting.

MISSED APPROACH: Climbing LEFT turn to 3000' via outbound ITO VOR R-079 to VEWES INT/ D5.0 and hold.

	CIRCLE-TO-LAND
	MDA
A	540'(502')-1½
B	600'(562')-1½
C	680'(642')-1¾
D	820'(782')-2½

MAP at D1.0

CHANGES: MSA , procedure altitude, minimums.

(Reproduced with permission of Jeppesen Sanderson, Inc. NOT FOR USE IN NAVIGATION.)

FLYING THE DME ARC

Well, you have made your decision, asked Approach Control, and they've cleared you for the 11-mile DME arc approach.

When do you turn on the arc? A good rule of thumb is to allow a one-mile lead for each 100 knots of airspeed. In a Cessna 172 at 100 knots you would start your turn at 12 DME, while in a DC-9 at 250 knots you'd start it at 13.5 DME. In both cases, you would use a standard-rate turn. This would bring you out just about on the arc. From there on in, a series of shallow bank corrections should hold you on the arc.

To get on the arc initially, turn 90° from your inbound track heading. In this case, if you have been approaching the Hilo (ITO) VOR on a heading of about 145°, a left turn to a heading of 055° should put you on the arc. This is because, whenever you cross an arc inbound, you cross it at a 90-degree angle. To fly an arc, you actually fly a series of tangents to it. After roll-out on the arc, check your DME. If it is exactly 11 miles, you have done everything perfectly. If it's a little less than 11 miles, you turned too slowly so just maintain your heading of 055° until you get back to 11 miles. If you rolled out a little over 11 miles, you should turn back toward the VOR (in this case the turn will be to the right) about 10-20°, depending on what you will need to compensate for the wind. After completing the turn, hold your heading until the DME changes slightly. You will have to continue slight turns toward the VOR as you progress around the arc.

As you turn on the arc, set the #1 OBS to the inbound course (259°), and set the #2 OBS to 345° FROM, so you can identify the IAF. As the #2 needle centers, you are crossing the IAF and can descend to 1800 feet MSL. During your descent you can reset the #2 OBS to 249° TO, which will give you a 10-degree lead-in radial to use as a guide. With such a long distance left to fly, you can review the chart, paying special attention to the missed approach procedure. If you have ADF equipment on board, tune it to POA and use it as a back-up for the DME for VEWES intersection. Remember, don't let your navigational equipment gather dust. Make use of everything you have on board.

If there happens to be a compass locator (NDB) at or near the VOR site, setting the ADF to that frequency will prove a big help, as the relative bearing to the VOR site should remain off your wingtip throughout the arc.

When you have everything set up to your satisfaction, you can sit back and relax until the needle on the #2 OBI centers (at which time the #1 needle should be coming off the peg). By using both needles, you can adjust your rate of turn to intercept the radial without overshooting it. Then re-tune the #2 OBS to 079° FROM the ITO VOR to set yourself up for the missed approach. By now you should also be at approach airspeed with the approach flaps set.

As you cross VEWES, lower the gear and go through the before-landing checklist. And be aware that, because this approach has a Visual Descent Point at 0.2 DME (prior to the VOR), normally you may not descend below the MDA until you pass that point, even if you have the runway environment in sight.

You should be at your minimums before you reach the VOR. Remember that the closer the VOR facility is to the airport, the more accurate your approach should be. Anytime you hit minimums and can see the runway environment when the safety pilot lifts the hood, you have made a good VOR approach.

If you don't have visual contact with the runway environment by the time you cross the VOR, apply takeoff power, retract flaps to the takeoff position, and when you have a positive climb indication, retract the gear and start a climbing right turn to intercept the 079-degree radial outbound. Then clean up the flaps and continue to climb to 3000 feet. While all of this is going on, set the #1 OBS to 079° FROM. Until you get around to this you have the #2 OBI to use for guidance.

By the example just presented, you can see that there are times when, as pilot-in-command, you will have to weigh expediency versus safety.

20

ILS and Localizer-Only Approaches

ON THE VOR APPROACHES WE'VE BEEN DEALING WITH SO FAR, YOU ARE NOT allowed to descend below the MDA until you have the runway environment in sight, but you usually have a little time to spot it before you have to make a missed approach. Now you'll thread the needle, so to speak, and work on the ILS approach. Its enhanced accuracy can best be illustrated by the fact that, if you fly the glide slope down to the ground and keep the localizer needle anywhere on the active area of the indicator face, your wheels will hit the runway when you touch down. What this means is that, at the threshold of the runway, a full deflection of the localizer needle amounts to less than 100 feet of lateral displacement from the centerline. That's cutting it pretty close. It means that if you have the localizer needle centered when you break out, you will be looking right down the runway centerline.

FIGURE 20-1 is Honolulu's ILS Rwy 8L approach. The airport diagram (FIG. 20-2) shows that Runway 8L/26R is 12,360 feet long, with a 655-foot overrun for Runway 8L and an 863-foot overrun for Runway 26R. Under "Additional Runway Information" you learn that Runway 8L has High Intensity Runway Lights and a standard, high intensity Approach Light System with Sequenced Flashing Lights in an ILS CAT I configuration (ALSF-1). There is a standard VASI on the left side of the approach, the runway is 150 feet wide, and it is grooved. You also see that the usable runway length for landing beyond the glide slope is 11,127 feet, which means that the glide slope transmitter is positioned about 1200 feet from the approach end of the runway.

THE DUCK-UNDER SYNDROME

Quite a few accidents result from aircraft diving below the glide slope after they break out. Called "duck under" maneuvers, they are caused by two factors. First, if the aircraft is on the glide slope and breaks out at minimums, it will still be between 50 and 100 feet above the runway at the threshold. This is enough to make some pilots feel that they're too high. The other problem is that they will see a black hole in front of them, and they will be afraid of losing sight of the field. In any case, these reasons will be enough to make some pilots "dip" below the glide path and either land short, or hit with such a high rate of sink that they severely damage their planes. It's such a problem that our big brothers in the FAA have made a regulation prohibiting large and turbine-powered aircraft from flying below the glide slope prior to passing the middle marker. If a runway is equipped with a VASI, aircraft (including small ones) are not allowed to fly below the VASI. (These two restrictions apply to controlled airports.)

Anytime you are flying an ILS approach, remember that the glide slope transmitter is located 750 feet or more from the approach end of the runway. With this in mind, you should realize two things.

First, that you will, of necessity, cross the threshold higher when flying the ILS glide slope than you usually do when flying VFR. That's why it's a good idea to fly the glide slope from time to time in visual conditions, so you will be used to that Threshold Crossing Height. It will look even higher to you in rain and snow when visibility is reduced.

Second, the designated touchdown point is between 750 and 1500 feet from the approach end so there will still be plenty of runway left on which to stop, even if you fly the glide slope to the ground.

MOUNTAINS AND MOVING OBSTACLES

Now take a look at the face of the chart in FIG. 20-1. On the plan view you are cautioned by the note to the north of the MM which tells you that you may encounter 205-foot ships in the channel—that's because the channel leads into Pearl Harbor, which is a busy Naval installation. The MM is just past the channel with a glide slope crossing height of 249 feet MSL, so if you are on the glide slope and one of these large ships is in the channel, you will have about 100 feet of clearance, more or less. You certainly don't want to be low on this approach.

The LOM is called EWABE. In addition to its ADF (NDB) signal, this fix can also be determined by radar or by 6.7 DME on the 268-degree radial of the Honolulu (HNL) VOR, which is on a frequency of 114.8 MHz.

Both from the plan view and the MSA circle, you can see that Oahu is a high island, and although the runway is near sea level (13 feet MSL), it has high mountains on three sides. You will see more proof of that on the takeoff minimums page later.

Fig. 20-1

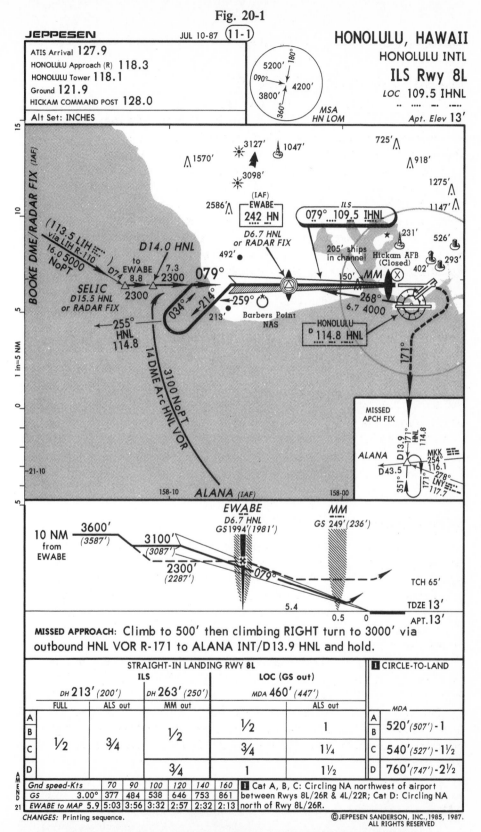

Fig. 20-2

HONOLULU INTL

N21 19.3 W157 55.5

Elev 13' Var 11°E

ATIS Departure 132.2	HONOLULU Departure (R)
HONOLULU Clearance 121.4	East 124.8
Ground 121.9	West 118.3
Tower 118.1	VOT 111.0

CAUTION: Birds in vicinity of airport.
Low level wind shear alert system.

HICKAM AFB

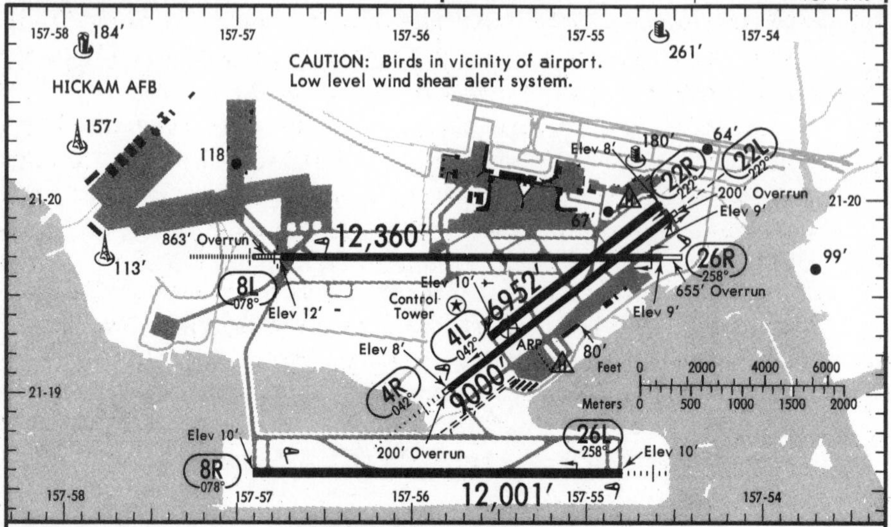

ADDITIONAL RUNWAY INFORMATION

RWY			USABLE LENGTHS — LANDING BEYOND —			
			Threshold	Glide Slope	TAKE-OFF	WIDTH
4R ❶	HIRL MALSR VASI-L	grooved		7949'		150'
22L	HIRL ❷VASI-L	grooved				
4L ❶	MIRL REIL VASI-L					200'
22R	MIRL REIL					
8R	HIRL VASI (3 bar)-L					200'
26L	HIRL MALSF ❸VASI (3 bar)-L					
8L ❹	❻HIRL ALSF-I VASI-L	grooved		11,127'		150'
❺26R	❻HIRL REIL ❼VASI (3 bar)-L	grooved				

❶ Closed to aircraft over 12,500 lbs for take-off sunset to sunrise.
❷ Unusable beyond 2 NM from threshold due to obstructions.
❸ System canted 5° south of rwy centerline.
❹ Rwy 8L closed to take-off for wide-bodied and 4 engine turbo jet. Not available for landing 1900-0700Z due to noise restriction.
❺ Rwy 8L-26R closed 0500-0700 FRIDAY except east 7400' rwy 8L for take-off.
❻ Runway lights are outside 200' pavement width; pavement striped 150' wide.
❼ Unusable beyond 3.6 NM from threshold due to obstruction.

For Take-Off Minimums and Departure Procedures see 11-1A.

FOR FILING AS ALTERNATE

	Precision	Non-Precision
A		
B	600-2	800-2
C		
D		

CHANGES: Runway 8L note.

No procedure turn is authorized on the straight-in approach from the IAF at BOOKE (which is off the chart to the left) or from the DME arc from ALANA (which is off the bottom of the chart). The procedure turn illustrated is for overhead approaches only, in which case EWABE is the IAF.

Let's take a look at some of the other information on the chart. On the plan view again, note the thin arrow crossing the DME arc which is the 255-degree radial of HNL VOR. It is the lead-in radial, marking the location where aircraft should begin to turn from the arc onto the final approach. You can see that the minimum altitude on the arc is 3100 feet MSL.

Over the runway symbol on the profile view is a note that reads, "TCH 65'." That is the Threshold Crossing Height for aircraft on the glide slope. The TCH appears on all ILS approach charts, because you usually want to know the height at which the glide slope crosses the threshold.

The solid line on the profile view shows the approach profile you would use if flying a full ILS, while the dashed line shows the step-down flight path you would use if flying a localizer-only approach.

MORE FACTS AND FIGURES

The minimums table shows how inoperative components will change your minimums. Just look under the appropriate column to see what minimums you should use.

You can determine an approximate rate of descent from the conversion table at the bottom of the chart, provided that you have your ground speed pretty well figured out. You can also see that the glide slope angle is 3°. Additionally, the conversion table tells you that the distance from the LOM (EWABE) to the MAP is 5.9 miles. Remember what you learned about the segment mileages shown above and below the ground reference line? In this case, it's 5.4 miles from the LOM to the MM and 0.5 miles from the MM to the runway threshold.

The MAP, indicated where the dashed horizontal line bends upwards, near the threshold, is the spot where you will begin a missed approach when flying a localizer approach. If flying the full ILS approach, you would be on the solid line and would be flying that down to a lower altitude—to the DH—which is just about the vicinity of the MM in this case. This is an absolute go/no-go point. When you reach the DH you either see the runway environment and land, or you initiate the missed approach. If you're on the localizer approach, get down to the MDA and fly out your time. When the MM is operational it will give you an additional check on your missed approach point, because you will have another half-mile to go (about 15 seconds in the average light aircraft) before the MAP.

Before we get into the actual approaches there are a few more items to consider. Note ∎ of the circle-to-land minimums tells you that Category A, B, and C aircraft are restricted from circling northwest of the airport between

Runways 8L/26R and 4L/22R, while Category D aircraft are restricted from circling north of Runway 8L/26R.

Near the bottom of FIG. 20-2 you see the note, "For Take-Off Minimums and Departure Procedures see 11-1A." So, look over at FIG. 20-3, which is one of those new pages Jeppesen has created for major airports. Under many of the take-off minimums you read, "If Special Departure Used or . . . ." Look down at the next-to-last listing on the page and you'll find the Special Departure explained as:

> Immediate climbing right turn, between headings 150° & 200° to be completed within 2 NM of runway departure end, then as cleared. Turn must be completed prior to HNL VOR D3.6. Caution: Steeply rising terrain north and east of airport. Tall vessels traverse Pearl Harbor channel.

LOCALIZER-ONLY APPROACH

Now that we've covered the information found on the approach charts, let's see how to incorporate it into a successful approach.

Begin with a localizer approach (no glide slope) as depicted by the dashed lines on the profile view, FIG. 20-1. The minimums box tells you that, for your type of aircraft, on a straight-in approach to Runway 8L, you will have an MDA of 460 feet MSL (447 feet AGL) and a visibility minimum, provided the ALS is operating, of ½ mile. If you lose the ALS, the visibility minimum will increase to one mile.

The 3600-foot MSL altitude shown on the profile view applies only to the procedure turn or overhead approach minimum altitude. Once you complete the procedure turn and are heading inbound, you can descend to 2300 feet MSL to the FAF which, in the case of this nonprecision approach, is EWABE.

The same 2300-foot minimum holds true for the two NoPT transitions. In the case of the 14-mile DME arc approach, you would start your descent from 3100 feet after you are established on the inbound course. If you were coming in from LIH (Lihue, Kauai), you would cross BOOKE intersection and descend to 5000 feet MSL until you got to SELIC (as in Tom!) intersection, which is 15.5 miles DME from the HNL VOR. It can also be identified by radar. At SELIC you would be established on the inbound track and could then descend to 2300 feet MSL. As you can see on the plan view, SELIC is 8.8 miles from EWABE and you would have 2700 feet to descend. If your ground speed was 120 knots, it would take about 4 minutes and 20 seconds to cover that distance, so you would want a descent rate of 700 FPM, or slightly greater, in order to get down to your minimums prior to the FAF.

Fig. 20-3

TAKE-OFF & DEPARTURE PROCEDURES

	Rwys 22L, 22R, 26R		Rwy 26L			Rwy 8R		
	Forward Vis Ref	STD	With Mim climb of 285'/NM to 3000'		Other	If Special Departure Used or With Mim climb of 212'/NM to 1000'		Other
			Forward Vis Ref	STD		Forward Vis Ref	STD	
1 & 2 Eng	¼	1	¼	1	300-1	¼	1	500-1
3 & 4 Eng		½		½			½	

	Rwy 8L					
	CAT A & B AIRCRAFT			CAT C & D AIRCRAFT		
	If Special Departure Used or With Mim climb of 210'/NM to 1000'		Other	If Special Departure Used or With Mim climb of 334'/NM to 1700'		Other
	Forward Vis Ref	STD		Forward Vis Ref	STD	
1 & 2 Eng	¼	1	600-2	¼	1	1500-2
3 & 4 Eng		½			½	

	Rwys 4L, 4R					
	CAT A & B AIRCRAFT			CAT C & D AIRCRAFT		
	If Special Departure Used or With Mim climb of 466'/NM to 2000'		Other	If Special Departure Used or With Mim climb of 524'/NM to 3500'		Other
	Forward Vis Ref	STD		Forward Vis Ref	STD	
1 & 2 Eng	¼	1	1800-2	¼	1	3200-2
3 & 4 Eng		½			½	

SPECIAL DEPARTURE

Immediate climbing right turn, between headings 150° & 200° to be completed within 2 NM of runway departure end, then as cleared. Turn must be completed prior to HNL VOR D3.6.
Caution: Steeply rising terrain north and east of airport. Tall vessels traverse Pearl Harbor channel.

IFR DEPARTURE PROCEDURE

Comply with SID or RADAR VECTORS, or: Rwys 4L, 4R, 8L, 8R, climbing right turn as soon as practicable, then as cleared. Rwys 22L, 22R, 26L, 26R, climb runway heading to 300' then left climbing turn as cleared. Left turn must be completed within 2 NM of runway departure end (HNL VOR D3.0).

AMEND7

CHANGES: Special departure.

(Reproduced with permission of Jeppesen Sanderson, Inc. NOT FOR USE IN NAVIGATION.)

Prior to SELIC you would want your #1 VOR tuned to the HNL ILS (assuming you're on radar vectors, and are not using the VOR receiver to navigate from LIH), and you will have identified it. You will have the OBS set on 079° and should have already checked the weather and completed the descent checklist. If your marker beacon receiver and/or ADF is operable, you will have the beacon switch turned to HI, and the speaker on. You will have checked the light bulbs in the marker beacon receiver for proper operation and will have tuned the ADF to EWABE. Naturally, you would have identified it as well. The #2 VOR receiver would be on the HNL VOR (also identified) for DME information, and you would have set the OBS to 171°, to be ready for the missed approach.

If I tend to keep repeating myself over proper radio identification it's only because, with the transistorized, digital equipment in use today, many pilots are getting sloppy about identifying the stations they're tuning to, and it's quite easy to make a mistake. Many times, this is caused by so many frequencies being so close together, both on the dial and on the ground. A good example of this is the frequency for the ILS approach to Runway 8L at Honolulu, 109.5, and the frequency for the ILS to Runway 4R at the same airport, 110.5. In the dark, or bouncing around in the clouds, it would be quite easy to miss by just one click of the knob, and end up flying the wrong approach. Also, there have been times when the frequency display is out of sync with the actual frequency being received. So, to implant it in the back of your minds, I'll repeat "and identify" each time I mention tuning radios.

There are two schools of thought regarding setting up your two VOR radios. One school prefers to have both radios tuned and identified on the approach frequency in order to detect a failure in one or the other. The second school says to have your primary radio set on your approach frequency, and your secondary radio set up for your missed approach.

If I am flying in a two-pilot cockpit, I adhere to the first method, as I can always tell the other guy to set up the missed approach on the radios while I am beginning the missed approach procedure. But if I am flying solo, I like to have the missed approach already set up, because I'll be busy enough doing everything else by myself.

Now, once you cross the FAF you can begin your final descent. You need to positively ascertain the FAF passage, however, and that can be done by the OM indicator light, the aural tone of the marker, the reversal of the ADF needle, the HNL 6.7 DME, or by Approach Control confirming it on radar.

When you cross the FAF, lower the gear and complete the pre-landing checklist, just as you did on the VOR approach. I have made it a habit of always calling for "gear down, landing checklist" whenever I cross the FAF, even if I'm flying solo, and even if I know I've lowered the gear earlier. By calling for it, it becomes a habit that will hopefully prevent me from landing with the gear up someday. Remember Murphy's Law—it's always waiting to catch us slipping up. In addition to calling for the gear down and the checklist, I also physically touch, or point to, the gear lights to ascertain that they are green.

I never fly closer to the airport than the FAF when the plane is clean. One reason for this is that I still won't be all that busy that far out, so there is plenty of time to get the gear down and the checklist completed properly. It's also nice to stabilize the approach far enough out so that you're not chasing the aircraft all the way to the runway.

To prevent chasing the plane all around the sky, try to get within 10° of the inbound track before crossing the FAF, and thereafter try to stay within 5° of the track. The heading required to stay on course will usually change somewhat as you descend, because the wind shifts around due to surface friction and the Coriolis force, and because the wind is deflected by ground objects such as stands of trees, small hills, and high buildings.

Keeping your heading changes this small requires a lot of practice and a fairly rapid instrument scan. Remember not to chase the needle. As I pointed out earlier, when flying the localizer, a full deflection of the needle will still put you over the runway. So if your needle starts drifting off center, make a small five-degree correction to try and stop that drift. Once the drift has stopped, a further correction of one or two degrees should start it back toward the center. Although it may not be considered good airmanship by some, I find it easier to apply a little rudder pressure to skid the nose around those few degrees. This keeps the gyro presentation steady and is actually easier on the passengers than a lot of wing waving. Once you have stopped the trend of the needle deflection, you have it made. If you can bring the needle slowly back to the centerline—and hold it there—you're a real pro.

The reason I emphasize just stopping the trend is that, if you work constantly at coming back to centerline as the aircraft gets closer and closer to the runway and the width of the localizer beam narrows to just a few hundred feet, you'll look as though you're doing Dutch rolls on the way in.

THE PRECISION APPROACH

Now—what about the full ILS? What's the difference? Well, it usually means that you'll be descending 200-250 feet lower than on the localizer-only approach, and you'll have one more needle to monitor.

You will go through the same procedure you used for the localizer approach, as far as the tuning and identifying of the navigational aids is concerned. You will also be completing the same checklists at the same time, as well as checking on the latest weather. The big thing you will notice is that finally, that little red OFF flag on the side of the OBI is gone, and a "live" horizontal needle has appeared in its place.

As you maneuver to bring the aircraft onto the final approach path, this extra needle will normally be near the top of the indicator. This is merely a guide telling you that you are below the level of the glide path for this distance from the runway.

Even though you will be flying an electronic glide path down to the runway, you will still tune and identify the LOM on the ADF and turn on the marker beacon receiver, because there are many times when you will be intercepting false glide paths that are sent out as ghost signals from the transmitter. The most dangerous of these would be the ones that give you too steep of a glide slope. One indication of such a false signal would be a rate of descent in excess of that shown for your ground speed in the conversion table. If you were to hit wind shear, though, with a resultant tailwind (as happens many times, especially around squalls), you would expect a high rate of descent. The best indications of wind shear or false glide paths is your altitude when you cross the outer marker. If it's not close to that shown on the profile view (in the case of the ILS Rwy 8L at Honolulu, it would be 1994 feet MSL), you're on a false glide path. If your altitude is close to what is shown at the outer marker, and you still have a high rate of descent, then you have a strong tailwind. If this is the case, and the wind at the field is reported as coming down the runway, then you should be aware that you will be experiencing wind shear prior to touchdown. If the winds have been strong and gusty in the area, you may even want to abandon the approach and go around once to allow the shear condition to abate.

The solid line at 3100 feet MSL on the profile view in FIG. 20-1 shows the altitude where you would intercept the glide slope. If you were cleared for an ILS approach, this is the lowest altitude you would descend to until intercepting the glide slope. (By definition, your glide slope intercept point *is* your FAF.) This is also the time you would extend the gear. That way you would have a stabilized approach all the way down. If you set up your normal descent speed at glide slope interception, but left the gear up until the outer marker, you'd have to add power to compensate for the extra drag of the gear. It's a lot smoother to put the gear down as you intercept the glide slope and then just make enough of a power adjustment to establish the required rate of descent.

The next question is: How do you fly the glide slope indicator? Just as if it were a horizontal OBI indicator. Am I kidding? Nope—that's all there is to it. As you fly into the glide slope the needle will move off the upper peg. As it centers itself, lower the gear and begin your descent. Adjust the rate of descent as necessary to keep the needle near the center. The rate shown in the conversion table will give you a great starting figure. If you suddenly find that the glide slope needle is off center, glance at the vertical speed indicator. Chances are good that you have allowed your rate of descent to get away from you.

Just as with the localizer needle, don't chase the glide slope indicator. Alter your rate of descent by 200 FPM to try and stop any trend the needle makes off center, and then, when you get the needle stopped, adjust the descent by 100-FPM increments to bring it back to the center again. As with the localizer, as long as you keep the needle from pegging-out, you are in good shape. The big problem here would be that, if the needle were a dot high, you would be too low and might hit your DH before you'd be close enough to the field to pick up the approach lights. If the needle were a dot low, you'd be too high crossing the approach lights and might not see them.

How low do you fly, you ask? *Only down to the DH and no lower*, at which time you are required to initiate a missed approach if you don't see the runway or other identifying features. To review what these identifying features are, take a look at FAR 91.116 back in Chapter 11.

When you make your first full ILS approach, the accuracy will astound you. It will give you the confidence you'll need when the weather goes sour and you end up "on the gauges."

There's very little that is more satisfying in flying than breaking out of the mist and rain, at minimums, and seeing those sequence flashers right in front of your nose. It makes all of the hard work, study, and financial expenditure worthwhile.

ANOTHER LOOK AT HONOLULU

Before we get into the NDB approach, I'd like to go back to FIG. 20-2, the Honolulu airport chart, to discuss some more of the notes it contains. In the first place, you can see two different Departure Control frequencies, depending on which direction you are going after takeoff. Normally, the Clearance Delivery people will tell you the frequency to use on departure, but if they don't, they expect you to know which way you're heading. Listed in the lower right corner of the communications block, below the departure frequencies, is the VOR test frequency on the field (VOT 111.0).

Because they don't want you to be too surprised when you see feathers flying past the windshield, they have a note telling you about birds in the vicinity of the airport. I don't know what you could do about it in flight, because it's impossible to dodge a flock of them.

Each of the runways is equipped with a VASI on the left side of the runway (except for 22R, which has no VASI). The VASIs on 8R, 26L, and 26R are three-bar configurations, the rest are two-bar.

Note ❸ tells you that the VASI on 26L is canted 5° south of the runway centerline. This is because the normal approach to that runway is from offshore to the south, and the canted angle of the VASI allows you to pick it up sooner. Other notes say that you can only expect to see the 22L VASI within 2 nautical miles of the runway, and the 26R VASI within 3.6 nautical miles, due to obstructions in both cases.

Notice in FIG. 20-3 that takeoff minimums for Runways 4L and 4R are much more restrictive than takeoff minimums for Runway 8L, which are, in turn, more restrictive than those for Runway 8R. This makes sense; in each case you will be farther from the obstructions after takeoff. On Runways 4L and 4R you will be heading right at the mountains. On 8L you will be just about parallel to them, and on 8R you will be almost completely offshore.

Why, though, do you suppose that the takeoff minimum ceilings for other than special departures are so much higher than straight-in and circling landing minimums? Furthermore, why are they so much higher for Categories C and D than for A and B?

It all boils down to performance, again. The Category A and B aircraft will be getting off the ground sooner and they will have more room in which to maneuver. Also, because of their lower speed they will have a tighter radius of turn than the big birds. The heavies will be using up most of the runway before they finally stagger into the air, so they will end up a lot closer to the mountains.

These are things that should concern you on every departure you make—and every arrival as well. Sometimes, you may be able to get into a field, only to find out that you may not be able to get out for awhile. Yet, if you chose another field nearby, you might have no problem. It's just one more thing you'll have to look at during preflight planning.

21

NDB and Back Course Approaches

NOW, LOOK AT FIG. 21-1, THE NDB APPROACH TO HONOLULU'S RUNWAY 8L. An NDB (Non-Directional Beacon) approach is the same as an ADF (Automatic Direction Finder) approach. Its relatively low degree of accuracy is evidenced by its lowest MDA being 540 feet MSL. Because the MDA is so high, the missed approach procedure is a simple climbing right turn. You don't have to climb to 500 feet before turning as you did on the ILS and localizer approaches to Runway 8L at Honolulu because you are already higher than that.

When you look at the chart your immediate reaction may be, "Wow, a simple, old, overhead approach." It could be, and it should be, but because of the infrequency of making this type of approach, many students don't really receive enough training in the use of the ADF. It's not only student pilots though. There have been so many incidents in air carrier operations lately that the FAA is requiring each pilot proficiency check to include at least one NDB approach.

Simply stated, FIG. 21-1 shows you crossing the LOM on what I call "high key," or "high station." Proceed outbound, tracking on the 259-degree bearing from the station (EWABE) and descending to 3600 feet MSL, which is the minimum procedure turn altitude. Notice once again that the procedure turn has to be completed within 10 nautical miles southwest of the facility and that it can be any type of reversal you care to fly.

You should get the latest weather report and take care of the descent and in-range checklists while on descent from the high station. Sometime before or during the procedure turn, take a quick look at the missed approach procedure.

After the turn inbound, descend to 2300 feet MSL and, when you pass the FAF (LOM) inbound, check the time, lower the gear, begin your descent, report the FAF inbound, and take care of the pre-landing checklist—all the while tracking on the 079-degree bearing from the station. As in the VOR and localizer approaches, descend to the MDA and fly out the time, which in this case will again bring you to about the runway threshold.

TRACKING WITH THE ADF

There are basically three types of ADF presentations. The flux gate, or radio magnetic indicator (RMI), which is found on most large aircraft, is the best. It has the ADF needle incorporated into the face of the instrument and utilizes a movable face. This works so well that we call it the "no think" gauge. The instrument does the thinking for us. The face of the instrument, or the azimuth, turns to keep lined up with magnetic north. The RMI is your directional gyro as well, so whatever number shows on the upper indicator is your magnetic heading. Because the ADF needle always points to the station, whatever number it points to on the azimuth is the magnetic bearing to the station. This is what makes it a "no think" instrument. All you have to remember is that, if you want to change your magnetic bearing to the station, you have to turn, and if you can't remember which direction to turn, just remember the old saying, "pull the tail" of the needle.

The second type of presentation has a manually rotatable dial. This requires a three-step procedure. First, check the magnetic compass to set the DG. Secondly, rotate the dial of the ADF to make it read the same as the DG, and finally, read the magnetic bearing to the station directly off the ADF needle—provided your heading hasn't changed in the meantime.

The least expensive and most common presentation found in general aviation aircraft is the one that uses a fixed-azimuth dial. On this dial, 0° (360°) is is always at the top of the face and the needle always reads the *relative* bearing to the station. That means that you have to mentally compute the magnetic bearing. I've seen a plastic accessory advertised which fits over the face of the fixed azimuth dial. You rotate the accessory to get the same results as in the manually operated dial. It's a good idea, but unfortunately you don't have one during this problem and are faced with flying an NDB approach using a fixed-azimuth ADF.

How do you figure it all out? Like any other type of navigation, one of the first things you have to know is where you are, so you will know which way you need to go. If you're a little confused, and are unable to convert all of the numbers at first, you can always turn the aircraft until the needle is pointing directly ahead (reading "0" on the dial), and then read the magnetic bearing to the station directly off of the DG.

"All right," you say, "but this procedure may not always be possible or practical. Then what?"

Fig. 21-1

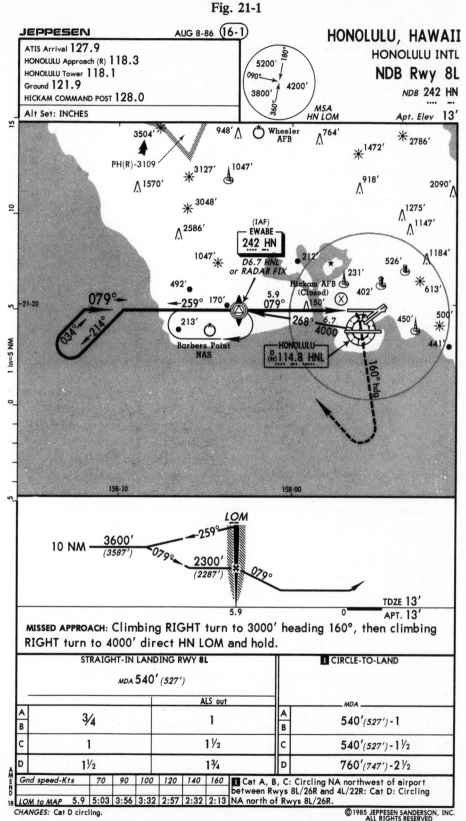

"Well," I say, "look here." The sum of your DG plus the azimuth reading (relative bearing to the station), if less than 360°, is the magnetic bearing *to* the station. Its reciprocal (add or subtract 180°) will be the bearing *from* the station.

If the sum of the DG plus the azimuth is more than 360°, simply subtract 360° from it, and the remainder will be the magnetic bearing to the station. If you find it difficult to do the math, invest a few dollars in a small electronic calculator.

Throughout this discussion I'll be mentioning bearings *to* and *from* the station, although technically speaking, when one refers to bearings in relation to NDBs, it should always be in terms of bearings *to*, which is the opposite of working with VORs, where the radials are defined as always *from* the station. However, usage of the terms "radial TO" and "bearing from" is becoming more common.

Setting Up an Example

Let's figure out some magnetic bearings. While we're at it, why not work out a problem showing how to track to the station on a given bearing, compensating for wind drift? It's all a simple matter of addition and subtraction as you can see in FIG. 21-2. In this example, you are directly south of the station in position A, and you want to track inbound *to* the station on the 330-degree bearing.

At position A, you are heading north, so the DG reads 0°, and because you are due south of the station, your azimuth is also 0°.

Your desired inbound course, of 330°, is found (on the ADF dial) to the left of the head of the needle. Now, if the head were on 330°, the tail would be on 150°, right? So, as I said earlier, to know which way to turn, remember to "pull the tail" of the needle. In this case you want to pull the tail to the right of the bottom of the dial, so you turn to the right. How *much* do you want to turn? That depends on how far you are from the station and what intercept angle you want to use, but to make this simple, turn 30° to the right.

At position B, at the moment you complete the turn to a heading of 030° on the DG (30° to the right of 0), and before you have moved off the 360-degree TO bearing, your azimuth will read 330°. If you add the DG (030°) and azimuth (330°) together, you get 360°, which is your magnetic bearing to the station at that moment.

If you continue on the heading of 030°, how will you know when you are crossing the desired track so that you can turn inbound? Well, you want to track inbound on the 330-degree TO bearing. By subtracting your heading (030°) from 330°, you get 300°. The needle will point to 300° (i.e., 300° will be the relative bearing on your azimuth) when you cross the 330-degree TO magnetic bearing at position C. When you turn inbound to a 330-degree heading, the relative bearing will be 0°, (position D).

Fig. 21-2

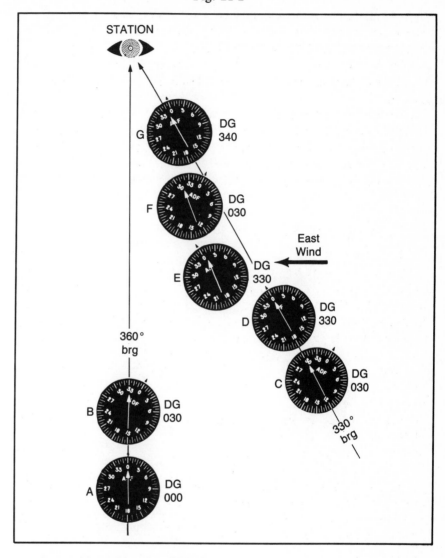

Correcting for the Wind

How do you correct for wind drift?

It's really just as easy. Let's assume that you have a wind from the east. This will cause you to drift to the west, and before long you'll end up 10° off course, as shown at position E. Your heading is still 330°, but your relative bearing is now reading 010°; 330° + 010° = 340°, which is now your new magnetic bearing to the station. To correct back to course, turn to a heading of 030° (position F). Here you see that your heading is 030° again, but because you were on the

340-degree magnetic bearing to the station when you made your turn, the relative bearing on the azimuth will be reading 310°. Is that correct? Let's confirm it. The DG is 030°, plus the relative bearing of 310°, which gives you a magnetic bearing to the station of 340°. Simple enough?

Once again you continue on a heading of 030° until the relative bearing is 300° and you'll be back at your desired magnetic bearing (330° TO).

This time, however, instead of turning inbound to the station and flying a 330-degree heading, which will only cause you to drift off course again, correct 10° to the right to compensate for wind drift. What will your instruments read now? Well, 10° right of 330° will give you a DG heading of 340°. This will provide a relative bearing 10° left of center on the ADF azimuth, or 350°. Are you still on the 330-degree magnetic bearing to the station? Check again. Your heading of 340°, plus the relative bearing of 350°, equals 690°. As this is more than 360°, you have to subtract 360°, which equals 330°. Easy? Well, maybe not, but at least this should take some of the mystery out of it.

The big thing to remember is that, when you are flying specific tracks on an NDB facility, decide on a heading to fly and then fly it. Any deviation of the azimuth needle will then be an indication of the wind drift involved. The biggest mistake beginning pilots make is to try to keep the azimuth needle centered. With a strong enough crosswind, and starting far enough from the station, you can conceivably end up flying an arc, reaching the station heading directly into the wind.

Tracking away from the station is similar, except you'll be working with reciprocals. Try it out both on paper and in the air.

If you're the type of person who does things easier pictorially rather than mathematically, look at it this way. In FIG. 21-2, to go from A to C, you have to change your relative bearing by 30° (360° magnetic bearing to 330° magnetic bearing). If you stay on the heading of 030°, you will fly until your relative bearing changes the 30° from 330° (at B) to 300° (at C), and you are there.

Either way, it all comes out the same, and although the NDB approach requires more mental labor than the others, once you have mastered the basic rules outlined above, and have practiced them a bit, you really will be able to say what you did in the beginning of this chapter—"Wow, a simple, old, overhead approach."

FLYING "AWAY" FROM THE NEEDLE

It is time to discuss one last approach—the localizer back course. The back course we'll study will be the Kahului, Hawaii, LOC DME (BACK CRS) Rwy 20 approach (FIG. 21-3).

Two main facts to remember concerning back course approaches are: (1) you cannot use the glide slope information, and (2) the localizer needle moves "backwards." This means that you have to be really cautious and think through the approach, as you'll have to consciously fight your previous training. On a back course, if the OBI moves to the left, you don't turn left to bring it back. You turn to the right. If it moves to the right, you turn to the left. You fly *away* from the needle. As long as you keep that in mind, you should have no trouble.

If you are making arc approaches from the east or west, you can see the lead-in radials indicated. From the east, OPANA is the IAF, which is where the 069-degree radial of the OGG VOR crosses the 13 DME arc. Remain at 3000 feet and fly the arc until passing the 032-degree radial from the OGG VOR, at which time you can begin the turn inbound to intercept the back course.

From the other direction, the IAF is PLUMB, which is 8.0 miles northwest of the 13.0 DME fix on the OGG 320-degree radial. The lead-in radial is the 017-degree radial. Remember now—you are flying the localizer back course, so the ILS will be tuned and identified on your #1 VOR receiver, while the OGG VOR should be on the #2 receiver. In fact, if you read the notes in the profile view, you will see that separate localizer and DME receivers are required, and that you are using the DME information from the OGG VOR.

You will use the DME to determine letdown points on this specific approach, as the approach is made over water. After you turn inbound at KRANE, you can descend to 1500 feet MSL. You have 1500 feet to lose, but you have eight miles (about four minutes) to lose them in, so if you keep a reasonable descent rate of between 500 and 600 FPM, you will get down there in plenty of time. Fly at 1500 feet to MUNCY, which is the 5.0 DME fix from the OGG VOR. It is also the FAF. After MUNCY, descend to your minimums, which are 400 feet MSL (375 feet AGL).

The MAP here, 1.0 DME from the OGG VOR, is 0.4 miles from the runway threshold. If you have to execute the missed approach, climb to 3000 feet MSL outbound on the 190-degree radial of the OGG VOR. You would have had set that heading on the #2 OBS upon turning onto final approach, so now all you have to do is fly it. You will be holding at DIPPS intersection, which can be identified by the intersection of the Lanai (LNY) 090-degree radial and the front course ILS to Kahului, by the LNY 090-degree radial and the OGG VOR 204-degree radial, or by the 22.2 DME fix on the LNY 090-degree radial.

If, after a missed approach on the back course, you want to try a front course ILS to Kahului, you would probably just turn the #1 OBS to the inbound (024-degree) ILS course. By the time you're about 10 miles south of the OGG VOR on the missed approach, you should have the heading pretty well tied down, so you can re-tune the #2 receiver to the LNY VOR, and set the OBS to 270° TO. Turn right (toward LNY) as the #2 needle centers, fly until the #1 needle (ILS) centers, and make a 30-degree turn to the right for a teardrop entry into the nonstandard (left-hand) holding pattern. While flying the one-minute outbound leg you would reset the #2 (LNY) OBS to 090° FROM, which will be the inbound holding pattern course.

VECTORS TO FINAL—A WARNING

On many approaches—not just the ones discussed in this chapter—you will be provided radar vectors to the final approach course. In such cases, it is critical that you be aware of the following from the *Airman's Information Manual*:

> After release to approach control, aircraft are vectored to the final approach course (ILS, MLS, VOR, ADF, etc.). Radar vectors and altitude or flight levels will be issued as required for spacing and separating aircraft. Therefore, pilots must not deviate from the headings issued by approach control. Aircraft will normally be informed when it is necessary to vector across the final approach course for spacing or other reasons. If approach course crossing is imminent and the pilot has not been informed that he will be vectored across the final approach course he should query the controller . . . The pilot is not expected to turn inbound on the final approach course unless the approach clearance has been issued . . .

Here we have a possible disaster. A low-time instrument pilot, suffering from fatigue, is vectored through the final approach course for separation purposes. The controller gets busy with another aircraft. The pilot, not familiar with the terrain, or perhaps misreading the chart, could conceivably fly into a mountain. This points out a good reason to study the entire approach chart, including the heights of all major obstructions—not just the diagram of the approach itself.

Fig. 21-3

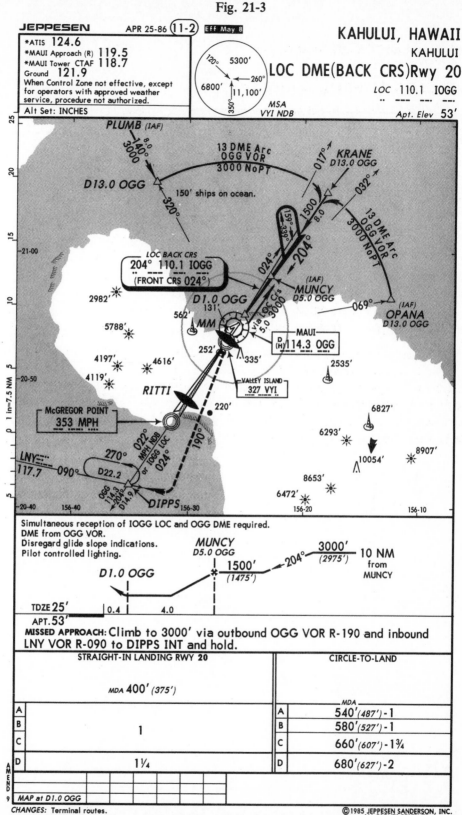

Conclusion

T HAT'S ABOUT IT. WE'VE COVERED PRACTICALLY EVERY TYPE OF APPROACH.
Now, let's review some of the more important DOs and DON'Ts as they
relate to instrument flying:

- DO learn to fly the basic maneuvers well before thinking
  about approaches.

- DO thoroughly study every current approach chart for every
  airport you will be using as a destination or alternate. Use
  a highlighter to make salient features such as the minimums
  for your category of aircraft, the missed approach procedures,
  and other important data.

- DO check all current NOTAMs.

- DO keep abreast of all changes that may occur in the symbols
  used on the charts.

- DO complete the descent checklist before initiating the
  approach. It would be very embarrassing to have your engine
  quit inside the outer marker because your mixture was still
  leaned out.

- DO get the latest weather before initiating an approach to ascertain whether or not the airport is above your minimums. It will also give you an idea of what to expect when you break out.

- DO identify every navaid you use. Make it standard practice to leave the speaker turned up on your primary navigational radio. If at any time you stop hearing the maddening identifier, you'll know that you've got problems.

- DO work to improve the speed of your instrument scan. The more effective and rapid your scan becomes, the more accurate your approach will be.

- DO have the proper approach plate handy. As you've seen, some airports have many different approaches, and sometimes the approach names sound similar.

- DO lower your gear and perform the pre-landing checklist when you cross the final approach fix inbound.

- DO use every bit of functioning navigational equipment you have on board. It won't do you a bit of good if you suddenly need it and it has to warm up.

- DO be sure to check, understand, and respect the weather. Remember that your instrument ticket has been issued to you not only because you have proven that you know how to fly on the gauges, but also because you have shown that you can exercise common sense and that you know that there is some weather out there that you really shouldn't be fooling around with. You don't have to get anywhere so badly that you should take unnecessary risks. No appointment is so valuable that it's worth dying for.

- DO practice instrument procedures and instrument flying at every opportunity. The more you practice the better you become—but you become very rusty, very quickly, when you don't use your skills.

- DON'T chase the needles on any approach, especially on the localizer or glide slope.

- DON'T be afraid to make a missed approach. In fact, just as you program your thinking to the possibility of an abort on each takeoff, you should program it for a missed approach on each approach. You don't have to wait until you get all the way to your MDA before you pull up. If, at any time, you feel that you're getting confused or behind your aircraft, pull up. Get some altitude under you where you'll be safe until you get your thinking and confidence back. Then, and only then, should you consider initiating a new approach. You'll only be taking an extra 15 minutes or so, but at least you'll still be alive.

- DON'T duck under the glide slope after you break out. Maintain a constant rate of descent to your normal flare-out altitude.

- DON'T use obsolete charts—ever.

- DON'T descend below the MDA or DH unless you actually see the runway or approach lights and are in a position to make a normal landing. And, naturally, as in all instrument work. . .

- *DO have faith in your instruments.*

Well, that's about it. I've tried to keep the tone general enough for most aircraft and most situations. Certain planes may operate a little differently, so check the aircraft operating manual carefully to be sure that you are operating within the proper guidelines.

I'm sure that once you've successfully completed your first *actual* IFR flight to a minimum type of landing, you'll feel even better than you did on your first solo flight.

"HAPPY LANDINGS!"

Glossary

The following glossary of instrument flight terms has been compiled from both the Jeppesen Chart Glossary and the FAA's Pilot/Controller Glossary. It is by no means complete.

Abbreviated IFR Flight Plans—An authorization by ATC requiring pilots to submit only that information needed for the purpose of ATC. It includes only a small portion of the usual IFR flight plan information. In certain instances, this may be only aircraft identification, location, and pilot request. Other information may be requested if needed by ATC for separation/control purposes. It is frequently used by aircraft which are airborne, desire an instrument approach, or by aircraft on the ground which desire a climb to VFR-on-top.

Advise Intentions— Tell me what you plan to do.

Aircraft Approach Category—A grouping of aircraft based on a speed of 1.3 times the stall speed in the landing configuration at maximum gross landing weight. An aircraft shall fit in only one category. If it is necessary to maneuver at speeds in excess of the upper limit of a speed range for a category, the minimums for the next higher category should be used. For example, an aircraft which falls in Category A, but is circling to land at a speed in excess of 91 knots, should use the approach Category B minimums when circling to land. The categories are as follows:

1. Category A—speed less than 91 knots.

2. Category B—speed 91 knots or more, but less than 121 knots.

3. Category C—speed 121 knots or more, but less than 141 knots.

    4. Category D—speed 141 knots or more but less than 166 knots.

    5. Category E—speed 166 knots or more.

aircraft classes—For the purposes of Wake Turbulence Separation Minima, ATC classifies aircraft as Heavy, Large, and Small as follows:

    1. Heavy—Aircraft capable of takeoff weights of 300,000 pounds or more whether or not they are operating at this weight during a particular phase of flight.

    2. Large—Aircraft of more than 12,500 pounds, maximum certificated takeoff weight, up to 300,000 pounds.

    3. Small—Aircraft of 12,500 pounds or less maximum certificated takeoff weight.

airport elevation/field elevation—The highest point of an airport's usable runways measured in feet from mean sea level.

Airport Reference Point/ARP—A point on the airport designated as the official airport location.

airport elevation/field elevation—The highest point of an airport's usable runways measured in feet from mean sea level.

    1. Indicated Airspeed—The speed shown on the aircraft airspeed indicator. This is the speed used in pilot/controller communications under the general term "airspeed".

    2. True Airspeed—The airspeed of an aircraft relative to undisturbed air. Used primarily in flight planning and en route portion of flight. When used in pilot/controller communications, it is referred to as "true airspeed" and not shortened to "airspeed".

airway—A control area or portion thereof established in the form of a corridor, the centerline of which is defined by radio navigational aids.

alternate airport—An airport at which an aircraft may land if a landing at the intended airport becomes inadvisable.

approach gate—An imaginary point used within ATC as a basis for vectoring aircraft to the final approach course. The gate will be established along the final approach course 1 mile from the outer marker (or the fix used in lieu of the outer marker) on the side away from the airport for precision approaches and 1 mile from the final approach fix on the side away from the airport for nonprecision approaches. In either case when measured along the final approach course, the gate will be no closer than 5 miles from the landing threshold.

approach speed—The recommended speed contained in aircraft manuals used by pilots when making an approach to landing. This speed will vary for different segments of an approach as well as for aircraft weight and configuration.

arc—The track over the ground of an aircraft flying at a constant distance from a navigational aid by reference to the distance measuring equipment (DME).

Area Minimum Altitude/AMA—This is an altitude defined by Jeppesen. The AMA is designed to provide terrain and obstacle clearance within AMA envelopes shown on area charts. It represents the upper limit of high ground or obstacles adjusted upward for vertical clearance. An AMA of 7000 feet or less clears all known obstacles and terrain by 1000 feet. An AMA greater than 7000 feet clears all known terrain and obstacles by 2000 feet.

area navigation/RNAV—A method of navigation that permits aircraft operation on any desired course within the coverage of station-referenced navigation signals or within the limits of a self-contained system capability. Random area navigation routes are direct routes, based on area navigation capability, between waypoints defined in terms of latitude/longitude coordinates, degree/distance fixes, or offsets from published or established routes/airways at a specified distance and direction. The major types of equipment are:

1. VORTAC referenced or Course Line Computer (CLC) systems, which account for the greatest number of RNAV units in use. To function, the CLC must be within the service range of a VORTAC.

2. OMEGA/VLF, although two separate systems, can be considered as one operationally. A long-range navigation system based upon Very Low Frequency radio signals transmitted from a total of 17 stations worldwide.

3. Inertial (INS) systems, which are totally self-contained and require no information from external references. They provide aircraft position and navigation information in response to signals resulting from inertial effects on components within the system.

4. MLS Area Navigation (MLS/RNAV), which provides area navigation with reference to an MLS ground facility.

5. LORAN-C is a long-range radio navigation system that uses ground waves transmitted at low frequency to provide user position information at ranges of up to 600 to 1200 nautical miles at both en route and approach altitudes. The usable signal coverage areas are determined by the signal-to-noise ratio, the envelope-to-cycle difference, and the geometric relationship between the positions of the user and the transmitting stations.

Automatic Direction Finder/ADF—An aircraft radio navigation system which senses and indicates the direction to a L/MF nondirectional radio beacon (NDB) ground transmitter. Direction is indicated to the pilot as a magnetic bearing or as a relative bearing to the longitudinal axis of the aircraft depending on the type of indicator installed in the aircraft. In certain applications, such as military, ADF operations may be based on airborne and ground transmitters in the VHF/UHF frequency spectrum.

bearing—The horizontal direction to or from any point, usually measured clockwise from true north, magnetic north, or some other reference point, through 360°.

below minimums—Weather conditions below the minimums prescribed by regulation for the particular action involved; e.g., landing minimums, takeoff minimums.

ceiling—The heights above the Earth's surface of the lowest layer of clouds or obscuring phenomena that is reported as "broken," "overcast," or "obscuration," and not classified as "thin" or "partial".

circle-to-land maneuver/circling maneuver/circling approach—A maneuver initiated by the pilot to align the aircraft with a runway for landing when a straight-in landing from an instrument approach is not possible or is not desirable. This maneuver is made only after ATC authorization has been obtained and the pilot has established required visual reference to the airport.

Circle To Runway (Runway Numbered)—Used by ATC to inform the pilot that he must circle to land because the runway in use is other than the runway aligned with the instrument approach procedure. When the direction of the circling maneuver in relation to the airport/runway is required, the controller will state the direction (eight cardinal compass points) and specify a left or right downwind or base leg as appropriate . . .

clearance limit—The fix, point, or location to which an aircraft is cleared when issued an air traffic clearance.

Clearance Void If Not Off By (Time)—Used by ATC to advise an aircraft that the departure clearance is automatically cancelled if takeoff is not made prior to a specified time. The pilot must obtain a new clearance or cancel his IFR flight plan if not off by the specified time.

Cleared As Filed—Means the aircraft is cleared to proceed in accordance with the route of flight filed in the flight plan. This clearance does not include the altitude, SID, or SID Transition.

Cleared for Approach—ATC authorization for an aircraft to execute any standard or special instrument approach procedure. Normally, an aircraft will be cleared for a specific instrument approach procedure.

Cleared For (Type of) Approach—ATC authorization for an aircraft to execute a specific instrument approach procedure to an airport . . .

Compass Locator—A low power, low or medium frequency (L/MF) radio beacon installed at the site of the outer or middle marker of an instrument landing system (ILS). It can be used for navigation at distances of approximately 15 miles or as authorized in the approach procedure . . .

compulsory reporting points—Reporting points which must be reported to ATC. They are designated on aeronautical charts by solid triangles or filed in a flight plan as fixes selected to define direct routes. These points are geographical locations which are defined by navigational aids/fixes. Pilots should discontinue position reporting when informed by ATC that their aircraft is in "radar contact."

contact approach—An approach wherein an aircraft on an IFR flight plan, having an air traffic control authorization, operating clear of clouds with at least 1 mile flight visibility and a reasonable expectation of continuing to the destination airport in those conditions, may deviate from the instrument approach procedure and proceed to the destination airport by visual reference to the surface. This approach will only be authorized when requested by the pilot and the reported ground visibility at the destination airport is at least 1 statute mile.

Cross (Fix) At (Altitude)—Used by ATC when a specific altitude restriction at a specified fix is required.

Cross (Fix) At Or Above (Altitude)—Used by ATC when an altitude restriction at a specified fix is required. It does not prohibit the aircraft from crossing the fix at a higher altitude than specified; however, the higher altitude may not be one that will violate a succeeding altitude restriction or altitude assignment.

Cross (Fix) At Or Below (Altitude)—Used by ATC when a maximum altitude at a specific fix is required. It does not prohibit the aircraft from crossing the fix at a lower altitude; however, it must be at or above the minimum IFR altitude.

Cruise—Used in an ATC clearance to authorize a pilot to conduct flight at any altitude from the minimum IFR altitude up to and including the altitude specified in the clearance. The pilot may level off at any intermediate altitude within this block of airspace. Climb/descent within the block is to be made at the discretion of the pilot. However, once the pilot starts descent and verbally reports leaving an altitude in the block, he may not return to that altitude without additional ATC clearance. Further, it is approval for the pilot to proceed to and make an approach at destination airport and can be used in conjunction with:

1. An airport clearance limit at locations with a standard/special instrument approach procedure. The FARs require that if an instrument letdown to an airport is necessary, the pilot shall make the letdown in accordance with a standard/special instrument approach procedure for that airport, or

2. An airport clearance limit at locations that are within/below/outside controlled airspace and without a standard/special instrument approach procedure. Such a clearance is NOT AUTHORIZATION for the pilot to descend under IFR conditions below the applicable minimum IFR altitude nor does it imply that ATC is exercising control over aircraft in uncontrolled airspace; however, it provides a means for the aircraft to proceed to destination airport, descend, and land in accordance with applicable FARs governing VFR flight operations. Also, this provides search and rescue protection until such time as the IFR flight plan is closed.

cruising altitude/level—An altitude or flight level maintained during en route level flight. This is a constant altitude and should not be confused with a cruise clearance.

Decision Height/DH—With respect to the operation of aircraft, means the height at which a decision must be made during an ILS, MLS, or PAR instrument approach to either continue the approach or to execute a missed approach.

Direct—Straight-line flight between two navigational aids, fixes, points, or any combination thereof. When used by pilots in describing off-airway routes, points defining direct route segments become compulsory reporting points unless the aircraft is under radar contact.

Distance Measuring Equipment/DME—Equipment (airborne and ground) used to measure, in nautical miles, the slant range distance of an aircraft from the DME navigational aid.

DME fix—A geographical position determined by reference to a navigational aid which provides distance and azimuth information. It is defined by a specific distance in nautical miles and a radial, azimuth, or course (i.e., localizer) in degrees magnetic from that aid.

Execute Missed Approach—Instructions issued to a pilot making an instrument approach which means continue inbound to the missed approach point and execute the missed approach procedure as described in the instrument approach procedure chart, or as previously assigned by ATC. The pilot may climb immediately to the altitude specified in the missed approach procedure upon making a missed approach. No turns should be initiated prior to reaching the missed approach point. When conducting an ASR or PAR approach, execute the assigned missed approach procedure immediately upon receiving instructions to "execute missed approach".

Expect (Altitude) At (Time) Or (Fix)—Used under certain conditions to provide a pilot with an altitude to be used in the event of two-way communications failure. It also provides altitude information to assist the pilot in planning.

Expect Further Clearance (Time)/EFC—The time a pilot can expect to receive clearance beyond a clearance limit.

final approach course—A published MLS course, a straight-line extension of a localizer, a final approach radial/bearing, or a runway centerline, all without regard to distance.

Final Approach Fix/FAF—The designated fix from or over which the final approach (IFR) to an airport is executed. The FAF identifies the beginning of the final approach segment of the instrument approach . . . FAF is charted only when specified by official source.

final approach—IFR—The flight path of an aircraft which is inbound to an airport on a final instrument approach course, beginning at the final approach fix or point and extending to the airport or the point where a circle-to-land maneuver or a missed approach is executed.

fix—A geographical position determined by visual reference to the surface, by reference to one or more radio NAVAIDs, by celestial plotting, or by another navigational device.

flight level—A level of constant atmospheric pressure related to a reference datum of 29.92 inches of mercury. Each is stated in three digits that represent hundreds of feet. For example, flight level 250 represents a barometric altimeter indication of 25,000 feet; flight level 255, an indication of 25,500 feet.

flight path—A line, course, or track along which an aircraft is flying or intended to be flown.

flight visibility—The average forward horizontal distance, from the cockpit of an aircraft in flight, at which prominent unlighted objects may be seen and identified by day and prominent lighted objects may be seen and identified by night.

gate hold procedures—Procedures at selected airports to hold aircraft at the gate or other ground location whenever departure delays exceed or are anticipated to exceed 15 minutes. The sequence for departure will be maintained in accordance with initial call-up unless modified by flow control restrictions. Pilots should monitor the Ground Control/clearance delivery frequency for engine startup advisories or new proposed start time if the delay changes.

glide slope/glide path—Provides vertical guidance for aircraft during approach and landing. The glide slope/glide path is based on the following:

1. Electronic components emitting signals which provide vertical

guidance by reference to airborne instruments during instrument approaches such as ILS/MLS, or

2. Visual ground aids, such as VASI, which provide vertical guidance for a VFR approach or for the visual portion of an instrument approach and landing.

3. PAR. Used by ATC to inform an aircraft making a PAR approach of its vertical position (elevation) relative to the descent profile.

glide slope/glide path intercept altitude—The minimum altitude to intercept the glide slope/path on a precision approach. The intersection of the published intercept altitude with the glide slope/path, designated on Jeppesen Terminal charts by the start of the glide slope/path symbol, is the precision FAF; however, when ATC directs a lower altitude, the resultant lower intercept position is then the FAF.

ground visibility—Prevailing horizontal visibility near the earth's surface as reported by the United States National Weather Service or an accredited observer.

Height Above Airport/HAA—The height of the Minimum Descent Altitude above the published airport elevation. This is published in conjunction with circling minimums.

Height Above Touchdown/HAT—The height of the Decision Height or Minimum Descent Altitude above the highest runway elevation in the touchdown zone (first 3000 feet of the runway). HAT is published on instrument approach charts in conjunction with all straight-in-minimums.

hold/holding procedure—A predetermined maneuver which keeps aircraft within a specified airspace while awaiting further clearance from air traffic control. Also used during ground operations to keep aircraft within a specified area or at a specified point while awaiting further clearance from air traffic control.

holding fix—A specified fix identifiable to a pilot by NAVAIDs or visual reference to the ground used as a reference point in establishing and maintaining the position of an aircraft while holding.

IFR conditions—Weather conditions below the minimum for flight under visual flight rules.

ILS Categories—

1. ILS Category I—An ILS approach procedure which provides for approach to a height above touchdown of not less than 200 feet and with runway visual range of not less than 1800 feet.

2. ILS Category II—An ILS approach procedure which provides for approach to a height above touchdown of not less than 100 feet and with runway visual range of not less than 1200 feet.

3. ILS Category III.

   a. IIIA—An ILS approach procedure which provides for approach without a decision height minimum and with runway visual range of not less than 700 feet.

 b. IIIB—An ILS approach procedure which provides for approach without a decision height minimum and with runway visual range of not less than 150 feet.

 c. IIIC—An ILS approach procedure which provides for approach without a decision height minimum and without runway visual range minimum.

Initial Approach Fix (IAF)—The fix(es) depicted on instrument approach procedure charts that identifies the beginning of the initial approach segment(s).

Inner Marker/IM/Inner Marker Beacon—A marker beacon used with an ILS (CAT II) precision approach located between the middle marker and the end of the ILS runway, transmitting a radiation pattern keyed at six dots per second and indicating to the pilot, both aurally and visually, that he is at the designated decision height(DH), normally 100 feet above the touchdown zone elevation, on the ILS CAT II approach. It also marks progress during a CAT III approach.

Instrument Approach Procedure (IAP)/instrument approach—A series of predetermined maneuvers for the orderly transfer of an aircraft under instrument flight conditions, from the beginning of the initial approach to a landing, or to a point from which a landing may be made visually. It is prescribed and approved for a specific airport by a competent authority . . .

Instrument Flight Rules/IFR—Rules governing the procedures for conducting instrument flight. Also a term used by pilots and controllers to indicate type of flight plan.

Instrument Landing System/ILS—A precision instrument approach system which normally consists of the following electronic components and visual aids:

 1. Localizer

 2. Glide slope

 3. Outer Marker

 4. Middle Marker

 5. Approach Lights

Instrument Meteorological Conditions/IMC—Meteorological conditions expressed in terms of visibility, distance from cloud, and ceiling less than the minima specified for visual meteorological conditions.

Instrument Runway—A runway equipped with electronic and visual navigation aids for which a precision or nonprecision approach procedure having straight-in landing minimums has been approved.

Landing Minimums/IFR Landing Minimums—The minimum visibility prescribed for landing a civil aircraft while using an instrument approach procedure. The minimum applies with other limitations set forth in FAR Part 91 with respect to the Minimum

Descent Altitude (MDA) or Decision Height (DH) prescribed in the instrument approach procedures as follows:

1. Straight-in landing minimums—A statement of MDA and visibility, or DH and visibility, required for a straight-in landing on a specified runway, or

2. Circling minimums—A statement of MDA and visibility required for the circle-to-land maneuver.

Descent below the established MDA or DH is not authorized during an approach unless the aircraft is in a position from which a normal approach to the runway of intended landing can be made and adequate visual reference to required visual cues is maintained.

localizer—The component of an ILS which provides course guidance to the runway.

Localizer-Type Directional Aid/LDA—A NAVAID, used for nonprecision instrument approaches with utility and accuracy comparable to a localizer but which is not a part of a complete ILS and is not aligned with the runway.

marker beacon—An electronic navigation facility transmitting a 75 MHz vertical fan or boneshaped radiation pattern. Marker beacons are identified by their modulation frequency and keying code, and when received by compatible airborne equipment, indicate to the pilot, both aurally and visually, that he is passing over the facility.

Maximum Authorized Altitude/MAA—A published altitude representing the maximum usable altitude or flight level for an airspace structure or route segment.

Middle Marker/MM—A marker beacon that defines a point along the glide slope of an ILS normally located at or near the point of decision height . . .

Minimum Crossing Altitude/MCA—The lowest altitude at certain fixes at which an aircraft must cross when proceeding in the direction of a higher minimum en route IFR altitude (MEA).

Minimum Descent Altitude/MDA—The lowest altitude, expressed in feet above mean sea level, to which descent is authorized on final approach or during circle-to-land maneuvering in execution of a standard instrument approach procedure where no electronic glide slope is provided.

Minimum En Route IFR Altitude/MEA—The lowest published altitude between radio fixes which assures acceptable navigational signal coverage and meets obstacle clearance requirements between those fixes. The MEA prescribed for a Federal airway or segment thereof, area navigation low or high route, or other direct route applies to the entire width of the airway, segment, or route between the radio fixes defining the airway, segment, or route.

Minimum IFR Altitudes/MIA—Minimum altitudes for IFR operations as prescribed in FAR Part 91. These altitudes are published on aeronautical charts and prescribed in FAR Part 95 for airways and routes, and in FAR Part 97 for standard instrument approach procedures. If no applicable minimum altitude is prescribed in FAR Parts 95 or 97, the following minimum IFR altitude applies:

1. In designated mountainous areas, 2000 feet above the highest ob-

Minimum Obstruction Clearance Altitude/Minimum Safe Altitude

stacle within a horizontal distance of 5 statute miles from the course to be flown; or

2. Other than mountainous areas, 1000 feet above the highest obstacle within a horizontal distance of 5 statute miles from the course to be flown; or

3. As otherwise authorized by the Administrator or assigned by ATC.

Minimum Obstruction Clearance Altitude/MOCA—The lowest published altitude in effect between radio fixes on VOR airways, off-airway routes, or route segments which meets obstacle clearance requirements for the entire route segment and which assures acceptable navigational signal coverage only within 25 statute (22 nautical) miles of a VOR.

Minimum Off-Route Altitude/MORA—This is an altitude derived by Jeppesen. The [route] MORA provides terrain and obstruction clearance within 10 NM of the route centerline (regardless of route width) and end fixes A grid MORA altitude provides terrain and obstruction clearance within the section outlined by latitude and longitude lines. A MORA values clear all terrain and obstructions by 1000' in areas where the highest terrain and obstructions are 5000' MSL or lower. MORA values clear all terrain and obstructions by 2000' in areas where the highest terrain and obstructions are 5000' MSL or higher. When a MORA is shown along a route as "unknown" or within a grid as "unsurveyed" a MORA is not shown due to incomplete or insufficient official source.

Minimum Reception Altitude/MRA—The lowest altitude at which an intersection can be determined.

Minimum Safe Altitude/MSA—

1. The minimum altitude specified in FAR Part 91 for various aircraft operations.

2. Altitudes depicted on approach charts which provide at least 1000 feet of obstacle clearance for emergency use within a specified distance from the navigation facility upon which a procedure is predicated. These altitudes will be identified as Minimum Sector Altitudes or Emergency Safe Altitudes and are established as follows:

   a. Minimum Sector Altitudes—Altitudes depicted on approach charts which provide at least 1000 feet of obstacle clearance within a 25-mile radius of the navigation facility upon which the procedure is predicated. Sectors depicted on approach charts must be at least 90 degrees in scope. These altitudes are for emergency use only and do not necessarily assure acceptable navigational signal coverage.

   b. Emergency Safe Altitudes—Altitudes depicted on approach charts which provide at least 1000 feet of obstacle clearance in nonmountainous areas and 2000 feet of obstacle clearance in designated mountainous areas within a 100-mile radius of the navigation facility upon which the procedure is predicated and normally used only in military procedures. These altitudes are identified on published procedures as "Emergency Safe Altitudes."

of obstacle clearance in designated mountainous areas within a 100-mile radius of the navigation facility upon which the procedure is predicated and normally used only in military procedures. These altitudes are identified on published procedures as ''Emergency Safe Altitudes.''

Minimum Vectoring Altitude/MVA—The lowest MSL altitude at which an IFR aircraft will be vectored by a radar controller, except as otherwise authorized for radar approaches, departures, and missed approaches. The altitude meets IFR obstacle clearance criteria. It may be lower than the published MEA along an airway or J-route segment. It may be utilized for radar vectoring only upon the controller's determination that an adequate radar return is being received from the aircraft being controlled. Charts depicting minimum vectoring altitudes are normally available only to the controller and not to the pilots.

Minimums/Minima—Weather condition requirements established for a particular operation or type of operation; e.g., IFR takeoff or landing, alternate airport for IFR flight plans, VFR flight, etc.

Missed Approach—

1. A maneuver conducted by a pilot when an instrument approach cannot be completed to a landing. The route of flight and altitude are shown on instrument approach procedure charts. A pilot executing a missed approach prior to the Missed Approach Point (MAP) must continue along the final approach to the MAP. The pilot may climb immediately to the altitude specified in the missed approach.

2. A term used by the pilot to inform ATC that he is executing the missed approach.

3. At locations where ATC radar service is provided, the pilot should conform to radar vectors when provided by ATC in lieu of the published missed approach procedure.

Missed Approach Point/MAP—A point prescribed in each instrument approach procedure at which a missed approach procedure shall be executed if the required visual reference does not exist.

No Gyro Approach/Vector—A radar approach/vector provided in case of a malfunctioning gyro-compass or directional gyro. Instead of providing the pilot with headings to be flown, the controller observes the radar track and issues control instructions ''turn right/left'' or ''stop turn'' as appropriate.

Nondirectional Beacon/Radio Beacon/NDB—An L/MF or UHF radio beacon transmitting nondirectional signals whereby the pilot of an aircraft equipped with direction finding equipment can determine his bearing to or from the radio beacon and ''home'' on, or track to or from, the station. When the radio beacon is installed in conjunction with the Instrument Landing System marker, it is normally called a Compass Locator.

nonprecision approach procedure/nonprecision approach—A standard instrument approach procedure in which no electronic glide slope is provided; e.g., VOR, TACAN, NDB, LOC, ASR, LDA, or SDF approaches.

No Procedure Turn/NoPT—No procedure turn is required or authorized without ATC clearance.

Outer Marker/OM—A marker beacon at or near the glide slope intercept altitude of an ILS approach. It is keyed to transmit two dashes per second on a 400 Hz tone, which is received aurally and visually by compatible airborne equipment. The OM is normally located four to seven miles from the runway threshold on the extended centerline of the runway.

Pilot's Discretion—When used in conjunction with altitude assignments, means that ATC has offered the pilot the option of starting climb or descent whenever he wishes and conducting the climb or descent at any rate he wishes. He may temporarily level off at any intermediate altitude. However, once he has vacated an altitude, he may not return to that altitude.

precision approach procedure/precision approach—A standard instrument approach procedure in which an electronic glide slope/glidepath is provided; e.g., ILS/MLS and PAR.

prevailing visibility—The greatest horizontal visibility equaled or exceeded throughout at least half the horizon circle which need not necessarily be continuous.

procedure turn/PT—The maneuver prescribed when it is necessary to reverse direction to establish an aircraft on the intermediate approach segment or final approach course. The outbound course, direction of turn, distance within which the turn must be completed, and minimum altitude are specified in the procedure. However, unless otherwise restricted, the point at which the turn may be commenced and the type and rate of turn are left to the discretion of the pilot.

procedure turn inbound—That point of a procedure turn maneuver where course reversal has been completed and an aircraft is established inbound on the intermediate approach segment or final approach course. A report of "procedure turn inbound" is normally used by ATC as a position report for separation purposes.

radar approach—An instrument approach procedure which utilizes Precision Approach Radar (PAR) or Airport Surveillance Radar (ASR).

radar contact—

1. Used by ATC to inform an aircraft that it is identified on the radar display and radar flight following will be provided until radar identification is terminated. Radar service may also be provided within the limits of necessity and capability. When a pilot is informed of "radar contact," he automatically discontinues reporting over compulsory reporting points.

2. The term used to inform the controller that the aircraft is identified and approval is granted for the aircraft to enter the receiving controller's airspace.

Radar Service Terminated—Used by ATC to inform a pilot that he will no longer be provided any of the services that could be received while in radar contact. Radar service is automatically terminated, and the pilot is not advised in the following cases:

1. An aircraft cancels its IFR flight plan, except within a TCA, TRSA, ARSA, or where Stage II service is provided.

2. An aircraft conducting an instrument, visual, or contact approach has landed or has been instructed to change to advisory frequency.

3. An arriving VFR aircraft, receiving radar service to a tower-controlled airport within a TCA, TRSA, ARSA, or where Stage II service is provided, has landed; or to all other airports, is instructed to change to tower or advisory frequency.

4. An aircraft completes a radar approach.

release time—A departure time restriction issued to a pilot by ATC (either directly or through an authorized relay) when necessary to separate a departing aircraft from other traffic.

reporting point—A geographical location in relation to which the position of an aircraft is reported.

Request Full Route Clearance/FRC—Used by pilots to request that the entire route of flight be read verbatim in an ATC clearance. Such a request should be made to preclude receiving an ATC clearance based on the original filed flight plan when a filed IFR flight plan has been revised by the pilot, company, or operations prior to departure.

Resume Own Navigation—Used by ATC to advise a pilot to resume his own navigational responsibility. It is issued after completion of a radar vector or when radar contact is lost while the aircraft is being radar vectored.

Roger—I have received all of your last transmission. It should not be used to answer a question requiring a yes or no answer.

Runway Visual Range/RVR—An instrumentally derived value, based on standard calibrations, that represents the horizontal distance a pilot will see down the runway from the approach end. It is based on the sighting of either high intensity runway lights or on the visual contrast of other targets, whichever yields the greater visual range. RVR, in contrast to prevailing or runway visibility, is based on what a pilot in a moving aircraft should see looking down the runway. RVR is horizontal visual range, not slant visual range. It is based on the measurement of a transmissometer made near the touchdown point of the instrument runway and is reported in hundreds of feet. RVR is used in lieu of RVV and/or prevailing visibility in determining minimums for a particular runway.

Runway Visibility Value/RVV—The visibility determined for a particular runway by a transmissometer. A meter provides a continuous indication of the visibility (reported in miles or fractions of miles) for the runway. RVV is used in lieu of prevailing visibility in determining minimums for a particular runway.

Segments of an Instrument Approach Procedure—An instrument approach procedure may have as many as four separate segments depending on how the approach procedure is structured.

1. Initial Approach—The segment between the initial approach fix and the intermediate fix or the point where the aircraft is established on the intermediate course or final approach course.

2. Intermediate Approach—The segment between the intermediate fix or point and the final approach fix.

3. Final Approach—The segment between the final approach fix or point and the runway, airport, or missed approach point.

4. Missed Approach—The segment between the missed approach point or the point of arrival at decision height and the missed approach fix at the prescribed altitude.

sidestep maneuver—A visual maneuver accomplished by a pilot at the completion of an instrument approach to permit a straight-in landing on a parallel runway not more than 1200 feet to either side of the runway to which the instrument approach was conducted.

Simplified Directional Facility/SDF—A NAVAID used for nonprecision instrument approaches. The final approach course is similar to that of an ILS localizer except that the SDF course may be offset from the runway, generally not more than 3 degrees, and the course may be wider than the localizer, resulting in a lower degree of accuracy.

speed adjustment—An ATC procedure used to request pilots to adjust aircraft speed to a specific value for the purpose of providing desired spacing. Pilots are expected to maintain a speed of plus or minus 10 knots or 0.02 mach number of the specified speed.

Standard Instrument Departure/SID—A preplanned instrument flight rule (IFR) air traffic control departure procedure printed for pilot use in graphic and/or textual form. SIDs provide transition from the terminal to the appropriate en route structure.

standard rate turn—A turn of three degrees per second.

Standard Terminal Arrival/STAR—A preplanned instrument flight rule (IFR) air traffic control arrival procedure published for pilot use in graphic and/or textual form. STARs provide transition from the en route structure to an outer fix or an instrument approach fix/arrival waypoint in the terminal area.

stepdown fix—A fix permitting additional descent within a segment of an instrument approach procedure by identifying a point at which a controlling obstacle has been safely overflown.

straight-in approach—IFR—An instrument approach wherein final approach is begun without first having executed a procedure turn, not necessarily completed with a straight-in landing or made to straight-in landing minimums.

straight-in landing—A landing made on a runway aligned within 30° of the final approach course following completion of an instrument approach.

surveillance approach—An instrument approach wherein the air traffic controller issues instructions, for pilot compliance, based on aircraft position in relation to the final approach course (azimuth), and the distance (range) from the end of the runway as displayed on the controller's radar scope. The controller will provide recommended altitudes on final approach if requested by the pilot.

threshold—The beginning of that portion of the runway usable for landing.

Threshold Crossing Height/TCH—The theoretical height above the runway threshold at which the aircraft's glide slope antenna would be if the aircraft maintains the trajectory established by the mean ILS glide slope or MLS glide path.

Touchdown Zone—The first 3000 feet of the runway beginning at the threshold. The area is used for determination of Touchdown Zone Elevation . . .

Touchdown Zone Elevation/TDZE—The highest elevation in the first 3000 feet of the landing surface. TDZE is indicated on the instrument approach procedure chart when straight-in landing minimums are authorized.

transition—

1. The general term that describes the change from one phase of flight or flight condition to another; e.g., transition from en route flight to the approach or transition from instrument flight to visual flight.

2. A published procedure (SID Transition) used to connect the basic SID to one of several en route airways/jet routes, or a published procedure (STAR Transition) used to connect one of several en route airways/jet routes to the basic STAR.

transmissometer—An apparatus used to determine visibility by measuring the transmission of light through the atmosphere. It is the measurement source for determining runway visual range (RVR) and runway visibility value (RVV).

Verify Specific Direction of Takeoff (or Turns after Takeoff)—Used by ATC to ascertain an aircraft's direction of takeoff and/or direction of turn after takeoff. It is normally used for IFR departures from an airport not having a control tower. When direct communication with the pilot is not possible, the request and information may be relayed through an FSS, dispatcher, or by other means.

Visual Approach Slope Indicator/VASI—A visual guidance system for aircraft used to ensure proper obstruction clearance and to provide a runway aiming point. It provides a fixed light path to be utilized for descent guidance during approach.

visual approach—An approach wherein an aircraft on an IFR flight plan, operating in VFR conditions under the control of an air traffic control facility and having an air traffic control authorization, may proceed to the airport of destination in VFR conditions.

Visual Descent Point/VDP—A defined point on the final approach course of a nonprecision straight-in approach procedure from which normal descent from the MDA to the runway touchdown point may be commenced, provided the approach threshold of that runway, or approach lights, or other markings identifiable with the approach end of that runway are clearly visible to the pilot.

VFR-On-Top—ATC authorization for an IFR aircraft to operate in VFR conditions at any appropriate VFR altitude (as specified in FAR and as restricted by ATC). A pilot receiving this authorization must comply with the VFR visibility, distance from cloud criteria and the minimum IFR altitudes specified in FAR Part 91. The use of this term does not relieve controllers of their responsibility to separate aircraft in TCAs/TRSAs as required by FAA Handbook 7110.65.

wind shear—A change in wind speed and/or wind direction in a short distance resulting in a tearing or shearing effect. It can exist in a horizontal or vertical direction and occasionally in both.

Abbreviations

ADF—Automatic Direction Finder
A/FD—Airport/Facility Directory
AGL—above ground level
AI—attitude indicator
AIM—Airman's Information Manual
ALS—Approach Lighting System
ALSF—ALS with Sequential Flashing Lights
AMA—Area Minimum Altitude
ARP—airport reference point
ARTCC—Air Route Traffic Control Center
ASR—airport surveillance radar
ATC—air traffic control
ATIS—Automatic Terminal Information Service
ATP—airline transport pilot

CAS—calibrated airspeed
CAT II—ILS Category II
CAT IIIA—ILS Category IIIA
CDI—course deviation indicator
CG—center of gravity
CTAF—Common Traffic Advisory Frequency

COP—changeover point

DF—direction finder
DG—directional gyro
DH—Decision Height
DME—Distance Measuring Equipment

EAC—expected approach clearance time
EFC—expected further clearance time

FAA—Federal Aviation Administration
FAF—final approach fix
FAR—Federal Aviation Regulation(s)
FL—flight level
FM—fan marker
FPM—feet per minute
FSS—Flight Service Station

G—force of gravity
GADO—General Aviation District Office
GCA—ground-controlled approach
GS—glide slope

HAT—height above touchdown
HF—high frequency
HIRL—High Intensity Runway Lights
hp—horsepower
Hz—hertz; cycles per second

IAF—initial approach fix
IAP—Instrument Approach Procedure
IAS—indicated airspeed
ICAO—International Civil Aviation Organization
IFR—Instrument Flight Rules
ILS—Instrument Landing System
IM—inner marker
IMC—instrument meteorological conditions
INT—intersection

kHz—kilohertz; 1000 cycles per second
KRM—instrument landing system used in eastern Europe

LDA—Localizer-Type Directional Aid

LF—low frequency
L/MF—low/medium frequency
LMM—middle compass locator
LOC—localizer
LOM—outer compass locator

MAA—Maximum Authorized Altitude
MAP—missed approach point
MALSR—Medium Intensity Approach Lights with RAIL
MCA—Minimum Crossing Altitude
MDA—Minimum Descent Altitude
MEA—Minimum Enroute IFR Altitude
MHz—megahertz; one million cycles per second
MLS—Microwave Landing System
MM—middle marker
MOCA—Minimum Obstruction Clearance Altitude
MPH—miles per hour
MRA—Minimum Reception Altitude
MSL—mean sea level
MSA—Minimum Safe Altitude/Minimum Sector Altitude
MVA—Minimum Vectoring Altitude

NDB—nondirectional beacon
NM—nautical miles
NoPT—no procedure turn
NOS—National Ocean Service
NOTAM—Notice to Airmen

OAT—outside air temperature
OBI—omni bearing indicator (same as CDI)
OBS—omni bearing selector
OCA—Obstruction Clearance Altitude
OM—outer marker
omni—VOR

PAR—Precision Approach Radar
PT—procedure turn

RAIL—Runway Alignment Indicator Lights
RCAG—Remote Center Air/Ground Facility
RCLM—runway centerline markings
RCLS—Runway Centerline Lighting System
RCO—Remote Communications Outlet

REIL—Runway End Identification Lights
RMI—Radio Magnetic Indicator
RNAV—area navigation
RVR—Runway Visual Range
RVV—Runway Visibility Value
Rwy—runway

SDF—Simplified Directional Facility
SFL—Sequenced Flashing Lights
SID—Standard Instrument Departure
SM—statute miles
SSALSR—Simplified Short Approach Lighting System with RAIL
STAR—Standard Terminal Arrival Route
SVFR—Special Visual Flight Rules

TACAN—Tactical Air Navigation
TCH—Threshold Crossing Height
TDZ—Touchdown Zone
TDZE—Touchdown Zone Elevation
TDZL—Touchdown Zone Lighting
TWEB—Transcribed Weather Broadcast

UHF—ultrahigh frequency
UTC—Universal Coordinated Time; Zulu time (Z)

V_a—design maneuvering speed
VASI—Visual Approach Slope Indicator
VDP—Visual Descent Point
VFR—Visual Flight Rules
VHF—very high frequency
VMC—visual meteorological conditions
V_{ne}—never-exceed speed
VOR—VHF Omnidirectional Range
VORTAC—VOR with TACAN
VOT—VOR test signal
V_r—rotation speed
VSI—vertical speed indicator

W/P—waypoint

Z—Zulu time; Universal Coordinated Time (UTC)

About the Author

J.R. Williams was born in the hard coal region of northeastern Pennsylvania in 1934. He graduated from the General Motors Institute in Flint, Michigan, in 1955, and spent 15 years in the automobile industry. During this time, he also drove professional race cars: midgets, sprint cars, and stock cars.

He learned to fly at the Wyoming Valley Airport in Forty-Fort, Pennsylvania, and worked in the area as a charter pilot and flight instructor until he went to work for Northeast Flying Service at Washington (D.C.) National Airport flying DC-3s before joining Hawaiian Airlines (HAL) in May 1964.

At HAL he has flown DC-3s, Convair 340/440s, Convair 640s, Nihon YS-11s, and DC-9 series 10, 30, 50, and super 80 aircraft. He is currently a Lockheed L-1011 captain based at San Francisco and flying between there and Honolulu, as well as internationally to London, Paris, Jamaica, American and Western Samoa, and Tonga. He first checked out as captain in 1972 and has more than 15,000 hours of flight time.

Williams was a contributing editor to *Private Pilot* for seven years and has written for *AOPA Pilot* and *Air Line Pilot* as well. He has published more than 150 articles on flying, motorcycles, sailing, health, and travel. His first novel was published in 1981.

Index

weather minimums for, 56-57
alternate minimums, 174, 181, 195, 197
NOS approach charts, 192
altimeters, errors in, 77
altitudes, 7, 32
control of, 31
reporting changes in, 83
antihistamines, 19
approach charts, 137-168
airports and, 150
conversion table on, 167
effective date of, 138
filing of, 138
format of, 138
frequencies for, 142, 143
heading of, 140, 141, 143
holding patterns and, 150
landing minimums on, 163-165
legend for, 139
missed approaches and, 148, 150, 160, 161
NAVAIDs on, 145
nonprecision approaches and, 153
NOS, 187-212
obstructions and, 150
plan view of, 137-152
precision approach and, 157, 159
procedure turns in, 154
profile view of, 153-168
transition information on, 144-149
approach lights, 170, 177
approach plates, 50
approaches, 93-100
aircraft categories and, 97, 98
back course, 252, 253
circling, 106-109
circling, minimums for, 105
contact, 103, 104
descent minimums, 97
DME, 223-233
FAR 91 requirements for, 230
final fix for, 154
ILS and localizer-only, 235-246
initial and final fix for, 146

inoperative components in, 97
localizer-only, 241-243
minimums for, 96
missed, 107, 108, 148, 150, 160, 161
missed, procedures for, 100
missed, reporting, 83
NDB and back course, 247-255
nonprecision, 95, 153
precision, 95, 159
safety in, 94
straight-in, minimums for, 105
visual, 102, 103
VOR, 213-222
area charts, 111, 128, 131
legend for, 133
Area Minimum Altitudes (AMAs), 128, 132, 133
at pilot's discretion, 78
attitude
indicator (AI), 6, 23, 25, 27, 28
unusual, 33
attitude instrument flying, 23-30
Automatic Direction Finders, 23
automatic sensing azimuth, 23

B

back course approaches, 247-255
barbiturates, 19
bearings, 120, 250
examples of, 250
bends, 19
bracketing, 218

C

call-up, 71, 81
canyon approach, 41
carbon monoxide, 21
carburetor ice, 53, 76, 77
CAT II and CAT IIIA approach profiles, 158, 159
Center, 71
centerline lights, 175
changeover points (COPs), 79, 123
circling approach, 106, 107, 108, 109

fixes, 120, 121, 207
flashlights, 50
flight computers, 50
flight kit, 50
flight plan
  filing of, 57, 67
  forms for, 51
  in-flight, 72
Flight Service Station (FSS),
  frequencies of, 116
flight track, 148, 149
flight visibility, 230
flux gate compasses, 23, 248
flying with a cold, 19
forecasting weather, 75-76
fuel requirements, 53-57

G

G forces, 12, 35
glide path intercept point, 157
glide slope, 244
  angle, 164
  intercept altitude, 206
gravity, 7
Grid MORA, 122, 126, 129
ground visibility, 230
gyro precession, see precession

H

H/L altitude charts, 112
head-movements, vertigo-causing,
  14
heading control, 23
heading indicators, 23
heads, 7
height above touchdown (HAT),
  161
High Intensity Runway Lights
  (HIRL), 96
holding pattern, 87-91, 207
  approach chart and, 150
  DME approaches, 224
  entry to, 88
  reporting change in, 84
hyperventilation, 22

hypoxia, 20, 21
  symptoms of, 21

I

icing, 52, 53, 76
IFR aircraft requirements, 51
ILS, NOS approach chart and, 188,
  189, 194
ILS and localizer-only approaches,
  235-246
  airport charts and, 245
  duck-under syndrome in, 239
  example of, 236, 237
  mountains and moving obstacles
    in, 239
  precision approach and, 243
inertia, 8, 12
inertial navigation system (INS),
  112
initial approach fix (IAF), 146
inner ear
  mechanics of, 13
  structures of, 16
  vertigo and, 12
instrument approach procedure
  (IAP) chart, 93, 137
instrument errors, 6
instrument interpretation, 1-10
instrument lag, 7, 9
Instrument Landing System (ILS),
  96
instrument scanning, 4, 5, 26
  common errors in, 29, 30
instrument takeoffs, 37, 38
instruments
  partial panel, 32
  vertigo and, 11
interpreting instrument information,
  4

J

Jeppesen Airway Manual, 60
Jeppesen charts, 111-136
Jeppesen, Elroy B. "Jepp", 94, 95